Heidegger:
A Critical Reader

𝕁𝔹

Heidegger:
A Critical Reader

Edited by
Hubert Dreyfus and Harrison Hall

BLACKWELL
Oxford UK & Cambridge USA

First published 1992

Blackwell Publishers
Three Cambridge Centre
Cambridge, Massachusetts 02142
USA

108 Cowley Road
Oxford OX4 1JF
UK

Library of Congress Cataloging in Publication Data
Library of Congress CIP data has been applied for.

ISBN 0–631–16341–7; 0–631–16342–5 (pbk.)

A CIP catalogue record for this book is available from the
British Library.

Typeset in 9$\frac{1}{2}$ on 11 pt Plantin
by TecSet Ltd, Wallington, Surrey
Printed in Great Britain by T. J. Press Ltd, Padstow, Cornwall
This book is printed on acid-free paper.

Contents

Contributors

William D. Blattner, Department of Philosophy, Georgetown University

Robert Brandom, Department of Philosophy, University of Pittsburgh

Hubert Dreyfus, Department of Philosophy, University of California, Berkeley

Joseph P. Fell, Department of Philosophy, Bucknell University

Charles Guignon, Department of Philosophy, University of Vermont

Michel Haar, Département de Philosophie, Université de Paris XII

Jürgen Habermas, Department of Philosophy, Johann Wolfgang Goethe-Universität

John Haugeland, Department of Philosophy, University of Pittsburgh

Randall E. Havas, Department of Philosophy, Yale University

Mark B. Okrent, Department of Philosophy and Religion, Bates College

Richard Rorty, Department of Philosophy, University of Virginia

Theodore R. Schatzki, Department of Philosophy, University of Kentucky

Charles Spinosa, Departments of English and Philosophy, University of California, Berkeley

Charles Taylor, Departments of Philosophy and Political Science, McGill University

Introduction

Hubert Dreyfus and Harrison Hall

For several generations leading thinkers in philosophy, the humanities, and the social sciences have acknowledged a debt to early or late Heidegger. Thinkers such as Jean-Paul Sartre, Maurice Merleau-Ponty, Hans-Georg Gadamer, Hannah Arendt, Michel Foucault, Pierre Bourdieu, Jacques Derrida, Charles Taylor, and Richard Rorty demonstrate the twofold way in which Heidegger has transformed our understanding of ourselves and our world. First we felt the effect of Heidegger's "existentialist" side on Sartre and Merleau-Ponty, both of whom were so close to Heidegger that they worked out their views in constant dialogue with *Being and Time*. Aside from philosophers, Heidegger inspired theologians such as Rudolf Bultmann and Paul Tillich and a postwar generation of writers and literary critics. These thinkers modified, extended, and applied Heidegger's ideas; they did not write *about* him.

Later generations were influenced by late Heidegger's abandonment of the residual subjectivity in *Being and Time* and his subsequent turn to Nietzsche. Michel Foucault is typical of this second stage of Heidegger appropriation. He has said, "Heidegger has always been for me the essential philosopher. . . I still have the notes I took while reading Heidegger – I have tons of them! – and they are far more important than the ones I took on Hegel or Marx. My whole philosophical development was determined by my reading of Heidegger."[1] Foucault recalls Heidegger's role in his reading of Nietzsche. "I tried to read Nietzsche in the fifties, but Nietzsche by himself said nothing to me. Whereas Nietzsche and Heidegger – that was a philosophical shock!"[2] Foucault felt so close to Heidegger that, as he tells us, he thought from within him and could not write *about* him. "But I've never written anything on Heidegger . . . I think it's important to have a small number of authors with whom one thinks, with whom one works, but on whom one doesn't write."[3]

Foucault is not the only one thinking from within the space opened by Heidegger. Early in his career Jacques Derrida doubted that he could write anything that had not already been thought by Heidegger. Pierre Bourdieu says that in philosophy Heidegger was his "first love." His own important concept of the social field is indirectly indebted to Heidegger by way of Merleau-Ponty.

Even Jürgen Habermas, who, as his essay here shows, is highly critical of later Heidegger, tells us that "an intensive engagement with the early Heidegger left its marks on [my] work," (p. 205) and acknowledges that with *"Being and Time* Heidegger proved himself, almost overnight, to be a thinker of the first rank." He concludes that "Heidegger's new beginning still presents the most profound turning point in German philosophy since Hegel." (p. 188).

The effect of Heidegger has been felt in ever-widening circles. Indeed, in looking through the many articles and books on Heidegger, what strikes one most is the peculiar range of his influence. It is not just that Heidegger wrote about almost all the important figures in philosophy from Anaximander to Nietzsche, nor that he wrote on issues that intersected all areas of philosphy from aesthetics, ethics, and religion to philosophy of science and logic. His thinking has another sort of range rarely found in other philosophers, in that he deals with the most abstract issues in ways that have everyday concrete practical implications. What could be more abstract than the question of the various senses of being and how they fit together, which Heidegger tells us has been his lifelong concern? Yet Heidegger wanted his work to "break through the narrowness of academic philosophy and reach much broader circles for the benefit of a large number of people."[4] And, indeed, Heidegger's work has had an enormous influence on contemporary life and thought. Wherever people understand themselves and their work in subjectivist or objectivist ways, Heidegger has enabled them to recognize the limitations of their approach and to discover appropriate alternatives – ways of understanding and acting available but neglected in our culture – which overcome these limitations. At an international conference in Berkeley on the occasion of the hundredth anniversary of Heidegger's birth, not only philosophers, political scientists, and literary critics, but also doctors, nurses, psychotherapists, theologians, management consultants, educators, lawyers, and computer scientists took part in a discussion of the way Heidegger's thought had affected their work.

This wide influence is due to the fact that Heidegger does not ground his thinking in average, everyday *concepts*, but in average, everyday *practice*; in what people do, not in what they say they do. This leads him to abandon our pervasive Cartesian way of thinking of human beings as subjects who represent objects to themselves. Rather than thinking of action as based on beliefs and desires, Heidegger describes what actually goes on in our everyday skillful coping with things and people and how we are socialized into a shared world. He describes simple skills – hammering, walking into a room, using turn signals, etc. – and shows how these everyday coping skills contain a familiarity with the world that enables us to make sense of things and "to find [our] way about in [our] public environment."[5] Thus, like Ludwig Wittgenstein, Heidegger finds that the only ground for the intelligibility of thought and action that we have or need is in the everyday practices themselves, not in some hidden process of thinking or of history.

But in spite of their common interest in the everyday world, Heidegger is, in an important way, unlike Wittgenstein. Whereas Wittgenstein thought that there was nothing general one could say about our shared practices, except that they were the background necessary for the application of rules and concepts,[6] Heidegger seeks to understand our practices not piecemeal, game by game, but in terms of what unifies them – what makes them all coherent.

Heidegger finds in our everyday dealings two types of unity. In *Being and Time* he lays out the structural unity of disclosive practices, which he maps onto the structure of temporality. (This is discussed below in the essays of John Haugeland, William Blattner, and Mark Okrent.) Later Heidegger then fills in this structure with an account of the series of concrete kinds of unified intelligibility that have governed thought and action in successive stages of our culture. Heidegger calls any such concrete unity an understanding of being. An understanding of being is that aspect of our everyday practices that lets things, people, institutions, etc., show up for us *as* some particular thing suited to a particular historical world.

That and how things show up as being equipment in terms of the everyday skills and purposes that constitute our everyday world is spelled out in *Being and Time*. Although later Heidegger is still interested in the world disclosing function of such practices, he nevertheless shifts his concern to our culture's changing understanding of what it is for something to be. So, on his account, everything showed up for the Greeks as *physis* (self-disclosing), for the Romans as being finished pieces of work, for the Medievals as creatures, for the early modern age as objects, and for us as resources to be ordered for efficient further enhancement.

Because he looks for what makes our practices hang together, Heidegger also discovers and thinks about marginal practices that do not fit in with the dominant ones. This brings him to the distinction between marginal and central practices and how history proceeds by the re-gestalting of this relationship. This understanding of history in turn requires an account of the cultural role of rituals, sagas, and gods – territory that fascinated Wittgenstein, but which he thought was beyond philosophy.

The breadth of Heidegger's thought has led to the curious double situation in Heidegger's reception mentioned at the beginning of this Introduction. On the one hand, we received our Heidegger by way of his decisive influence upon most major contemporary thinkers. The first wave, led by Sartre and Merleau-Ponty, thought of existential phenomenology as rooted in concrete experience; the second wave, exemplified by Foucault, Bourdieu, and others, took from Heidegger his insight that everyday practices are the source of intelligibility. This insight freed these thinkers from looking for a hidden intelligibility whose secret truth they had to reveal, and enabled them to recognize how pervasive practices produced meaning in their own domains, as well as allowing them to see what the practices they studied excluded. But on the other hand, the professional interpreters of Heidegger have been attracted to Heidegger's typically Continental claim to write a philosophy that did what religion and philosophy had done in the past – give a ground (in Heidegger's case, an ungrounded ground) for our understanding of everything. Heidegger's tragic-romantic-sounding resoluteness and his later secularizing of religion in his account of the absent god who must return, seemed to these professional interpreters to promise that the ground for understanding the meaning of everything lay in an intelligibility that was concealed from the common run of people. And for Heidegger, it seemed, the name of this concealed order of intelligibility was "being."[7]

But what was the meaning of being for these interpreters? Certainly, it could not be everyday practices. Such practices were, after all, objects of study for sociology. Moreover, our everyday practices, by some of Heidegger's own words, seemed corrupted by the philosophical tradition and by a particular kind of "falling" behavior induced by everyday activity. Where was a scholar to search for Heidegger's elusive meaning of being? Once everyday practices are eliminated, there simply is no other place, no point of reference for seeing what Heidegger is talking about, except the Heideggerian texts themselves. For this reason, for decades, the professional Heideggerians confined themselves to looking for the meaning of being by comparing sentences from various Heideggerian texts. With little recourse to any phenomena outside the text, such interpretations resembled interpretations of sacred writings. Indeed, hermeneutics, originally the interpretation of sacred texts, was practiced on Heidegger's own writings to recover their mystical meaning. And, as critics from Adorno to Bourdieu and Habermas have pointed out, the Heideggerian texts do seem calculated to promote adulation and exegesis rather than down to earth understanding. Didn't Heidegger invent a new obscure jargon and speak in a dark oracular prose, which was supposed to lead us to think the unthought and to listen to the mystery?[8]

After several generations of adulation, however, the tone has now turned to disappointment with the master. It looks like Heidegger never fully freed himself from the tradition's attempt to find a ground for all meaning, and this failure left him attracted to totalizing and anti-democratic politics. Indeed, Heidegger turned out to be more reactionary than he had led his followers to believe, and his sustained support of National Socialism could not be divorced from a seemingly romantic and nationalistic strain in his thought. In the light of these revelations, many of those who had been engaged in extolling Heidegger now follow Derrida in attempting to deconstruct and "go beyond" him.[9]

All this explains why the reception of Heidegger's work up till now reveals a peculiar pattern. On the one hand, Heidegger's interpretation of practice has had a profound impact on many of the most important thinkers of the late twentieth century, especially outside of academic philosophy and even outside of academia altogether. On the other hand, the secondary literature on Heidegger that tries to capture Heidegger's powerful new insights by looking solely within his texts has been largely a huge and growing wasteland that gives little hint of what Heidegger is saying and why his works are so influential.

What was left out in both the mystification and demystification of Heidegger was a serious attempt to understand him – to put his jargon into clear terms, to examine and extend the range of phenomena he introduced into philosophy, and to continue his attempt to relate his thinking to current practices. The essays collected in this volume do just that. Included are essays by those few established philosophers who have always approached Heidegger with an eye to some aspect or other of the phenomenon he was discussing. But this volume is primarily a collection of essays representing a new approach in Heideggerian studies that stresses simple, everyday practices and how they convey an inexhaustible understanding of being. The essays that follow are intended to inspire others to try to make sense of Heidegger's often dark and difficult prose, not by poring over the words, but by looking for that to which the words are intended to point: our everyday practices, not as studied by objective social science, but as interpreted with an eye to the meaning of being they embody.

We have not attempted to be exhaustive. There are many important themes in Heidegger that this volume does not address. These include, notably, his account of the absent god and his account of the "turning" (*Kehre*) in the culture that must precede that god's return. This volume also leaves out Heidegger's controversial critical dialogues with the pre-Socratics, Aristotle, Descartes, Leibniz, Kant, Hegel, and Hölderlin. (Havas takes up Heidegger's dialogue with Nietzsche and Taylor that with Plato.) Nor are all those who are seriously attempting to make sense of Heidegger included. Writers such as Albert Borgmann, Frederick Olafson, John Richardson, Joseph Rouse, Ernst Tugendhat, and Michael Zimmerman have all attempted to clarify, criticize, and apply Heidegger's thinking, but they have chosen to work out their ideas in book rather than essay form. Nonetheless, the following essays offer a variety of approaches to a wide range of issues. Haugeland, Brandom, Fell, Schatzki, Blattner, and Guigon address themes in *Being and Time*. Okrent and Haar focus on Heidegger's constant concern with how a world is opened up and the difference between the world and what shows up in it. Dreyfus traces Heidegger's development by following his changing understanding of equipment. Rorty, Havas, and Taylor focus on nihilism, language, and nature in the later works. Finally, Spinosa looks at Derrida's attempt to go beyond Heidegger. Habermas's essay fits into this collection focused on practice, since he commends the influence of Heidegger upon the "investigation of life-world practices" (p. 203) and denounces "merely socializing people into an unclarified language game" (p. 203). But the essay is included mainly because it represents the most serious and illuminating attempt thus far to deal with the "internal relations" (p. 203) between Heidegger's philosophy and his political involvement with National Socialism.

We take as our task in this Introduction to help the reader by highlighting the contribution of each essay while filling in some of what it presupposes.

John Haugeland's essay is the natural starting point for this volume. Our theme is making sense of Heidegger and Haugeland's topic is Heidegger's own conception of making sense – disclosing – and is a paradigm case of the kind of Heidegger scholarship we wanted to collect and bring to the attention of English-speaking readers.

Haugeland uses the notion of normative holism and the constraints such holism places on (Davidsonian radical) interpretation to make sense of the kind of interconnections Heidegger claims to exist among equipmental things and between these things and the human beings who deal with them. Starting with such artificial "worlds" as those carved out by the interrelated practices, norms, and roles of games like chess and baseball, Haugeland is able to extend the account to the everyday world and make sense of a number of Heidegger's mysterious sounding claims about us, the world, and the hyphenated relations that tie all the pieces together ("being-in," "being-amidst," "being-with"). The norms implicit in our everyday know-how and tacit sense of propriety make our ordinary dealings with things a disclosing of them by casting them into their socially instituted (public) roles. To be an item of equipment, that is, to be available, just is to have a place in such a system of roles, and to be disclosed or made sense of just is to be appropriately cast.

What makes the constituents of being-in-the-world into an inseparable whole is that each requires the others for its intelligibility, each being constituted as what it is by its relationship to the rest. The normative framework within which things can be disclosed makes no sense independent of available things with their publicly articulated roles and accountable users whose employment of equipment can be assessed in terms of the tacit public norms governing such skillful use. And the human beings whose dealings with equipment institute this normative framework are themselves disclosed in terms of the public roles into which they cast themselves.

Robert Brandom approaches Heidegger's two fundamental categories of things – the ready-to-hand (the available) and the present-at-hand (the occurrent) – in terms of the notion of criterial dominion or authority. Brandom argues that Heidegger is a pragmatist about such authority, seeing it as rooted in social practice rather than objective fact. This guides Brandom's account of Heidegger's categories and of the ontological priority of the ready-to-hand. If the ultimate court of appeal as to what counts as what kind of thing is social practice, then the categories of social practice will enjoy a consequent priority over the categories of objective or independent reality.

Human beings always find themselves in the midst of a world of equipmental things whose significance consists in their appropriateness (or inappropriateness) for various practical roles. This significance or appropriateness, construed broadly enough to include the interrelations of roles that hold items of equipment together in equipmental complexes (pen, ink, paper; hammer, nails, saw, boards), constitutes the readiness-to-hand of such things. The readiness-to-hand or practical availability of a hammer is its appropriateness for hammering. Brandom's concern is with the criterion for such appropriateness, and his claim is that it is social response. Our responding to a certain object with the appropriate performance, in this case driving a nail with it to fasten one board to another, is what makes it count as a hammer. This significance is social in the sense of being instituted by social practice.

Brandom believes that the criterion for recognizing someone as another (Dasein) is also located in patterns of social response. To recognize someone as a communal other, another member of one's own community, is to see his responses as having the same criterial authority as one's own, that is, to see him as instituting by his behavioral responses the same appropriateness classes (kinds of things) as oneself, including the co-recognition of oneself as a member of the same community.

The concluding section of Brandom's paper argues against the popular (mis)conception of the present-at-hand as what is left when the practical or social world is abandoned entirely and ready-to-hand things completely de-contextualized as a result. Brandom contends that the present-at-hand involves instead a re-contextualization of the ready-to-hand and can be understood in terms of the same sort of account using social behavioral response. The details of how practical understanding is transformed into conditional deliberation and finally into linguistic assertion we will leave to Brandom. The bottom line of the story is that the present-at-hand is to be identified with a specific kind of behavioral response or performance, namely, making assertions. And assertions are themselves a very special kind of equipment or ready-to-hand thing, by virtue of being appropriately useful for one purpose only, namely, inference. But since inferences can be practical as well as theoretical, resulting in action rather than simply in further assertions, the present-at-hand cannot be divorced entirely from the social world of practical concerns and involvements. What accounts for our sense of the objectivity and independence of us of present-at-hand things is their inability to figure directly in practical activity. We can make practical use of assertions about the present-at-hand, but not of the present-at-hand itself. Nonetheless it is social behavior that generates both categories and gives to the present-at-hand its sense of objectivity and independence of our practical concerns.

In his own way, Joseph Fell continues something begun in Brandom's essay, namely, correcting the overemphasis on readiness-to-hand and ordinary practical activity as the only important part of early Heidegger's ontology. Fell goes further, however, in identifying a sense of presence-at-hand which is prior to or more fundamental then readiness-to-hand. That is, Fell argues that the ontological priority of the practical which everyone finds in *Being and Time* is only part of a larger ontological story – and that there is another very important part of that story in which the priorities are completely reversed.

Fell distinguishes two sorts of priority or primacy in Heidegger and at least three senses of presence-at-hand. One sort of priority is in terms of ordinary chronology, and this sort is frequently attributed by Heidegger to the practical world of everyday life and the things encountered within it. The everyday world is certainly where we find ourselves "first and for the most part." From the starting point of everyday life, the theoretical attitude is secondary and involves a modification or re-contextualization of ready-to-hand objects and our typical comportment toward them. But Fell is quick to warn that priority in ordinary chronology is not equivalent for Heidegger to ontological priority or primacy. In fact, Fell contends, there is no one answer to the question of which category of things enjoys ontological primacy over the other. The trick is to avoid such oversimplification and appreciate the details of Heidegger's complicated ontological account of things and our understanding of them.

Fell finds at least three senses of presence-at-hand which can be arranged in order of decreasing connection to the everyday practical world as follows. First, there is the way that things show up during local breakdowns in useability (the head flies off the hammer, etc.). This sense is normally characterized as unreadiness-to-hand. The item of equipment involved is no longer available for use, but the referential context of practical relations remains intact. In fact, Heidegger uses such breakdowns to reveal those relations which are transparent when everything is functioning smoothly. Such presence-at-hand is clearly present but unnoticed within the everyday world.

Fell's second sense of presence-at-hand is that treated in Brandom's essay and discussed above. This is the sense things have as objects of assertion or of scientific inquiry into their natural or inherent properties, and Fell's account of the relations between this sort of object and inquiry and the objects and world of everyday practical activity is consistent with Brandom's analysis.

It is the third kind of presence-at-hand, normally characterized as pure presence-at-hand to distinguish it from the second sense of the term, which is of special interest to Fell. This is the sense of things disclosed in anxiety. Here there is a universal breakdown and the everyday world of significance is reduced to nothing. Although this sense of presence-at-hand is not first in the order of everyday temporality, it is described by Heidegger as brought out of hiding by anxiety and as an original and primordial disclosure of beings. What is disclosed in anxiety is the brute otherness of things, nature in its aspect of complete independence of human concerns, both practical and theoretical. Such disclosure is more fundamental than the everyday disclosure of the social and practical significance of things. The very meaning of nature includes independence of all human meaning and design, and that is precisely the aspect of things that shows up in anxiety, their lack of dependence on the world of significance.

Understood in this way, the experience of pure presence-at-hand is the original disclosure of natural beings. Any further disclosure, whether practical or theoretical, will require a world of significance with its categories of readiness-to-hand and the less extreme sorts of presence-at-hand. If Fell is right, there are no absolute ontological priorities in Heidegger, and the relative priorities that are there are missed or misconceived in the usual attempt to establish the absolute priority of the ready-to-hand.

Theodore Schatzki approaches early Heidegger in terms of a concept fundamental to all of Heidegger's thought – namely that of the clearing in which things can show up as what they are. In early Heidegger it is human understanding whose projection of possibilities constitutes this clearing. In later Heidegger the relation of human beings to the clearing is much less active, but that is another story.

Schatzki clarifies early Heidegger's account of the clearing by pursuing two questions which Frederick Olafson raises but claims Heidegger cannot satisfactorily answer.[10] The first question is as follows. If human understanding is individual and there are as many clearings as there are human beings, how can being or the reality which shows up in them be singular? Second, if the clearing is identified with human existence and understanding, does this mean that entities would no longer exist or would never have existed if human beings were no longer to exist or had never existed?

Schatzki contends that several points are missed or misunderstood by Olafson, which render the plurality of clearings and the singularity of the being or reality which shows up in them compatible for Heidegger. Although it is true that each individual human understanding projects possible ways of being in terms of which things can be encountered, this multiplicity of clearings does not entail a multiplication of realities. A single reality does not require that there be a single clearing. All that is required is that there be sufficient commonalities across multiple clearings to make sense of a common reality which shows up in each. And early Heidegger has the resources for demonstrating such commonalities.

In the first place, all human beings project the same most general ways in which things can be. Heidegger refers to these as the that-, how-, and what-being of entities. Slightly less general are the categories of present-at-hand (occurrent), ready-to-hand (available), and being-there-with (the general way in which other people are encountered). Since all clearings involve an understanding and projection of possible ways of being differentiated along these same general lines, it follows that the general ways of being are the same in each of the many different clearings there are. Secondly, there is Heidegger's emphasis on the socio-historical character of individual understanding, and hence of the clearing it projects. We encounter things and others for the most part in what we do. And what we tend to do is what anyone (*das Man*) would do, what is normal or acceptable according to the open-ended totality of individuals whose behavior institutes social norms and who exert pressure on us to conform to them. Since understanding is active for Heidegger, entities being understood for the most part in terms of the ways they fit into what we are doing, social conformity in ways of acting means conformity in ways of understanding and encountering entities as well. In addition, the social norms are handed down and carry the weight of tradition, so that the understanding and possible ways of acting and being which constitute the clearing are relatively stable over time and across large numbers of individuals. The commonalities associated with the anyone and tradition are not universal, but they are sufficiently extensive to guarantee that what people and things show themselves as being is largely the same from clearing to clearing.

The final source of commonalities across multiple clearings for Heidegger is the fact that the same realm of present-at-hand (occurrent) entities enters each clearing. It is this final point which Schatzki develops into Heidegger's answer to Olafson's second question, explaining the nature of Heidegger's realism (and idealism) along the way. Presence-at-hand is a possible way for things to be and hence is only as projected by human understanding. Nonetheless, as present-at-hand, entitities show themselves as being what they are independent of human understanding and encountering of them. Had there never been any human understanding, any projection of possible ways for things to be, presence-at-hand would not be such a possibility and the independent existence of things would be inconveivable. But once this possibility has been projected, present-at-hand things show themselves to have been as thus encountered all along, independent of such encountering.

William Blattner distinguishes Heidegger's originary or existential temporality from everyday or pragmatic temporality. Understanding originary temporality in the way Blattner suggests solves a number of puzzles surrounding early Heidegger's discussions of temporality and time, and explains why Heidegger cannot be interpreted as a pragmatist.

Blattner argues that, contrary to standard interpretations, originary time is not associated exclusively with authentic human existence. The reason that Heidegger's discussion of originary temporality occurs so late in *Being and Time* is that it depends upon the discussions of death as a possibility and guilt as the nullity of Dasein's being the ground for its own projections. But these phenomena are not intrinsically authentic at all. It is our response to them which makes the distinction between authentic and inauthentic human existence. Originary temporality turns out to be the temporal structure of human existence, whether authentic or inauthentic. And it is temporal in a way that, at least at first glance, has little to do with our ordinary, everyday sense of time. The projection of possibilities that constitutes the "futureness" of human existence is a casting oneself into roles which is incompletable in principle and makes no reference to the future in the ordinary sense of a time yet to come. The "alreadiness" of things showing up for us as mattering in certain ways, which constitutes the "pastness" of our existence, likewise makes no reference to an actual time which was once but is no longer present. And the "enpresenting" of the entire pragmatic context which gives the everyday world its significance and intelligibility – relying on the wherewithal that has already been made available in our present use of a particular piece of equipment in order to accomplish a task in the foreseeable future – is neither confined to a momentary present nor about to become past.

The connection between originary temporality and our everyday sense of time is a complicated explanatory dependence of the latter upon the former. However, Blattner argues, the special nature of the originary present is such that the entire structure of everyday temporality – past, present, and future – is incorporated within it. Everyday temporality *is* pragmatic temporality. It is the time that shows up in our ordinary taking care of things and finding our way about in the world. Originary temporality is non-sequential and so does violence to our ordinary sense of time. It "lies beneath" the time of everyday practice. It is temporal in the deeper sense of being the source of our everyday pragmatic understanding of time. And this is what keeps Heidegger from being a pragmatist.

Charles Guignon uses the charge by Habermas and others that Heidegger's early philosophy gives a decisionistic view of human choice as arbitrary – free of real ties to history or tradition – as a vehicle for investigating Heidegger's account of historicity and authentic commitment. He finds Heidegger indebted to both Dilthey and Nietzsche in ways that shed light on the discussions of temporality and history in *Being and Time*. From Dilthey, Heidegger takes over the idea that human existence forms a continuous, connected whole whose meaning is prior to that of its parts, each part of a life being understood in terms of what it contributes to the whole. And, as with Dilthey, the future has a special role to play in determining the meaning of a life, since the meaning we give to the whole is a function of where we see the life as going.

Most importantly, both Dilthey and Heidegger see the temporal development of a life as inseparable from the historical culture of the public world in which it is embedded. "For Dilthey, we only *become human* by becoming participants within a concrete historical culture" (p. 134). For Heidegger, we understand ourselves in terms of the culturally available possibilities we project and out of a public world of shared significance to which we are implicitly attuned. So the historical situatedness of human existence is guaranteed by the public understanding of being into which we are thrown, at least for inauthentic human existence which is entirely "lost" in the public sense of itself and its world. But authentic existence is described by Heidegger as free of such "lostness." How is Habermas's charge to be answered with respect to authentic human decision and action?

Guigon points out that, for Heidegger, not being lost in the public world is not equivalent to being outside of it. We never escape the understanding of things embodied in the shared practices of our current world. Authenticity is rather a matter of encountering public possibilities in a special manner. The authentic individual grasps the cultural past as a heritage, a source of heroes or role-models and of a shared or communal destiny. Heidegger describes the relation of the authentic individual to the past in terms of "retrieval" and "repetition." Such an individual draws on the possibilities opened by a shared heritage and grasps them as such.

Heidegger uses Nietzsche's description of the three kinds of historiography[11] to describe the three temporal phases of authentic action. The authentic individual is able to grasp the "monumental" or utopian possibilities for the future, to see what the current situation demands in order to achieve a shared destiny. And this requires, for Heidegger, the "antiquarian" relation to the past, reverently preserving the existence in which the monumental possibility one is retrieving first became manifest. Finally, authentic existence is "critical," not in relation to the past as in Nietzsche, but in relation to the conventional wisdom of the present. This conventional wisdom must appear to lack authority in contrast to "the potential built into our heritage and the . . .aims definitive of our destiny" (p. 138).

Authentic existence for Heidegger, far from severing our ties to history and tradition and making our choices absolutely free, binds us more closely to our history. The authentic individual understands his fundamental task to be the preservation and transmission of a tradition.

Mark Okrent's essay marks the turn in our anthology to the later Heidegger by way of addressing the common theme that unites all of Heidegger's thought. Whereas early Heidegger had been in search of an ahistorical sense of being as temporality, later Heidegger after his "turning" (to be distinguished from the turning of the culture, mentioned above) is interested in the various understandings of being that have succeeded one another in the West. Each of these understandings of being has been articulated by a metaphysical thinker who formulated it as *the* meaning of being. (Okrent points out that Heidegger's use of the term "being" both for what makes the various metaphysical accounts possible and also for what each metaphysician was trying to name has created much confusion.)

Okrent clearly distinguishes Heidegger's account of the *understanding of being*, from the metaphysical concern with what Heidegger calls *the being of beings*. Being as discussed by the metaphysical tradition always names what beings show up *as*, what Heidegger calls "beingness"; whereas being, as the understanding of being, does not show up directly at all. Even the pre-Socratic understanding of being as presencing, which Heidegger finds the deepest in our tradition, is one more account of *how* entities show up, not of what makes it possible for entities to show up or to presence. As Heidegger puts it, the clearing that makes presencing possible necessarily "withdraws." To what extent we can talk about and point out the clearing – the meaning in our background practices – is a serious question for Heidegger, and its difficulty explains both why he was led to talk about the unthought of a thinker and the mystery of being, as well as to introduce strange accounts of the working of the artwork and of the thinging of the thing (to be discussed below).

Okrent argues that Heidegger's clearing is not a transcendental condition of experience, but what he calls "a pre-thematic articulation of the world by language." His paper shows how far one can get with rigorous Heidegger exegesis provided one has an understanding of Heidegger's reliance on practices – in Okrent's case, linguistic practices – to distance oneself from the tradition. But although Okrent explains the clearing, which is a great step forward, we still need to know how the clearing governs the way particular beings show up. A pragmatic account of linguistic practices as arbitrary, however, does not provide enough concrete detail for him to explain this governing. His account of Heidegger's important notion of *Ereignis*, which he sees points to Heidegger's answer to this question of the clearing's governing, leaves *Ereignis* an empty place holder. He sees *Ereignis* as an "entirely formal feature of historical worlds." As Charles Spinosa shows, however, only by turning to a concrete account of how linguistic practices tend to cohere and to highlight what matters to a culture can we see how everyday activity mediates between the understanding of being and the way particular beings show up.

So far the writers described have focused on shared activity as opening up a shared clearing or world. In *Being and Time* an equally important source of a shared world is the way we are attuned – the way things and ways of acting matter to us. Heidegger calls our receptiveness to mattering *Befindlichkeit*. The term is meant to convey our always finding ourselves already affected in some way or other, so we will translate it "affectedness." The specific way we are affected is experienced as mood. As Heidegger uses the term, mood can refer to the *sensibility* of an age (such as the romantic), the *culture* of a corporation (such as aggressive), the *temper* of the times (such as revolutionary), as well as the *mood* in a current situation (such as the eager mood in the classroom) and, of course, the mood of an individual. These are all ontic specifications of affectedness, the ontological existential condition that things always already affect us.

That we are always in some mood and touched by some concerns, and that this is not a mere psychological fact but performs the ontological function of opening a world – all this, Heidegger points out, has been passed over by the philosophical tradition. The neglect continues, for this aspect of Heidegger's thought has been little discussed in the secondary literature. This is in part Heidegger's own fault, since the examples of affectedness in *Being and Time* are restricted to individual moods, and the focus is almost exclusively on the special mood of anxiety that, Heidegger claims, reveals the ungroundedness or nothingness of human existence.

Now, however, with the publication of Heidegger's lectures from the 1930s, especially those on Hölderlin, we can see that Heidegger gave an important place to public moods or cultural sensibilities in establishing the succession of clearings that make up the history of being in the West. Michel Haar shows that, indeed, in several volumes of Heidegger's posthumously published lectures, Heidegger delegates to mood, rather than to practical activity, the most basic job of opening up a world. Haar also shows a hitherto unknown aspect of Heidegger's later thought; namely, that just as there is a history of the being of equipment and of the understanding of being in general, there is a concomitant historical story to be told about the West's changing cultural climates or sensibilities.

The three basic historical moods turn out to be: Greek astonishment, Enlightenment assurance, and contemporary distress. These basic attunements do not simply occur *in* history. Rather they make history possible by giving everything that shows up a certain tone which thought then seeks to articulate. The individual mood of anxiety that early Heidegger held to be an ahistorical experience of the abyss of groundlessness definitive of the human condition, and that on Fell's account required the active response of making sense of brute nature, is now rethought as revealing the radical powerlessness and necessary receptivity of human beings. We will say more about this receptivity below.

In his essay, Haar contributes a detailed analysis of the ontological function of affectedness. Thanks to his account of Heidegger's dense Hölderlin lectures, one can see that Heidegger's interpretation of cultural sensibility is original and important. One also senses, however, the difficulty Heidegger faces in describing *Befindlichkeit*, and it is clear that much more work needs to be done before Heidegger's insights into moods can be made as down to earth and extendible as are his insights into the functioning of everyday practices. Spinosa's notion of *styles of revealing* as a phenomenon that encompasses the practices as well as the sensibility of an age, is, as we shall see, a suggestive way to specify and extend Heidegger's account of basic cultural moods and their importance.

While Okrent and Haar make the move to later Heidegger by examining the phenomena that remain the constant concern throughout Heidegger's thinking, another way is to trace the changing interests that distance Heidegger's later works from *Being and Time*. Dreyfus contributes such a study by focusing on Heidegger's various discussions of the being of equipment which make it especially clear that Heidegger is interested in our changing everyday practices. Specifically, Heidegger contrasts the way wood shows up for a cabinetmaker as soliciting an appropriate response, with the way it is treated by nineteenth-century manufacturers as raw material in industrial production, and contrasts both with the way nature shows up for modern technology as a source of energy to be ordered and enhanced.

Because he is so sensitive to the current practices, Heidegger goes beyond the banal romantic claim that technology objectifies and dominates nature. That, Heidegger would say, is the way nature was treated during the rise of industrial production. Modern technology is something essentially different. It involves a new mode of revealing he calls *enframing* or ordering, which forces whatever is revealed to show up as ordered for use as a resource. Heidegger's account of this new way our practices order everything in our world shows us how our technological understanding of being is nihilistic. For, since this understanding is dedicated solely to the pursuit of efficient ordering merely for its own sake, technology progressively levels those differences such as noble and ignoble, just and unjust, saved and damned, mature and immature, which once gave meaning and direction to human activity in the West.

Now that we have discussed both Heidegger's early account of our relation to history and his later story of the history of being in the West with its final arrival at a dead end in technological nihilism, we are in a position to appreciate both the depth and limits of Habermas's powerful attempt to demonstrate the internal relations between Heidegger's philosophy and his politics.

When it comes to showing the relation of Heidegger's philosophy to his conservative politics, Habermas uses different strategies for early and later Heidegger. In dealing with early Heidegger, Habermas seeks to show that *Being and Time*, in claiming that all choices are arbitrary, is *decisionist*, and in denigrating the everyday social world, is *anti-democratic* as well. Guignon, as we have noted, argues in response that for Heidegger we are always choosing from among our cultural possibilities against the cultural background of intelligibility into which we have been thrown. It is this essential feature of being human that separates Heidegger's existentialism from the Sartrean variety with its absolute freedom, its unmotivated rather than situationally motivated choices, and its emphasis on the chooser's radical independence from his past and his society. As Guignon argues, his emphasis on our embeddedness in history distances Heidegger from the "decisionism" Habermas finds in the authentic "resolute-ness" of *Being and Time*.

Heidegger's anti-democratic disdain for the masses, however, is undeniably evident in *Being and Time*. But in claiming further that, due to this disdain, Heidegger has no positive account of the social, Habermas accepts uncritically an old objection to *Being and Time*, picked up from Michael Theunissen, that in "attributing a merely derivative status to *Mitsein* (Being-with others) [Heidegger] misses the dimension of socialization and intersubjectivity." Or, as Habermas puts it, completing the list of received complaints, "Concrete history remained for [Heidegger] a mere 'ontical' happening, social contexts of life a dimension of the inauthentic, propositional truth a derivative phenomenon, and morality merely another way of expressing reified values." (p. 191).

Heidegger does take over from Kierkegaard a distrust of the crowd, but this does not entail for Heidegger, as it may have for Kierkegaard, that the social contexts of life are a dimension of the inauthentic. Guignon stresses that for Heidegger the authentic individual is embedded in his culture and his current society, and Haugeland, Brandom, and Schatzki, each in his own way, show that in *Being and Time* Heidegger takes being-with to be an essential structure of human being and bases his whole account of intelligibility on the functioning of shared social practices. Brandom also makes clear that Heidegger is concerned with legitimizing propositional truth and theory, so that Heidegger's holding that "propositional truth [is] a derivative phenomenon" cannot be taken as a criticism of propositional truth. The account of Heidegger's "social pragmatism" that emerges in these essays should lay to rest once and for all the assumption that Heidegger is a methodological solipsist.

As to Heidegger's view of morality, Habermas is right. Heidegger does consider recourse to moral conscience to be inauthentic. But rejection of a morality based on inner voices or abstract principles need not be taken as an example of existentialist nihilism. It can be read as a critique of inwardness and of the abstract moral principles sought by Plato and Kant, all in the name of an Aristotelian appreciation of the wise man's appropriate response to the particular situation. In saying that authentic Dasein does not follow general moral principles and does not engage in moral deliberation, but "responds to the specific situation," Heidegger revitalizes the Aristotelian account of the wise person who knows in most situations intuitively what to do and "straightaway" does it.[12] Nonetheless, Habermas's concern over Heidegger's repudiation of moral principles cannot be easily dismissed. Heidegger's phenomenology of ethical conduct does deny the possibility of context-free rational grounds from which to criticize current practices – in Heidegger's case the conservative and nationalistic practices, which the Nazis encouraged and Heidegger enthusiastically endorsed. The question remains open, however, as to whether in the absence of such rational grounds we might still have a basis for criticizing political practices.

Habermas's more serious accusation, however, is that after 1929 Heidegger gave up philosophical argument and responsibility to the phenomena altogether, and used his jargon to disguise and lend credibility to his neo-conservative, nationalist, authoritarian politics in a mystified form. Habermas does not claim that Heidegger's later philosophy *dictated* his political engagement, but rather that his later works present "'diagnoses of the present' taken up ad hoc" (p. 188) first to legitimate and later to excuse his support of National Socialism.

In 1933 Heidegger appears to have thought that following Hitler as a charismatic leader was the only way to save and refocus local and traditional German practices.[13] Even after he became disenchanted with the way the Nazi program was being carried out, he still held that the rooted Germans under the Nazis would save the world from rootless global technology, as exemplified by the Soviet Union and the United States. This view underlies the claim, inserted by Heidegger into his 1935 course, *Introduction to Metaphysics*, that the "inner truth and greatness" of [National Socialism] consists in "the encounter between global technology and modern man."[14]

Then, around 1936, as Habermas recognizes, Heidegger changed his stand on National Socialism completely. It is clear that by 1938, in "The Age of the World Picture," Heidegger sees technology as a problem of the *West*, and National Socialism rather than the USSR and the United States, as the most dangerous form of what he calls, in Nazi terms, "total mobilization."[15] Heidegger also criticizes the Nazi idea of the *Volk*. The nation and the people are seen as just social versions of the Cartesian foundational subject:

Man as a rational being of the age of the Enlightenment is no less subject than is man who grasps himself as a nation, wills himself as a people, fosters himself as a race, and, finally, empowers himself as lord of the earth.[16]

Heidegger's rejection of the Nazi program and its idea of the *Volk*, however, did not change his conviction that Germany was the place where the history of being in the West would be decided. As Habermas points out, "Whereas previously national revolutions with their leaders at the head represented a *counter movement* to nihilism, now Heidegger thinks that they are a particularly characteristic *expression* of it, and thus are a mere symptom of that fateful destiny of technology against which they were formerly supposed to be working" (p. 197). Total mobilization now becomes, for Heidegger, the "greatest danger" and Germany the vanguard of nihilism. So, although Heidegger no longer supports the regime, he continued to believe in "the German people . . . as the metaphysical people from which alone a turning of the planetary fate can be expected . . . [A]nd he remains convinced of the world-historical importance and of the metaphysical meaning of Nazism to the bitter end" (p. 196).

Habermas cites evidence that, at least to the end of the war, Heidegger held to an "essentially unchanged, nationalistic estimation of the Germans as the 'heart of all people'" (p. 195). It is this conservative nationalism that Habermas finds most offensive. Surprisingly, Habermas seems to attach little significance to the fact that Heidegger's history of the West led him to a rejection of all forms of totalitarianism, including National Socialism.

Habermas is right in warning that Heidegger's obsession with technological nihilism and his belief that the answer must be found in Germany led him to demand a charismatic leader and so made his disastrous political choice possible. As Habermas sees it, Heidegger's philosophy is dangerous because it seeks to convince us that first we are up against nihilism and then only a charismatic figure or some culturally renewing event can save us. He notes with repugnance, "even at the end of his life, Heidegger placed his hopes in 'a' god who can save us" (p. 192).

Heidegger does, indeed, see nihilism as the problem of our age and he sees no hope of overcoming nihilism by accepting the notion of rational autonomy central to the Enlightenment. In fact, as Charles Taylor emphasizes, Heidegger sees Enlightenment autonomy as the cause of our contemporary nihilistic condition, and so sees receptivity to a new understanding of being as essential no matter what the risk. Indeed, if our culture is to survive, which for Heidegger means not just endure, but remain true to its historical essence, it must, in Heidegger's view, retain its identity as a receiver of unified understandings of being.

Habermas agrees with half of Heidegger's critique of Enlightenment autonomy, viz. that it is too individualistic. That is why he holds that "Heidegger pursues critical insights about reason that have not been superseded even today" (p. 195). But, as is well known, Habermas holds that the Enlightenment is basically on the right track; that a less individualistic, more communitarian understanding of rationality tells us that and how mature human beings can and must shape their own destiny.

Heidegger, on the contrary, counters Enlightenment autonomy with a non-theological version of the Christian message that Western man cannot be saved by autonomy, maturity, equality, and reciprocity alone, but must rather relearn to be receptive to something which is the basis of our being and beyond our understanding and control. In the end, it is Heidegger's rejection of any active controlling subject, whether that subject be the individual, the *Volk*, or even a community of rational human beings in undistorted communication, that Habermas cannot accept.

To Heidegger's critique of all Enlightenment political programs Habermas has a simple, but unfortunately question-begging, response. Stories about the failure of the Enlightenment and our cultural identity can only be taken seriously if they are based upon the results of objective social science – Enlightenment science. Otherwise, "unfiltered by any knowledge of the social sciences" (p. 188), they can only be self-interested ideological pronouncements – "a dark dalliance with scientifically unexamined diagnoses of the times" (p. 193). However, since Habermas grants that Heidegger's great achievement is to show us the phenomenon of *Welterschliessung* – world disclosure – he would have to admit that to think about such a phenomenon can neither amount to reporting one's subjective feelings, nor amount to making objective scientific statements which correspond to the facts, since there are facts only relative to a particular disclosed world. It would seem to follow that for Habermas, discussion of the current meaning of being should not be "the egalitarian business of science" (p. 203), but rather should be the job of an interpretive discourse similar to that of art criticism.

Heidegger, then, must be seen as giving an *intepretation* of our current condition as manifesting the absence of a god, and of our current distress as the result of this absence. He attempts to focus on and augment our distress, and to show that it can be accounted for only by the progressive totalization of the understanding of being in our history and our related loss of our sense of receptivity. This progressive totalization is the greatest danger because the wasteland *grows*. That is, the way our current technological practices work they tend towards ever greater unity, wiping out all marginal and local practices, and thus closing off our access to new understandings of being. Such an interpretation has to convince us by the illumination it casts on our current condition, especially our sense of ontological distress or emptiness, if we have one. By Habermas's own standards Heidegger's discourse should be judged by interpretive criteria, even if it is homologous to discourse in the political sphere that must be judged politically.[17]

Heidegger's writings, nonetheless, seem to Habermas a clear case of "ideological infiltration" (p. 202) and rationalization. The emphasis on receptivity, so central to later Heidegger's writings, is, Habermas claims, the result of Heidegger's "retreat from the disappointing history of the world" (p. 198). "Only after Heidegger gave up hope [for the nationalist revolution]," he tells us,

> and had to demote fascism and its leaders into symptoms of the disease they were originally supposed to heal . . ., did the overcoming of modern subjectivity take on the meaning of an event that is only to be undergone. Until then the decisionism of self-assertive Dasein . . . had retained a role in disclosing being. Only in the final phase of working through his disillusionment does the concept of the history of being take on a fatalistic form. (pp. 197–8)

Habermas thus pictures early Heidegger as "faithful . . . to the stubborn logic of his problematic" (p. 202), but later Heidegger as "removed from all empirical (and ultimately all argumentative) grasp" (p. 193) – a thinker claiming "a privileged access to truth" (p. 202). Following this line, Habermas is led to the same conclusion that sustains some of Heidegger's most devoted followers. Like those who seek the mystical meaning of being, Habermas thinks of later Heidegger as "severing the emphatically extraordinary from its roots in ordinary, everyday experience and practice" (p. 203).

To determine whether Heidegger has abandoned all discipline, even a phenomenological hermeneutic faithfulness to the meaning in our everyday practices, for a flight to a fatalistic otherworldly history of being, we must turn back to a detailed discussion of Heidegger's history of the West. We must ask, is Heidegger's anti-Enlightenment emphasis on receptivity justified by his interpretation of the phenomena? Is his claim that only a god can save us integral to his philosophy or an expression of personal disillusionment? The essays by Rorty, Havas, Taylor, and Spinosa all cast light on these questions. They represent an ongoing discussion of whether our everyday practices do, indeed, receive a succession of understandings of being and even gods, and if so, how they do it. In short, they seek to describe the structure that a cultural clearing must have to be a clearing, and how such a clearing works.

Rorty opens the discussion by interpreting understandings of being as final vocabularies. "A final vocabulary," he tells us, "is one which we cannot help using, for when we reach it our spade is turned" (p. 216). As examples of final vocabularies, Rorty cites the Heideggerian account of the history of being in terms of the "elemental words" coined by the thinkers in each epoch. The elemental words we just happen to use, Rorty tells us, determine our fate because they are our last recourse. Rorty makes a persuasive case for the view that all final vocabularies are contingent (in that they might have been otherwise), and yet they have authority for us. These contingent elemental words are the ones that poets and thinkers make up, but they have authority for us because the people whose fate they determine experience themselves as thrown into them. As the ground for the knowledge and morality claims of those who share them, they cannot be undercut. So, while there is no deep ground for any linguistic clearing, the elemental words and way of experiencing they make possible furnish all the ground we need. As candidates for what Heidegger means by the clearing, final vocabularies have the following promising characteristics:

1 Final vocabularies are not necessary. There have been and will be others in the course of history.
2 There are no criteria of correctness for final vocabularies. A particular final vocabulary cannot be justified as being in any sense better than any other.
3 Final vocabularies depend on human beings, especially poets and thinkers, who use words in new ways.
4 Final vocabularies, nonetheless, act as grounds for those who use them because these words allow things to show up *as* something.

All this is summed up in Rorty's claim that final vocabularies are contingent, historical clearings. But, since all final vocabularies are equally contingent, there is no reason for preferring one clearing to another. Indeed, it is precisely the attempt to prove that one's current final vocabulary is true – that it corresponds to the way being really is – that Rorty, following Heidegger, rejects as the misguided goal of traditional metaphysics. But, following this illuminating line of thought, Rorty, as he frankly admits, can make no sense of Heidegger's story about the decline of the West: "[Heidegger] makes all sorts of invidious comparisons between the less forgetful people . . . – The Greeks – and the more forgetful ones . . . us. . . . The question of Heidegger's relation to pragmatism can be seen as the question: does Heidegger have any right to [this] nostalgia?" (p. 217). Rorty is thus led to ask: "Should we read [Heidegger] as telling a story about the contingency of vocabularies or about the belatedness of our age? Or rather: since he is obviously telling both stories, can they be fitted together?" (p. 217). He concludes that they cannot, and, therefore, that Heidegger must give up his claim that our understanding of being is inferior to that of the ancient Greeks. Our technological practices are no more or less contingent than any others. The only thing wrong with them, it would seem, is that, in their assured sense of superiority and rationality, they may, more than previous vocabularies, cover up their own contingency.

Rorty hopes that once we get over our modern metaphysical stance and accept our technological practices and the elemental words like "progress" and "efficiency" that sustain them, we will see clearly that our vocabulary is just one more contingent vocabulary that is no better or worse than any other. Once this is achieved, speakers will be grateful for having whatever vocabulary they have, even though there is no sense in which the poets and thinkers whose elemental words and metaphors created the vocabulary were responding to something to which they had to be responsible. Indeed, Rorty holds that the poets and thinkers who create new world-views or final vocabularies have to free themselves from their thrownness into the current one. Only then can they create new metaphors and thus open up radically new worlds and let new sorts of beings be. There is thus no place for obedience to the call of being in Rorty's account of the activities of thinkers and poets. Rather Rorty, like Habermas, finds he can make no sense of Heidegger's claim that thinkers and poets gain their authority from something beyond them.

Randall Havas's study of Heidegger's confrontation with Nietzsche can be read in this context both as completing Rorty's sketch of Heidegger's history of being by focusing on Nietzsche, the last metaphysical thinker, and as showing one way Heidegger argues for the thinker's receptivity. Havas's point is that, according to Heidegger, Nietzsche as a thinker has authority precisely because he was receptive to something going on in the everyday practices of his time. But, paradoxically, Nietzsche has authority as the last metaphysician precisely because he consistently denies all receptivity.

Havas convincingly argues that, if one grants Nietzsche's assertion that everything is "will to power," the only status that Nietzsche is entitled to claim for his thought is that of being one more world-view. That is, Nietzsche sees that it has become impossible in our age, when *to be* means to be willed by us, for anyone or any practices to claim authority over us.

As *the* thinker of the present age, however, Nietzsche is not simply providing us with one more interpretation of modernity or one more world picture. For this reason, Heidegger sees his task as one of presenting the peculiar source of Nietzsche's otherwise inexplicable authority for us. Heidegger maintains that, as a thinker, Nietzsche is the *receiver* of the current and final stage of the understanding of being in the West. But since Nietzsche has no room for receiving in his account, it is impossible for Nietzsche to legitimate his own authority.

To put this in an historical context, Heidegger maintains that at each earlier stage in the history of the understanding of being in the West, philosophers could give philosophical arguments for what they took to be *the* understanding of being, i.e., the beingness of beings. But what Nietzsche was receptive to, and what his thinking gave voice to, is that the very sense of a right understanding of being has become completely implausible to us. In Rorty's terms, Nietzsche saw and accepted the contingency of all final vocabularies. Nietzsche was thus receptive to the total withdrawal of even a trace of a sense of the understanding of being that could give authority to a thinker's words.

Obviously in denying that there is anything that reveals a truth to which one must be receptive, Nietzsche must in effect deny his own receptivity. Heidegger's charge, then, that Nietzsche's metaphysics completes the oblivion of being is not a criticism of Nietzsche. As the thinker who is receptive to our modern technological nihilistic understanding of being, Nietzsche could not express himself otherwise.

Havas thus shows us the peculiar source of the last thinker's authority. But for that very reason, he cannot show us the source of the authority of thinkers in general. Nietzsche is a special case in that he was responding to the total withdrawal of the understanding of being. But to what were the other thinkers in the West responding? Even if metaphysical thinkers, as Heidegger claims, were responding to the withdrawal of the clearing, there is also a series of understandings of being that they are able to name with their elemental words. Moreover, there was something to which the pre-Socratic thinkers were responding and for which they were thankful. And Heidegger suggests an account of what they were responding to as well as of the kind of authority and gratitude it entailed. If the elemental words that name being are not just words the thinkers make up and are also not metaphysical terms which purport to name reality as it is in itself, then what do these terms designate and how do they function?

To understand both the authority of thinkers and how our current practices could be belated, we would have to discover certain characteristics that a vocabulary or clearing *must* have in order to do its job of letting things show up for us. As Rorty says, we would need to discover "the ahistorical conditions for the occurrence of history" (p. 218–219). But, Rorty claims, "Heidegger never tells us how we can be historical through and through and yet ahistorical enough to step outside our world-view and say something neutral about the 'structure' of all actual and possible world-views" (p. 220). Yet only then could we understand Heidegger's claim that thinkers and poets are receptive to being, and only then could we rank some clearings as doing their job better than others. Rorty is right that in later Heidegger we cannot expect to find talk of transcendental, or better, existential, structures whose necessity early Heidegger tried to demonstrate by deriving them from temporality; nonetheless, Taylor and Spinosa claim that later Heidegger gives us an account of how historical practices must work that is based on letting the phenomenon of our historical clearing show itself through artworks and other focal things and practices. In this way, they claim, Heidegger seeks to reveal the invariant characteristics of all cultural clearings we know or can imagine.

As we have seen, Rorty, whose pragmatist reading of Heidegger is meant not as a faithful exegesis but as a "strong reading" that salvages what is useful in Heidegger, concludes that final vocabularies, especially in the form of metaphors, can *create* our various understandings of what it means for things and people to be. Taylor, drawing on Heidegger, describes the role of language quite differently. Language for him has the power to *articulate* what is already taking place in the practices, and thus to make what is implicitly shared, explicitly shared. For Taylor, the clearing's *telos* or goal is to disclose itself, to bring itself undistortedly to light. It follows that, although the articulation of the clearing is dependent on us, what is articulated is not within our power or at our command. As Taylor says,

[W]hen we can bring [the way that language opens a clearing] undistortedly to light, we see that it is not something we accomplish. It is not an artifact of ours, our *Gemächte*. It must be there as the necessary context for all our acting and making. We can only act insofar as we are already in the midst of it. (p. 263)

Thus the need to find the right articulation can place a demand upon us. Even artists and poets do not just make up vocabularies; they have to find the right expression, the *mot juste*.

Taylor uses his account of the importance of articulating the shared concerns of a culture to explain Heidegger's views concerning how art works. Since this is an important topic and, as Habermas has pointed out, has dangerous implications, we will elaborate on Taylor's remarks. In the "Origin of the Work of Art," Heidegger holds that a work of art is a thing with a special function. In his language, it is "a being in the Open . . . in which the openness takes its stand and attains its constancy."[18] The Open for Heidegger is the world of a culture. The understanding of being that the artwork sets up cannot be captured as a set of beliefs. Indeed, it cannot be directly described at all. As the pervasive background of what shows up it does not show up – it withdraws – yet it can show itself in an artwork such as a temple, an epic, a painting, etc. Things function as works of art when they unify a people and show them their understanding of being. When a work of art functions in this way – when an artwork works, Heidegger would say – it intensifies the coherence of, and thereby transforms, the practices it manifests. "It gives to things their look and to men their outlook on themselves."[19]

Heidegger's work of art functions as a cultural paradigm, and the fact that the paradigm can never be completely articulated gives rise to what Heidegger calls the struggle between earth and world. For Heidegger a working artwork tends to make all relevant practices explicit and coherent – this is its world aspect. But at the same time it exhibits a resistance to paraphrase and totalization – this Heidegger calls "showing forth the earth." Thus the work of art shows at the same time what is at stake in the culture and that the culture's understanding of being (which is what is at stake) cannot be made fully explicit and settled once and for all. Still, since what the cultural paradigm shows forth grips members of a culture as crucially important, they must try to articulate and interpret it. This sets up a conflict of interpretations – a fruitful struggle between world and earth that generates the culture's history. Whenever a new work occurs, history begins anew.

Heidegger generalizes the notion of a cultural paradigm to any being in the clearing that can refocus and so renew cultural practices. There are, he tells us, several ways "in which truth establishes itself in the beings it has opened up. One is truth setting itself into work [the work of art]. Another way in which truth occurs is the act that founds a political state."[20] An example of the latter for us might well be the US Constitution. Because it focuses what our way of life is supposed to be about, when we try to get clear about who we are as US citizens, we try to make it explicit and consistent, and applicable to all aspects of our current situation. In 1935 when Heidegger first mentions a founding political act, however, the renewing event would almost certainly be taken by the Germans to refer to a leader such as Hitler. And Habermas is probably right when he says, "The leaders [*Führer*] are, then, the great creators, who put truth to work" (p. 194).

Once one sees that language and artworks articulate and so gather or collect our practices, one can understand another important theme in later Heidegger – his attempt to recover an understanding of simple things and of nature not collected by the ordering power of our current technological style of coping. Taylor looks to the account of practices implicit in Heidegger's essay, "The Thing," to show how humble but significant things and events gather together human beings in their natural and social context. Thus, Taylor is able to find a deep continuity in later Heidegger's writings. Language, artworks, and things all unify our shared practices and make explicit that they are shared. Things are examples of local centers where "the rich web of practices can be sensed" and where one can see and be grateful for how our practices fit into a more inclusive nature and a wider world. If this is a way in which a clearing *must* work, then we can see that our technological clearing which has no place for such inefficient local practices is deficient and belated.

The above argument shows, in effect, that Rorty was right; thinking of linguistic practices, and by extension all cultural practices, as contingent is not compatible with thinking of our understanding of being as belated. Taylor can account for belatedness only because he rejects the idea that final vocabularies are contingent. But, of course, Rorty would not accept Taylor's account of the receptivity of linguistic practices. He would no doubt respond that thinking of articulation or expression as the teleology of our practices constitutes one more attempt to find a correct representation of ultimate reality. He would claim, we suppose, that Taylor writes as if there were only one understanding of being in the West that thinkers have progressively lost and must now recover. This is why the ecological understanding of being is presented as restoring to us those aspects of the clearing with which we have increasingly lost touch during our history. Taylor, Rorty would hold, does not do justice to the genuinely creative power of language to produce incommensurate clearings.

Charles Spinosa, in explicating Heidegger's term *Ereignis* – Heidegger's most elemental word (usually translated "event of appropriation") – is led to an account that preserves the truth in both Taylor's and Rorty's positive descriptions of linguistic practices and in their implicit critique of each other. Noticing that any language works from the start by naming and thus highlighting the importance of some things, and not naming and thus downplaying others, Heidegger sees that language implicitly imposes various ways of understanding and dealing with things, thus focusing the attention and activities of the people who use the language. This sets up the possibility of a work of art that focuses on the marginalized practices producing a gestalt switch, which transforms the self-understanding of the culture. Given that language, then, has an inner tendency toward focusing practices, but not necessarily focusing all of them around any single central practice, Spinosa says Heidegger would want to make clear that cultural praradigms neither *create* a cultural understanding *ex-nihilo* as claimed by Rorty, nor *reveal one that is already there* as Taylor seems to hold. Rather the work of art *re-gestalts* the practices by letting some practices be seen as central while making others appear irrelevant or insignificant.

Spinosa refers to the tendency of cultural practices to cohere as the tendency to exhibit a "style" – and his paper shows how Heidegger's account of the background practices as moving toward a consolidation of a cultural style is opposed to Jacques Derrida's account of the role of linguistic and other background practices as shifting and dispersing shared, taken-for-granted styles of coping. Spinosa shows how, by focusing on marginal discontinuities and shifts of style, Derrida can account for our sense of wonder and its role in our being related to the clearing; while Heidegger, by focusing on the ways of revealing in our everyday lives, can account for the meaningful interconnectedness or resonance in our practices, and thus for our being indebted to the clearing as a source of stable meaningful differences.

Taken together Havas's, Taylor's and Spinosa's essays suggest that Heidegger's insistence on the necessity of our receptivity to the understanding of being and our need for a new god are not an arbitrary addition to his later work – not an excuse for resignation to the decrees of some otherworldly power or for a passive obedience to the edicts of a charismatic leader. Heidegger's notion of receptivity to the call of the practices for articulation and celebration is internal to the working of the practices themselves. Nor is Heidegger's final stance apolitical. As Taylor shows, Heidegger's withdrawal from active politics goes along with the advocacy of a certain life-style and the support of an approach to nature that sees natural things as making demands on us which justify some forms of communal action and condemn others.

But part of what makes the Habermas story about Heidegger convincing is that he depends on something Rorty, Havas, and Taylor all grant – what Habermas calls Heidegger's fatalism. On this view, what is deepest about our practices is that they received at some point a particular understanding of being as presencing and that, in working out what this meant, they had to go through metaphysics and nihilism to come out either with the acceptance of ungrounded technological practices as a gift, as Rorty and Havas would have it, or with an ecological understanding of being such as Taylor describes. This sort of historical necessity – a secular version of the familiar structure of the fortunate fall – makes Habermas's account of a Heideggerian fatalism compelling. It makes it plausible that for Heidegger, following Hölderlin, Nazism had a deep truth, because, as Heidegger repeatedly said, the saving power lies in the darkest moment. This interpretation implies that we ought to be thankful to the Nazis for providing us with the darkest moment or, worse, with bringing us toward an even darker moment. Such thinking seems dangerous to say the least. For is not thinking in terms of one total, compelling, non-rational truth that our culture must work out at the heart of any fascist thinking?

Derrida, for one, would argue that any single, totalizing, or as he would put it, excluding, understanding of a culture's practices is, indeed, the heart of fascism.[21] But Spinosa suggests that such readings of Heidegger miss an important aspect of his thinking. Spinosa shows that for Heidegger *Ereignis* is a fundamental characteristic of any clearing, rather than any particular total style that gives a culture a single dominant understanding of what it is about. According to Spinosa, Heidegger ought to be understood rather as the philosopher of what Heidegger himself called poetic dwelling, of dwelling with resonance. Granted that *Ereignis* is the tendency of any shared practices to gather together in ways that resonate with each other, this resonance does not require that everything gathered by it have the same kind of being. Rather, it requires just the opposite. For if everything had the same kind of being (such as being resources for efficient use), there would be no multiple centers of enriching resonance, but just a single monotonous form of life; and language, as the place where artworks occur and where marginal yet resonant strains of revealing reside, would cease to be language. Moreover, history, which as Heidegger understands it requires marginal practices, would end.

But, then, what about the supposed centrality and necessity of the work of art, and Heidegger's notorious pronouncement that only a god can save us? Heard in a monotheistic way this might well sound totalitarian, but one must remember that Heidegger's examples come from the polytheistic side of our culture. The Greek temple was not the only being in the Greek clearing that focused what their culture was up to. Granted that in 1935 Heidegger's account of a renewing event refered to the National Socialists, it would be more in line with later Heidegger's account of the gathering power of things for his saving god to provide a shared style that allowed room for other centers of resonance.

The point of this collection, however, is not to whitewash Heidegger, nor to decipher the hidden meanings of his writings, nor even to decide which of our authors has most deeply grasped the working of our practices. It is to show that even questions about gods saving us can be brought down to earth and must finally be settled not by looking to Heidegger's texts or to another world, but rather by looking to the extraordinarily subtle and varied way our everyday practices actually work to give us an understanding of what it means for us and everything else to be.

NOTES

1   Michel Foucault in an interview conducted by Gilles Barbadette and Andre Serla, which first appeared in *Les Nouvelles*, June 28–July 5, 1984. Reprinted in a translation

by John Johnston as "The Return of Morality," in *Foucault Live*, Semiotext(e), Columbia University, New York: 1989, p. 326. For a detailed account of this influence, see Hubert Dreyfus, *On the Ordering of Things: Being and Power in Heidegger and Foucault*, Berkeley: University of California Press, forthcoming.

2 Ibid.

3 Ibid.

4 *Zolikoner Seminare*, ed. Medard Boss, Frankfurt am Main: Klostermann, 1987, p. x.

5 Martin Heidegger, *Being and Time*, trans. Macquarrie and Robinson, New York: Harper & Row, 1962, p. 405.

6 Wittgenstein says: 'How could human behavior be described? Surely only by showing the actions of a variety of humans, as they are all mixed up together. Not what *one* man is doing *now*, but the whole hurly-burly, is the background against which we see an action, and it determines our judgment, our concepts, and our reactions' (*Remarks on the Philosophy of Psychology*, vol. 1, ed. G. E. M. Anscombe and G. H. von Wright, Chicago: University of Chicago Press, 1980, p. 97, (629).

7 The word "*Sein*", which is capitalized like all nouns in German, is often translated by Being, with an upper case "B". But this only exacerbates the tendency to read Heidegger as what some opponents have called a "Being-mystic." We use a lower case "b" as part of our attempt to combat this reading, but we have not attempted to impose this convention on our contributors.

8 In contrast, many of the posthumously published lectures eschew dark sayings and barbarous etymologies, and offer instead straightforward accounts of everyday practices supported by examples from student life such as walking into a lecture room, listening to a boring lecture, or the contagion of moods at a party.

9 See especially, Jacques Derrida, *De l'esprit, Heidegger et la question*, Paris: Galilée, 1987.

10 Frederick Olafson, *Heidegger and the Philosophy of Mind*, New Haven: Yale University Press, 1987.

11 Friedrich Nietzsche, *On the Advantage and Disadvantage of History for Life*, trans. Peter Preuss, Indianapolis: Hackett Publishing Co., 1980. Nietzsche describes three styles of history writing: the monumental, the antiquarian, and the critical.

12 See H. Dreyfus and S. Dreyfus, "What is morality? A phenomenological account of the development of ethical expertise," *Universalism vs. Communitarianism: contemporary debates in ethics*, ed. David Rasmussen, Cambridge, Mass.: MIT Press, 1990.

13 For a detailed account of how this conviction is both justified and criticized by Heidegger's account of the work of art as a renewing event, see H. Dreyfus, "Heidegger on the connection between art, nihilism, technology and politics," in *The Cambridge Companion to Heidegger*, ed. Charles Guignon, Cambridge: Cambridge University Press, forthcoming.

14 Martin Heidegger, *Introduction to Metaphysics*, New York: Doubleday, 1961, p. 166.

15 Martin Heidegger, *The Question Concerning Technology and Other Essays*, New York: Harper Torchbooks, 1977, p. 137, Gesamtausgabe 5 97.

16 Ibid., "The Age of the World Picture," p. 152.

17 See Pierre Bourdieu, *Martin Heidegger's Political Ontology*, Stanford: Stanford University Press, 1991.

18 Martin Heidegger, *Poetry, Language, Thought*, p. 61.

19 Ibid., p. 43.

20 Ibid., pp. 61–2.

21 This seems to be the heart of his argument in *De l'Esprit*.

1
Dasein's Disclosedness

John Haugeland

Dasein is its disclosedness.[1] This formula, while not exactly an equation, is at least an announcement that Dasein cannot be understood apart from its disclosedness, nor disclosedness apart from Dasein; each can be understood only with, and indeed *as*, the other. Here, I shall begin with an interpretation of disclosedness, and use that as a guide to interpreting Dasein.

Heidegger says a variety of things about disclosedness, and it is not always clear how they are connected, or even mutually compatible. Since any interpretation must address this diversity, it is appropriate at the outset to list (some of) the claims:

1 Intraworldly entities can be discovered only because of, or in terms of, a prior disclosedness; disclosedness *makes discoveredness possible.*[2]
2 What is disclosed is not the same as the entities that are discovered in terms of it. According to some passages, what is disclosed is the *being* of those entities;[3] but according to others, it is *Dasein*,[4] or even the *world*.[5] In the meantime, and despite the disclaimers, a few passages seem to speak of this or that intraworldly entity as itself disclosed.[6]
3 Disclosedness is *primordial truth*; and as such, it is the condition of the possibility of the truth of assertions.[7]
4 *Publicness* and *resoluteness* are modes of disclosedness.[8]
5 The basic structure or make-up of disclosedness is: *so-foundness, telling*, and *understanding.*[9]

According to the first thesis, disclosedness is the condition of the possibility of discovering intraworldly entities. But there might seem to be any number of such preconditions. For instance, scientific discoveries are impossible in principle without scientific evidence; and, *mutatis mutandis*, the same could be said for mathematical, criminological, geographical, and even treasure-hunting discoveries. So, maybe, to disclose is to be *evidence* for. (That fits the connotations of revealing what is hidden, or divulging a secret, and is also related to truth.) But another undeniable prerequisite for discovery is *discoverers*: scientific discoveries are made by scientists, and even an accidental discovery of lost treasure requires someone to stumble across and recognize it. So maybe to be disclosed is to be a discoverer. (That fits the suggestion that Dasein is what is disclosed.) And there are other possibilities: maybe to be disclosed is to be proven or provable – that would connect well with truth (and the German verb *erschließen* can also mean "to infer"); or maybe disclosedness is consciousness – that would not only fit well with the main strands in modern philosophy, but also with Heidegger's explicit discussions of mood and understanding.

Each candidate, however, really accommodates only a fraction of what Heidegger says about disclosedness. Thus, whatever so-foundness, telling, and understanding are, they are unlikely prospects for the structure of evidence or provability; on the other hand, neither discoverers nor consciousness can easily be identified with primordial truth. What is worse, Heidegger's principal example of discovering is that of equipment and paraphernalia in the course of Dasein's everyday taking care of business; and such discovering is precisely *not* dependent on evidence, proof, or consciousness – at least, not in any traditional senses. Finally, none of the four jibes with the suggestion that what is disclosed is the world or the being of entities. Clearly, what is called for is a more penetrating account of the preconditions on discovery, something that might at the same time account for the possibility of evidence, discoverers, proof, and even consciousness.

Consider, as a contrived but transparent example, playing chess. A player might discover, in the course of a game, a weakness in the opposing position, an unexpected opportunity, or a cunning avenue of attack. To be sure, a sort of evidence, discoverer, proof, and even consciousness are prerequisite to such discoveries – though again, perhaps not in their traditional senses. But the most characteristic and peculiar precondition on any and all chess discoveries is the game of chess itself. In periods or places where chess is not played (e.g. before it was invented), discovering chess weaknesses, or even pieces and positions, would be quite impossible – because it would not make any sense. Without the game of chess, in terms of which they can make sense, there can be no such things as chess pieces or chess weaknesses, and hence they cannot be discovered. The sense that pieces and positions make is part and parcel of the sense that chess-playing makes as a whole; pursuing the analogy then, it is *the game of chess* as played that is disclosed, and its *making sense* is its disclosedness.

The game of chess is a condition of the possibility of chess discoveries not only negatively, as a *sine qua non*, but also positively, as enabling or rendering possible; it is precisely in terms of the game that there *can be* such discoveries at all.[10] Chess evidence (e.g., from looking ahead), chess discoverers (canny players), chess proof (winning and losing), chess consciousness (whatever it is) – these too are positively made possible by the sense that the game and playing it make as a whole. We can even say that the game as such is the "world" within which chess discoveries are made. But does it also amount to the "being" of the entities thus discovered, or anything that we might call "chess Dasein" or "chess truth"? What, indeed, is "making sense of chess-playing as a whole"? These are difficult questions, which can only be approached by a longer route.

We can further work out the idea of disclosedness as making sense by turning to some examples which, though still not Heideggerian, are at least not as contrived as chess. In a series of influential articles, Donald Davidson distinguishes mental and physical events as two distinct sorts of entity.[11] The distinction between sorts of entity is made out in terms of a distinction between kinds of explanatory theory, each with a characteristic vocabulary. Explanatory theories are essentially ways to *make sense of* (render intelligible in general) some domain of entities and associated phenomena. Distinctive *kinds* of explanatory theory make distinctive kinds of sense, or make sense of things in distinctive ways. Davidson carefully avoids claiming to have articulated the distinctive character of either the mental or the physical; but the tenor of his view is clear. Physical events and conditions make sense as such – hence count as *physical* – in so far as they are subsumable with others under *strict causal laws* in a closed, comprehensive system of such laws. Mental events and states, by contrast, make sense as such – hence count as *mental* – in so far as they are ascribed in a holistic account that shows some individual's behavior to be generally *rational*.

It is part of Davidson's purpose to show that, because of the difference between these ways of making sense, there can be no strict laws connecting the mental and physical as such – that is, laws expressed in a mixed psychophysical vocabulary. In a revealing passage he writes:

> There are no strict psychophysical laws because of the disparate commitments of the mental and physical schemes. It is a feature of physical reality that physical change can be explained by laws that connect it with other changed and conditions physically described. It is a feature of the mental that the attribution of mental phenomena must be responsible to the background of reasons, beliefs, and intentions of the individual. There cannot be tight connections between the realms if each is to retain allegiance to its proper source of evidence.[12]

The notions of "commitment," "allegiance," and "proper evidence" are used here without elaboration or defense; yet they suggest a deep (and, I think, deeply right) intuition to the effect that different schemes or realms entail different *standards* or criteria of adequacy to which descriptions of the phenomena must "live up." Or, to put it another way (accepting Davidson's connection between vocabulary and domain): entities themselves must live up to these standards, if they are to count as entities in that domain at all. Thus, being rationally related to other mental states and events is a standard that any proposed candidate must meet if it is to join the mental club; being interrelated with others according to strict causal laws is the analogous entry condition for physical phenomena.

The notion of standards for entities themselves introduces the *being* of those entities. When Davidson tells us (if not quite in so many words) that *to be* a mental entity is to be rationally ascribable to a rational individual, he is telling us something about the *being* of the mental as such. Following Heidegger (and, via him, the history of philosophy), we may distinguish between the *how* of an entity's being and its *way* of being.[13] The "how" of its being is how it has a

determinate character, how it is *as* it is, how it is "what it's like." In the case of
things, we might say that how they are determinate in general is by having
intrinsic properties – those properties that, for each particular thing, make it what
it is. The "way" of an entity's being is the way or manner in which it is at all, as
opposed to not. In the case of things, we might say that the way they are is by
actually occurring, being present, at particular times and places. Thus, the how
concerns *what* the thing is, whereas the way concerns *that* (or *whether*) it is. In
medieval ontology (oriented to the thing), this distinction shows up as that
between essence and existence.

The standards for the entities in a domain effectively establish both the how
and the way of their being. Thus, the standard of overall rationality establishes
both how mental entities are determinate and the way that they are at all. Mental
states are determinate in general as attitudes to propositions, and, in each
instance, by which attitude it is to which proposition.[14] According to Davidson,
they have that determinacy in terms of (and only in terms of) their respective
"places" in an overall rational pattern of talk and behavior. Even on the face of it,
this is quite unlike the determinacy that intrinsic properties afford particular
things. What Davidson would say about the *way* in which mental states
(propositional attitudes) are is less clear. But it must be something like this: an
individual indeed has a given attitude just in case ascribing that attitude is part of
an optimal "theory" of that individual as rational. The optimality of such a theory
is a kind of global equilibrium among many competing constraints; hence, by its
very nature, it is subject to occasional global readjustments in response to local
changes. As a result, a person can sometimes gain or lose a belief, not by a change
of mind on that topic, but by a revision on some other, which shifts the
equilibrium.[15] Clearly, such a way of being is radically different from the actual
occurrence (presence at a place and time) of a thing.

When Heidegger says that it is the being of entities that is disclosed, he means
both their how and their way of being; for they go together. He does not mean by
such disclosedness, however, that their how and way of being, or the standard
that establishes them, is articulately worked out. A region or domain is disclosed,
"pre-ontologically" as Heidegger says, in so far as its standard is effectively
applied in practice. Thus, Europeans in the Dark Ages may very well have
understood one another as having beliefs and desires, by tacitly[16] relying on
standards of rationality, albeit with no explicit idea thereof; if so, the realm of the
mental was disclosed to them, but only pre-ontologically. Such tacit or in-effect
application of standards happens, unspoken and unnoticed, in the everyday
adoption and transmission of social practices – what everybody knows "we" do
or say under conditions like this. By way of contrast, Dark Age Europeans could
not have begun to understand anything as physical, in Davidson's modern
scientific sense, since nothing in their practices reflected the strict law standard,
even tacitly; the being of the physical was not disclosed to them at all.

Heidegger nowhere treats the being of either the physical or the mental in
Davidson's senses. Instead, he begins with an account of the being of everyday
equipment. Both the differences and the similarities between his discussion and
Davidson's are instructive. In the first place, Heidegger, unlike Davidson, does

not appeal to explanatory theory as a paradigm of making sense of a domain of entities. Rather, he says, equipment is most properly understood in its appropriate and successful use; for instance, a hammer is best understood as a hammer in the course of smoothly hammering in nails with it. Accordingly, the understanding of equipment need not be mediated by any descriptive vocabulary, nor, therefore, by the standards for employing such a vocabulary. Hence, finally, this understanding is also in some sense not cognitive, but, perhaps, "pragmatic" or "embodied in know-how"; originary understanding is skillful mastery.

Despite these significant differences, the convergences are at least as important. According to Heidegger, the being of equipment is its *involvement*; and, as with the rationality of mental phenomena, equipmental involvements only make sense holistically. Thus, much as Davidson says: "My general strategy . . . depends, first, on emphasizing the holistic character of the cognitive field", and "the content of a propositional attitude derives from its place in the pattern";[17] Heidegger says: "To the being of any equipment there always belongs an equipmental whole, in which it can be this equipment that it is"; and "In accord with its equipmentality, equipment always is from its belonging to other equipment: inkstand, pen, ink, blotter, table, lamp, furniture, window, doors, room."[18] The *whole* that is invoked here is in each case the *concrete* whole of "actual" propositional attitudes or items of equipment; attitudes and equipment are intelligible as such only as "placed in" or "belonging to" the whole of their concrete circumstances or context.

To characterize a whole, however, it is not enough simply to identify what it comprises; one must also specify the relationships that make of what it comprises a whole. Thus, when Davidson says that the attitudes are placed in a pattern, he means a pattern of rational relationships – that is, a pattern defined in terms of rational *norms*. When Heidegger speaks of equipment belonging to other equipment, he also means a pattern of normative relationships – though not rational in Davidson's sense. To say that a hammer is a hammer only as belonging to nails, boards, wooden structures, and the like, is to say that the equipmental/functional *role* of hammers as such is to drive nails into boards, and so on.[19] The normative relationships among equipment that make for a concrete equipmental whole are role-relationships: e.g., what a hammer is *for* is driving in nails. Such relationships are called *assignmments*; and, as I interpret Heidegger, the roles themselves are *involvements*.[20]

Involvements are the *how* of equipmental being; they answer the question of *what* something is as equipment; a hammer is a *hammer*, for instance, in so far as it plays *that* role, the role of being a hammer. What is the way of being that belongs together with this how? The *way* of equipmental being, its "actuality," lies in the actual *playing* of an equipmental role, something actually *having* that role. Equipment can play or have its role, of course, even while it is not currently being used, so long as it stands available for such use ("ready-to-hand"). To be available, it is neither necessary nor sufficient that something be workable or effective in a certain role. Thus, home remedies, though ineffective, may be readily available for various ailments; and common chemicals whose healing powers remain unsuspected are not therapeutically available today. Something actually plays a role if, according to the customs and practices of a community, it is taken to play that role. *Availability* is the *way* of equipmental being.[21]

Differences notwithstanding, the ontologies of the mental and the equipmental converge in the notion of normative holism. To pursue the presuppositions of this convergence, we must consider more carefully the idea of disclosing as making sense of. "Makes sense of," like "discloses," has the formal structure of a two-place relation: Y makes sense of Z (or Z makes sense to Y). Each of our examples so far – chess, equipment, the physical, and even the mental – has approached making sense from the direction of Z, that which gets made sense of. To understand making sense, however, we shall also, and perhaps especially, have to consider Y, that to which sense is made, that which somehow "does" the sense-making. This presents a curious doubling: if we are to understand Y in its capacity as making sense of things, then we must, in effect, *make sense of Y* in that capacity. In other words, Y has to occupy both argument places, once as what we make sense of, and again as itself making sense of something else. This structure is not paradoxical, any more than helping someone to help someone else; but it requires care, if we are to avoid confusion.

Davidson characteristically keeps the issues clear by adopting the formal mode: consider X (an anthropologist or linguist, say) making sense of Y (some foreigners, say) *as* making sense of Z (their environment, say). What can we (philosophers) say about X's problem, the problem Davidson calls *radical interpretation?*[22] Notice first that it is the general case, of which mental state ascription and radical translation are but special cases; in effect, "making sense of things" is just a broader characterization of what we earlier called "rationality." Indeed, as Davidson was a pioneer in emphasizing, the special cases are essentially impossible, because the holism of interpretation applies to them all simultaneously. That is, not only do the translations of various terms depend on one another, and the ascriptions of various mental states depend on one another, but translations, ascriptions, interpretations of behavior, and so on, are all equally interdependent. Making-sense-of must make sense as a whole.

We can work our way toward Heidegger by examining further what is presupposed in radical interpretation. Our guide will be the idea of normative holism, beginning in the familiar confines of linguistic interpretation, and then generalizing. There are three main points. First, whatever is interpreted must be taken in its *full concretion*; in particular, each item must be taken in its complete concrete context – not just physical circumstances, but also conversational, biographical, political, and what have you. Of course, what these circumstances are is itself determined only in the interpretation; but that is just to acknowledge that the interpretation must be holistic. Thus, as everyone knows, speech behavior can only be interpreted "in context," where this means two things: (1) utterances must be interpreted in relation to other utterances, and (2) they must be interpreted in relation to (nonlinguistic) circumstances of utterance. The point generalizes easily to all interpretable behavior: a baseball batter laying down a sacrifice bunt can only be understood in the context of a runner on base with at most one out; voting for president only makes sense in the context of being a registered voter with a valid ballot during a presidential election; and so on. In sum, if behavior is to be interpreted as making sense of things, it must itself be understood as situated and busy *in the midst of* those things.[23]

Second, whatever is to be interpreted must always already belong to and be construed in terms of a *common institutional framework*. Thus, obviously, if a body of utterances is to be interpreted, they must be taken as uttered "in" a common language, and construed in its terms. To say that the language is common is to say that all the utterances are "in" the same language – the same vocabulary and the same grammar, roughly. (If each utterance were in a different language, holistic constraints could not get a grip, and interpretation would be impossible.)[24] To say that the language is an institutional framework is to say that it is a nexus of interdefined norms and roles; and, to say that utterances are "in" that framework is to say that they are subject to and made possible by those norms. Again the point generalizes easily: no behavior could be a sacrifice bunt except in terms of the norms and roles of baseball, or a vote except within democratic institutions. As a rule, of course, institutions are not so "institutionalized" as these, but work tacitly in the background: the nexus of equipmental roles is a case in point, but most of our other everyday norms are comparably inarticulate and inconspicuous. Notice that the institutional framework is itself holistic; but this should not be confused with the holism of the concrete context. Thus, the norms and roles of baseball (batters, pitchers, fielders, etc.) make sense in relation to one another and as a whole; likewise, the tactical moves and plays in a particular game situation (showing bunt, taking a big leadoff, playing the infield up) make sense in relation to one another and as a whole; but these are not the same. The former, the institutional framework as a whole, is, I believe, what Heidegger calls *world*.[25]

Third, interpreted behavior must always be apportioned among *accountable agents*. Imagine a scrambled (or alphabetized) list of all the sentences ever uttered on some distant planet, and consider the problem of making sense of them. We have already seen that they must be situated in their concrete contexts, and also allocated to their respective languages. But in addition, they must be apportioned among distinct speakers – the ones *who said* them. Why? *Prima facie*, because rational coherence is basically intra-individual. Imagine a disagreement in which two people hold incompatible views, each trying to convince the other. If the claims are considered all together, they are a jumble of contradictions, saying first one thing then the other; but if they are apportioned to two interlocutors, then not only does each position become coherently intelligible, but also the exchange, as point and counterpoint.

Indeed, the very idea of making a claim, inasmuch as that entails taking responsibility for what is said, either to back it up or to back off, requires there to be *someone* whose claim it is; and the obvious generalization extends not only to promises and apologies, but equally to bunts and votes. In general, agents – the "who" of actions – must be understood as having *continuing* statuses, most basically in the form of lasting commitments and entitlements.[26] Thus, just as the institution of promising presupposes a single speaker who first promises and then must deliver, so democratic elections presuppose self-identical voters who first register and later vote, not to mention enduring candidates who first establish their credentials, then run for office, and, if elected, serve.

Two deeper questions, however, remain unanswered. First, not all norms are of the sort that entail responsibility – commitment and entitlement – on the part of that to which they apply. Thus, the parts of a complex organism or system can often be understood as having functional roles, defined by norms of performance. For instance, a heart is "supposed to" pump blood, much as a carburetor is "supposed to" mix fuel; these are their normal roles, and we may even call them "faulty" if they fail. But they are in no sense committed or obliged (still less entitled) to fill these roles; hence they cannot be found culpable, or blamed as irresponsible if they fail. The structure of the who – of accountable agents – is, by contrast, precisely that of entities who *are* responsible for what they do: they *can* be committed and entitled, and hence held to account for how they perform. What we have yet to see, however, is *why* this should be so. What does radical interpretation, making sense of something as itself making sense of something else, have to do specifically with the sort of norms that entail responsibility?

Second, although it is clear enough from the examples how a commitment or entitlement can be regarded as a continuous line or link from one performance to another (a strand of obligation from promise to fulfillment, for instance), it is not yet clear what such strands can have to do with one another. If the registrant and voter must be selfsame (as the enduring entitlement implies), and likewise the claim-maker and claim-justifier, what further unity can tie these together? Why aren't the various strands of accountable agency scattered and unrelated? What, in short, weaves the separate threads of continuous responsibility into the durable coats of personal identity?

Leaving these questions aside for the moment, we have nevertheless already exposed, among the presuppositions of radical interpretation, an essential structure in whatever can be so interpreted: to make sense as making sense of things, behavior must be concretely situated in the midst of those things, in terms of a common institutional world, and assigned to the agent who did it. This structure is by no means arbitrary (any more than that of context-language-speaker), for it is basically just spelling out what is implicit in normative holism. In articulating it, however, we have made an important transition from Davidson to Heidegger, for this structure is precisely *being-in-the-world*.

According to Heidegger, being-in-the-world is the basic structure, make-up, or constitution of Dasein; it is what Dasein basically amounts to.[27] Such a thesis could, in principle, be informative either about being-in-the-world or about Dasein, depending on which was understood already. Here, we have just elaborated an account of being-in-the-world; so the thesis tells us about Dasein: in its basic make-up, Dasein has the structure who/being-amidst/world, as spelled out in the presuppositions of radical interpretation.

On the face of it, this structure looks like a relation: being-amidst as a relation between self (agent, who) and world. The difficulty with such a view, however, emerges as soon as we ask about the relata. An institutional framework, like a language, is not a self-subsistent entity,[28] which can exist apart from concrete behavior, and then be brought, through such behavior, into relation with selves or speakers. Rather, the framework or language is itself determinate only as an essential normative structure tacitly instituted within the whole of concretely situated social behavior. Similarly, agents or selves, understood as loci of accountability, are just a different essential structure instituted within that same behavior. The two structures presuppose and enable one another: behavioral norms require accountable agents if they are to be normative for anyone; and accountable agents require behavioral norms if they are to be accountable for anything. In effect, instead of a relation between two entities, being-in-the-world is a single entity with two interdependent structural aspects: self and world are like two sides of one coin, the actual "metal" of which is the whole of concrete being-amidst.

This reading illuminates an otherwise cryptic passage in Heidegger's introductory discussion of being-in as such:

> But then what else presents itself with this phenomenon than the occurrent commercium *between* an occurrent subject and an occurrent object? Such an interpretation would get closer to the phenomenal content if it said: *Dasein is the being* of this "between." Still, orientation to the "between" is misleading. It partakes uncritically in an ontologically indefinite assessment of the entities between which this between as such "is." The between is already conceived as the result of two occurrent entities coming together.[29]

And it is supported also by Heidegger's explicit account of self and world as jointly determining Dasein: "Self and world belong together in one entity, Dasein. Self and world are not two entities, like subject and object, or like I and thou; rather, self and world are the basic determination of Dasein itself, in the unity of the structure of being-in-the-world."[30] Evidently, "Dasein" is not equivalent, not even extensionally, with "person" or "individual subject," both because it (somehow) comprises more than one person and because it comprises more than just people. Yet, unquestionably, "Dasein" is Heidegger's technical term for whatever it is that is essentially distinctive of people; and, in each case, we *are* it. How can this all be?

I shall sketch an interpretation according to which Dasein is a "living" (currently being lived) *way of life*. Thus, the Polynesian way of life, surviving (though not unchanged) on many Pacific islands, is Polynesian Dasein. Likewise, the "yuppy" way of life, flourishing among the upper middle classes, is yuppy Dasein. Again, there is academic Dasein, modern western Dasein, swashbuckling fighter-pilot Dasein, and so on. By contrast, the Aztec and ancient Egyptian ways of life have died out – there is no more Aztec or ancient Egyption Dasein. Like natural languages, ways of life evolve slowly through the years, and vary gradually across the landscape; like dialects, lingo, and professional jargon, many ways of life can intermingle and overlap in a single community, and even a single individual.[31]

Nevertheless, a living way of life, Dasein, is an *entity* – something that there *is*. It is, to be sure, no sort of material thing or property of things; nor is it an abstract entity, like a universal or a set; nor, indeed, is a way of life plausibly understood as an event, a process, a pattern, a state, or any other traditional category, ideal or real – any more than is a "living" language. As entities, ways of life do not sit well with the motto "No entity without identity" for their "identity conditions" are anything but well defined. They are definitely mundane, ephemeral, and contingent, yet they are not physical or tangible; like a language, a way of life can be well known, yet it is not obvious how it can be a cause or an effect. In sum, though ways of life in some way *are*, their ontology is surely peculiar. Given all that Heidegger says about the ontology of Dasein, such peculiarity seems a point in favor of the interpretation.

If Dasein is a living way of life, with being-in-the-world as its basic make-up, what is an *individual person*? What can Heidegger mean when he says we *are* Dasein? Remembering the constitutive structure of the who – accountable speakers or agents – we can, I think, take a cue from linguists, who have extrapolated the notion of a local dialect to its logical limit: a living language, as spoken by only one speaker, is an *idiolect*. By analogy, a living way of life, as lived by only one agent or "liver,"[32] would be an idio-way-of life, or *idio-Dasein* – your way of life or mine, for instance. Idio-Dasein, like any Dasein, has the full structure of being-in-the-world: concrete being-amidst in terms of common institutions to which this one agent is accountable. In fact, of course, an idio-way-of-life is nothing other than the peculiar integration and adjustment of various "public" ways of life as idiosyncratically adopted and lived by one person. To say that we *are* Dasein is to say that each of us *is* his or her own personal living way of life: we *are* what we do.[33] For convenience and euphony, I prefer to call idio-Daseins *cases of* Dasein; so, people are cases of Dasein – hence, Dasein (viz., their[34] Dasein).

We have seen that the whole of concrete being-amidst has, on opposite sides as it were, the two interdependent structures, who and world. This tells us, in general terms, that people live and interact accountably, according to common norms, and, in so doing, let equipment be as filling roles. But it does not provide any detail about *how* they do that. How is it that cases of Dasein in the midst of things – busily living their lives – constitute the overall structure of being-in-the-world and make sense of things? Heidegger works out a three-part analysis of being-in as such, an analysis which, at the same time, gives the ontological constitution of disclosedness.[35] The terms of this analysis are *Befindlichkeit*, *Rede*, and *Verstehen* – which I translate as *so -foundness*, *telling*, and *understanding*. In the course of explicating (interpreting) the analysis itself, the point of the translations should also become apparent. Heidegger says that each of these constitutive items must reflect the full structure of who/being-amidst/world.

In asking how Dasein is in the midst of things, it will be helpful to resume, as a simplified comparison, our earlier example of chess-playing. If we take it in the sense of "living" chess – chess as currently being played – it has, in its limited way, the full structure of being-in-the-world: accountable players, in the midst of play, in terms of the common chess framework. Thus, our questions about being in the midst of things in "real life" can be introduced and elucidated by simpler parallel questions about being in the midst of play – i.e., in the midst of a game.

How, then, is Dasein "in the midst of" living its life? Or, to begin with the simplified version, how is chess play in the midst of a game? Well, in the first place, in the midst of a game, play always finds itself already in some definite position – the current position; chess play always takes place in the current position. Living (Dasein), likewise, always finds itself already situated; being in the midst of things is being, in each case, already in some definite situation. The expression "finds itself" is Heidegger's.[36] With it he is clearly adverting to the constitutive item in being-amidst that he calls *Befindlichkeit*: that essential character of living Dasein that, in each case, it always finds itself already situated. Hence my *"so-foundness."*[37]

What is it for life or play to find itself already situated in the midst of things, and how does it reflect the full structure of being-in-the-world? It is, first, to find itself confronted with things to be dealt with, ongoing business to be taken care of. Thus, there is the business of your pawn threatening my rook – which I can deal with by capturing your pawn with my knight. This is the way so-foundness reflects being-amidst as such; Heidegger expresses it by saying that so-foundness first makes possible a self-directing upon – that is, dealing with. Such confronting, however, only makes sense in so far as the things confronted are found already significant, such that they can call for and admit of determinate dealings, need to and can be taken care of. Thus, your pawn's angle on my rook is, as a chess position, a threat, and, as a threat, important; likewise, as an opportunity, my knight's angle on your pawn. This is the way so-foundness reflects the world; Heidegger expresses it by saying that so-foundness grounds the possibility of things mattering. But in concrete confronting, things do not just "call" for attention; rather, they can matter only because Dasein is somehow stuck with them as they stand. The only way I can carry on with my game is by dealing with the current position, including your pawn and my rook; I cannot but deal with that position (hence it matters), because it is the position I find myself, so to speak, "plunked down in." For Dasein in each case, the current situation is, inevitably, the first situation of the rest of its life. This is how the who is reflected in so-foundness; Heidegger expresses it by saying that so-foundness discloses Dasein in its thrownness.

Telling (Rede) is the articulation of significance or intelligibility, both in the sense of separating or carving up, and in the sense of expressing in words. The carving up is not a matter of focusing attention or arbitrary subdividing, but an essentially public or shared way of distinguishing determinate entities in determinate regards. Thus, in playing chess, I deal with your pawn and my rook (two pieces), with regard to one's threatening the other, and as pieces that you likewise deal with. *Because* the intelligibility of the position is articulated in this shared way, I can say to you, "Your pawn is threatening my rook"; and you could reply, "I'm sorry" (or remain tellingly silent); but equally, I think, *because* we share that language, the position can have that shared intelligibility.[38] Though Heidegger does not make this explicit, we may surmise that concrete being amidst is reflected in telling what the current position is, the world in telling what a rook or a threat is, and the who in the sharing or communicating.[39] Needless to say, so-foundness presupposes such telling, and vice versa.

I am inclined to believe, though there is almost no basis for it in the text, that the ur-phenomenon of telling is telling whether behavior does or does not accord with the common norms – in effect, telling right from wrong. Such telling would indeed be the originary articulation of significance, and would, at the same time, be fundamental to the possibility of correctness – e.g., of assertions. It might also account for Heidegger's architectonic vacillation between falling and telling, for falling is essentially "falling in with" public norms as the determination of right.

Finally, this interpretation would connect telling directly with norms, tightly integrating it therefore with the rest of my account.

Understanding, Heidegger says, is projecting in terms of possibilities. But projecting is not predicting the future direction of things, nor is it planning or sketching out a project (even implicitly); and possibilities are not things or states of affairs that might or might not be or become actual.[40] Rather, *possibilities* in Heidegger's sense are the new options and alternatives opened up by norms: roles that things can play, and ways that they can play them. Thus, being a pawn, and therefore moving as a pawn does, and attacking rooks, are possibilities in the world of chess; being a hammer, and therefore being used to drive in nails, are possibilities in the world of carpentry. What then is "projecting" in terms of possibilities?

Well, how is it that equipment can have the possibilities that it has – that is, have a role? The world, the common institutional framework of roles, is, of course, prerequisite to any entity having a role. But the world itself does not assign any concrete entities to any determinate equipmental roles; nor do intraworldly entities adopt their roles themselves. Rather, it is only in virtue of Dasein's concrete being-amidst – selves actively dealing with things and taking care of business – that those things have roles. Dasein deals with things *as* having roles and proper uses, and in virtue of this they *do* have them. You and I and all chess players move rooks only along ranks and files; and we all expect each other to do likewise. We do so move and expect because that is how rooks are supposed to move; but *also*, that is how rooks are supposed to move because that is what we all do and expect. In Dasein's practical know-how and sense of propriety, tacitly manifested in concrete taking care of business, dealing with things and one another, those things are effectively "given" roles and understood in terms of them; or, in Heidegger's words, Dasein *projects* things in terms of possibilities. In English, we can make a pun on "projecting," and say that, according to Heidegger, understanding is tacit *role-casting*.

Dasein's practical casting of the entities it finds itself in the midst of, in terms of publicly articulated roles, just *is* its *making sense of* those entities. Earlier we saw *that*, without seeing *why*, radical interpretation presupposes the sort of norms that entail an accountable who; here we see why. It is only because the who is accountable for how it deals with equipment that Dasein's concrete being amidst can institute the normative framework in terms of which that equipment then becomes intelligible as playing roles. Equipmental roles, unlike the functional roles of organic and mechanical subsystems, are essentially *instituted*: they arise only in conjunction with norms of use – that is, norms to which not the equipment itself but its *users* are accountable. Because, and only because, accountable Dasein institutes equipmental roles (tacitly, in socially transmitted skillful mastery) does Dasein understand equipment as equipment (in its skillful employment). In sum, it is only because Dasein is normatively accountable for how it uses equipment, hence (in that use) institutes intelligible roles, that it can itself be understood as understanding – that is, be radically interpreted.[41]

Dasein's originary understanding is active, tacit in the normal exercise of socially transmitted skillful mastery. It reflects being-amidst as such because it is only in the course of concrete intraworldly dealings that equipment is cast into its worldly roles, and thereby made sense of as what it is; Heidegger calls this the *fore-grasp* of understanding. Active understanding reflects the world in that it is worldly norms to which the skillful behavior is accountable, and hence worldly roles into which the equipment is cast; the institutional framework is always already the background in terms of which any active understanding is possible. Heidegger calls this the *fore-having*. Active understanding reflects the who in that, in each case, skillful dealings belong to and are guided by some job or endeavor undertaken by an accountable agent – something somebody is doing; Heidegger calls this the *fore-sight*.

When Heidegger introduces his account of understanding as projecting in terms of possibilities, he speaks first and foremost of *self*-understanding. On the present reading, self-understanding would be casting oneself into roles; part of my self-understanding, for instance, might be my casting myself as a school-teacher or a chess-player. These roles which a case of Dasein plays determine not what but *who* it is; even though they are socially instituted and worldly, they differ fundamentally from equipmental roles precisely in that cases of Dasein are accountable for how they perform. Thus, if a hammer fails to fill its role properly, it may be defective, but it is not reprehensible; on the other hand, a teacher who deliberately missed classes, or a chess-player who deliberately broke the rules, would be culpable and blameworthy. To cast oneself into such a role is to *take on* the relevant norms – both in the sense of undertaking to abide by them and in the sense of accepting responsibility for failings.

Dasein's abiding self-understanding – casting itself into roles – is the essential "continuity" that is presupposed by accountability. Promising is possible as an institution only in so far as cases of Dasein who make promises can, by virtue of having undertaken that commitment, be expected to keep them; in other words, it depends on cases of Dasein *who* cast themselves (understand themselves) as promisers, and hold themselves to it. Likewise, mere moving of the pieces of a chess set in accord with the rules, even on purpose, does not automatically amount to chess-playing – one might be acting, unaware that it is a game, or indifferent to the outcome. For the moves to constitute a chess game, the players must not only move according to the rules, but also cast *themselves* as chess-players. Thus, Dasein's *self*-understanding is essential to any understanding, and hence to disclosing being-in-the-world as such.

Self-casting into roles, however, can never be simple. Even so focused a commitment as keeping a single promise entails anticipating and satisfying prerequisites, recognizing and overcoming obstacles, being able to tell when it has been kept, and sticking with it until done. Each of these, in multifarious ways, can also require normatively accountable dealing with the world, and thus a re-identifiable who. But if they are all to be understood together, as the responsibilities of a promiser, then these separate threads of accountability must be strands in a *single* who. More complicated social roles, such as running for and holding political office, obviously integrate innumerable strands of commitment and entitlement into individual accountable agents. What is more, many of these *same* strands will also be integral to complex roles, such as upstanding citizen, responsible parent, loyal patriot, and so on; thus, the same individual simultaneously plays many roles. In order that anything be understandable as a claim, a checkmate, a bunt, a vote, and so on, it is essential not only that the equipment be cast into the relevant roles, but also the people: they must understand themselves as responsible role-players.

In so far as cases of Dasein make sense of themselves, we have instances of the formula "Y making sense of Y," with Y in two of the argument places of the radical interpretation formula, "X making sense of Y making sense of Z." But, as we saw earlier, there are two ways in which Y can occupy a second argument place in the larger formula. On one reading, Y is substituted in the formula for Z (things); that is, Y makes sense of itself in more or less the way that it makes sense of things – by casting itself in terms of publicly defined worldly roles (and in more or less the same way that everybody else casts into those roles). This, I think, is what Heidegger means by everyday or "unowned" self-understanding, and disclosedness in the mode of publicness. On the other reading, however, Y would be substituted in the formula for X (Davidson's anthropologist); in that case, Y makes sense of itself *as* itself making sense of things – Y understands itself not at all as a thing but as a *sense-maker*. This possibility, implicit in the story as told so far, but not here worked out, is, I believe, what Heidegger means by *owned* self-understanding, and disclosedness in the mode of resoluteness.

NOTES

I am indebted to audiences at the 1989 Spindel Conference at Memphis State University and at the University of of Toronto for comments and suggestions, and to Bert Dreyfus and Bill Blattner for years of inspiration and instruction.

1 *Sein und Zeit* (hereafter *SZ*), p. 133.
2 *SZ*, 85, 137, 220, 297, 350, 437; *Die Grundprobleme de Phänomenologie* (hereafter *GP*), 101f.
3 *SZ*, 357, 437; *GP*, 101–2.
4 *SZ*, 85; *GP*, 307.
5 *SZ*, 86, 137, 364.
6 *SZ*, 151, 341.
7 *SZ*, 220f, 297, 396; *GP*, 24f, 307f.
8 *SZ*, 167, 297.
9 *SZ*, 180, 220, 295f; Heidegger is not consistent about this structure, however: sometimes falling is substituted for telling (*SZ*, 349), and other times all four are given (*SZ*, 269, 335). "So-foundness" and "telling" are my translations of *Befindlichkeit* and *Rede*; they will be explained below.
10 Note that the game of chess not only positively enables actions that are otherwise impossible (such as checkmates and knight forks), but even enables the invention or discovery of possibilities that are unprecedented and hitherto unimagined (such as a new combination, or a new strategy for the opening). One of the limitations of the chess example, however, is that the game does not offer the resources for its own elaboration (the introduction of new rules or practices); by contrast, *Sein und Zeit* (to take only one example) not only says unprecedented things with the resources of German, but also elaborates and extends those resources themselves (through the introduction of new terminology and new uses of extant terms, for example). For a fuller treatment of these distinctions, see Robert Brandom, "Freedom and constraint by norms," especially section III.

11 See, for instance, "Mental Events" (hereafter ME), "Psychology as Philosophy" (PP), "Belief and the Basis of Meaning" (BBM), and "Thought and Talk" (TT). Of course, Davidson also maintains that every mental event is a physical event; but that is the conclusion of an argument requiring further factual and conceptual premises. It is not built into his notions of mental and physical events *per se*.

12 ME, 222.

13 See *GP*, ss. 10–12 (especially ss. 10a and 12c); "how" and "way" translate "*wie*" and "*Weise*."

14 For fluency of exposition, I am diverging from the details of Davidson's formulation (for instance, in speaking of states rather than events); but the view presented remains Davidsonian in general character. Note that the "determinacy" discussed here is not incompatible with Quinean indeterminacy; for Quine's point was never that meaning is *totally* indeterminate, but only that it is not totally determinate.

15 Compare this with Davidson's argument for the "nomological slack" between the mental and the physical: "The point is rather that when we use the concepts of belief, desire, and the rest, we must stand prepared, as the evidence accumulates, to adjust our theory in the light of considerations of overall cogency: the constitutive ideal of rationality partly controls each phase in the evolution of what must be an evolving theory. An arbitrary choice of translation scheme would preclude such opportunistic tempering of theory; put differently, a right arbitrary choice of translation manual would be of a manual acceptable in the light of all possible evidence, and this is a choice we cannot make" (ME, 222–3).

16 I'm using "tacit" semi-technically in a sense related to but distinct from that of "implicit." Both terms indicate something that is meant or done, but not explicitly or articulately. They differ, however, in that "implicit" suggests something which, although not itself explicit or said, is implied by something else that is explicit; whereas "tacit" suggests nothing explicit, but rather silence. Thus, fear of spiders might be implicit in calling (or thinking) them mean and ugly, while it might show tacitly in giving wide berth to woodpiles and dank corners. Standards of decorum and politeness can be applied tacitly, often quite unconsciously, in, for instance, responsive tone and body language.

17 PP, 231; ME, 221.

18 *SZ*, 68.

19 The terms "norm" and "role" are not Heidegger's. They are also not prominent in Davidson's vocabulary, though he does not abjure them, as the following passages attest: "The interpretation of verbal behavior thus shows the salient features of the explanation of behavior generally: we cannot profitably take the parts one by one (the words and sentences), for it is only in the context of the system (language) that their role can be specified" (PP, 239). And: "We have the idea of belief only from the role of belief in the interpretation of language, for as a private attitude it is not intelligible except as an adjustment to the public norm provided by language" (TT, 170).

20 The distinction between a nexus of interrelated equipment and a nexus of interdefined involvements – two different wholes – is often overlooked. It is clearly drawn, however, by both Brandom and Okrent, who also both interpret involvements (Okrent's translation is "functionalities") as roles. See "Heidegger's Categories," (p. 50), and *Heidegger's Pragmatism* (hereafter *HP*), 42. This is the same as the distinction we will later note between concrete context and world.

21 See *GP*, 432. "Availability" translates "*Zuhandenheit*." Heidegger refers to both involvement and availability as the *being* of equipmental entities (*SZ*, 69, 71, 84f)

22 Interestingly, Davidson himself uses the "make sense" locution in both ways: "Making sense of the utterances and behavior of others, even their most aberrant

behavior, requires us to find a great deal of reason and truth in them" (BBM, 153). And: "In our need to make him make sense, we will try for a theory that finds him consistent, a believer of truths, and a lover of the good (all by our own lights, it goes without saying)" (ME, 222).

23 "Amidst" and "in the midst of" are my attempt to render Heidegger's use of "*bei*" in the crucial phrase "*Sein-bei (innerweltlich begegnendem Seienden)*" (*SZ*, 192) and its many variants. As I interpret it, the point is that Dasein is by nature busily engaged in the midst of (or "in the thick of") things – not an indifferent outsider or passive spectator. This use is correlative with that of "*mit*" in "*Mitsein*" (or "*Sein mit*"), which I take to mean that Dasein is by nature communal – in each case, one "among" the others (i.e., not an outsider socially either).

24 Perhaps this position should be associated more specifically with what might be called "vintage Davidson," for more recently (see "A Nice Derangement of Epitaphs"), he has backed off the idea that linguistic communication depends on a language (or way of interpreting utterances) that is (1) systematic, (2) shared by speaker and hearer, and (3) conventional (or otherwise known in advance). Rather, speaker and hearer need only share a systematic "passing theory" for each utterance – a theory which each generates *ad hoc* on the basis of a "prior theory" of the other, plus current evidence. Without argument, let me suggest (in what I take to be a Heideggerian vein) that this view founders on the assumption that people normally *interpret* – that is, produce "interpretations" of – one another's speech. (I deny that radical interpretation begins at home.) Instead, primarily and usually, they "know how to go on" (in the conversation and elsewhere) on the basis of what has gone before (in the conversation and elsewhere). This is analogous to the claim that carpenters do not normally "interpret" the feel of the hammer and the look of the nail, but just carry on, fluidly and skillfully. Of course, in conversation as in carpentry, something can go awry, bringing one up short, and *then* interpretation (a passing theory, perhaps) may be needed and helpful.

Two points are crucial here (and hence most in need of argument). First, whatever talkers and carpenters have in advance (their normal skills and know-how), in terms of which they understand what is going on, must be different in kind from the interpretations or passing theories they come up with to handle difficulties; for otherwise, it would itself just be some prior (and presumably unconscious) interpretation or theory. Second, the sort of interpretation or theory that arises in response to routine glitches is essentially derivative and local; that is, it merely effects an adjustment or "work around" within the prior skillful repertoire, which remains fundamentally intact.

25 This interpretation is supported by the distinction Heidegger draws between the world as a totality of entities, and the world as that wherein Dasein "lives" and understands itself and in terms of which entities are freed (the latter is his official sense; for the former, he reserves quote marks) (*SZ*, 64f, 85f), and perhaps also by the thesis that significance is the worldliness of the world (*SZ*, 86f, 123). It must be conceded, however, that Heidegger's usage is not entirely clear, nor, I think, entirely consistent.

26 Compare Brandom's "Asserting."

27 Heidegger's word is "*Grundverfassung*," which Macquarrie and Robinson translate as "basic state," and Hofstadter translates as "basic constitution." The latter is better. The term "state" suggests a condition that something could be in or not be in, and hence is incidental to the entity itself. Thus, a squadron might be in a state of readiness (or not), a closet might be in a disordered state (or not), a neon atom might be in an excited state (or not). By contrast, as Heidegger emphasizes, it is incoherent

to say that Dasein might be "in-the-world" or not. But, if we understand being-in-the-world as a "state," this only invites the question: *Why* does Dasein *have to be* in that state? Why is the alternative incoherent? The problem is in thinking of Dasein as one thing (a thinking substance, an ego, a person) and in-the-worldness as another (a condition that it might – or, must – be in). The root of the problem lies in misconceiving Dasein: Dasein is not something that *has* being-in-the-world, whether necessarily or contingently; rather, Dasein *is* being-in-the-world. (My only hesitation in following Hofstadter in translating "*Verfassung*" as "constitution" is avoiding conflict with the technical term "*Konstitution*," and all that is associated with it.)

28　Saying that it is not a self-subsistent entity is far from saying that it is not an entity at all.

29　*SZ*, 132.

30　*GP*, 422; cf. *GP*, 237; *SZ*, 64, 364.

31　This collage-like structure of slowly varying, broader and narrower, criss-crossing unities and subunities is evident not only in Dasein as such and languages, but also, for instance, in professions, religious traditions, literary genres, Kuhnian disciplinary matrices, and so on. Needless to say, each of these can be seen as a kind of microcosm of being-in-the-world; indeed, Heidegger explicitly says that sciences (*SZ*, 11; cf. 357) and language (*BP*, 296) have Dasein's sort of being (existence in his technical sense).

32　Barbara Haugeland, psychologist and pâté chef, says: "Where there's life, there's a liver."

33　Compare *SZ*, 126, 239, 322; and *GP*, 226.

34　This possessive is the one expressed also in Heidegger's "*Jemeinigkeit*," "in each case mineness" (*SZ*, 41f); it is implicit also in the slogan "We *are* what we do" (cited above), for what we "do" is, of course, *our* behavior and roles. This "ownership" of our selves and our actions, grounded in accountability, is not the same as, but is the condition for the possibility of, that distinctive self-understanding that Heidegger calls ownedness or authenticity (*Eigentlichkeit*).

35　Compare *SZ*, 133 and 180. Note that Heidegger's use of "in" is seriously ambiguous. At *SZ*, 53, he distinguishes three constitutive moments in the structure of being-in-the-world: the "in the world," the "who" (or self, cf. *SZ*, 190), and being-in as such. This division is more or less echoed in the topics of the next three chapters, and again in the definition of care as the being of Dasein (*SZ*, 192, 249). But "in" means fundamentally different things in the first and third items. In the latter, being-in as such, it means engaged and caught up in concrete activities and communities; its modes are the amidst and among (of *Sein-bei* and *Mitsein*). But the "in" of the first item, the "in the world", can mean no such thing, for the world is not a concrete situation but rather an institutional framework of norms and roles: here the "in" is the same as (or a generalization of) the "in" of "in English": "Hobbes wrote both *in* English and *in* Latin."

36　e.g., *SZ*, 135, 188, 340, 346.

37　The awkward fact that "so-foundness" is not an English word is somewhat mitigated by the corresponding fact that "*Befindlichkeit*" is not a German word. Macquarrie and Robinson's translation, "state-of-mind," is really hopeless in that *Befindlichkeit* is neither a state nor of mind. Kisiel's "disposition" has the advantage that mood or attunement (*Stimmung*) sounds natural as an ontical mode; but it risks suggesting subjectivity, and in any case conflicts with an established philosophical usage. Dreyfus's and Blattner's "affectivity" has the same advantage as "disposition" and also accords with Heidegger's remarks about things mattering to Dasein, and sensory affect; but it sounds too much like Kant's "receptivity" and thus again suggests being on one side of a subject/object distinction. Guignon's "situatedness," which I like the best of these, lacks only the sense of Dasein "finding itself" situated, which is relevant to *Befindlichkeit* as disclosure. Finally, for what it's worth, "so-foundness" is more or less "literal."

38 I am not sure that Heidegger accepts the second clause; but he should, and I suspect he does.

39 "Telling" is a better English term for this phenomenon than "talk" or "discourse," even though it is not really correct as a translation of "*Rede,*" because it is broader, and in the direction of Heidegger's meaning. Expressly, I can tell you not only about the position, but also how to play, what to do, how I feel, and what someone said; without expression, I can tell your pawn from my rook, that the rook is threatened, and what to do about it.

40 More carefully put, these are not the basic phenomena of projection and possibility; in the ontologically derivative case of explaining occurrent (*vorhanden*) entities and events, however, projecting can, perhaps, amount to predicting, and possibility can be the same as not necessarily actual.

41 By the same token, not every way of having to do with things, or being directed toward them, is role-casting or understanding in this Heideggerian sense. Thus, if a tiger homes in on an antelope, or a guided missile homes in on a target, neither one is behaving accountably, in accord with collectively instituted norms and roles, in terms of which it could cast anything *as* an antelope or target. Because they are not themselves accountable to norms, they cannot "inhabit" an institutional frmework in terms of which things could make sense to them. (The tiger/antelope example is Okrent's – see *HP*, chapter 5 – but my interpretation of it is contrary to his).

REFERENCES

Brandon, Robert "Freedom and constraint by norms," *American Philosophical Quarterly* 16: 187–96.

——(1983a), "Asserting". *Noûs* 17: 637–50.

——(1983b), "Heidegger's categories," *The Monist* 66: 387–409.

——(1970), "Mental events," in *Experience and Theory*, Lawrence Foster and J. W. Swanson (eds), Amherst: University of Massachusetts Press. Reprinted in Davidson (1980); page references are to the latter.

—— (1974), "Psychology as philosophy," in *Philosophy of Psychology*, S. C. Brown, (ed.), London: Macmillan. Reprinted in Davidson (1980); page references are to the latter.

——(1974), "Belief and the basis of meaning," *Synthèse* 27: 309–23. Reprinted in Davidson (1984); page references are to the latter.

——(1980), *Essays on Actions and Events*. Oxford: Clarendon Press "Thought and talk," in *Mind and Language*, Samuel Guttenplan (ed.), Oxford: Clarendon Press (1975). Reprinted in Davidson (1984); page references are to the latter.

——(1984), *Inquiries into Truth and Interpretation*. Oxford: Clarendon Press.

Davidson, Donald (1986), "A nice derangement of epitaphs," in *Philosophical Grounds of Rationality*, Richard Grandy and Richard Warner (eds), Oxford: Clarendon Press.

Heidegger, Martin, (11th edition, 1967) *Sein und Zeit* Tubingen: Max Niemeyer Verlag. First published as a special edition of: *Jahrbuch für Philosophie und phänomenologische Forschung*, Vol. 8 (1927), Edmund Husserl (ed.). Translated as *Being and Time* (1962), by John Macquarrie and Edward Robinson, New York: Harper & Row.

——(1975), *Die Grundprobleme der Phänomenologie*. Frankfurt-am-Main: Vittorio Klostermann. (Marburg lectures, summer 1927). Translated as *The Basic Problems of Phenomenology* (1982), by Albert Hofstadter, Bloomington: Indiana University Press.

2
Heidegger's Categories in *Being and Time*

Robert Brandom

Introduction

In Division I of *Being and Time* Heidegger presents a novel categorization of what there is, and an original account of the project of ontology and consequently of the nature and genesis of those ontological categories. He officially recognizes two categories of Being: *Zuhandensein* (readiness-to-hand) and *Vorhandensein* (presence-at-hand). *Vorhandene* things are roughly the objective, person-independent, causally interacting subjects of natural scientific inquiry. *Zuhandene* things are those that a neo-Kantian would describe as having been imbued with human values and significances. In addition to these categories, there is human being, or Dasein, in whose structure the origins of the two thing-ish categories are to be found. This essay concerns itself with three of Heidegger's conceptual innovations: his conceiving of ontology in terms of self-adjudicating anthropological categories, as summed up in the slogan "fundamental ontology is the regional ontology of Dasein," his corresponding anti-traditional assertion of the ontological priority of the domain of the *Zuhandensein* to that of the *Vorhandensein*, which latter is seen as rooted in or precipitated out of that more basic (Heidegger says "primordial") world of human significances, and the non-Cartesian account of awareness and classificatory consciousness as social and practical.

  Section 1 presents an interpretation of Heidegger's notion of fundamental ontology, and its relation to the "vulgar" ontology practiced by previous philosophers. Section 2 introduces *Zuhandensein* – the world of equipment, each element of which is experienced *as* having some practically constituted role or significance. Section 3 offers a reading of *Mitdasein*, the social mode of being, which institutes the world of equipment. Finally, section 4 discusses the move from a world of equipment, about which there are no facts over and above how things are *taken* to be by all the bits of Dasein involved, to a realm of things which have properties not exhausted by the possible roles in Dasein's practical dealings.[1]

(1) What is most striking about Heidegger's account of categories is his distinction between "vulgar" ontology and "fundamental" ontology, and the co-ordinate claim that fundamental ontology is the regional ontology of Dasein (the kind of being we have). Vulgar ontology is the cataloging of the furniture of the universe. Fundamental ontology is said to be deeper and more difficult than the vulgar variety, requiring the investigation of the significance of ontological categorization. For vulgar ontology in its most careful versions, whether we consider Leibniz, Hegel, Frege, or Quine, a specification of such general kinds takes the form of a specification of *criteria of identity* and *individuation* for entities of those kinds. As an ontologist in this tradition, Descartes inaugurated the modern era with a bold reincarnation of a Plantonic idea: things are to be distinguished according to criteria of identity and individuation couched in terms of *epistemic* privilege. In particular, he invented a new kind of thing, according to the scheme: an event or object is *mental* (or subjective) just in case it is whatever it is taken to be by some individual.[2] The rest of the (nondivine) universe he relegated to the physical or objective realm. These were things which are what they are regardless of how any individual takes them to be.[3] The contribution of the nineteenth century to this scheme was Hegel's notion (see section 3) of a third category of *social* entities. What is at issue here is the domain of social *appropriateness* in which, as in etiquette, social practice is the highest court of appeal. Thus a group or community can be thought of as having the same sort of criterial dominion or authority over, and hence, privileged access to, social things that individuals have over subjective things.

Before describing how Heidegger develops this idea into a detailed model of social practice and significance in *Being and Time*, let us consider some consequences which adding such an ontological category to the Cartesian two-sorted ontology can have. In particular, we can ask the question of fundamental ontology: What is the ontological status of the distinction of entities into three kinds (subjective, social, and objective) based on the source of criterial authority for them? In particular, is the division of things into subjective, social, and objective a subjective distinction (as Berkeley would have it), a social distinction, or an objective one?[4] The conceptual status of such a question is unusual enough to warrant the citation of a few more familiar examples which exhibit the same structure.

First, consider the distinction between differences of *quality* and differences of *quantity*. Is this difference, we may ask, a qualitative or a quantitative one? Engels notoriously takes himself to have transformed the philosophical tradition by suggesting the latter response in place of the former. Whatever merit that suggestion may have, the issue it seeks to respond to seems to be perfectly intelligible.

Another example can be observed in the medieval notions of "*distinctio rationis*" and "*distinctio realis.*" The distinction between form and matter is only a distinction of reason, for we can never have one without the other. Only by, e.g., rationally considering the relations a bronze cube stands in to a bronze sphere and a marble cube can we "separate" its being bronze from its being a cube. Between a piece of bronze and a piece of marble, on the other hand, there exists a real distinction, for these can be nonmetaphorically separated without reliance on rational abstraction by comparison. But now we must ask, as did the Scholastics, whether the distinction between rational and real distinctions is itself a rational or a real distinction. Although issues of great moment for the debate about the ontological and epistemological status of universals turn on the answer to this question, our concern is with the structure of the question rather than with the plausibility of various answers to it.

A final example should make clear the phenomenon being pointed out. The US constitution gives the three broad branches of the Federal government distinct responsibilities and jurisdictions. As part of the relations of authority and responsibility which exist between the branches (the "checks and balances" that regulate their interaction), the judiciary is given the authority and responsibility to interpret the proper region of authority and responsibility of *each* branch, itself included. In matters of constitutional import, we may say, the judiciary is given the authority to draw the boundaries between its own authority and that of the executive and legislative branches.

It is not easy to describe the structure which these examples share. In each case a family of concepts pertaining to identity and individuation is examined, and the root of the identity and individuation of those concepts is found to reside in one of them. (In the last example, instead of a concept with an extension including various things, we have a social institution with a jurisdiction including various things.) In each case the question can be raised whether one of those concepts (institutions) is *self-adjudicating* in the sense that it applies to the sort of identity and individuation which distinguishes it from the other concepts or institutions in that family. To raise this second-order sort of question about a scheme of ontological categories is to engage in fundamental ontology. And Heidegger's claim that fundamental ontology is the regional ontology of Dasein is the claim that Dasein-in-the-world-of-the-ready-to-hand is ontologically self-adjudicating in this sense. Not only is the distinction between the ontological categories of the ready-to-hand and the present-at-hand intelligible only in terms of the sort of being that Dasein has, but the difference between Dasein's sort of being and readiness-to- and presentness-at-hand must itself be understood in terms of Dasein. It is this central feature of his early work which led the later Heidegger to dismiss *Being and Time* as "merely anthropological."

The ontological primacy of the social can be justified by appeal to a more specific thesis: pragmatism concerning *authority*. This is the claim that all matters of authority or privilege, in particular *epistemic* authority, are matters of social practice, and not objective matters of fact.[5] The pragmatist about authority will take the criterial distinctions between ontological categories to be social in nature, for those categories are distinguished precisely by the locus of criterial authority over them. The category of the social must then be seen as self-adjudicating, and hence as ontologically basic, so the broader claim of the ontological priority of social categories follows from the narrower doctrine concerning the social nature of authority. In what follows it will be argued that Heidegger develops precisely this line of thought in Division I of *Being and Time*.

(2) According to Heidegger, Dasein finds itself always amidst an already existing world of equipment, consisting of significant things each of which is

experienced *as* something. The readiness-to-hand of a piece of equipment consists in its having a certain significance. This significance in turn consists in its appropriateness for various practical roles and its inappropriateness for others. "But the 'indicating' of the sign and the 'hammering' of the hammer are not properties [*Eigenschaften*] of entities . . . Anything ready-to-hand is, at worst, appropriate [*Geignet*] for some purposes and inappropriate for others" (p. 114). Properties, by contrast, are what characterize the present-at-hand independently of human practical ends – what would be taken to be true of objects before human beings "attach significances" to them on the neo-Kantian picture Heidegger wishes to invert. Heidegger's problem in the first part of *Being and Time* is to explain how such a category of objective Being could be constructed or abstracted out of the primitive system of appropriatenesses and significances which makes up the world in which we always already find ourselves.

How are we to understand this category of the ready-to-hand? To inhabit a *world* is to *take* each thing in that world *as* something. A piece of equipment is something experienced *as* something. Several points about this "as"-structure must be appreciated in order to understand the ready-to-hand as the kind of being or significance a thing exhibits by being taken *as* something. First, the something$_1$s which are taken as something$_2$s must be understood as themselves things which are ready-to-hand as ways of taking still other pieces of equipment. "In interpreting we do not, so to speak, throw a 'signification' over some naked thing which is present-at-hand, we do not stick a value on it."[6] The something$_1$s which are given with respect to one set of takings must themselves have been socially constituted. Second, it must be understood how thoroughly non-Cartesian and unsubjective is Heidegger's notion of the classificatory activity in virtue of which things show themselves *as* something$_2$s. The world of the ready-to-hand is what we can be aware of, *as* we are or would be aware of it. For Heidegger, as for others, there is no awareness or experience without classification. But the "awareness" which is the appropriation of some bit of equipment *as* having a certain significance is a public behavioral matter of how the thing is treated or responded to, not a mental act. For Heidegger the confused notion of the subjective arises when the category of the present-at-hand has been achieved, as that co-ordinate mental realm which must be invoked when one mistakenly takes the present-at-hand as ontologically primary, and looks for something to *add* to it to explain the everyday world of the ready-to-hand. If this anti-subjectivism is overlooked, the use of the notion of classification to bridge the gap between Heidegger's "as"-structure and traditional notions of consciousness will be misleading. Finally, it must be noted that modeling understanding on taking-as is a device for interpreting the text, not a rendering of its terminology. Officially, discussions of "as-structure" are restricted to the level of interpretation (which develops out of understanding) where something is noticed *as* a hammer not when it is hammered with (as the model of understanding would have it) but only when it is discarded as inappropriate for, or searched for as required by some practical project. The broader usage has an exegetical point, however, and the specific differences between understanding and interpretation can be accommodated within it, as we shall see. The positive account of treating or taking *as* has three features. First, takings are public performances which accord with social practices. Second, such performances are individuated as and by *responses*. Third, the responsive dispositions which constitute the social practices are related to one another so as to satisfy a strong systematicity condition. We examine these points below.

Where do the sorts or kinds or characters which are the something$_2$s according to which something$_1$s are classified come from? Any concrete object or event is similar to any other in an infinite number of respects, and dissimilar to it in an infinite number of others. For a respect of similarity is just a shared possible partial description, and these can be gerrymandered as we like. The practical discrimination of objects and performances into those appropriate for or according to some practice and those not is precisely the recognition of *some* of these infinitely numerous abstractly generable respects of similarity as having a special privilege over the rest. Heidegger should be interpreted in accord with the pragmatist thesis about authority, as taking this privilege to consist in its social recognition, that is, as a matter of how some community does or would respond to things. Something$_2$s are response-types, and classifying something$_1$s as a particular something$_2$ is simply responding to it with a performance of that type. Equipment is originally introduced in section 15 as consiting of *pragmata*, "that which one has to do with in one's concernful dealings." The ready-to-hand is generically characterized by serviceability (*Dienlichkeit*): "Serviceability . . . is not an appropriateness of some entity; it is rather the condition (so far as Being is in question) which makes it possible for the character of such an entity to be defined by its appropriatenesses" (p. 115. H, 83). "Serviceability" is thus the potential which objects have to be caught up in the practices which institute specific respects of appropriateness. For something$_1$ to be so caught up is for it to be *involved*: "The Being of an entity within the world is its involvement [*Bewandtnis*]" (p. 116, H, 84). Such involvement in turn comprises a system of references or assignments: "To say that the Being of the ready-to-hand has the structure of reference or assignment [*Verweisung*] means that it has in itself the character of *having been assigned or referred*" (p. 115, H, 84). The appropriatenesses which are the significance of a particular entity exist in virtue of such reference or assignment. Referring or assigning is instituting relations among equipment (pen, ink, paper, etc.) and clearly is something that is *done*, though we must not assume for that reason that it is something any one of us can do, or even that it is something the whole community can do (except in a derivative sense), rather than something done by the community's practices as constitutive of those practices . . .[7] These assignments exist in virtue of the responsive dispositions which are appropriate in a community.

A further doctrine is that "An entity is discovered when it is assigned or referred to something, and referred as that entity which it is" (p. 115, H, 84). Discovering an entity is taking it *as* something (the non-Cartesian notion of awareness as behavioral classification). Referring or assigning is to be understood not only as instituting the social appropriatenesses which are the significances of objects and performances, but also as making possible the appropriation of such significances by those who discover objects in terms of them. "Appropriation" [*Zueignung*] is Heidegger's nonsubjective epistemic activity. To discover something ready-to-hand, to appropriate it, is to take it *as* something, to respond to it in a certain way. In one of his rare examples, after telling us that signs can be taken as paradigmatic of equipment in general, Heidegger says that "the kind of behaving (Being) which corresponds to the sign [a turn-signal arrow] is either to 'give way' or stand still with respect to the car with the arrow" (p. 110, H, 79). Here it is precisely how it is appropriate to respond to the turn-signal in a context that makes it the bit of equipment it is. To take it *as* such a signal (discover it as such) is just to respond to it with the appropriate behavior.

The systematicity requirement may be put broadly by the claim that "Taken strictly, there 'is' no such thing as *an* equipment. To the Being of any equipment there always belongs a totality of equipment, in which it can be the equipment that it is" (p. 97, H, 68). Anything ready-to-hand is so only in virtue of the role it plays in a "referential totality of significance or involvements." "As the Being of something ready-to-hand, an involvement is itself discovered only on the basis of the prior discovery of a totality of involvements" (p. 118, H, 85).

In terms of what relations are such roles to be understood, and how must they fit together to form the appropriate kind of totality? Heidegger gives his answer in section 18, "Involvement and Significance – the Worldhood of the World." Although the account offered there deploys an unfamiliar set of technical terms, its basic characteristics may be straightforwardly set out. The bearers of the social significances making up readiness-to-hand are of two kinds: objects and performances. Objects and performances are what can be constitutively judged to be (in the sense of being responded to as) appropriate or not according to the social practices which are the medium of social significance. Heidegger calls those practices "in-order-to's" (*das Umzu*). Fastening one board to another by driving a nail would be an example. An object can be caught up in such a practice either by being used in the practice, or by being produced in that practice. In the former case, Heidegger calls the object (for example, a hammer or a nail, used in the different senses of "employed" and "consumed" respectively) the "with-which" (*das Womit*) of the practice, and in the latter case he calls the object which is produced the "towards-which" (*das Wozu*). The assignments of objects are the relations between them instituted by relations between the practices in which they are involved in these two ways. The role of an object (its involvement) is determined by those practices in which it is appropriately used, and those practices in which it can appropriately be produced.

Particular performances are called "in whiches" (*das Wobei*). A social practice may be thought of as a class of possible performances, that is as a performance *type*. Such an in-order-to consists, namely, of just those performances which are or would be (taken to be) appropriate according to it. For something to be (ready-to-hand as) a hammer is for it to be appropriate to respond to it with a performance of the hammering type, i.e., to hammer with it. It is performances of using and producing objects which make up the social practices in virtue of which those objects acquire their involvements and significances. Social object -types are then instituted by social practice types of the performances in which they are appropriately used or produced. In the world of the ready-to-hand, in which things are whatever they are (or would be) responded to *as*, then, the individuation of objects (by their roles as with- and towards-whiches) is determined by the individuation of social practices. Object types are instituted by performance types. So where do the appropriateness equivalence classes of performances, which are the social practices, come from?

As with objects, performance tokens exhibit infinite numbers of objective respects of similarity and dissimilarity. The privilege which one type or co-appropriateness class of performances exhibits as a practice can only have its source in its social recognition, that is, in how the type-privileged (co-typical) performance tokens would be treated or taken, or more generally responded to by the community in question. The performances comprised by a social practice are of the same type in that there is some other responsive performance type (something$_2$) such that each of the tokens of the instituted performance type (something$_1$) is, according to the community whose recognitions are constitutive in this domain, appropriately responded to by some performance belonging to the instituting type. A performance is recognized as being of the type by being responded to as such. For instance, what makes a certain class of performances all instances of the type *constructings of tribally appropriate dwelling huts* is that each of those possible performances would be appropriately responded to by a performance of the type *tribe members treating the produced object as a dwelling* – that is *being prepared to dwell in it under suitable circumstances*. Whenever what is produced by one practice is used by another, the using practice plays the role of responsive recognition performance type(rrpt) with respect to the producing practice. The role of a social performance type in a "totality of involvements" is specified by saying what performance type is its rrpt, and what performance type it is an rrpt for.

The requirement of systematicity or of the autonomy of significance may then be stated in two parts. First, with respect to objects, every object-type appropriately produced by one social practice must be appropriately useable in or by some other practice. The converse need not hold, for Heidegger says several times that *natural* objects are ready-to-hand as objects useable in human practice, but not requiring to be produced by it.[8] Second, with respect to performances, every performance type which is an rrpt for some performance type must have some other performance type as its own rrpt. Again the converse need not hold, since we can respond to natural events. To specify the role of an object in such a system is to specify those practices with respect to which it functions as towards-which, and those with respect to which it functions as a with-which. To specify the role of a performance (in-which) is to specify the practice, that is the performance type to which it belongs. And to specify such an in-order-to is to specify its rrpt and what it functions as an rrpt of. Doing so determines all of the assignment relations and involvements which hold between socially significant objects as such, as well as the instituting responsive relations defining social performance types. The non-Cartesian epistemic notion of appropriation of significance or discovery of the ready-to-hand is also given a natural social-behavioral reading on this account. For to grasp the involvement of an object is to achieve practical mastery of its various assignments. And such mastery consists simply in being able to act (use, produce, and respond) appropriately according to the practices which institute those involvements. To respond to an object or performance which is appropriate according to a practice *as* appropriate according to that practice, that is, to respond appropriately to it, is to discover it as what it is, as ready-to-hand for what it is ready-to-hand for. Such practical capacities can be described without invoking anything subjective on the part of the practitioners. The inhabitant of a Heideggerian world is aware of it as composed of significant equipment, caught up in various social practices and classified by the involvements those practices institute. But this awareness is practical, social, and behavioral, consisting entirely in the exhibition of differential responsive dispositions according appropriately with those of the community.

The account suggested of the nature of the referential totality of significance within which we encounter the ready-to-hand explains the concept of the worldhood of the world in at least one straightforward sense. For the remarks above can be expressed in a first-order quantificational language. Such a language would need two different sorts of indivdual constants, to stand for object types and performance types, and three different predicates (corresponding to the three sorts of "assignment or reference" distinguished above); U (o,p), interpreted as saying that object o is used in practice p, P(p, o), interpreted as saying that object o is produced by practice p, and R(p,p'), interpreted as saying that p' is the rrpt of p. It is easy to see that the two halves of the systematicity condition can be expressed as quantificational sentences in such a language. It is equally easy to see how the model theory for such a language might go. Theories in the specified language that include the sentences codifying the systematicity conditions would be interpreted by model structures which consisted of domains of object and performance types (represented as sets of tokens) and relations between them of using, producing, and responding. A Heideggerian world is such a structure satisfying in the usual sense a first-order theory of the sort described which contains the systematicity conditions.[9] At the end of section 18 Heidegger summarizes the structure he discerns:

> The "for-the-sake-of-which" signifies an "in-order-to"; this in turn a "towards-this"; the latter, an "in-which" of letting something be involved; and that in turn the "with-which". These relationships are bound up with one another as a primordial totality; they are what they are *as* signifying . . . The relational totality of this signifying we call "significance." (p. 120, H, 87)

This passage emphasizes the systematic structure of social significance and retraces the relations of use and response described above. It mentions the further technical expression "for-the-sake-of-which" [*das Worumwillen*] which marks the point of contact of the categorial structure with the existential concerns of Division II and so cannot be discussed here. A practical "in-order-to" gives a point to performances of some type by providing a use for the "towards-this" (a particular "towards-which") produced by such performances. Those performances are "in-which"s individuated as types by their overall role or involvement in use of "with-which"s as means or production of "towards-which"s, as those "towards-which"s are individuated by their involvement not only in being produced by performances of a certain kind from raw materials of a certain kind, but also by their involvement in a further practice (an "in-order-to" whose performances are themselves "in-which"s) which makes use of them. The communities whose responsive recognitive practices generate these structures of social significance will be considered next.

(3)   We have interpreted worldhood as that referential totality which constitutes significance. In Being-familiar with this significance and previously understanding it, Dasein lets what is ready-to-hand be encountered as discovered in its involvement. In Dasein's Being, the context of references or assignments which significance implies is tied up with Dasein's ownmost Being . . . (p. 160, H, 123)

Nothing like a full account of Dasein's kind of Being can be essayed here; that's the topic of the whole of *Being and Time*. On the other hand, something must be said about the constitution of the community in whose dispositions (for appropriate responsive recognitions or takings) significance originates. Happily the features of Dasein's kind of Being which must be understood if the precipitation of the present-at-hand out of the ready-to-hand is to be intelligible can be explained with the materials already available.

The first point, of course, is that Dasein's Being is *social* in nature: So far as Dasein *is* at all, it has Being-with-one-another as its kind of Being (p. 163, H, 125)

Not only is Being-toward-Others an autonomous, irreducible relationship, as Being-with, it is one which, with Dasein's Being, already is (p. 162, H, 125).

Dasein in itself is essentially Being-with (p. 156, H, 120).

Next, Dasein's sociality is essential to the practical activity which constitutes worldly significance: "Dasein-with remains existentially constitutive for Being-in-the-world" (p. 157, H, 121: compare also p. 163, H, 125). Third, it is only in the context of such Dasein-with that individuals can be spoken of: "In Being with and towards Others, there is thus a relationship of Being [*Seinsverhaltnis*] from Dasein to Dasein. But it might be said that this relationship is already constitutive for one's own Dasein" (p. 162, H, 124). "In terms of the 'they' [*das Man*] and as the 'they', I am given proximally to myself" (p. 167, H, 129).

These doctrines can be understood according to the Hegelian model of the synthesis of social substance by mutual recognition. To belong to a community, according to this model, is to be recognized as so belonging by all those one recognizes as so belonging. Hegel's idea was that community constitutive recognition is transitive *de jure* – that one must recognize those who are recognized by those one recognizes. The reflexive self-recognition that makes one a Hegelian individual will then follow if one can establish *de facto* symmetry, that is achieve recognition by those one recognizes. To be entitled to recognize or regard oneself as an excellent chess-player one must be entitled to be regarded as such by those one so regards.

Of course, for an account along these lines to be helpful in interpreting Heidegger, recognition must not be taken to be a mental act, but as with awareness and classification must be given a social behavioral reading in terms of communal responsive dispositions. What sort of response (rrpt) is taking or recognizing someone *as* one of us, a member of *our* community? Clues are to be found in two passages: "In that with which we concern ourselves environ-mentally, the Others are encountered as what they are; they *are* what they do" (p. 163, H, 126). What is it that other community members as such do? They take objects and performances *as* ready-to-hand with respect to various practices *by* using them and responding to them in various ways. How does such behavior constitute the practioners as other members of one's own community? "By 'Others' we do not mean everyone else but me – those against whom the 'I' stands out. They are rather those from whom for the most part one does not distinguish oneself – those among whom one is too" (p. 154, H, 118).

Not everyone is a communal Other, but only those one recognizes or responds to as such. To respond to them as such is not to distinguish them from oneself. But in what regard? The previous passage said that the Others are what they do, so it is their doings which one does not distinguish from one's own. And this is to say that one treats their *responses* and dispositions as one's own. What they take to be appropriate performances and usings and producings of equipment, one also takes as such. To give one's own responses no special status or priority in this way is to treat the kinds they institute as social. It is to take the authority over appropriateness boundaries to reside in the community, which is constituted by that very recognition.[10]

The suggestion is that my recognizing someone as a co-community member is responding to him in a certain way. That way is for me to respond to his responses as having the same authority to institute kinds and appropriateness equivalence classes that my own responses have. In particular, my recognitions of others *and myself* as members of the community have no special authority. My recognitions of myself as community member count only if they are taken to count by those I take to be community members. Their so taking my recognitions is in turn simply a matter of their recognizing me, that is treating my responses as equally authoritative as theirs in determining appropriatenesses. The commun-ity, *Mitdasein*, then differs from the ready-to-hand in that its members are constituted not only by being recogniz*ed* or responded to in a certain way, but also by their recogniz*ings* and responses as recogniz*ers*.

Being-together-with in the sense of forming a recognitive community is accordingly the existential basis of the consilience of practice which constitutes the category of the ready-to-hand and hence, as we shall see, the category of the present-at-hand as well. The distinction between the existential and the categorial terminologically marks that between recogniz*ers*, and the merely recogniz*eds* which do not have the kind of being of one of us. The practical agreement of recognizing each other's recognizings can be called "communication" "in a sense which is ontologically broad":

"Communication" in which one makes an assertion – giving information, for instance – is a special case of the communication which is grasped in principle existentially. In this more general kind of communicating the Articulation of Being-with one another understandingly is constituted. Through it a co-state-of-mind [*Mitbefindlichkeit*] gets "shared," and so does the understanding of Being-with. (p. 205, H, 162)

In the next section we investigate the genesis of the category of the present-at-hand out of the sort of understanding which consists in shared recognitive pratice permitting communication about a world of equipment each bit of which is whatever it is recognized-by-us as.

(4) The claim to be developed in this section is that the category of the present-at-hand consists of ready-to-hand things which are appropriately responded to by a certain kind of performance, *qua* things that can *only* be appropriately responded to by such a performance. That categorially constitutive kind of responsive recognition performance type is *assertion*. Since Heidegger holds that "assertion is derived from interpretation, and is a special case of it,"[11] the story must begin with the notion of interpretation (*Auslegung*)

Interpretation is a co-ordinate notion to that understanding which consists in the practical mastery of a totality of significations or assignments required if one is to live in a world at all. For "we never perceive equipment that is ready-to-hand without already understanding and interpreting it."[12] Four features of interpretation must be recognized. First, interpreting characterizes practical activity: "Interpretation is carried out primordially not in a theoretical statement but in an action of circumspectful concern . . . [e.g.] laying aside the unsuitable tool" (p. 200, H, 157). Second, interpreting involves making something one's own. Interpretation is described as "the working-out and appropriation of an understanding."[13] "In understanding there lurks the possibility of interpretation – that is of *appropriating* what is understood" (p. 203, H, 161. See also p. 191, H, 150). Taking something as something was the form of the act of understanding, that discovery of a bit of equipment which also disclosed a totality of equipmental involvements. What is it practically to appropriate such an understanding?

The answer is offered by a pair of passages, worth citing at length, which for the third point introduce the crucial *conditional* structure of interpretation, out of which the possibility of inference and hence assertion develops.

> Circumspection operates in the involvement-relationships of the context of equipment which is ready-to-hand. What is essential is that one should have a primary understanding of the totality of involvements . . . In one's current using and manipulating, the concernful circumspection . . . *brings* the ready-to-hand *closer* to Dasein, and does so by *interpreting* what has been sighted. The specific way of bringing the object of concern closer we call *deliberating* [*Ueberlegung*]. The schema particular to this is the "if . . . then . . ."; if this or that, for instance, is to be produced, put to use, or averted, then some ways, means, circumstances or opportunities will be needed. (p. 410, H, 359)

Interpretation classifies according to personal ends or projects, and hence appropriates. What new element is indicated by the invocation of the "if . . . then . . ." as what is in this way brought closer to oneself?

But if deliberation is to be able to operate in the scheme of the "if . . . then . . .", concern must already have "surveyed" a context of involvements and have an understanding of it. That which is considered with an "if" must already be understood as *something or other* . . . . The schema "something-as-something" has already been sketched out beforehand in the structure of one's pre-predicative understanding. (p. 411, H, 359)

Understanding appropriates equipment. It is exercised in taking something as something, e.g., as a hammer. Interpretation at the level of deliberation adds to this use and appropriation of equipment, the use and appropriation of equipmental *understanding* of particular involvements. One can not only take something as a hammer, but can take a hammer as one of the tools required for a certain pratical project. What is appropriated is then the conditional serviceabilities of things. One uses and produces conditional understandings of the significance of particular something$_1$s as something$_2$s.

The fourth point is that this non-Cartesian cognitive notion of interpretation as the personal practical appropriation of a conditional appropriateness of equipmental involvement brings us closer to the notion of linguistic assertion.

In the significance itself, with which Dasein is always familiar, there lurks the ontological condition which makes it possible for Dasein, as something which understands and interprets, to disclose such things as 'significations'; upon these, in turn, is founded the Being of words and of language. (p. 121, H, 87)

"Significations" are the conditional appropriatenesses into which the totality of significations can be "dissolved or broken up."[14] What makes the transition to language possible is that one can come to respond differentially to (and hence disclose practically) not just things and performances but the significations which are their conditional dependencies. Deliberation develops towards asserting when what is surveyed from the point of view of a practical end is a field of "if . . .then . . ."s, each of which may then itself be used or laid aside, just as with first-order equipment. Deliberation accomplishes a special kind of abstraction, requiring responsive recognition of the serviceabilities of equipment, rather than merely of the equipment itself.

The key to the precipitation of the present-at-hand out of the ready-to-hand lies in assertion:

The levelling of the primordial "as" of circumspective interpretation [the "existential-hermeneutical 'as'"] to the "as" with which presence-at-hand is given a definite character [the "apophantical 'as'"] is the specialty of assertion. Only so does it obtain the possibility of exhibiting something in such a way that we just look at it. (p. 201, H, 158)

The articulation leading to the discovery of the present-at-hand begins in the "if . . . then . . ." of interpretation of the ready-to-hand. What matters is "what is awaited"[15] in the "then . . ." part. In the basic case of interpreting something merely ready-to-hand, what is "awaited" is the useability or producibility of some actual or envisaged object or performance – that is, the projection of a practical possibility. In presence-at-hand, the primary consequence of an "if (something as something) . . ." is the appropriability of some *claim* or assertion. The difference between responding to something as present-at-hand and as merely ready-to-hand is that things which are present-at-hand are appropriately responded to as such only by producing a particular kind of performance, namely assertions. The "then" is still something ready-to-hand when we thematize (i.e., respond to something as present-at-hand), but it is an assertion, a very special kind of equipment.

The question is then: "By what existential-ontological modification does assertion arise from circumspective interpretation?" (p. 200, H, 157). The answer in brief is that assertions are equipment appropriately used for *inference*. Assertion is the topic of section 33, which offers three "significations" of assertion. The central one of these is that "assertion means communication."

> As something-communicated, that which has been put forward in the assertion is something that Others can 'share' with the person making the assertion . . .. That which is put forward in the assertion is something which can be passed along in further retelling. (p. 197, H, 155)

> What is expressed becomes, as it were, something ready-to-hand within-the-world which can be taken up and spoken again. (p. 266, H, 224)

Asserting thus has the significance of issuing a *re*-assertion license to other community members. The assertion is produced as something useable by others.

The other two features by which assertion is introduced are "pointing-out" some subject of assertion, and "giving it a definite character" by predicating something of it. What is shared, in other words, is the taking of something as something. Where before taking something as something (pointing it out and characterizing it) was something one could only *do*, now it becomes something one can *say*. What was implicit in performance now becomes an explicitly producible and usable bit of equipment, which one can appropriate and make available for others to appropriate. The pointing-out of a subject is socially transitive acros authorized reassertions, and so guarantees communication in the sense of securing a common topic: "Even when Dasein speaks over again what someone else has said, it comes into a Being-towards the very entities which have been discussed" (p. 266, H, 224). Such social preservation of a common subject-matter is a necessary condition for the possibility of agreement and disagreement of assertion, as opposed to mere change of topic.

Predication, as explicitly communicable characterization, further extends the authorizing dimension of asserting. For predicates come in inferential families: *if* what is pointed out is appropriately characterizable by one speaker as red, *then* it is appropriately characterizable by another as colored. The practical conditional appropriatenesses of assertion which make up such familes of predicates guarantee that an asserting licenses more than just re-assertion, licensing others to draw conclusions beyond what was originally claimed. As members of inferential families, the predicates used to characterize objects in assertions codify the conditional significations responded to as such already in deliberation. It is in virtue of the socially appropriate inferential consequences of an asserting that it conveys information, authorizing a specific set of performances (including other assertions) which would have been inappropriate without such authorization. The taking of something$_1$ as something$_2$ of pre-predicative understanding becomes explicitly usable and sharable once linguistic terms are available as equipment for publicly pointing out something$_1$s, and predicates codifying as inferential significances the conditional serviceabilities discerned by deliberative interpretation are available as equipment expressing explicitly the involvements implicit in the something$_2$s things were taken as.

Understanding asserting as authorizing reassertion and inference specifies the *use* to which assertions, as bits of equipment, may appropriately be put. The recognitive responsive performance type of any asserting-type will be the set of assertions which it may appropriately be seen as licensing, namely those which follow from it according to the inferential practices of the community. But this is only half the story. What about the appropriate circumstances of *production* of this new sort of ready-to-hand equipment? Corresponding to the dimension of authority governing the use of assertions as equipment-for-inference is a dimension of responsibility governing their production. For in producing an assertion one does not simply authorize others to use it inferentially, one also undertakes the responsibility to justify one's claim.

> Assertion communicates entities in the "how" of their uncoveredness . . .
> If however, these entities are to be appropriated explicitly with respect to their uncoveredness, this amounts to saying that the assertion is to be *demonstrated* as one that uncovers. The assertion expressed is something ready-to-hand. (p. 266, H, 224, emphasis added)

As ready-to-hand, assertings are subject to social appropriatenesses of production as well as use. These concern when one is entitled to commit oneself to the claim, or in Heidegger's terminology, "appropriate" it, so that the inference and reassertion license is in force: "It is therefore essential that Dasein should explicitly appropriate what has already been uncovered, defend it against semblance and disguise, and assure itself of its uncoveredness again and again" (p. 265, H, 222).

The responsibility to justify or defend one's claims undertaken as a matter of course in their appropriate production is essential to the special sort of communication which emerges with assertion. For even when Dasein speaks over again what someone else has said, though it comes into relation to the things pointed out and uncovered "it has been exempted from having to uncover them again, primordially, and it holds that it has thus been exempted."[16] That is, he who relies on the authority of a previous speaker in reassertion is absolved of the responsibility to justify his claim which he would otherwise have undertaken by his performance of producing that assertion. His reliance upon the authority of the first assertor just is his acquisition of the right to defer justificatory responsibility for his own assertion to the original speaker. The response which socially constitutes taking someone to have appropriately made an assertion (fulfilled or be able to fulfill his justificatory responsibility) is to treat his assertion as genuinely authoritative as licensing others, that is, to recognize as appropriate any deferrals of justificatory responsibility for that claim and its consequences to the original assertor by those relying upon that authority. It is in this way that the dimensions of responsibility and authority, of appropriate production and use, are related so as to constitute assertions as equipment-for-communicating.[17]

This sketch of Heidegger's notion of assertion puts us in a position to understand the category of the present-at-hand. The crucial point to understand here is that the move from equipment ready-to-hand, fraught with socially instituted significances, to objective things present-at-hand, is not one of decontextualization, but of *re*contextualization. Asserting and the practices of giving and asking for reasons which make it possible are themselves a special sort of practical activity. Responding to something by making an assertion about it is treating it *as* present-at-hand. Presence-at-hand is constituted by special appropriatenesses of response.

> In characterizing the change-over from manipulating and using and so forth which are circumspective in a "practical" way, to "theoretical" exploration, it would be easy to suggest that merely looking at entities is something which emerges when concern *holds back* from any kind of manipulation . . . . But this is by no means the way in which the "theoretical" attitude of science is reached. On the contrary, the tarrying which is discontinued when one manipulates can take on the character of a more precise kind of circumspection . . . (p. 409, H, 357–8)

Claims, equipment for asserting, represent "more precise" interpretive responses because in them the significations which are merely implicit in ordinary equipment become explicit or "thematized," accessible to claims and inferences and hence to demands for justification. Treating something as present-at-hand is not ignoring its social significance, but attending to a special sort of significance it can have, namely significance for the correctness of assertions about it. Corresponding to a new social mode of response, asserting, there is a new kind of being, presence-at-hand, constitutively uncovered by that response: "Thematizing objectifies. It does not first 'posit' the entities, but frees them so that one can interrogate them and determine their character "objectively". Being which objectifies and which is alongside the present-at-hand within-the-world is characterized by a *distinctive kind of making-present*" (p. 414, H, 363).

The present-at-hand may thus be defined as what is ready-to-hand as a with-which for the practice of assertion, that is, as what is responded to as such only by making a claim about it. We have seen what kind of performance assertings are. What is the relation between what is responded to as ready-to-hand for assertion and what is pointed out as present-at-hand in the assertion? Heidegger explains this in terms of a transformation:

The entity which is held in our fore-having – for instance the hammer – is proximally ready-to-hand as equipment. If this entity becomes the "object" of an assertion, then as soon as we begin this assertion, there is already a change-over in the fore-having. Something *ready-to-hand with which* we have to do or perform something turns into something *"about which"* the assertion that points it out is made. Our fore-sight is aimed at something present-at-hand in what is ready-to-hand . . .. Within this discovery of presence-at-hand, which is at the same time a covering-up of readiness-to-hand, something present-at-hand which we encounter is given a definite character in its Being-present-at-hand-in-such-and-such-a-manner. Only now are we given access to *properties* or the like . . .. This levelling of the primordial "as" of circumspective interpretation to the "as" with which presence-at-hand is given a definite character is the specialty of assertion. Only so does it obtain the possibility of exhibiting something in such a way that we just look at it. (p. 200, H, 158)

The present-at-hand is first discovered *in* something already ready-to-hand which we are related to by being practically involved with it. It is then possible to adopt a special stance, shifting from the original practical context to that of assertion. The referentiality of the relation to the original piece of equipment is inherited by assertions about the object discovered in it. Dealing with the object in such a context, where practical significance is restricted to significance for inference, is attributing properties to something present-at-hand pointed out in the assertions about it.

One question remains. In what sense does responding to something by making an assertion about it count as treating it as having objective properties? What sort of independence of the social appropriatenesses of use and production constitutive of the ready-to-hand is attributed to the present-at-hand when we understand its defining recognitive responsive performance type to be asserting? Equipment as such is always equipment serviceable for the pursuit of some practical end. Significance flows from the practically orienting projects to the "with-which"s and "towards-which"s whose involvements are their roles in instrumental practices. The objectivity of the present-at-hand consists in the indifference of the appropriatenesses of assertion to the practical ends motivating assertors. Taking something as a hammer is taking it as appropriate for hammering. When the property of heaviness is discerned in the present-at-hand object which was ready-to-hand as a hammer, a claim is made whose appropriateness is not a matter of serviceability for or obstruction of any particular practical ends or projects. The justifiability and hence appropriateness of such a claim is not a matter of answering to some practical need.

The autonomy of justification and inference with respect to the pursuit of practical projects is the source of the autonomy of the properties of the present-at-hand with respect to the appropriatenesses of practice. It is this autonomy that is invoked when it is said that the truth of assertions answers to the things pointed out in assertion. Authority is a social matter, and in the game of asserting and giving and asking for reasons authority over the appropriateness of claims has been socially withdrawn from the sphere of usefulness for practical ends.

The claim that the objectivity of the present-at-hand consists in its insulation by assertion from Dasein's practical activity can be given a strong or a weak reading, and it is important to distinguish these. On the strong reading, the present-at-hand would be entirely irrelevant to practical concerns. On this account, the only appropriate response to something present-at-hand is an assertion, the only use which can be made of assertion is inference, and inference is restricted to *theoretical* inference, that is inference whose conclusion is another assertion. Assertions are seen as irrelevant to practice, as mere representations of an independent reality indifferent to practical projects. This practical indifference is then inherited by the present-at-hand, since it can only be the subject of such assertions. This idea is present in Heidegger. It is not presence-at-hand however, but what he calls the doctrine of *pure* presence-at-hand (or, sometimes, "Reality").

> ["Reality"] in its traditional signification stands for Being in the sense of pure presence-at-hand of Things . . . [But] *all* the modes of Being of entities within-the-world are founded ontologically upon the worldhood of the world and accordingly the phenomenon of Being-in-the-world. From this arises the insight that among the modes of Being of entities within-the-world, Reality has no priority, and that Reality is a kind of Being which cannot even characterize anything like the world or Dasein in a way which is ontologically appropriate. (p. 211, H, 254)

Presence-at-hand corresponds to a weaker reading of the insulation assertional practices provide between the objects present-at-hand and practical projects. For although it is correct to see assertions as the only appropriate responses to the present-at-hand as such, and although the only use that can appropriately be made of assertions is inference, it is simply a mistake to think of all inference as theoretical inference. There is also practical inference, whose premises are assertions and whose conclusion is a practical performance which is not an assertion but, in virtue of its genesis as the result of such deliberation, an action. Assertions about the present-at-hand can be practically relevant. We can use information about the merely present-at-hand properties of things, such as the heaviness of the hammer. Without the possibility of language exits through non-assertional performance, theoretical or intralinguistic inference would lose much or all of its point.[18]

If it is then incorrect to see the present-at-hand as completely irrelevant to practical pursuits, as in pure presence-at-hand, what *is* meant by its objectivity? Just this. The *only* way in which the present-at-hand can affect Dasein's projects is by being the subject of an assertion which ultimately plays some role in practical inference. It is not that the present-at-hand is irrelevant to non-assertional practice, it is that its relevance is *indirect*. Assertions are the only interface between the present-at-hand and the rest of our practice. The mistake of the doctrine of pure presence is to see no interface at all.[19] The genuine difference between the present-at-hand (which can be thought of in an extended sense as ready-to-hand for the practices of assertion and inference) and what is ready-to-hand is that one can only make practical use of assertions about the present-at-hand, never of what is present-at-hand itself. Its assertional proxies are serviceable equipment, but the present-at-hand itself is not. Only as represented in assertions can the present-at-hand partake of the equipmental totality of significance which is the world within which Dasein lives and moves and has its being. Discovery of the present-at-hand is an authentic possibility of Dasein's being, instantiated by all human communities ever discovered. Pure presence-at-hand is a philosopher's misunderstanding of the significance of the category of presence-at-hand, and a bad idea.

The categorial nature of the present-at-hand, no less than that of the ready-to-hand (or for that matter the existential nature of Dasein itself as Mitdasein) is constituted by its being appropriately responded to in a certain way, in this case by assertions. In this fact resides Heidegger's ontological pragmatism, and the self-adjudicating nature of Mitdasein-in-the-world. Heidegger sees social behavior as generating both the category of equipment ready-to-hand within a world, and the category of objectively present-at-hand things responded to as independent of the practical concerns of any community. In virtue of the social genesis of criterial authority (the self-adjudication of the social, given pragmatism about authority), fundamental ontology (the study of the origin and nature of the fundamental categories of things) is the study of the nature of social being – social practices and practitioners. Only because Dasein as socially constituted and constituting masters communal practices classifying things according to kind which are whatever they are taken to be "can Dasein also understand and conceptualize such characteristics of Being as independence, the 'in-itself', and Reality in general. Only because of this are 'independent' entities, as encountered within-the-world, accessible to circumspection" (p. 251, H, 207).

We have been concerned with three conceptual innovations presented in *Being and Time*. One of these is Heidegger's hierarchy of non-Cartesian cognitive notions. At its base is understanding – the disclosure of a totality of social significance and the discovery within it of individual pieces of equipment by mastery of communal responsive practices. At the next level is deliberative interpretation by appropriation of the conditional significances implicit in the understanding of the ready-to-hand. Finally there is the discursive appropriation of the present-at-hand through assertion of sentences which in virtue of their social inference potentials explicitly thematize the significations one becomes aware of in interpretation. Second, we have seen how the category of presence-at-hand arises within and yet is distinct from the more fundamental category of readiness-to-hand. Third, in terms of the first two points it is clear that the ready-to-hand is first among equals among the categories because of the self-adjudicating nature of the social (*Mitdasein* in a world which is a totality of practical significance). Understanding in this way the basic ontological structure of Heidegger's account in Division I is the necessary preparation for understanding both his account of the individuation of Dasein and the institution of temporality by the personal appropriation of projects in Division II, and his profound reading of that tradition of philosophy which has left us in such a mistaken position that "in general our understanding of Being is such that every entity is understood in the first instance as present-at-hand."[20]

NOTES

1 The general orientation of this essay owes much to John Haugeland, particularly to his account of transcendental constitution as and by social institution in "Heidegger on being a person," *Noûs*, March 1982, I would also like to thank my fellow staff members and the seminar participants at the Council for Philosophic Studies 1980 Summer Institute, "Phenomenology and Existentialism: Continental and Analytic Perspectives on Intentionality," for their responses to an earlier version of the ideas presented here.

2 See Rorty's "Incorrigibility as the mark of the mental," *Journal of Philosophy* vol. 67, no. 12 (25 June 1970).

3 Of course, Descartes held other views about the substances to which these categories applied as well. He filled in the abstract ontological categorization of epistemic kinds with specifications, e.g., of the objective realm as having its essence exhausted by geometric extension, and of the epistemic subject whose incorrigible "takings" define the mental as itself identical with the sum of mental things it is aware of. The current concern is with the ontological framework rather than with Descartes' theories about the entities it categorized.

4 In "Freedom and constraint by norms" (*APQ*, April 1977) I investigate the sort of norm inherent in the appropriatenesses instituted by social practices. I took it to be significant that the socialTobjective distinction can be seen as the origin of the valueT fact distinction, and that both naturalists, who want to reduce one category to the other, and non-naturalists, who do not, presumed that it was an *objective* distinction between facts and values which was at issue. I explore the consequences of treating the socialTobjective, and hence the valueTfact, distinction as itself social rather than objective, that is, as a matter of how the community responds to various things, not how they are independently and in themselves.

5 As Rorty has argued (*Philosophy and the Mirror of Nature*, Princeton, NJ: Princeton University Press, 1979) on the plausibility of such a claim rest Sellars' and Quine's twin attacks on the two varieties of unjustified justifiers ("privileged representations") which foundationalists, particularly positivistic ones, had relied on as the foundations of our inferential structures. Thus Quine dismantled the picture of *language* as a source of authority immune to social revision ("intrinsic credibility," "self evidence," etc.) for some sentences thought to be true-in-virtue-of-meaning, and Sellars performed the same service for the picture of the mind as a source of supposedly socially impervious privilege for "reports" of thoughts and sensations.

6 p. 190, H, 150.

7 Cf. the "*sich verweisenden Verstehen*" of p. 119.

8 See, e.g., p. 100, H, 70.

9 Such a model must be used with caution, however. Heidegger is concerned that the structures so taken as worlds involve *concrete* relations of use, production, and response, rather than simply structurally analogous relations. He says, "The context of assignments or references, which, as significance, is constitutive for worldhood, can be taken formally in the sense of a system of Relations. But one must note that in such formalizations the phenomena get levelled off so much that their real phenomenal content may be lost . . . the phenomenal content of these "relations" and "relata" –

the "in-order-to," the "for-the-sake-of," and the "with-which" of an involvement – is such that they resist any sort of mathematical functionalization" (pp. 121–2, H, 88).

10 This view represents a normative version of the 'conformism' discussed by Haugeland (op. cit.), without what I take to be the ontologically irrelevant account of its ontic genesis which he offers.

11 p. 203, H, 160

12 p. 190, H, 150.

13 p. 275, H, 231.

14 p. 204, H, 161.

15 p. 411, H, 360.

16 p. 266, H, 224, following the passage on speaking-over quoted above.

17 I have presented the details of an account of asserting along these lines in "Asserting," *Noûs* 17: 637–50.

18 Here "theoretical" inference refers to language-language moves, by contrast to "practical" inference involving language-exit moves (in Sellars' sense). In a different sense "theoretical" claims are those which can *only* be arrived at inferentially, and not as non-inferential reports. Discussion of the relevance to the understanding of presence-at-hand of claims which are theoretical in this sense is beyond the scope of this essay.

19 The semantics of the points of view generated by such "interfaces" – where a set of claims can make a difference to practical deliberations only in so far as it makes a difference to some other set of claims which then affects the deliberations – is discussed in my "Points of View and Practical Reasoning," *Canadian Journal of Philosophy*, June 1982.

20 p. 268, H, 225.

3
The Familiar and the Strange:
On the Limits of Praxis in the Early
Heidegger

Joseph P. Fell

(1) In his description of the disclosure of environing things in *Being and Time*, Martin Heidegger sought to deprive theoretical seeing and knowing of the priority they have enjoyed in the philosophical tradition ever since Parmenides. It is a matter of showing that neither the theoretical activity nor the theoretical object is primary. The *locus classicus* for interpreting what activity and what sort of entity *are* primary has been sections 15–18 of *Being and Time*. There Heidegger says that "The Greeks had an appropriate term for 'things': *pragmata* – that is to say, that which one has to do with in one's concernful dealings (*praxis*)," even if "ontologically, the specifically 'pragmatic' character of the *pragmata* is just what the Greeks left in obscurity."[1] Heidegger indicates specifically pragmatic entities by the term "equipment" (*Zeug*) and by the ontological category "readiness-to-hand" (*Zuhandenheit*).[2] The praxis by which this kind of being is disclosed he calls a kind of "concern" (*Besorgen*) whose pretheoretical way of seeing is "circumspection" (*Umsicht*).[3] What Heidegger especially wishes to show is that the disclosures of this circumspective practice are *intraworldly* – that they are oriented and made possible by a totality of references or significative meanings that Heidegger calls a "world."[4]

There is high drama in the reversal of traditional priorities which this analysis of praxis and its pragmata brings about. Both the *way* of seeing and the kind of *entity* taken as primary from Parmenides to Husserl are shown to be made possible only by a modification of a prior practice and its intraworldly disclosures. Heidegger indicates this ontological reprioritization by the following sequence:[5]

1. the being of those entities within the world which we first of all [*zunächst*] encounter – readiness-to-hand. 2. the being of those entities which we can come across and whose nature we can determine if we discover them in their own right [*eigenständig*] by going through the entities first encountered – presence-at-hand.

Thus the practical takes ontological priority over the theoretical, and everyday experience or comportment takes priority over scientific cognition. The drama of Heidegger's violent act of insubordination toward the philosophical tradition has not been lost on his interpreters, who have found grounds in sections 15–18 for holding that Heidegger is a pragmatic philosopher,[6] that Heidegger finds any and every thing to be ready-to-hand,[7] that nothing is ever discovered as merely present-at-hand,[8] and that the referential totality wholly determines the being of aₙ entity.[9]

In the 1969 Le Thor seminar Heidegger complained that the analyses of equipmental structures in *Being and Time* were "misunderstood."[10] Apparently, misunderstanding of the point of these analyses began very early, for in the winter semester of 1929–30 Heidegger told the students in his course on *The Basic Concepts of Metaphysics*:[11]

> In distinction to this *historical way* into the understanding of the concept of world, I attempted in *Being and Time* a first characterization of the *phenomenon of world* through an interpretation of *how we move about first and for the most part in our world everyday*. In so doing, I started with what is ready-to-hand for us everyday, what we use and manage . . . The point was to press on, by and through this first characterization of the phenomenal world, to an exhibition of the phenomenon of world as a problem. But it was never my intention to assert or establish through this interpretation that the essence of man consists in his wielding a spoon and fork and riding on the streetcar.

Heidegger is emphasizing here that the way in which *Being and Time* arrives at the phenomenon of world – via analysis of average everyday praxis – is not the sole possible way or a privileged way. In those 1929–30 lectures, Heidegger takes instead the path of what he calls a "comparative consideration," and the "historical way" he refers to is the path taken in *The Essence of Reasons*, which had just been published.[12] Secondly, Heidegger is warning against misinterpreting the equipment analyses of Division I of *Being and Time* as claiming that the human being is essentially a practical user of practical instruments. He notes (1) that *Being and Time* attempts only a "first" characterization of the phenomenon of world, and (2) that it is based on ordinary chronology: how we "first and for the most part" (*zunächst und zumeist*) comport ourselves in everydayness. And that is what he had indeed said in *Being and Time*: that the analysis in Division I was of "average everyday" comportment or was of our experience "first and for the most part."[13] Heidegger has more than one notion of primacy, and clearly the interpreter of *Being and Time* must be careful not to conflate what is "first and for the most part" with what is "fundamental" or "primordial" (*ursprünglich*).

In *The Essence of Reasons* Heidegger issues a similar warning against misinterpretation of the equipment analyses of *Being and Time*, but here he makes specific reference to *nature*:[14]

> If we somehow equate the ontical system of useful things (of tools) with the world and explain being in the world as traffic with useful things, we then

abandon any understanding of transcendence as being in the world in the sense of a "basic constitutive feature of Dasein."

On the other hand, a study of the ontological structure of "environmental" being (in so far as it is discovered as tool) has one singular advantage for a *preliminary characterization* of world: it leads over to an analysis of this phenomenon and prepares the way for the transcendental problem of world. As is indicated clearly enough in the outline and arrangement of sections 14–24 of *Being and Time*, this is the sole intention of the analysis of environment, which itself, considered in terms of the *guiding aim* of the book, remains subordinate.

There are reasons why the concept "nature" seems to be missing in the Analytic of Dasein – not only "nature" as the object of natural science but also "nature" in a primordial sense (cf. *Sein und Zeit*, p. 65 *et infra*). The decisive reason is that we encounter nature neither within the compass of the environment [*Umwelt*] nor in general primarily as something *to which* we *relate* ourselves. Nature is primordially manifest in Dasein because Dasein exists as situated and disposed [*als befindlich-gestimmtes*] in the midst of beings. But only in so far as situatedness (thrownness) belongs to the essence of Dasein and is expressed in the unity of the full concept of *care* can we attain the *basis* for the *problem* of nature.

Heidegger is evidently thinking here of the need to counterbalance the claims made for everyday praxis in *Being and Time* by the claims made by nature, and he notes that the analysis of environmental being plays only a "subordinate" role in *Being and Time*. Neither the everyday *Umwelt* nor natural science presents nature in a "primordial sense." The "preliminary" characterization of world in *Being and Time* has not done justice to the relation of world and nature. (The oft-noted infrequency of the term "earth" in *Being and Time* seems one sign of the incompleteness of that book's treatment of the being of nature.) If one starts philosophically with Dasein's everyday preoccupation with practical equipment, one reaches nature as such only secondarily, by a derivation or shift of focus that brings presentness-at-hand to the fore – if we can assume for the moment that by entities disclosed "in their own right" (*eigenständig*) Heidegger means to include natural beings disclosed *as* natural. So it can appear to the interpreter of *Being and Time* that nature is a *derivative* phenomenon and a *deficient* phenomenon, dependent for its being on the prior showing of an apparently primordial readiness-to-hand. Yet Heidegger never says that readiness-to-hand is "primordial"; it is the kind of being that is experienced "first and for the most part" in "average everydayness," which is a "fallen" and "inauthentic" experience.[15] He goes so far as to observe in *Being and Time* that "Perhaps even readiness-to-hand and equipment have nothing to contribute as ontological clues in interpreting the primitive world," although the primitive is already Dasein and "an understanding of being is constitutive for primitive Dasein and for the primitive world in general."[16] Whereas in the note to *The Essence of Reasons* I have quoted, Heidegger asserts that "Nature is primordially manifest in Dasein." My point is not that the primitive is the primordial. My point is that if nature is *primordially* manifest in Dasein, it must be manifest in Dasein as such, including primitive

Dasein. But readiness-to-hand and equipment may *not* be manifest in the primitive world. Thus it is not necessarily the case that nature is disclosed to Dasein on the basis of a prior disclosure of ready-to-hand equipment.

Heidegger was evidently taken aback by an interpretation of *Being and Time* which concluded that nature is *not* primordially manifest *in* Dasein – that is, in Dasein's world which, as a world of praxis, first discloses equipment, by comparison with which nature seems to have only a dependent being. There are many indications that in the years 1927–30 Heidegger thought he had to make a series of efforts to nip this interpretation in the bud. Among those efforts were the passages I have cited from *The Basic Concepts of Metaphysics* and *The Essence of Reasons*. I shall try to show that both *The Basic Problems of Phenomenology* (summer 1927) and *What is Metaphysics?* (1929) contribute to this corrective effort.

(2)   If average, everyday practical comportment is an experience of *the familiar*, to it must be counterposed a disclosure of *the strange*. If the accent in the disclosure of the practical *Umwelt* falls on what is readily *understood*, the accent in the disclosure of nature will fall instead on *disposition* and *thrownness*. Thus Heidegger says in the note I have cited from *The Essence of Reasons*:

> Nature is primordially manifest in Dasein because Dasein exists as situated and disposed [*als befindlich-gestimmtes*] in the midst of beings. But only in so far as situatedness (thrownness) belongs to the essence of Dasein . . . can we attain the *basis* for the *problem* of nature.

It is to Dasein's being disposed or being mooded that we must turn, then, in order to find Heidegger's account of the disclosure of primordial nature and so his account of the limits of praxis. Behind average everyday fallen comportment there is a mood that, according to *What is Metaphysics?*, has been "repressed,"[17] for what it discloses represents a threat to ready familiarity. That mood is anxiety.

Heidegger claims that moods disclose, and that anxiety is a "ground-mood."[18] This means that anxiety discloses the ground, or at least an aspect of the ground, from which it follows that anxiety is at least partially disclosive of being (for Heidegger characterizes being as meaning and ground).[19] It is anxiety that discloses Dasein's *Befindlichkeit*, the ground-state in which Dasein finds itself as unaccountably thrown, so that Dasein, finding no metaphysical ground outside itself, has to be its own ground, has to throw itself into its own grounding.[20] Thus the ground disclosed by anxiety is Dasein itself, its own temporal way of being. As a "groundless ground,"[21] Dasein has to provide a meaning that is not otherwise given.

But there is more. Anxiety is doubly disclosive. Anxiety discloses something about the world as well as about Dasein itself – but since world is an existential of Dasein itself, and since anxiety shows this to be so, these are but two aspects of a single disclosure. Here we should turn directly to Heidegger's description of anxiety in *What is Metaphysics?*[22]

In anxiety beings as a whole [*das Seiende im Ganzen*] become superfluous. In what sense does this happen? Beings are not annihilated by anxiety, so that nothing is left. How could they be, when anxiety finds [*befindet*] itself precisely in utter impotence with regard to beings as a whole?

"Beings as a whole," as the context makes clear, means beings in the world, in their everyday context of significance, i.e., as routinely understood and interpreted within a "referential totality." Anxiety "nihilates" ("nothings," reduces to nothing) this world-context. Since this world-context is ordinarily projected in understanding as a condition for disclosure of beings in their whatness, it would seem that anxiety is simply an experience of the failure of disclosure of beings. But just because of the lapse of projective understanding in anxiety, anxiety is able to disclose something else: "Nihilation . . . discloses these beings in their full but heretofore concealed strangeness as the pure other [*das schlechthin Andere*] – as opposed to nothing."[23] The blanking out of everyday significance does not leave us with nothing at all; beings remain, but now as strange, stripped of their ordinary familiarity. Abruptly, they stand out like sore thumbs, all by themselves, independent of any grounding context. Not nothing, they *are* – but for no evident reason or purpose, without "whence and whither." This is the original but routinely concealed human experience of the disclosure of sheer givenness, sheer contingency, the disclosure of naked "that-being":[24]

In the clear night of the nothing of anxiety the original [*ursprüngliche*] openness of beings as such arises: that [*dass*] they are beings – and not nothing. But this "and not nothing" we add in our talk is not some kind of appended clarification. Rather it makes possible in advance the revelation of beings in general. The nature of the originally nihilating nothing lies in this, that *it brings Dasein for the first time before beings as such.*

Anxiety is thus the beginning and a basis of all specifically human ontic experience and ontological understanding. The "original openness of beings" of which Heidegger here speaks is, on the one hand, the disclosure of "beings as such" and, on the other hand, the opening of the opening (the clearing, the *da*) itself. The expanse of nothingness one experiences around beings is at once the *absence* of given meaning (*was-sein*) and the disclosure of an opening *for* meaning, the place in which meaning can be projected. The disclosure of the given, "beings as such" – and in anxiety both that-being and nothing are given – is the ground-possibility of the projection of what-being. So in anxiety one is confronted by the phenomenal evidence for the claim made in *Being and Time* that:[25]

. . . all beings whose kind of being is of a character other than Dasein's must be conceived as *unmeaning*, essentially devoid of any meaning at all . . . And only that which is unmeaning can be contrary to meaning [*widersinnig*]. The present-at-hand, as encountered in Dasein, can as it were assault Dasein's being – for example, natural events that break in and destroy.

Anxiety is thus at once disclosure of that-being and nothing: both the ground-lessly given and the ground-possibility of its meaning. This remarkably multi-disclosive ground-mood of anxiety also reveals the basic temporality of being, both human and non-human. Dasein here finds itself groundlessly thrown, and thrown into the midst of beings which, if they are going to be significant, are going to have to have a meaning-ground projected for them in that open future which is Dasein's own possibility of meaning. Thus are both Dasein's *having been* (thrown) and its *possible meaningful future* disclosed to it. At the same time, beings other than Dasein are disclosed both as *already simply given* and as *possibly significant* (interrelatable, referable to each other). This gives us, Heidegger argues, the ground-possibility of science ("scientific existence is possible only if in advance it holds itself out into the nothing").[26] If, for example, the causal relation is projected as an aspect of the what-being of environmental beings, then these beings can refer to each other as cause to effect or effect to cause.[27] Scientific presentation is thus grounded in the temporality of anxiety – in its disclosure of "beings as such" as already there in their naked thatness, as "inherently devoid of meaning" but understandable on the ground of possible projective meaning. It is this same anxious disclosure that makes possible the disclosure of the ready-to-hand. That is, the original experience of the strange is the ground-possibility of any practical comportment, of any becoming-familiar with equipment.

So Heidegger has characterized the beings other than Dasein disclosed by anxiety in the following terms: as "beings as such," as "strange," as unaccoun-tably there in their sheer "that . . . ," and as "inherently devoid of meaning." Now in section 68 of *Being and Time* Heidegger leaves no doubt that these terms describe sheer presentness-at-hand. He writes:[28]

> Anxiety is anxious in the face of the nothingness of the world; but this does not mean that in anxiety we experience something like the absence of what is present-at-hand within the world. The present-at-hand must be encoun-tered in just such a way that it does not have any involvement *whatsoever* and can show itself in an empty mercilessness.

That beings other than Dasein are "originally" or "primordially" (*ursprünglich*) present-at-hand is also confirmed by Heidegger in *The Essence of Reasons*, where he writes:[29]

> The world gives itself to Dasein as an actual wholeness for Dasein's own sake, but that means for the sake of a being that with equal originality [*Gleichursprünglich*] is: being amidst . . . the present-at-hand [*das Sein bei . . .Vorhandenem*], being with . . . the Dasein of others and being toward . . . itself.

What this means is that disclosure of beings *as present-at-hand* in anxiety is the original ground-possibility of both the presentness-at-hand of the theoretical object of science and the readiness-to-hand of the equipment of everyday praxis. This suggests that the presentness-at-hand, which in section 18 of *Being and Time* is secondary, reached only by "going through" the ready-to-hand, is not the fundamental or original disclosure of the present-at-hand.

(3)   It should be observed that Heidegger discriminates at least four senses of the term "presentness-at-hand" – three proper senses and one improper sense. Let us first dispose of the improper sense. This Heidegger calls "the present-at-hand in the widest sense," in which *all* beings whatsoever, including the human being, are thought of and spoken of as "present-at-hand" with entire disregard of the "manifold senses of being" they really exemplify. Here all differentiation between "kinds of beings" is lost in a "levelled-down uniformity" of "indistinction."[30] This tradition-enforced sense of presentness-at-hand is challenged by the whole of Heidegger's thought. Heidegger calls it a "misinterpretation" on the part of "vulgar common sense."[31]

What are the three proper senses of the term? In the first case, presentness-at-hand denominates beings as disclosed in anxiety; here all referentiality fails – there is a "universal" breakdown – and the world of significance is reduced to nothing, or is only a future possibility. It is crucial to observe that while *in everyday chronology* this disclosure is *preceded* by a practical preoccupation with familiar ready-to-hand beings, none the less according to *What is Metaphysics?* the anxiety that rarely breaks out overtly was already there, "but sleeping": already covered over or "repressed" (*niedergehalten*) in a falling, inauthentic comportment.[32] The distinction between *average everyday time* and *primordial authentic time* makes all the difference here. This fundamental sense of presentness-at-hand, while not "first and for the most part" in everyday chronology, is none the less brought out of hiding by overt anxiety as an "original" or "primordial" disclosure of beings. Here we should remark that Heidegger asserts that "*in*authentic temporality arises out of finite authentic temporality"[33] or "primordial authentic temporality"[34] and that the ready-to-hand is disclosed in inauthentic temporality. The inauthentic temporality in which Dasein "first and for the most part" encounters the ready-to-hand is the same inauthentic temporality in which "Dasein flees" – first and for the most part – in the face of . . . thrownness, which has been more or less explicitly revealed."[35] Thus in routine disclosure of the ready-to-hand the anxious disclosure of present-at-hand nature is already being covered over.

In the second case, presentness-at-hand denominates certain beings as disclosed through a *local* breakdown in useability (e.g., the sail rips), but the referentiality of regions of the world other than the region of my immediate present praxis remains unaffected.[36] And it is the presentness-at-hand *of* the perhaps only temporarily unusable and repairable ready-to-hand being which obtrudes. We should note, however, that this is the experience of a presentness-at-hand that was *already there* but which in my practical preoccupation I was simply not attending to.

In the third case, presentness-at-hand denominates a range of beings, or all beings whatsoever, as "objects" of objectifying assertions, or objects of an inquiry (a science) into the "natural" or "inherent" properties of these objects.[37] Beings are in this last-named case made objects of an "objective seeing" (theory), and there is once again no universal breakdown, for the beings inquired into are presumed to be intelligible in their own right, and the inquirers are likely to count on ready-to-hand instruments in investigating the properties of these objects as part of the specific sort of praxis of theoretical science. (Not to mention that the inquirers are likely to count on a significant world when they leave their laboratories and drive home for supper with their families.)

Which of these senses of presentness-at-hand is the "fundamental" one? Or is this an improper question? It is worth taking to heart Justus Buchler's notion of "ontological parity," which warns against the very sort of "hierarchizing" of modes of being into levels, such that some are more real than others, of which phenomenology in general and Heidegger in particular have sometimes been accused.[38] All three senses represent genuine kinds of disclosure, and none of them, when properly interpreted, is incompatible with readiness-to-hand as a genuine kind of disclosure. But this is not to deny that there are certain relative priorities, derivations, or dependencies in the ways different senses of being are related to each other. Heidegger carefully observes the different but complementary priorities indicated by the traditional terms *ordo cognoscendi* and *ordo essendi*: the order of thought in which beings become disclosed, as distinct from the order in which beings occur in a state of nature or independently of thought. Thus for example:

1 In the order of everyday practice, readiness-to-hand has priority, and presentness-at-hand is derived from it through instrumental breakdown, or through a shift to the apophantic "as" of the assertion, or through a shift to the theoretical attitude, or through an outbreak of overt anxiety. But:
2 In the order of authentic recognition or retrieval, the presentness-at-hand disclosed in anxiety is seen to have a certain priority over a still merely possible readiness-to-hand, as well as over a still merely possible "objective" sense of presentness-at-hand (e.g., Cartesian theoretical objects, as distinct from beings as disclosed in anxiety).
3 In the order of fundamental disclosure, Dasein's temporal self-disclosure has a certain priority over disclosure of all beings other than Dasein, whether artifactual or natural. But:
4 In the order of nature, natural process has priority over Dasein's temporal being. This particular priority deserves our further attention.

(4) It looks like the notion of presentness-at-hand has some relation to the notion of *nature*, a notion which of course itself has multiple meanings. Might Heidegger's consideration of the meanings of "nature" aid our effort to comprehend the interrelation of the meanings of presentness-at-hand and the interrelation of presentness-at-hand and readiness-to-hand? Are there not different senses of "nature" in routine everydayness, in science, and in outbreaks of anxiety? Is "nature" – whatever its meaning – always a mode of presentness-at-hand? In Heidegger's initial treatment of nature in *Being and Time*, nature's kind of being is in fact readiness-to-hand. The context of his discussion (Division I) is, of course, the order of disclosure in average everydayness. "Nature" here has the meaning of that kind of readiness-to-hand which has not been produced by the human being (a non-artifactual readiness):[39]

The production itself is a using *of* something for something. In the work there is also a reference or assignment, to materials . . . So in the environment certain beings become accessible which are always ready-to-hand but which, in themselves, do not need to be produced. Hammer, tongs, and needle refer in themselves to steel, iron, metal, mineral, wood, in that they consist of these. In equipment that is used, "nature" is discovered along with it by that use . . .

There follows perhaps the most frequently cited Heideggerian passage on nature:

Here, however, nature is not to be understood as that which is only present-at-hand . . . The wood is a forest of timber, the mountain a rock quarry, the river is water-power, the wind is wind "in the sails." As the "environment" [*Umwelt*] is discovered, the "nature" [*Natur*] thus discovered is encountered too. If its kind of being as ready-to-hand is disregarded, it itself can be disclosed and determined in its pure presentness-at-hand. But when this happens, the nature that "stirs and strives," that assails and enthralls us as a landscape, remains hidden. The botanist's plants are not the blossoms on the ridge, nor is the geographically established "source" the "spring in the dale."

This passage forms part of Heidegger's demonstration that beings as routinely experienced are not formed dualistically, by the imposition of a "subjective coloring" on "a world-stuff at first present-at-hand in itself."[40] Nature as pre-scientifically experienced has a validity of its own and the natural sciences cannot justify the claim that valid disclosure of the environment is their private property. Heidegger drives the point home by arguing that botanical or geographical disclosure closes something off in the very process of disclosing. Yet we cannot interpret this argument as claiming that everyday disclosure is *full* disclosure which the sciences replace with a *partial* disclosure or with a warped disclosure. Heidegger is not asking us to choose between the validity of science and the validity of ordinary experience. He is broadening and deepening the phenomenon of truth, not transferring it from one set of disciplines to another. The point is that *true* disclosure cannot be equated with *total* disclosure. And if scientific disclosure is partial, hiding something in the very act of revealing something else, the same must be said of everyday disclosure. Thus Heidegger claims in *Being and Time* that disclosure in everyday routine preoccupations is obtained at the price of a deep self-forgetting in which the very ground of disclosure (the human being's original and temporal way of being) is covered up.[42] And we have seen that in *The Essence of Reasons* Heidegger says that it is not in the everyday *Umwelt* that nature is "primordially manifest."[41] Unless one insists *a priori* and arbitrarily that there is one and only one method of disclosing, and one and only one true aspect of beings, one can be open to the possibility of different *but complementary* disclosures of one and the same being. We need not, perhaps cannot, choose between the blossoms on the ridge and the botanist's plants. "Being" has "manifold senses," which must not be reduced to a single sense by a metaphysics insistent on unity at any cost.

But it is true that the blossoms on the ridge or the wind in the sails have a certain priority. Were it not for an artificial narrowing of the notion of truth and of the proper method of reaching it in the history of philosophy, it would go without saying that it is the (quite real) blossoms on the ridge that the botanist makes the object of his inquiries. What Heidegger asks scientists (and the rest of us) to recognize is that genuine disclosure *occurs on a thrown-projective temporal ground* which requires a human projection of meaning of more than one possible sort – a precondition that is covered up in *both* ordinary everydayness and ordinary scientific comportment. The covering up of this thrown-projective temporal ground may hide the real relation of both everyday equipment and the scientific object to the nature that is "primordially manifest in Dasein . . ."

(5)   Now we must revert to a strange and estranging phenomenon. If it can be shown that the everyday and the scientific disclosures of nature are complementary and both valid, *both* of them go up in smoke in anxiety – a *third* mode of disclosure of nature. Is it really possible to turn the trick of somehow making *this* mode of disclosure compatible with the other two? How is a disclosure of nature as utterly insignificant in any way compatible with either the everyday or the scientific modes of intelligibility?

Yet is the disclosure in anxiety really a disclosure *of nature*? The very term "nature" seems to imply some order or intelligibility, whether it is that of the blossoms on the ridge or that of the botanist's plants. Furthermore, Heidegger quite explicitly takes nature to be "intraworldly," while "Anxiety is anxious in the face of the nothingness of the world."[43] The anxious lapse of world would thus seem the loss of the condition under which alone nature could be disclosed as nature. At this juncture we need to consider Heidegger's analysis of the relation of nature to world in *The Basic Problems of Phenomenology*:[44]

An example of an intraworldly entity is nature. It is indifferent in this connection how far nature is or is not scientifically uncovered, indifferent whether we think this being in a theoretical, physico-chemical way or think of it in the sense in which we speak of "nature out there," hill, woods, meadow, brook, the field of wheat, the call of the birds. This being is intraworldly. But for all that, *intraworldliness does not belong to nature's being* [*zu seinem Sein*]. Rather, in commerce with this being, nature in the broadest sense, we understand that this being *is* as present-at-hand, as a being that we come up against, to which we are delivered over, which on its own part [*von sich her*] always already is. It is, even if we do not uncover it, without our encountering it within our world. Being within the world *devolves upon* [*fällt zu*] this being, nature, solely when it is *uncovered* as a being . . . Intraworldliness belongs to the being of the present-at-hand, nature, *not* as a determination of its being, but as a *possible* determination, and one that is necessary for the possibility of the uncoverability of nature . . . Intraworldliness, being within the world, is not an ontological structure or, more carefully expressed, it does not belong to nature's being. We say "more carefully" because we have to reckon here with a restriction, so far as there is a being which *is* only in so far as it is intraworldly. There are beings, however, to whose being intraworldliness belongs in a certain way. Such beings are all those we call *historical* entities – historical in the broader sense of world-historical, all the things that the human being . . . creates, shapes, cultivates: all his culture and works. Beings of this kind only are or, more exactly, arise only and come into being only *as* intraworldly.

Nature must occur within the world if it is to be disclosed, but this intraworldly disclosure precisely shows nature as having its own wholly independent extraworldly being. Heidegger here observes the traditional distinction between the *ordo cognoscendi* and the *ordo essendi*. But if being *(Sein)* means meaning and ground,[45] and if meaning, as projected in Dasein, belongs to world rather than to nature, how can one say that nature has any being (meaning) at all? When Heidegger writes that intraworldliness is a *possible* determination of nature's being, this can be construed as saying that nature will in effect accept the meanings "nature," "independent," "present-at-hand," and "essentially devoid of meaning" as conditions or grounds of its disclosure – always bearing in mind that for Heidegger "*x* means *y*" does not say that "*x* has the (inherent) property *y*" but rather "*x* is disclosable on the ground of *y*." This is but another way of saying that meaning is "ontologically different" from the beings meant. When Heidegger asserts that nature has its own being, this in effect says that it must be *meant as* existing *apart from* all meaning and all human design.

But that is precisely the aspect beings show in anxiety, and we can thus claim that the disclosure of beings in anxiety as *not* dependent on the world for their being is just what originally enables the human being to make the basic distinction between historical (including artifactual and equipmental) beings and natural beings – between Dasein-dependent and Dasein-independent beings. This would seem to answer the question I posed: anxiety is indeed a disclosure *of nature*. But, I should immediately stress, a disclosure of *an aspect* of nature, its sheer that-being in its utter otherness or strangeness. For any further disclosure, for a revealing of any other aspect of nature, a *significant* world will be required. In other words, it will be necessary to return to the referential world either by lapsing back into inauthentic average everydayness or by authentically throwing oneself with resolve into a modification of everydayness. These are two ways of overcoming the condition that Heidegger, in *What is Metaphysics?*, calls "rest" or "suspense," to which one is reduced by anxiety, and returning to "movement."[46] Anxiety in effect sits between inauthenticity and authenticity. It does not have the character of an "evasive forgetting," nor does it have the character of a "remembering."[47] It is a highly partial experience, for it fails to throw itself into the active projection of meaning that, together with thrownness, is constitutive of Dasein's authentic being. If one returns to the everyday practical world in the comportment of authentic resolve, one "remembers" and "repeats" what anxiety has disclosed: the original contingency of nature as devoid of meaning, and so also the necessity of oneself projecting meaning in a future now grasped not inauthentically as something simply passively "awaited," but as something actively meant. Authentic resolve thus consists in a proper *co-ordination* of anxious having-been and future anticipation: of the *limit* imposed on praxis by the sheer contingency of nature and the *possibility* afforded to praxis by the opening for meaning. So the present-at-hand turns out to have a *fourth* proper sense: it is disclosed in anxiety as the *possibly* significant. Since they happen to be given, beings are available for . . .

(6) Let us now step back and try to summarize what has been established.

As I have just noted, from the vantage-point of anxiety presentness is the possibility of readiness – although it is also the case that from the vantage-point of an undisturbed everydayness readiness is the possibility of presentness. The priorities or sequences of disclosure in anxiety and in average everydayness are not the same. But which, then, is the "real" priority? They both are. This means that there is a very important sense in which both anxiety-disclosure and everyday-disclosure are *partial* disclosures of the being of beings and of the relation of Dasein to these beings. Givenness and usability are complementary aspects of beings. Were this not so, Heidegger would be guilty of contradicting himself in maintaining both that beings are truly disclosed as "strange" and truly disclosed as "familiar." He maintains *both* that primordial nature is disclosed as worldless and that historical beings are originally disclosed as worlded.

He says that Dasein is "primordially familiar" with its world and that this primordial familiarity goes to make up Dasein's understanding of being.[48] This means that Dasein has always projected meaning as a ground for disclosing intraworldly beings. But it does not entail that this meaning has always been or always will be essentially readiness-to-hand. Not does it entail that, when readiness-to-hand is the meaning projected first and for the most part, that this readiness-to-hand gives the being of *all* entities, both artifactual and natural. Nor does it entail that all original or basic disclosure of the beings surrounding me is a confirmation of understanding, for the presentness-at-hand of primordial nature is disclosed in an anxious *failure* of understanding. Thus one can speak of no absolute categorial priority in the early Heidegger. One can speak only of *relative* priorities. The "priority" is always "priority in some respect." We can then employ this notion of "priority in some respect" to assess the real relations of presentness-at-hand and readiness-to-hand in Heidegger's early thinking.

1 In the order of average everydayness, equipmental things are first and for the most part disclosed as ready-to-hand and already have been, and their disclosure as present-at-hand requires a shift in attitude or mode of praxis. This is true disclosure *of artifacts* in their "being in themselves" as artifacts.[49]

2 In the order of anxiety, things are disclosed as purely present-at-hand and their disclosure as ready-to-hand requires a practical projection which has been suspended or is as yet only a future possibility. This is true disclosure *of independent nature* and it makes possible true disclosure of the natural *aspect* of ready-to-hand beings.

3 Both of these orders are simultaneously there in human experience but *at different levels*. In the "surface chronology" of average everydayness Dasein interprets both natural and artifactual things first and for the most part as ready-to-hand. But repressed and so concealed underneath this surface chronology is what Heidegger calls the "peculiar"[50] temporality of anxiety

that is moodedly centered on *having-been* as thrown rather than on *future* practical preoccupations.

4   Experiencing (as opposed to thinking about) either of these orders normally relegates the other to the background. In average everydayness, the anxious disclosure of beings as purely present-at-hand – inherently devoid of meaning – is repressed, and so concealed. In overt anxiety, the disclosure of beings as ready-to-hand has lapsed or is in suspension.

5   Overt anxiety is the rare experience of the raw nature that historical praxis has already domesticated. *Overt* anxiety discloses the *hidden* anxiety that has always already been the suppressed premise of the human projection of the meaning of things.

6   Thus everyday disclosure has always already been real *foreground* disclosure of environmental things but has always already been premised on real *background* disclosure of nature as sheerly contingent and inherently devoid of meaning.

7   Especially since the category readiness-to-hand may not characterize the experience of "primitive Dasein," the categories readiness-to-hand and presentness-at-hand are not of equivalent primordiality. Readiness-to-hand is a category of post-primitive "historical things," while the presentness-at-hand of anxiety is a category denominating an extra-historical being disclosed to anxious Dasein of all eras as existing independently of and ground of all everyday practical things.[51] Thus Heidegger notes in *Being and Time's* analysis of anxiety: "That kind of being in the world which is tranquillized and familiar is a mode of Dasein's uncanniness, not the reverse. *From an existential-ontological point of view, the 'not-at-home' must be conceived as the more primordial phenomenon.*"[52]

I shall conclude with a few very general implications of the foregoing points for the relation of nature and praxis. Although, first and for the most part, average everyday disclosure of the ready-to-hand is genuine disclosure, its interpretation of the temporality of this disclosure is inauthentic or guilty of a self-forgetting. This self-forgetting consists in a flight from the structure of its own temporality as originally disclosed in anxiety. What has been disclosed by anxiety is one's having been thrown without ascertainable reason into the midst of brute and meaningless nature and one's having to project a sense for what would otherwise remain senseless. By dimming down or repressing the brute nature that resists and can destroy one, one attempts in routine praxis to domesticate, to make familiar and to master, what at heart one understands to be strange and over-mastering. Even though one's "first and for the most part" experience is a praxis disclosive of practical things, that praxis is *already a response to what it tries to conceal and forget*: an original anxious disclosure of contingent and unmeaning nature. While that praxis is unavoidable and is indeed genuinely disclosive, an authentic remembering of its anxious temporal basis would require recognition of and resignation to the severe limits of praxis. But this will mean recognition that the ready-to-hand thing of praxis that is first in the order of average everydayness is *not* first in the underlying order of anxious temporality. What is original in the mostly repressed order of anxious temporality is exposure to a sheer presentness-at-hand that both cries out for and limits the human effort to make it familiar and controllable. On the one hand, the everyday practical demands made on nature make it possible for nature to show itself as *resisting* those demands.[53] On the other hand, those demands are motivated by an original disclosure of nature as existing in its own right, indifferent to all praxis and all meaning.

NOTES

This paper is dedicated to Robert D. Cumming

References to volumes of *Martin Heidegger: Gesamtausgabe*, Frankfurt-am-Main: Vittorio Klostermann, will be indicated by "GA" in their first occurrence, followed by the volume number and the date of its publication.

1 *Sein und Zeit* (GA 2 [1977]; hereinafter *SZ*), p. 92 (*Being and Time*, London: SCM Press, 1962; hereinafter *BT*), pp. 96–7.
2 *SZ*, pp. 92–3 (*BT*, pp. 97–8).
3 *SZ*, p. 93 (*BT*, p. 98).
4 *SZ*, ss. 16–18.
5 *SZ*, pp. 117–18 (*BT*, p. 121).
6 Richard Rorty, *Philosophy and the Mirror of Nature*, Princeton: Princeton University Press, 1979, p. 368 and passim.
7 John Sallis, *Delimitations*, Bloomington, Ind: Indiana University Press, 1986, p. 142.
8 Laszlo Versényi, *Heidegger, Being and Truth*, New Haven, CT: Yale University Press, 1965, p. 12.
9 Charles B. Guignon, *Heidegger and the Problem of Knowledge*, Indianapolis: Hackett Publishing Company, 1983, p. 99
10 *Vier Seminare*, Frankfurt-am-Main: Vittorio Klostermann, 1977, p. 100. The specific misunderstanding Heidegger singles out here is that which interprets *Being and Time* as claiming that everyday Dasein's preoccupation with beings is somehow not proper unless Dasein is led back to a thematizing of being.
11 *Die Grundbegriffe der Metaphysik* (GA 29/30 [1983]), pp. 262–3.
12 Ibid., pp. 261, 263.
13 *SZ*, pp. 58–9 (*BT*, p. 69).
14 "Vom Wesen des Grundes," *Wegmarken* (GA 9 [1976]; hereinafter W-WG), pp. 155–6 (*The Essence of Reasons*, Evanston, Ill.: Northwestern University Press, 1969; hereinafter ER, pp. 80–3; translation slightly modified).
15 *SZ*, pp. 28–9 (*BT*, pp. 42–3). Heidegger *does* say that "world" is "primordially familiar" (*SZ*, p. 116 [*BT*, p. 119]) and he speaks of "the primordial 'as' of an interpretation . . . which understands circumspectively" (*SZ*, p. 210 [*BT*, p. 201]). In *Erkennen und Handeln in Heideggers "Sein und Zeit,"* Freiburg/Munich: Alber, 1977, Gerold Prauss construes such passages as giving a "primacy" [*Primat*] to *Zuhandenheit*. If I only half-agree with this interpretation, that is because I place more stress than does Prauss on (1) the distinction between the "first and for the most part" and the "primordial" as types of primacy and between inauthentic and authentic temporality; (2) the historicality of the category *Zuhandenheit*; and (3) the temporality of anxiety and its disclosures.
16 *SZ*, p. 110 (*BT*, p. 113).
17 "Was ist Metaphysik?", in *Wegmarken* (GA 9; hereinafter W-WM), p. 117; "diese ursprüngliche Angst wird im Dasein zumeist niedergehalten. Die Angst ist da. Sie schläft nur. Ihr Atem zittert ständig durch das Dasein" (*Basic Writings*, ed. D. F. Krell, New York: Harper & Row, 1977, p. 108: "the original anxiety in existence is

usually repressed. Anxiety is there. It is only sleeping. Its breath quivers perpetually through Dasein").

18 W-WM, p. 111 (BW, p. 102).
19 *SZ*, p. 202 (*BT*, pp. 193–4).
20 *SZ*, pp. 376–9 (*BT*, pp. 329–31).
21 W-WM, p. 122 (BW, p. 112).
22 W-WM, pp. 113–14 (BW, pp. 104–5).
23 W-WM, p. 114 (BW, p. 105).
24 W-WM, p. 114 (BW, p. 105). Italics added.
25 *SZ*, pp. 201–2 (*BT*, p. 193).
26 W-WM, p. 121 (BW, p. 111).
27 The whole possibility of logical and scientific reasoning is grounded in this original disclosure of being and its temporality. Cf. Joseph Fell, "The crisis of reason," in *Heidegger Studies*, II (1986), 41–65.
28 *SZ*, p. 454 (*BT*, p. 393).
29 W-WG, p. 163 (ER, pp. 100–1). Translation modified.
30 See *Die Grundbegriffe der Metaphysik* (GA 29/30), pp. 398–400.
31 Ibid., p. 422. Cf. *SZ*, p. 298 (*BT*, p. 268): "in general our understanding of being is such that every entity is understood in the first instance as present-at-hand." For a primary case of the philosophical analogue of this vulgar universalization of presence-at-hand (in Descartes), cf. *SZ*, s. 20.
32 See note 17 above.
33 *SZ*, p. 437 (*BT*, p. 379).
34 *SZ*, p. 461 (*BT*, p. 399).
35 Ibid.
36 *SZ*, pp. 98–9 (*BT*, pp. 102–3).
37 See *SZ*, ss. 33 and 69(b).
38 See Buchler, *Metaphysics of Natural Complexes*, New York: Columbia University Press, 1966, pp. 30–51. In my judgment, Buchler's inclusion (p. 31) of Heidegger among the violators of the principle of ontological parity is questionable. R. Schürmann (*Heidegger on Being and Acting*, Bloomington: Indiana University Press, 1987, pp. 128–9) rightly argues that Heidegger is not inquiring into "a hierarchy of grounds."
39 *SZ*, pp. 94–5 (*BT*, pp. 99–100). For another account of nature as "pre-scientifically directly experienced," see *Logik: Die Frage nach der Wahrheit* (GA 21 [1976]), pp. 314–15.
40 *SZ*, p. 95 (*BT*, p. 101).
41 Cf. *SZ*, p. 468 (*BT*, p. 405): "A specific kind of *forgetting* is essential for the temporality that is constitutive for letting something be involved. The Self must forget itself . . . On such a basis circumspection can encounter the ready-to-hand *as that being* which it is."
42 See note 14 above.
43 *SZ*, p. 454 (*BT*, p.393).
44 *Die Grundprobleme der Phänomenologie* (GA 24 [1975]), pp. 240–1 (*The Basic Problems of Phenomenology*, Bloomington: Indiana University Press, 1982, pp. 168–9). Italics, in part, added. In one of his direct references to nature in SZ, Heidegger speaks of the ready-to-hand as "within the present-at-hand" (p. 545 [*BT*, p. 465]). Such a passage clearly shows that Heidegger recognizes the sense in which nature's being exceeds human being and its practical concerns and instruments.
45 See note 19 above.
46 On "rest" and "suspense" in anxiety, see W-WM, p. 111 ("Ruhe") and p. 112 ("*Wir 'schweben' in Angst*") (BW, pp. 102, 103). On "movement" or "motion" (*Bewegung*),

see Joseph Fell, *Heidegger and Sartre*, New York: Columbia University Press, 1979, esp. pp. 123–4.

47 *SZ*, p. 454 (*BT*, p. 394).
48 *SZ*, p. 116 (*BT*, p. 119).
49 *SZ*, p. 87 (*BT*, p. 120).
50 *SZ*, p. 455 (*BT*, p. 394): "The temporality of anxiety is peculiar, for anxiety is grounded primordially in having been, and only out of this do the future and the present temporalize themselves . . . In this, Dasein is taken all the way back to its naked uncanniness . . ."
51 This is the case since anxiety is definitive of Dasein, and anxiety is disclosive of sheer presentness-at-hand, while experience of ready-to-hand equipment cannot be said to be definitive of Dasein.
52 *SZ*, p. 252 (*BT*, p. 234).
53 *SZ*, p. 471 (*BT*, p. 407).

4
Early Heidegger on Being, The Clearing, and Realism

Theodore R. Schatzki

Perhaps the most prominent concept in Heidegger's philosophy is that of a clearing in which entities can be, a space or realm of illumination in whose light things can show or manifest themselves to people. Heidegger's central concern, throughout his philosophical career, was to understand the nature and constitution of this clearing. In his earlier writings, the clearing is identical with human existence because the light that constitutes the clearing is human understanding, the *lumen naturale* in man.[1] In his later writings, however, Heidegger no longer identifies the clearing with human understanding. The light in whose illumination things manifest themselves to us is something distinct from human understanding and existence, and the latter are now viewed as that by which we apprehend (in Heidegger's language, are "open for") this light and what appears in it.

In this chapter, I explore Heidegger's early views on (1) the clearing and its relation to human existence, and (2) realism and the oneness of reality. I will organize my discussion by addressing two questions, which Frederick Olafson has recently raised about Heidegger's ideas in his excellent study of Heidegger's thought, *Heidegger and the Philosophy of Mind*.[2] These two issues are, first, how can the clearing, which is the realm in which things can be, be identified with human existence given that there exists a plurality of human existences whereas being and reality are presumably one? And second, if the clearing is identified with human existence, does this mean that entities would no longer exist, or would never have existed, if suddenly there were no more, or had never been, any people? Olafson claims that Heidegger is unable to answer the first question and that

> The central paradox of Heidegger's philosophy stems from the fact that he wants to say that Dasein is the clearing and also that being is the clearing. If Dasein is inherently plural and being is just as inherently singular and unique, it is not apparent how both these assertions can be true. (*OL*, 226)

Olafson contends, further, that Heidegger fails to resolve the second question. I shall argue, on the contrary, that Heidegger does answer the second question and that this answer is part of his solution to the first issue. *Pace* Olafson, Heidegger's positions at the time of *Being and Time* on realism and on the compatibility of the singularity of being and reality with the plurality of human existences are coherent, although they are perhaps too individualist for the tastes of many twentieth-century philosophers.

1   Dasein and individual people

Heidegger does not employ everyday expressions such as "person" and "people." In order to refer to people, he uses, instead, a term of art: Dasein. It is obvious that the object of Heidegger's existential analytic in *Being and Time* is the nature of individual ongoing human existence and that, correspondingly, the term "Dasein" refers, in some sense, to individual people. Complications arise only because this term is not a count noun (nor a mass noun) and has no plural form, whereas people are denumerable and plural. This apparent complication is easily dissolved, however, by noting Heidegger's comment that he chose this term to denote "This entity which each of us is himself" (*BT*, 27) because it expresses this entity's way of being (*BT*, 33). "Dasein" means being-the-there, and this is man's way of being (*BT*, 47). Thus Dasein refers to entities of a certain kind, while at the same time expressing the way of being peculiar to and definitive of that kind. These entities are people and not also dogs and baboons, on the one hand, or corporations, nations, and sports franchises on the other.

It is important to stress that Dasein refers to individual people, not only because the problems that Olafson raises presuppose this fact, but also because failing to grasp it makes understanding Heidegger's view on the socio-historical nature of human existence and understanding impossible. Heidegger's conception of socio-historical embeddedness is one of the topics we shall discuss later. Here, in order to nail down the equation of Dasein with individual people, I shall mention five reasons for reading Heidegger this way.

1   Heidegger says repeatedly that the existence that is an issue for Dasein is in each case mine (e.g., *BT*, 67). Existence, that is, is characterized by mineness. In each instance, consequently, Dasein's existence is someone's existence. As a result, Heidegger remarks, one must always use personal pronouns when addressing *Dasein* (*BT*, 68). These claims, and others like them, strongly suggest that Dasein refers to individual people. Whereas people speak out the mineness of their own existence with the expression "I" and must be addressed with personal pronouns, these facts are not true, for instance, of corporations, nations, and sports franchises. It is important to realize, however, that the two expressions, Dasein and human being, the latter thought of as a term standing for members of a particular biological species, are not coextensive. Not all human beings are Dasein – for instance, infants and severely brain-damaged individuals. Rather, Dasein are functional human beings able of their own initiative to

interact intentionally with and to take account of the things in the world amidst which they exist.

2   The second reason is closely connected with the first. The possibility of authenticity, the mode of existence in which Dasein leads a life of its own (choosing), as opposed to one prescribed to it by the state of the world and the way things are customarily understood and done (inauthenticity), is grounded in the fact that Dasein is in each case mine (*BT*, 68). This shows again that instances of Dasein are individual people. Even if it is possible for a corporation to take over and make its being something of its own, this possibility cannot be grounded in the fact that the corporation's existence is intrinsically mine. For mineness does not pertain to the being of corporations. Only in the case of individual people can the possibility of authentic existence be grounded in mineness. Further support for identifying the referents of Dasein as individual people is furnished by Heidegger's thesis that, in authenticity, a Dasein is individualized in the consciousness of death as a possibility of its own (e.g., *BT*, 308). Neither individualization, consciousness of death, nor the transformation in manner of being (authenticity) consequent upon these two phenomena can be ascribed to anything but individual people. In fact, these phenomena capture something extremely individualistic about individuals, something that pertains to each individual alone in isolation from others.[3]

These remarks do not deny, incidentally, that entities such as corporations and nations partake to some extent of the mode of being belonging to people. After all, such entities consist, at least in part, in people (more precisely: in particular aspects of people's lives). These entities consist also, however, in entities which, according to Heidegger, have modes of being different from that of individual people, e.g., buildings, telephone systems, and sidewalks. Consequently, the mode of being belonging to social formations is more complex than, and thus different from, that of individual people. Hence, these formations are not among the referents of Dasein. On the other hand, unlike in the case of social formations, Heidegger believes that animals share hardly any of Dasein's way of being. His conception of animal life, however, is closely tied to the biology of his day (Driesche, Uexkull): animal existence is a series of blind, nonconceptually mediated, instinctual reactions activated by an animal's meeting up with certain entities in its environment.[4] It is true that, on a more contemporary view of animal life, creatures such as dogs and baboons do share certain components of Dasein's way of being, for instance, conceptually mediated apprehension of the environment. Even so, only if an animal's way of being is identical with Dasein's way of being, and thus only if the animal exhibits all the components of the latter, can the animal be a Dasein. The extent to which any animal shares in Dasein's way of being is, I believe, an empirical question. It seems unlikely, however, that any animal partakes in all of it, since it seems unlikely, for instance, that being-toward-death and the possibility of authenticity are features of anything other than human lives.

3   A third reason is furnished by Heidegger's practice, occasional in *Being and Time* and widespread in *The Basic Problems of Phenomenology* and *The Metaphysical Foundations of Logic*, of identifying Dasein as the "subject." This manner of speaking indicates that Heidegger considers his analysis of Dasein to be a more

adequate analysis of what was intended by the Cartesian concept of the subject but misanalyzed by that philosophical tradition.[5] In a nutshell: whereas the subject was traditionally viewed as essentially outside and distinct from the world, in Heidegger it is analyzed as being-in-the-world. The point in the present context, however, is that, since individual subjects have been traditionally associated with individual people, Heidegger's use of the term "subject" reinforces the impression that Dasein refers to individuals (cf. also Heidegger's use of the expression "the individual Dasein," e.g., *BT*, 219, 221; *GB*, 429). These linguistic facts do not, of course, prove my reading. Philosophers have advocated various notions of subjects that transcend individual people; and purely linguistically, the expression an "individual Dasein" could encompass corporations and dogs. Still, in combination with the other reasons, Heidegger's language here supplies supplementary evidence.

4   A fourth reason, which I shall merely mention, lies in the fact that the object of much of Heidegger's analysis in chapters 3 and 4 of Division I of *Being and Time* is how Dasein encounters (*begegnen*) entities. Heidegger believes that the notion of encountering applies solely to people's lives. For encountering something means experiencing it *as* something; and, as indicated, animals, in Heidegger's view, do not experience the objects they run up against in their environment *as* objects. Rather, these objects serve simply as causal releases for instinctual drives. Accordingly, if encountering is discussed as part of an account of Dasein's way of being, it follows that, in Heidegger's view, Dasein refers to individual people.

5   Finally, a fifth reason is contained in Heidegger's remark that, although Dasein is not the "ontic isolated" individual, in the sense of an egotistical individual acting for his or her own interests in oblivion to the interests of others, talking about Dasein does imply the "metaphysical isolation" of the human being (*MFL*, 137). Part of what he means is that Dasein is the way of being of an individual person taken in and for itself. He is also saying something, however, about the metaphysical self-sufficiency of a person *vis-à-vis* being, namely, that each individual, taken for itself, is a clearing of being in which things can show themselves. This interpretation is supported by his later implication that each *Dasein* has its own transcendence (*MFL*, 190). I think that this remark shows conclusively that Dasein refers to individual people. In fact, Heidegger claims that a consequence of the metaphysical isolation of the human being is that Dasein, as factual, is in each case dispersed into a body and into a particular sexuality (ibid.: for further references to Dasein's body, see *BT*, 419; *HCT*, 232). Corporations and nations are neither embodied nor sexed and thus cannot be Dasein.

2   The clearing and being

Now that it is clear that Dasein refers to functional men, women, and children, we can begin examining the two questions that Olafson poses about Heidegger's early thought. The first of these questions, the subject of the current section, is: How do the facts (1) that human existence is a clearing, (2) that there is a plurality of people and thus, presumably, a plurality of clearings, and (3) that being is unique and singular, cohere? Doesn't a multiplicity of clearings entail a multiplication of realities, therewith raising the specter of incommensurability?

What does Heidegger mean when he claims that Dasein is a clearing? As indicated in the Introduction to this chapter, a clearing is an openness, or space, in which things can be, a lit-upness in whose light things can manifest themselves as themselves. Less matephorically, Heidegger conceives of this space as a space of possibilities, an indefinitely complex space of possible ways for things (including people) to be (e.g., *BT*, 183–5). Existing and not existing are two such possibilities. Others include being red and being green, being hard and being soft, being useful for hammering or being unusable for hammering, going to school and going home, being happy and being piqued, and so on. The clearing is a clearing of being in the sense that what constitutes it (the light in which things can show themselves as being some way) is a totality of possibilities pertaining to the what, how, and that of entities.

Heidegger connects the clearing to people by way of the phenomenon of understanding (and also the phenomenon of *Befindlichkeit*, attunement, although I shall set this aside in what follows).[6] Human understanding opens up the clearing. For the possible ways of being that constitute a clearing are objects of understanding. More strongly: these possible ways of being do not exist except as objects of understanding (cf. *BT*, 117–18). Understanding clears, i.e., establishes the clearing in which things can be, for it is only as understood that the possible ways in which things can be themselves are. Understanding, as the *lumen naturale* in man, is the light in which things can be manifest (cf. *MFL*, 147).

It is now possible to describe what Heidegger means by "being." Analytically, the term "being" embraces all modalities of "is": that something is (*Dass-sein*), how something is (*Wie-sein* or *So-sein*), and what something is (*Was-sein*).[7] Being is also the mode of the possible manifestation of entities to people; that is, entities show themselves to people as things that are such and such (or that are not such and such), that are a certain sort of thing (or that are not a certain sort of thing) and that are (or that are not). That being is the mode of the possible manifestation of entities helps explain why Heidegger believes that all encountering of entities occurs and is possible only on the basis of an understanding of the being of the encountered entities (e.g., *BT*, 363, 371; *BP*, 325). Entities are encountered existing, being such and such, and being a certain sort of thing because entities are encountered in the ways of being already projected as possibilites in Dasein's understanding. In sum, being is the "how" of the possible accessibility of entities, the mode in which entities can manifest themselves as entities (cf. *GB*, 484).[8]

The idea that understanding projects ways of being in which things can be manifest is not unknown in the history of philosophy. Its most important forerunner is embodied in Kant's picture of experience. In Kant, experience is something in which things manifest themselves, or in Kant's language, "appear." How things manifest themselves in experience, moreover, what they appear as, depends on understanding; more specifically, on the categories, the most general, *a priori* concepts contained in the understanding (and also on the forms of intuition contained in the sensibility). The possibilities of appearances are laid

down, at a high level of generality, in these categories; more precisely, in the
schemata of these categories, since everything that appears instantiates the latter.
Everything in experience is something of a particular extensive and intensive
magnitude, connected with other things, and either possible, actual, or necessary. The analogy between Kant's and Heidegger's views of human understanding
is thus unmistakable, even though Kant does not think in terms of possibilities of
being, and understanding in Heidegger is not the faculty of a subject but a
component of the structure of ongoing lived existence. In both philosophers,
understanding sets up a clearing of possible being in whose terms things can
manifest themselves as something, either in the experiences of a subject or in the
encounterings of a person involved in the world.

In both Kant and Heidegger, moreover, there are as many clearings as there
are people. In Kant, each person (i.e., subject) has its own understanding (and
experiences). Thus, because there exists a plurality of people, there exists a
plurality of clearings, in each of which things can manifest themselves in the
experiences of a particular subject. (Kant, of course, never talks in this way.) In
Heidegger, similarly, each person has his or her own understanding (and
encounterings). (Understanding, Heidegger writes, is an ontic characteristic of
Dasein; e.g., *BT*, 33.) Thus, because there exists a plurality of persons, each with
his or her own numerically distinct understanding, there exists a multiplicity of
clearings in each of which entities can manifest themselves in the encounterings
of a particular person. In Kant and Heidegger, there are as many clearings as
there are entities – people or subjects – to whom other entities can manifest
themselves. Notice too that, in both philosophers, the clearing is the realm of
possible, as opposed to actual, experiences/encounterings.

Now that we have established that there are as many clearings as there are
people, we can turn to the problem Olafson raises about this idea. The issue is
whether a plurality of clearings entails a pluralization of being and reality, where
being is understood as the clearing, and reality is understood as things being
certain ways. Each clearing is a realm of ways in which entities can be. What,
however, if these clearings differed, i.e., if the range of possible ways in which
entities can be varied from one clearing to the next? If such were the case, it
would seem that, instead of there existing one realm of being and thus one reality,
there would exist a plurality of such realms and thus a plurality of realities, each
associated with a different individual. As Olafson says, however, being and
reality are "most naturally thought of as unitary and single" (*OL*, 70). This
means that one and the same being and reality are there for each of us in our
individual existences. The aspects of this reality that a given individual appre-
hends often differ from those that others apprehend, but these aspects are still
aspects of the same one reality. How, then, does this presumption cohere with
the picture of a plurality of clearings?

Olafson believes that the two ideas are incompatible. He writes:

> it might seem just as plausible to hold that in each case the uncoveredness
> belongs to the Dasein that realizes it, and that being as presence [i.e., as the
> realm of possible manifestation], like Dasein, is essentially plural in
> character. But such an assumption would miss entirely the dimension of

being as presence in which it is independent of any particular Dasein. (*OL*, 146)

What, for Olafson, the independence of being from particular Daseins amounts to is that being is a realm in which entities can be "for a plurality of existing subjects" (*OL*, 144). The independence of being, in other words, consists (1) in the existence of a single clearing of being that is common to people as opposed to belonging to any one of them, and (2) in the consequent fact that, when entities manifest themselves in the clearing, they become accessible to an indefinite multiplicity of people in common. This single clearing is a single realm of being on the basis of which things are able to show themselves to any creature in the position and with the capacities to apprehend them.

In Olafson's view, the singularity and uniqueness of both being and reality require that there exists a single clearing in whose terms things are able to show themselves to people. If there were to exist a plurality of clearings, then, on this view, being would be "essentially plural in character." As I shall now explain, however, the singularity and uniqueness of being and reality can be understood in a second way, as the existence of certain commonalities between multiple clearings; and when it is so understood, the oneness of both being and reality is compatible with a plurality of clearings.

This commonality between clearings has three dimensions. The first consists in universal features of the notion of being as such. Being, Heidegger reiterates in several places, is a complex rather than simple concept. This means that there exists a multiplicity of general ways, or senses, of being in which entities can be. Entities, for instance, can be encountered as present-at-hand (i.e., occurring), ready-to-hand (e.g., usable/not usable), or being-there-with (*Mitdasein*; this way of being pertains to other people). More generally, as discussed earlier, Heidegger, in his lectures, identifies that-, how-, and what-being as the most general modalities in which entities can be manifest. Heidegger believes that these various general ways of being are universal among people. Any clearing happens, in part, as an understanding and projecting of possible ways of being differentiated along these lines (*GB*, 519, 528–30). Since each clearing happens as the same differentiations, being is "common" to and thus one in all clearings. Being, consequently, is singular, i.e., the general ways of being are one and the same in all clearings, even though clearings are multiple.

The second dimension of commonality is a socio-historical one. Olafson claims that the alternative to the view which, in treating being as plural in character, misses the dimension of being in which it is independent of any particular Dasein, is to construe being *qua* clearing as social and historical in character. He then claims that, although Heidegger emphasizes the notion of being-with (*Mitsein*) in *Being and Time*, this notion remains so undeveloped as to be unable to specify the sociohistorical character of the clearing and to ensure thereby the clearing's singularity and independence from individual people. Heidegger certainly should have said a lot more in this context about *Mitsein*. Olafson misses the significance of what Heidegger does say about it, however, because Olafson wants this notion to perform a task it is not designed to perform: establishing a single clearing in relation to a plurality of individuals. In Olafson's eyes, the notion of being-with should help define the "relationship in which one *Dasein* stands to another in grounding the same world" (*OL*, 72), the way in which disclosing is "joint" and "co-operative" (*OL*, 146, 71). In other words, this notion should help explain how people co-operate in opening up a single clearing on the basis of which things can be for them in common. On the view that there are as many clearings as there are people, on the other hand, the role of *Mitsein* looks quite different. It then denotes the existence of commonalities and references between numerically distinct clearings. These commonalities and references are part of the story about why these distinct clearings are the same (i.e., the same possibilities constitute them) and why, as a result, being can be "one" even though clearings are multiple.[9]

The two most important notions expressing these commonalities are the anyone (*das Man*) and tradition. The anyone is Heidegger's term for a particular structure found in every indivdual's existence: that an individual, in the first place and for the most part (*zuerst und zumeist*), acts in ways in which anyone acts. That is, a person acts, firstly and mostly, in either normal and customary or acceptable ways. In Heidegger's view, in other words, the possible ways to act that an individual understands and actualizes are, for the most part, ways of acting either accepted by or common to and approved by an open-ended totality of individuals who exert pressure on others to conform to them:

> We take pleasure and enjoy ourselves as *one* takes pleasure; we read, see, and judge about literature and art as *one* sees and judges; likewise we shrink back from the "great mass" as *one* shrinks back; we find "shocking" what *one* finds shocking. The anyone, which is nothing definite, and which all are, though not as the sum, prescribes the kind of being of everyday-ness. . . . The anyone-self, for the sake of which Dasein is in an everyday manner, articulates the referential context of significance. When entities are encountered, Dasein's world frees them for a totality of involvements with which anyone is familiar, and within the limits which have been established with the anyone's averageness. (*BT*, 164, 167; translation modified)

In saying that individuals project and realize ways of acting that anyone projects and realizes, Heidegger claims that individual existence is intrinsically social in character. Heidegger's object of analysis is individual existence, but his analysis construes sociality as part of the essence of this existence. As he writes, being-in-the-world is constituted by being-with (*BT*, 156).

Moreover, Heidegger contends that, since people encounter themselves and others in what they themselves and others do (*BT*, 163), the ways in which people can encounter themselves and others is determined by the possibilities of action they understand. He further demonstrates that what entities manifest themselves to people as being also depends, in certain cases, on the possible ways of acting people project. For some entities show themselves as usable/unusable or as servicable/unservicable (*dienlich/undienlich*). Heidegger calls such entities "equip-ment." And things showing themselves as equipment depends on people realizing ways of acting since it is in relation to particular ways of acting that things *are* usuable or unusable, servicable or unservicable. Thus, because most of the ways of acting any given individual projects are ways of acting anyone projects, and because these ways of acting are projected in an indefinite plurality of individual existences, it follows that there exist extensive commonalities in what individuals can encounter themselves, other people, and equipment as being.

It turns out, therefore, (1) that clearings are largely the same, i.e., are constituted largely by the same (anyone) possibilities, and (2) that what people and entities can and do show themselves as being is thus largely the same from clearing to clearing. Being is unitary and common even though there exists a plurality of clearings.

> Thown into its "there," every Dasein has been factically submitted to a definite "world" – its "world". At the same time those factical projections which are closest to it, have been guided by its concernful *lostness* in the anyone. (*BT*, 344).

In sum, the commonality of being, in so far as it is effected by being-with, lies not in the existence of a single realm of being independent of and prior to any particular projecting of it, but in a commonality that holds between a plurality of clearings concerning the specific ways of being in which things can manifest themselves (cf. *MFL*, 172).

Of course, whereas the first dimension of commonality, common general modalities of being, embraces all clearings whatsoever, the different sociohistorical commonalities constituting the second dimension embrace various lesser sized sets of clearings. Being is less "singular" at the sociohistorical level than at the level of being as such. This lesser degree of singularity reflects (1) the fact that what other people and the entities we use show themselves as depends on what these people do and how we use the entities, and (2) the fact that possibilities of activity vary between societies, communities, and the like. The range of possible being-there-with and readiness-to-hand of people and entities varies between societies, etc., whereas being-there-with and readiness-to-hand as such are common to all.

Now, Heidegger maintains that people always fall into the anyone, into acting and encountering entities and people in the ways anyone does. People are *thrown* into this kind of existence – inextricably. Olafson simply overlooks this aspect of Heidegger's thought. (It is significant that the extremely important term "thrownness" appears almost nowhere in Olafson's account.) He writes: "it may sound as though a radical and original uncovering were effected in each case by an individual Dasein, unless, of course, it has relapsed into the unauthentic and anonymous mode of *das Man*" (*OL*, 147). Relapsed? Dasein is constantly and always already in the mode of *das Man*. Because of this, there are always considerable commonalities between the clearings of different people. Olafson reveals his misunderstanding of Heidegger, therefore, when he writes, in criticism of Heidegger: "What I am suggesting is that, if the [projections] of one Dasein were not made in such a way as to relate them, at least to some minimal degree, to the [projections] of other Daseins, it is hard to see how the specific uncoverings they effect could be shared" (*OL*, 148). The anyone ensures not merely that different people's projections (understandings) are "related" to one another, but that they are for the most part the same. So the anyone helps ensure that clearings are "shared," i.e., the same.

Moreover, the contrast Olafson sets up in the above quotation from page 147, that between _das Man_ and a radically individual and original clearing, further discloses his undervaluation of the breadth and domination of the anyone. If there could be an original and radically individual uncovering (which, given the contrast, presumably corresponds to the general way of being Heidegger calls "authenticity") it would indeed seem doubtful whether clearings were shared and being/reality one. Heidegger emphasizes at a number of places, however, that the authentic mode of existence cannot escape the anyone but, instead, involves merely a transformation in a person's relation to and cognizance of the anyone (e.g., _BT_, 168, 224, 422). The possibilities that an authentic individual projects and from which he or she chooses him- or herself are always still for the most part anyone possibilities. Thus an original and radically individual clearing is, in Heidegger's eyes, impossible. Such a clearing would nullify the sociality and commonality intrinsic to human life.

Of course, the authentic individual chooses him- or herself from a range of possibilities that is broader than that offered by the anyone. This broader range of possibilities is found in tradition. Tradition contains possibilities beyond those carried by the anyone since there always exist possible ways of acting handed down through tradition which have fallen into disfavor or disuse. The authentic individual, no longer blindly held captive to the anyone, is able to see that more is possible in the current situation than what is prescribed by the anyone and offered by the entities with which he or she is currently dealing (e.g., _BT_, 345). These further possibilities, in Heidegger's view, are all drawn from tradition (_BT_, 435–7).[10] It is from tradition, he thus writes, that the authentic individual can "choose a hero" (_BT_, 437). Tradition is not, however, a broader envelope or clearing within which individual clearings are suspended. An individual person is always already projecting some traditional possibilities, namely, those belonging to the past of his or her generation, which past he or she "has grown up both into and in" (_BT_, 41). Other traditional possibilities are preserved in entities encountered in existence, e.g., books, sayings, and stories. The key point here is simply that tradition is a second dimension of the sociohistorical commonality between clearings; and, as indicated, it consists in both a commonality in the possibilities that constitute clearings and a commonality (and similarity) in the possibility-preserving entities encountered in clearings. (The latter component of this commonality is an example of the topic of section 3.) Heidegger's notion of the destiny of a community reflects this second dimension of sociohistorical commonality. The destiny of a community, he writes, is not something put together out of individual fates and situations (_BT_, 436). Rather, it is a commonality in the situations and fates faced by the members of a community, a commonality constituted and made possible by commonalities both in projected possibilities and in the entities and people which people encounter or have to deal with.

Incidentally, Olafson's belief that a plurality of clearings is incompatible with the singularity and uniqueness of being is based, in part, on his misconception of the "choice-like" character of understanding and projection. In his view, the possibilities that any given person projects are subject to choice, and since choice varies between individuals, so too do the possibilities projected. In arguing this way, Olafson misunderstands the nature of the shared projections of the anyone and tradition. Olafson is correct to use the facts (1) that what equipment at any moment shows itself to someone as being depends on what that person is doing, and (2) that what a person is doing depends on that for the sake of which he or she acts (his or her end), to argue that what things show themselves as is determined by choice, at least in so far as choice determines a person's ends and how he or she acts so as to realize them: "choice figures not only as a partial determinant of what will actually be the case . . . but also as defining the practical meaning of the state of the world that does result" (*OL*, 69). In Heidegger's view, however, inauthentic action-determining choices are always choices from among, and thus they occur on the background of, the totality of possible anyone actions and ends that each individual projects.[11] The projection of anyone possibilities itself, however, is not a matter of choice – in Heidegger's eyes, it is simply a universal structure of human existence. Inauthentic individuals do not choose to project anyone possibilities (cf. *BT*, 312). And authentic individuals are unable to choose not to project them. Consequently, the clearing, *qua* space of anyone possibilities, is not subject to choice. Choice helps determine the range of projected actions only when authentic individuals take over nonanyone possibilities from tradition. These possibilities are few in number, however, in comparison to those constituting the anyone. So the facts that inauthentic choice varies between individuals and that authentic choice can occur do not nullify the sameness of people's clearings.

Finally, the third dimension of the singularity of being and reality, when singularity is construed as commonalities between clearings, is one and the same realm of present-at-hand entities entering each clearing. This idea is the topic of section 3. At this point, section 2 can be summarized as follows: resolving the paradox that Olafson raises about Heidegger's philosophy, how being can be one and clearings multiple, requires a correct understanding of the multiplicity of clearings and the oneness of being. A multiplicity of clearings consists in the existence of a plurality of people together with the fact that what things can show themselves to any one of these people as being is governed by the particular space of possible ways of being understood by that individual. The singularity of being, on the other hand, consists in possible ways of being being common to a plurality of clearings, i.e., to different people's understandings, with regard to both the specific and the types of possibilities involved.

3 Realism

For my purposes here, the issue of realism versus idealism is the issue of whether the entities that people encounter in lived experience exist, and are what they are, independently of people. If the answer to this question is yes, then even if there were suddenly no more (or had never been) any people, entities other than people would nonetheless continue to be and to be what they are. If, on the other hand, the answer to this question is no, then, if there were suddenly no more people, other entities too would no longer exist and be that which they are. The distinction between that-being and how-being, of course, multiplies the possible flavors of realism and idealism. This distinction plays a secondary role in Heidegger's views on this issue, however, since he takes a single position with respect to being in general.

Heidegger clearly thinks that entities exist, and are what they are, independently of people. A sample of quotations proves this beyond a shadow of a doubt: "Entities *are*, quite independently of the experience by which they are disclosed, the acquaintance in which they are discovered, and the grasping in which their nature is ascertained." (*BT*, 228). "[This] does not signify that only when Dasein exists and as long as Dasein exists, can the real be that which in itself it is" (*BT*, 255). "[Nature] is, even if we do not uncover it, without our encountering it within our world . . . Nature can also be when no Dasein exists" (*BP*, 169, 170; cf. *BP*, 222–3). "Beings are in themselves the kinds of beings they are, and in the way they are, even if, for example, Dasein does not exist" (*MFL*, 153; cf. 194). The interpretive issue, in this context, is whether Heidegger's avowals of realism are consistent with another sort of statement he sometimes makes, usually in conjunction with these avowals: "But being 'is' only in the understanding of those entities to whose being something like an understanding of being belongs" (*BT*, 228); "only as long as Dasein is . . . 'is there' being" (*BT*, 255).

Statements of these two sorts are *prima facie* inconsistent. Existing and being such and such are modalities of being. Hence, if there is being only in the understanding of being, entities can exist and be what they are only because and hence so long as there is understanding of being. If there are no people, however, there is no understanding of being. In such a situation, consequently, it would seem to follow that entities could neither be nor not be in any modality of being. Yet Heidegger clearly claims that beings are and are what they are even if there are no people.

The resolution of this *prima facie* incompatibility is only hinted at in *Being and Time*, appearing more prominently in Heidegger's subsequent lecture courses. To see it, we must first understand what Heidegger means by statements of the second sort. As sketched earlier, being is the "how" of the possible (and thus actual) manifestation of entities to people. What was not emphasized earlier, however, is that being is *nothing more* than the how of uncoveredness. Since being is nothing more than the how of uncoveredness, however, it cannot be independently of uncoveredness. So because there is no uncoveredness apart from understanding, there is no being apart from understanding. This is what Heidegger means, then, when he writes that "being 'is' only in the understanding of . . . being." Being, as the how of possible uncoveredness projected in the understanding, "is" only in this projection and thus so long as there is this projection and the accompanying uncovering of entities. Heidegger thus writes: "Being is there primordially and in itself, when it gives access to . . . beings." (*MFL*, 153).

This interpretation of statements of the second sort, however, only seems to make it harder to understand how entities can be and be what they are independently of and thus even when there are no people. Doesn't the latter independence require, contrary to the interpretation just given, that being characterizes entities even when there are no people, thus no understanding of being, and hence no being for entities to manifest themselves in? Heidegger claims that there is one particular modality of being, presence-at-hand, which is such that, when something present-at-hand shows itself to be a certain way, it shows itself to have been already or all along that way. Whenever, for instance, Newton's laws disclose something, "the entity which is uncovered with the unveiled laws was precisely in the way in which it showed itself after the uncovering and now is as thus showing itself" (*BP*, 220; connect with *BT*, 269). Heidegger does not explain why this is the case, although it might have something to do with the fact that "present-at-hand" (*Vorhandensein*) as we understand it means something like occurring or abiding. In any case, an entity that, in showing itself, shows itself as having been already what it shows itself to be, is what it shows itself to be independently of its showing itself. Hence, it lies in the meaning of one modality of being that entities that show themselves in this modality exist, and are what they show themselves in this modality as being, independently of their showing themselves thus. The independence of present-at-hand entities is an implication of presence-at-hand *qua* modality of being that itself is only as something understood (cf. *BP*, 169; see *BP*, 315 for a similar formulation pertaining to perceivedness). As Heidegger says, it is only in so far as Dasein gives itself being that beings can emerge in their in-themselves, i.e., it is only in so far as Dasein gives itself being that it is possible to understand that beings are in themselves the kinds of beings they are, and in the way they are, even if people do not exist (*MFL*, 153).

This reading of Heidegger's position reveals that, in the preceding passage from *MFL*, 153, as well as in others quoted earlier, Heidegger does not use the expression "in itself" as Kant does. In Kant, the thing in itself is how something is independently of how it is for us, thus how it is independently of any possible knowledge we can have of it. In Heidegger, on the other hand, what something is "in itself" is what it is independently of our actually encountering it. Thus, when Heidegger claims that what present-at-hand things show themselves to us as being is what in themselves they are, he means only that they are the present-at-hand entities they show themselves as being – and not something else – even if no one encounters them. Heidegger, in other words, is an empirical, and not a transcendental, realist. That this is so is in fact presupposed by the phenomenological character of his enterprise, which enterprise aims to "let that which shows itself be seen from itself in the way it itself shows itself to be" (*BT*, 58, retranslated). At the same time, even though what entities in themselves are is what they are independently of our actually encountering them, what they are independently of our actually encountering them is not, as we have seen, independent of our understanding of being. Heidegger is also an idealist.

This reading also enables us to explain the enigmatic second full paragraph in *Being and Time*, p. 255. Heidegger opens by saying that there is being only so long as Dasein is. He then writes:

> When Dasein does not exist, "independence" "is" not either, nor "is" the "in-itself." In such a case this sort of thing can be neither understood nor not understood. In such a case even entities within-the-world can neither

be disclosed nor lie hidden. *In such a case* it cannot be said that entities are, nor can it be said that they are not.

In other words, if there is no Dasein, and hence no understanding of being, there doesn't exist the understanding of that modality of being (presence-at-hand) by virtue of which either the independence of things or what things in themselves are can show itself or even be conceived. More radically, in fact, if there is no understanding of being, there is no understanding of any modality of being, and thus nothing by virtue of which to say or to understand anything, positive or negative, about the being of entities. Nonetheless, Heidegger concludes: "But *now*, as long as there is an understanding of being and therefore an understanding of presence-at-hand, it can indeed be said that *in this case* entities will still continue to be," i.e., given our understanding of being and thus our understanding of presence-at-hand, we do have something on the basis of which to answer (and, indeed, pose) the question about the independence of things in themselves; and in accordance with our understanding of presence-at-hand, the answer is yes, entities would still be.

Now, since present-at-hand entitities exist as such independently of their showing themselves, they form a realm of entities that can show themselves to an indefinite number of people. Existing independently of all encounterings, their showing themselves is not intrinsically tied to any particular encountering or person. Of course, as noted, present-at-hand entities can show themselves thus only because people understand presence-at-hand: "beings, among which Dasein also factually is, get surpassed by" Dasein's projection of possible ways of being which "first makes it possible for these [beings], previously surpassed as beings, to be ontically opposite [to Dasein] and as opposite to be apprehended in themselves" (*MFL*, 166). Still, because all people understand presence-at-hand, it is possible for present-at-hand entities to manifest themselves as themselves to an indefinite number of people while remaining what they are regardless of whether they show themselves or not.

It is even possible to speak of one and the same realm of entities "entering" different clearings. Olafson claims that Heidegger has no business talking about present-at-hand entities "entering the world." His claim is based, however, on the mistaken idea that Heidegger lapses into transcendental realism. Olafson begins his criticism from the idea that, since a clearing is constituted by the totality of possible ways of being that someone understands, it embraces the totality of what that person can understand as being in any way. He then claims that this characterization of a clearing entails that anyone who speaks of present-at-hand entities as "entering," and thus as "outside" of, clearings, presupposes that she can understand how entities are (i.e., present-at-hand) when they lie outside the totality of what can be in any way for her; outside, that is, the totality of what she can understand as being in any way (*OL*, 51; cf. 183). Such an understanding is unavailable to finite creatures such as ourselves. Consequently, Olafson concludes, Heidegger should abandon talk of entities "entering" the clearing. Of course, Heidegger himself, as the discussion of the paragraph from *BT*, 255 demonstrates, denies that people have access to a nonfinite viewpoint. In saying this, however, he is not, *pace* Olafson, being inconsistent. For Olafson misunderstands what Heidegger means by entities "entering" the clearing.

The happening of a clearing is the occurrence of possible ways of being in which things can show themselves. Entities "enter" a clearing when the clearing happens, when, that is, possibilities are projected (i.e., when Dasein exists; *MFL*, 194). And what it means to say that entities enter the clearing is simply that, with the occurrence of possible ways of being, it *becomes possible* for entities to show themselves (cf. ibid., 166, 193–5). The entities that are able to show themselves whenever Dasein exits, furthermore, are already what they are prior to their being able to do this. As Heidegger writes, "World-entry and its occurrence is solely the presupposition for extant things announcing themselves in their not requiring world-entry regarding their own being" (ibid., 195) In entering the clearing, moreover, they undergo no change in being: "Entry into the world is not a process of extant things, in the sense that beings undergo a change thereby and through this change break into the world. The extant's entry into the world is 'something' that happens to it" (ibid., 194; cf. *GB*, 406). As discussed earlier, however, the pre-existence and independence of entities follows from the meaning of one of the modalities of being (presence-at-hand) we understand. To speak of entities as "outside" of and as "entering" the clearing, therefore, is to conceive of them in one of the modalities of being we understand. So thinking of entities of a certain kind as "entering" the clearing does not require, as Olafson claims it does, that we understand how these entities are when they lie outside the totality of what we can understand as being in any way. It requires merely the understanding of being that we possess.

In other words, what it is for an entity to be "outside" a clearing is not for it to lie outside the totality of ways we can understand things to be. Rather, it is an entity's not having the possibility of showing itself. Consequently, Heidegger is not being muddle-headed in claiming that what something is "outside" a clearing, i.e., prior to its being possible for it to manifest itself to some person, i.e., prior to the existence of this person, is what it can show itself to that person as being.[12]

Although Heidegger is a realist, we must not forget the idealist character of his views. Things show themselves in the modalities of being because they show themselves in the possibilities grasped by understanding. Unlike Kant, however, Heidegger does not treat understanding as the "property" of a transcendental subject analytically distinct from the empirical subject. (I here pass over the issues of whether the transcendental and empirical subjects are identical and whether it makes sense to attribute understanding to the empirical subject). Since there are no Kantian things in themselves in Heidegger, there are likewise no transcendental subjects. As a result, the understanding on the basis of which a person encounters entities is the property of one of the entities that that same person encounters, namely himself. That is, the understanding in whose light entities manifest themselves to someone is an ontic property of that entity which in this light is revealed to that person as himself. Heidegger, finally, also surpasses Kant's idealism. For, in treating existence in the same way that he treats how and what being, Heidegger indicates that to speak of something as existing is to conceive of it in terms of the modalities of being that we understand.

Thus he would side with Hegel against Kant and claim that, since Kant attributes existence to the thing in itself, the Kantian conception of the thing in itself is a conception of a way things are for us and not a conception of how things are independently of any way they are for us.

4 Conclusion

The existence of one and the same realm of present-at-hand entities which enter into a multiplicity of clearings completes the story of how such a multiplicity is compatible with the singularity and uniqueness of being and reality. Not only are certain general modalities of being common to all clearings, but the same entities that show themselves to any given person can and do show themselves to others. Reality is a single totality of entities which show themselves to people in common as existing, being such and such, being of certain kinds, and so on. Furthermore, since the same possibilities of present-at-hand being are found in different clearings, what present-at-hand entities show themselves to any one person as being can be and often is what they show themselves to others as being. The anyone and tradition, lastly, embrace additional commonalities between varying pluralities of clearings in possibilities of ready-to-hand and being-there-with being. Because of these lesser commonalities, entities show themselves to different people as the same, and as the same types of, ready-to-hand entities; and people show themselves to themselves and to others as performing the same, and the same sorts of, actions.

In this essay, I have endeavored to show the consistency of Heidegger's earlier views on clearings, being, and reality. I also have been concerned to explore the individualist, idealist, and realist character of these views, together with the way *Being and Time* combines these elements with an analysis of the intrinsic sociohistoricity of human existence. This coexistence of idealist, realist, individualist, and historicist elements lends Heidegger's early position unique contemporary and historical philosophical significance.[13]

NOTES

1 Cf. Martin Heidegger, *Being and Time*, trans. John Macquarrie and Edward Robinson (Oxford: Basil Blackwell, 1962), p. 171. References to this work are henceforth indicated by *BT*. Other abbreviations for Heidegger's works are as follows: *BP* = *The Basic Problems of Phenomenology*, trans. Albert Hofstadter, Bloomington: Indiana University Press, 1982; *GB* = *Die Grundbegriffe der Metaphysik*, Volume 29/30 of the *Gesammtausgabe*, Frankfurt-am-Main: Vittorio Klostermann, 1983; *HCT* = *History of the Concept of Time*, trans. Theodore Kisiel, Bloomington: Indiana University Press, 1985; *MFL* = *The Metaphysical Foundations of Logic*, trans. Michael Heim, Bloomington: Indiana University Press, 1984.

2 Frederick Olafson, *Heidegger and the Philosophy of Mind*, New Haven, CT: Yale University Press, 1987. References to this work are henceforth marked by *OL*.

3 Additional evidence for this reading of Heidegger is provided by his comments about authentic community. If communities were instances of Dasein, then a discussion of

authentic community would seem to offer an especially favorable moment at which to indicate this, say, by stipulating that authentic individuality presupposes authentic community as something distinct from it. Heidegger, however, propounds the opposite thesis. Authentic community is the coming-together of authentic individuals (*BT*, 159, 344–5; *BP*, 288). This emphasis on individuals reinforces the claim that Dasein refers to individual people.

4   See the long discussion of animals at *GB*, part II, chapters 3–5.

5   For this way of describing Heidegger's relation to Cartesianism, cf. *BT*, 366, and his comments on Husserl's concept of intentionality at *HCT*, 303–4.

6   In the end for Heidegger, human existence is a clearing because human existence is the ecstatic, self-opening temporalizing of temporality. For the purposes of this essay, however, it is clearer to discuss Heidegger's position in terms of understanding.

7   Cf. *GB*, part II, chapter 6, passim. Elsewhere, Heidegger often differentiates only what-being and that-being, or what-being and how-being.

8   Olafson very nicely points out that, since existing, being such and such, and being a certain sort of thing are states of affairs, and since being is the "how" of the uncoveredness of entities, it follows that entities show themselves to humans as articulated into states of affairs. A red apple, for instance, shows itself as red and as existing when someone looks at it. Olafson then makes the immensely productive suggestion that the difference between entities and being in Heidegger corresponds roughly to the difference between things and states of affairs (facts). So understood, the irreducibility of being to entities is analogous to the irreducibility of states of affairs to things. See *OL*, 232ff.

9   For the purpose of space, I will not discuss the references that link clearings. What I have in mind is that, when Heidegger says that being-in-the-world is constituted by being-with, part of what he means is, first, that it is always the case that some of the ways of being in which (1) things can be manifest and (2) Dasein itself can exist contain references to others. For instance, an entity might show itself to someone as John's pliars or as usable for pulling John's teeth, whereas helping Maud and acting for the sake of Maud's well-being might be disclosed to him as possible ways (for himself) to be (see *BT*, 153–63). References such as these clearly establish linkages and dependencies between clearings. In saying that Dasein is essentially being-with, part of what Heidegger means is, second, that it is always the case that some of the ways of being that constitute the clearing are ways for others to be. On this point, see *BP*, 278–9; and *BT*, 183.

10 Notice that it is a bit difficult to see where, on Heidegger's view, new possibilities come from; that is, how tradition evolves.

11 The choices people make, moreover, quite often are the choices that "anyone" would make. So even to the extent to which what things show themselves as depends on choice, what things show themselves to different people as is not necessarily different.

12 These remarks explain the sense in which Heidegger believes that readiness-to-hand is "projected upon" entities. Heidegger certainly does not believe that this projection works as follows: in using, say, a hammer we first cognize the existence of a present-at-hand entity; second, project a "function predicate" (e.g., "for hammering") upon it; and third, on the basis of this projection, use it for hammering. Rather, in the flow of ongoing activity, entities are often immediately encountered in a "practical meaning" without an explicit projection of this meaning occurring. At the same time, however, ready-to-hand entities are not ready-to-hand independently of human existence. For something's being ready-to-hand, unlike its being present-at-hand, is relative to possible projects, purposes, and ends. So entities cannot be ready-to-hand "outside" a clearing, even though outside of one, i.e., prior to and following the existence of the particular understanding on the basis of which they can

show themselves to a particular person, they can be what they show themselves to that person as being when he or she encounters them as present-at-hand. From the reconstructive point of view made available by our acquaintance with present-at-hand entities, consequently, it is possible to say that, even if something is *encountered* in the first place as ready-to-hand, (1) it can be present-at-hand prior to, and even during, its being something ready-to-hand (cf. *BT*, 103), and (2) it first becomes, and remains, ready-to-hand when it is swept up into, and so long as it remains involved in, human activity. As Heidegger says, there are ready-to-hand entities only by reason of present-at-hand entities (*BT*, 101). From the reconstructive point of view, therefore, it makes good sense to speak of human activity "projecting" a meaning on entities.

13 I would like to thank Dan Breazeale, Hubert Dreyfus, and Jürgen Habermas for comments on earlier versions of this essay.

5
Existential Temporality in
Being and Time
(Why Heidegger is not a Pragmatist)

William D. Blattner

In chapter 2 of the Introduction to his *Being and Time*,[1] Martin Heidegger tells us that he will interpret Dasein as originary temporality (*S&Z*, 17). He adds that his concept of originary temporality (*ursprüngliche Zeitlichkeit*) differs dramatically from what we ordinarily think time is, and the way we ordinarily think we are in time (*S&Z* 17–18). It is also notoriously true that Heidegger's discussion of originary temporality is one of the most difficult passages of *Being and Time*. In this paper I shall investigate what originary temporality is and how it relates to Dasein's understanding of the now of world-time (which is, roughly, time as it shows itself in the everyday encountering of entities).

Consider a dilemma posed by the literature on Heidegger's originary temporality. Why does the account of originary temporality occur just where it does in *Being and Time*? In Division I, Heidegger presents his preliminary existential analysis of the being of Dasein, and he does this in terms of Dasein's "everydayness" – the way that Dasein can be found in its everyday goings about the world. In Division II, Heidegger engages in two seemingly disjoint enterprises: he argues for a series of classically "existentialist" claims (e.g., that Dasein's existence is fundamentally conditioned by its relation to its death); and he presents a systematic reinterpretation of Dasein in terms of its "originary temporality," which culminates in an account of the nature of time as ordinarily understood. Why do these two projects fall into one division? What links them together? And what is the relation between the temporal reinterpretation of Dasein's being and the analysis of the same phenomenon in Division I?

There are two standard ways of approaching these two questions. The first, and by far the most common, way of laying out the terrain is to claim that Heidegger's concept of "originary temporality" characterizes the being of Dasein in so far as it is authentic (*eigentlich*). According to this view, that temporal phenomenon is the temporal form of authentic, human existence, or perhaps the form of time encountered by authentic Dasein. Since Heidegger describes the patterns of existence that make up authenticity at length in Division II of *Being and Time*, this view makes good sense of why Heidegger offers the temporal analysis in the final quarter of *Being and Time*. However, as I shall argue below, Heidegger clearly indicates that originary temporality is *not* authentic. A second strategy understands originary temporality as the temporal, indeed usually historical, structure of human existence. It is the way of being in time that is implicated in the characterization of Dasein given in Division I. This temporal form is usually argued to be teleologically organized, so that we must – on pain of distorting Dasein's sort of being – understand the phases that make up the course of life of a human being to be tied in with one another as phases of the execution of projects. This strategy does justice to Heidegger's presentation of originary temporality as indifferent between authentic and inauthentic modes of human existence. However, it is by no means clear, on this reading, why Heidegger waits until *after* his introduction of authenticity to present originary temporality. Thus, we seem to be faced with a dilemma. Either we do justice to the feature of originary temporality that it is indifferent between authenticity and inauthenticity, but then not be able to understand why that phenomenon is introduced only in s.65 of *Being and Time*. Or we do justice to Heidegger's delayed presentation of originary temporality, but misconstrue originary temporality as authentic. How can we find a way out of this dilemma?

We must accept *both* that originary temporality is indeed indifferent between authenticity and inauthenticity, *and* that it is crucially important to the structure of *Being and Time* that the analysis of originary temporality not only *was* not presented until s.65, but *could* not be presented until then. I want to argue that there are two features of human existence – one of them a precondition for what Heidegger calls "death," and the other what he calls "the nullity of Dasein's being the ground" – that force the temporal analysis of Dasein's being to the phenomenon of originary temporality. These features emerge in the discussion of the "choice" between authenticity and inauthenticity, because this choice is a response to those features. But the features themselves are neither authentic nor inauthentic. So Heidegger could not simply have appended his analysis of temporality to the end of his analysis of everydayness, even though temporality is not essentially authentic. Thus, we have our way out of the dilemma, and a more satisfactory analysis of the place of temporality in *Being and Time*.

Furthermore, the second sort of view above underlies recent attempts to represent Heidegger as a pragmatist, in a way that I shall identify more carefully below. In undermining this view, then, I am undercutting the basis on which rests the attempt to view Heidegger as something of a pragmatist. Although the second view is right to interpret originary temporality as indifferent, Heidegger was not a pragmatist, and his doctrine of originary temporality lies at the center of why he was not. Recall that Heidegger called his philosophy "existential phenomenology," not "pragmatic phenomenology." The following interpretation of originary temporality will bear out Heidegger's choice.

Originary temporality is indifferent

Throughout s.65 of *S&Z* Heidegger seems to treat temporality as if it were the form of the existence only of authentic Dasein. For example, he says, "*temporality unveils itself as the sense of authentic care*" (*S&Z*, 326). In the same paragraph Heidegger says, even more distressingly, "In coming back to itself futurally, resoluteness enpresentingly brings itself into the situation. Only in so far as Dasein is determined as temporality, is the indicated authentic ability-to-be-a-whole of forerunning [*Vorlaufenden*] resoluteness possible for it. We call this phenomenon, which is unitary in the form of the future that has been and enpresents, *temporality*" (*S&Z*, 326). This seems to state that temporality is the temporal structure of authentic Dasein, for "resoluteness," i.e., authentic disclosedness, is linked here with temporality.

Despite this, there are strong indications that "temporality" should be taken to be a phenomenon that characterizes all forms of Dasein, not just the authentic ones. Section 65 does focus on authentic temporality, which is the reason why so many commentators have taken originary temporality to be authentic temporality.[2] But what s.65 says about authentic temporality is that it is only possible because Dasein is temporal in a more fundamental way. In the passage above, I suggest, the second sentence is the key. Compare this sentence with: "Forerunning [i.e., the *authentic* version of the future] makes Dasein *authentically* futural, and indeed in such a way that forerunning itself is only possible in so far as Dasein, *as an entity*, always already comes towards itself at all [*überhaupt*], that is, in so far as it is futural in its being at all" (*S&Z*, 325). And: "If resoluteness makes up the mode of authentic care, but it [viz., care] itself is only possible through temporality, then the phenomenon that has been attained with respect to resoluteness [viz., the temporal form of authentic existence] must itself only represent a modality of temporality, which makes care possible as such at all" (*S&Z*, p. 327).[3] In other words, Heidegger says that Dasein can only be authentically futural in so far as it is futural at all, or futural in a more general sense. Since s.65 follows upon the discussion of forerunning resoluteness, Heidegger begins the discussion of Dasein's temporality by focusing on authentic temporality. However, in order to understand how authentic temporality is possible, he must show how it is a mode of a more basic sort of temporality, the sort of temporality that Dasein cannot help but have, the sort of temporality that characterizes Dasein's being as such. Thus, in the passages in which Heidegger seems to say that temporality is an authentic phenomenon, he in fact says quite the opposite: *authentic temporality is merely one mode of originary temporality*.

Care and originary temporality

When Heidegger turns to the topic of this more basic sort of temporality (*S&Z*, 327), he appears to change the subject: he beings abruptly to discuss the "being-totality" (*Seinsganzheit*) of Dasein, namely care. Why would he do this? If temporality is the temporal structure of care in general (abstracted from its existentiell modes), however, then it makes sense for Heidegger to return to care (in general) to launch the discussion of temporality. He says,

> The being-totality of Dasein as care means this: being-ahead-of-itself-already-being-in (a world) as being-amidst (intraworldly encountering beings). When we first determined this articulated [*gegliederten*] structure, we pointed out that the ontological question with respect to this articulation must be pursued even further until we lay open the unity of the totality of the structural manifold. *The originary unity of the structure of care lies in temporality.* (*S&Z*, 327)

For each element of the care-structure Heidegger offers a temporal interpretation or sense (*Sinn*) of it. What are the elements of the care-structure, and what are their temporal interpretations? "The ahead-of-itself is grounded in the future. Already-being-in . . . announces in itself beenness [*Gewesenheit*]. Being-amidst . . . is made possible in enpresenting" (*S&Z*, 327).

How can we set about interpreting this? If we stick to the idea of interpreting originary temporality with the aid of the care-structure, we cannot get very far, for Heidegger devotes just about as little explanation to care as he does to originary temporality. We need another clue: "The temporal Interpretation of everyday Dasein should begin with the structures in which disclosedness is constituted. These are: understanding, affectivity [*Befindlichkeit*], falling and telling [*Rede*]. The modes of temporalization that are to be laid bare in light of these phenomena provide the ground for determining the temporality of being-in-the-world," (*S&Z*, 334–5).

Here Heidegger refers us to his disclosedness-structure, which leads us to chapter 5 of Division I.

Care is the articulated structure of the being of Dasein. Disclosedness is the manner in which Dasein's "There" is open, revealed, or unhidden. The "There" is the context in which being, Dasein, its world, and things are revealed or "there" for Dasein. (In some sense, disclosedness is the Heideggerian heir to the traditional notion of consciousness.) Dasein is its disclosedness, because for Dasein to be is for it (and being, things, etc.) to be disclosed; furthermore, Dasein is its world, is the very context in which anything can show up. Consequently, Dasein is self-disclosed, that is, an entity that is "there" for itself.[4] Since Dasein is self-disclosed, for each element of care, there is a correlative element of disclosedness, namely the disclosedness of that element of care. Being-ahead is disclosed in understanding, being-amidst is disclosed in falling, and being-already-in is disclosed in affectivity.[5]

Understanding, being-ahead, and the future

For Heidegger, understanding is not a cognitive activity (which is not to say that there isn't a version of it that is cognitive).[6] Understanding is practical: it is competence. He says,

In ontical discourse we often use the expression "to understand something" in the meaning "to be able to manage a thing" [*"einer Sache vorstehen können"*], "to be equal to it" [*"ihr gewachsen sein"*], "to be able to do something" [*"etwas können"*]. In understanding, as an existentiale, that which can be done is not a What, but rather being as existing. (*S&Z*, 143).

In other words, one understands something not when one cognitively grasps its content, its What, but rather when one can cope with it.[7] I understand being a teacher, because I am competent to be one. I understand a hammer because I can use it. I don't understand pianos, however, because I cannot play them.[8] Understanding something is competence with it.

Now, projection is Heidegger's analysis of this competence. To understand something is to let it play some role for you, to cast it in the role.[9] I understand a hammer in letting it play the role of hammer. (One way to misunderstand something is to let it play the wrong role, where right and wrong are codetermined by social custom and practical success). Heidegger introduces projection in the context of self-understanding. He says, "understanding has the existential structure that we call *projection[Entwurf]*. It projects the being of Dasein upon its for-the-sake-of-which just as originarily as upon significance, which is the worldliness of its current world" (*S&Z*, 145). What is self-understanding? According to the formula above, self-understanding is competence with oneself. What is self-competence? It is the ability to play one's role. According to Heidegger, whenever I act, I do so in accordance with some role that I am throwing myself into. When I vote I try to accord with the role of good citizen. My specific actions, for example, walking to the voting booth, are subservient to being a good citizen. This role that I am trying to play is the for-the-sake-of-which (*Worum-willen*). The for-the-sake-of-which is for Heidegger always a way to be Dasein. I have tried to anticipate this by using the example of *being* a good citizen. In acting, I constitute myself as who I am.[10] In going to the voting booth, I constitute myself as a good citizen. This is why Heidegger says, "The 'for-the-sake-of' ['*Umwillen*'] . . . always concerns the being of *Dasein*, for whom in its being this very being is essentially always at issue" (*S&Z*, 84). The for-the-sake-of-which is a way to be Dasein, and it is the point of my action.[11]

Now, the future of originary temporality is supposed to be the sense of this self-competence. What is the connection between this interpretation of Dasein as bound up with its ability to play a role and any view about time or temporality? To answer this question, I want to work off of the pragmatist interpretation of Heidegger, and in particular the views of Okrent and Olafson. Okrent says, the distinctive "future" of originary temporality "refers to the act in which Dasein expects, anticipates, or intends a possible future being for itself" (1988, p. 193). He continues,

some *x* can be correctly interpreted as acting toward such an end just in case *x* intends a possible future for itself in light of an awareness of what it has been doing, which involves a making-present of that with which *x* is dealing; and all of this is the case only if *x*'s behavior has a certain organized unity through time in which each act is tied to those that precede and those that follow it. (Okrent, 1988, p. 196).

So, since Dasein must try to bring about its future through action, Dasein's actions must exhibit a certain form of unity: for Jones now to be practicing for the basketball team, she must in a few moments be doing something that makes sense as an attempt to bring about the end of being an athlete. According to Okrent, Dasein's originary futurity just is this fact about it, that its current state of being is bound up with what it is trying to make itself be in the future.

Similarly, Olafson discusses two "ways of having a future," namely by thinking about the future and by bringing it about. He says,

> It is widely assumed that one could have a future in a purely theoretical or representational mode that would include even one's own future actions and without its making any difference that they were one's own actions. But [the way Dasein actually has] a future is a way of having it as what we are about to do or bring about. The linkage here among the notions of the future, possibility, and choice is clearly a very close one. (Olafson, 1987, pp. 91–2)

The one way to have a future is to represent it or think about it; the other, and presumably more originary, way to have a future is to bring it about, to carry it out. Jones aims to get on the basketball team, and her present relation to her future is not just one of thinking about it, or even of planning for it, but rather one of trying to make it happen. So, Dasein is an entity that "has time" in a very special way. It is not just that Dasein exists or endures through time, but rather Dasein acts and brings its future about.

We can tell immediately that something is wrong here. There is much to what Okrent and Olafson say, but it is not at all clear whether the facts they point to have any temporal-ontological significance. Even if these putative facts help to determine how we must conceive Dasein, do they in any way influence how we must conceive *time*? Okrent does not address this question. Olafson's idea, however, seems to be that Dasein must bring together its future and its present: in order to understand who I now am, I must try to bring about some future. I cannot confine my interest and knowledge just to the present; rather, I must not only think about the future, but also aim to make it be in some definite way. Even given this, however, it is still not clear that this has any significance for time. Olafson's central argument seems to be that this view entails that we cannot entirely distinguish the present and the future, because each is implicated in the other. What I bring about tomorrow is implicated in who I am now. Thus, he says, "but the future is not some gratuitous addition that thought contributes to what is already solidly given; it is that to which we are committed" (Olafson, 1988, p. 87). In picking up the basketball, Jones is committing herself to being a basketball player, and this means that her current identity cannot be specified without reference to her intended future.

The conclusions offered by Okrent and Olafson do not harmonize well with the rather dramatic sounding claims that Heidegger makes:[12] "'Future' does not here mean a Now, which *not yet* having become 'actual,' sometime *will be*, but rather the coming, in which Dasein comes towards itself in its ownmost ability-to-be" (*S&Z*, 325). And: "Temporalizing does not mean a 'succession' ['*Nacheinander*'] of the ecstases. The future is *not later* than been-ness and this is not earlier than the Present [*Gegenwart*]" (*S&Z*, 350). Is there anything in the accounts offered by Olafson and Okrent to warrant the claim that the future is *not later* than the present?[13] I see nothing that can. It is in fact crucial to their readings that the future is later than the present, that it is a later time in which I aim to realize my ends, make myself who I am. Moreover, all talk of trying to realize my ends, which I am, seems to imply that I can actualize or realize myself by bringing myself (or my future states) about in the future. Yet Heidegger says that this future that I am as coming towards myself is not something that could be actual.

Something must be missing from Olafson amd Okrent, something which could account for the dramatic language Heidegger uses in these contexts. Let me suggest that Olafson and Okrent both "over-pragmatize" Heidegger. In particular, they leave out his "existentialist" bent, and it is this existentialist bent that accounts for the distinctive features of his view.

The sense of "possibility" on which Heidegger relies is not that of "possible actuality," for it can never (come to) be that I have (already) made myself a lawyer, for example.[14] The point is not that there are conditions on being a lawyer that no one can ever satisfy, as for example there are unsatisfiable conditions (in different ways) on being someone who has counted to the end of the natural numbers. The point is rather that adopting a role (casting oneself in it) is not attempting to bring about some possible, future state of myself. Casting myself as a lawyer does not terminate in accomplishment or failure, because it does not terminate.[15] The possibility or role of being a lawyer is not an end-state aimed at by Dasein.[16] Casting myself as a lawyer is something that is always futural with respect to action. Casting myself in a role is not something that I can have behind me and take for granted. I am a lawyer only so long has I cast myself thus. When I stop casting myself as a lawyer, I am not a lawyer anymore. But as long as I do cast myself thus, being a lawyer is a possibility that stands before me. Thus, the role of lawyer never describes what I have been, but only what I can be.[17]

"But surely I can have become a lawyer! When I pass the Bar exam and take up a legal practice, I am a lawyer!" Responding to this objection requires us to distinguish the temporalized modalities of the two claims made in it. No, I *have not become* a lawyer, even after I have started a legal practice, for my being a lawyer is never a fact about me, as my height is (or even as being too heavy for this job is a fact about a hammer). But indeed I *can be* a lawyer, in the sense that I can be what I cast myself as.[18] This is why Heidegger refers to the "the ability-to-be, which [Dasein] itself *is*" (*S&Z*, 191–2, my emphasis). So, the factical (*faktisch*) sense in which I am something, a lawyer or a defeated person, is not the same as the factual (*tatsächlich*) sense in which I am so many feet tall, or brown-haired. The senses of "being something" are different.[19] (Dasein tolerates both senses of "being something" only because it is primarily existent, and secondarily occurrent in its own, bodily way.)

Correlative with the divergent senses of "being something," there are divergent senses of "possibility." This is why Heidegger says,

> Possibility, which Dasein in each case is existentially, is distinguished just as much from empty, logical possibility as from the contingency of

something occurrent, in so far as with the latter this and that can "happen" ["*passieren*"]. As a modal category of being-occurrent, possibility means the *not yet* actual and the *not ever* necessary. It characterizes the *merely* [*nur*] possible . . . Possibility as an *existentiale*, on the other hand, is the most originary and last, positive, ontological determination of Dasein . . . (*S&Z*, 143–4)

One would expect that if something were possible, then it would be possibly actual; but Heidegger here claims that this holds only for the sense of "possible" that belongs to an ontological framework alien and unsuited to Dasein. He calls that framework, the ontology of being-occurrent.[20] To say that the hammer can be destroyed is to say that destruction is something that could, but has not yet, happened to it. But what I *can be* is not something I *can have become*, not is it something that can come to happen to me. Also, in contrast with the interpretations of Olafson and Okrent, what I *can be* is not something I *can do*. As I argued above, what I can do is something that can be complete, finished, accomplished. But what I can be is something that I can cast myself as, and I have never cast myself in a role in such a way that I need no longer cast myself in that role.

Heidegger makes similar remarks concerning "not yet." There is a sense of potency, ability, of "not yet," that characterizes Dasein, but that cannot be cashed out by saying that Dasein can or is able to become, or that Dasein is not yet, but will be later. Thus, Heidegger says, "The 'ahead' ['*Vor*'] does not mean the 'in advance' ['*Vorher*'] in the sense of the 'Not-yet-now – but later' ['*Noch-nicht-jetzt – aber später*']; and just as little does the 'already' mean a "No-longer-now – but earlier" (*S&Z*, 327). So, Heidegger's analysis of understanding culminates in the conclusion that in order for Dasein to be a self-understander, it must project for itself a "not yet," but that this "not yet" is not a "not-yet-now – but later." It is the sense of "not yet" that we get when we strip from the concept of possibility that it is a possible actuality, understand it instead as a possible role for Dasein. My roles are not possible characteristics of me, not possible accidents of me *qua* substance or quasi-substantial thing, but rather my abilities-to-be. Thus, being-ahead requires that Dasein confront, in its self-understanding, a future, a "not yet," but one that must be distinguished from a "not yet now."[21]

Affectivity, being-aleady-in, and beenness

This claim – that I have never made myself a lawyer, let's say – would rouse suspicion from the pragmatists. It seems, from their perspective, that I have misunderstood Dasein's futurity because I have misunderstood its pastness (beenness, *Gewesenheit*). Okrent formulates that pragmatist understanding of beenness very succinctly:

Similarly, when Heidegger uses the term "past," or "having been" in his definition of "temporality," he is referring to the way in which any project of Dasein's is an ongoing enteprise that presupposes a set of initial conditions and activities already carried out: something is done for the sake of x only if it is a stage in a process that has determined Dasein as having done, and thus been, such and such. (Okrent, 1988, p. 194)

Okrent spells this out by saying that Dasein must retain what it has been, that is, it must have a grasp on what it has been doing in order that it can carry out its course of action. Jones's practicing to be a basketball player only makes sense as a stage in her development into a basketball player, a stage that began by shooting baskets on her childhood street, continued through signing up for Varsity Basketball at the University, etc. The point is that she already is her goal of being a basketball player, and she is already bound up with her actions in pursuit of that goal.

This understanding of the originary past meshes well with the reading of both Dasein and originary temporality that Okrent and the pragmatists offer. They understand the future, as we have seen, to be our making ourselves who we are by undertaking to realize some human possibility. The past is thus the initial conditions in terms of which we confront ourselves and the world around us, the initial conditions to which we respond by taking up the projects and possibilities that we aim for. So, as Jones confronts the option whether to sign up for Varsity Basketball, she departs from the initial conditions that she can play well, that she has always wanted to play major college basketball, that she has been working towards this goal for a long time, etc.

We see in these interpretations of the originary future and the originary past two cardinal tenets of pragmatism, namely, (1) the view that humans make themselves who they are by throwing themselves into socially constituted projects, and (2) the view that all human life is always situated *in medias res*. It is the ascription of these two doctrines that I take to constitute the relevant sort of pragmatism. But again, there must be something wrong here. When Heidegger discusses what Dasein has already been, he launches into his existential interpretation of moods as attunements. Neither Okrent nor Olafson ever connects Heidegger's discussion of attunements with temporality.

In the midst of his presentation of understanding and possibility, Heidegger distinguishes existential possibility from the "liberty of indifference":

> Possibility as an *existentiale* does not mean the free floating ability-to-be in the sense of the "indifference of the will" (*libertas indifferentiae*). Dasein is, as essentially affective, in each case already caught up in determinate possibilities . . . This means, however, that Dasein is a being-possible that is delivered over to itself; through and through it is *thrown possibility* [*geworfene Möglichkeit*]. (*S&Z*, 144)

Consider my current projection of my way of life. Certainly I have options in how to project this. (This is part of the point of calling my projects "possibilities.") There are very clearly physical and cultural limits on this range of possibilities: I cannot cast myself as a professional basketball player, because I cannot cut it physically; I cannot cast myself as a witch doctor, because that is not culturally possible around here. But we must also note limitations not on the *range* of possibilities, but rather on the *indifference of my projection* of these possibilities. Suppose that I must decide what career to pursue, either law or medicine. Heidegger says that I do not have the liberty of indifference, that is, that as I confront this decision I do not find myself indifferent between the possibilities. Each possibility means something to me: perhaps law means power, and medicine means helping others. How I incline in this decision depends certainly on how these various possibilties show up for me. It depends on what sort of a person I find myself to be.

But this finding myself to be a certain sort of person is not essentially cognitive or mental, but a basic way of being attuned to the way things matter: "In affectivity Dasein is always already brought before itself, it has always already found itself, not through perceptive appearing before itself [*wahrnehmendes Sich-vor-finden*], but rather through attuned affecting itself [*or*, attuned finding itself: *gestimmtes Sichbefinden*]" (*S&Z*, 135). In other words, I find myself as a person who cares about power, and thus turn my energies towards law. Affectivity lets possibilities show up in determinate ways, as mattering to me in determinate fashions. I already care about power, or money, or helping others, or whatever, and this already caring guides my decision. It is essential to remember, however, that the guidance here is *not* like the sort perhaps offered by recommendations; it is not as if I must refer to my list of things that matter to me and then decide on that basis which possibility to pursue. My encounter with my possibilities is itself modified by my affectivity. Or better, the possibilities themselves show up for me in the light of the affectivity: law seems worthwhile to me, for I care about power.

Heidegger refers to this form of self-encounter as *attuned* affecting itself. (He offers attunedness (*Gestimmtheit*) as an existential interpretation of moods (*Stimmungen*)). Through my affectivity I am attuned to various sorts of considerations. I am attuned or sensitive to the power inherent in the law, or the self-sacrifice inherent in medicine. This attunedness, however, is not an indifferent attunedness, not the mere ability to perceive. It is rather a caring attunedness, an attunedness to what does and does not matter, and the ways in which it does or does not matter.

My attunements are the grounds[22] for my action; they make my projections possible. I act on the basis of my attunements. Without an attunement, I would have no way to settle upon one project or another: they would all be equally indifferent and uninteresting to me. Thus, attunement is essential to projecting oneself into possibilities, and for this reason it is a part of the care structure, equally originary with being-ahead. Heidegger says, "Being-ahead-of-itself does not mean something like an isolated tendency in a worldless "subject," but rather characterizes being-in-the-world. Along with this, however, Dasein, as delivered over to itself, is in each case already thrown *into a world*. . . . Being-ahead-of-itself means, more fully stated, this: *ahead-of-itself-in-being-already-in-a-world*" (*S&Z*, 192). The second moment of care is being-already-in-the-world. I find myself already enmeshed within the possibilities made available by my culture. At each moment, I am not a "worldless subject," that is, I do not stand naked, uncaring, and indifferent before these possibilities. I am worldly, for I come fully armed with attunements which modify the way these possibilities show up for me.

Why does Heidegger call this "being-already-*in-a-world*," rather than something like "already-caring?" Already caring about the possibilities that are available to me in my world is *how* I am already in that world. This becomes clearer if one contrasts two "sub-worlds" or social arenas, one in which I am already situated and another in which I am not. I am already situated in (participant in) the world of teaching. As a teacher, I differentially confront the possibilities among ways to be a teacher: being an easy teacher and being a challenging teacher matter to me in contrasting ways. But I am not situated in the world of golf. The possibilities of being a finesse golfer or a power golfer do not matter to me, one way or the other. I could never choose between the many ways to be a golfer, and the many options among ways to play golf if I were asked to do so. (The only basis on which to make such a choice would be an external one: the live tournament is twenty miles away, etc. This, however, is not an issue in so far as we confront the world *tout court*.) So, already caring is not just already being qualified by certain affective states. It is already being situated in the world, already being a participant in the real, social world.

Dasein is not already someone by being involved in acting – though it surely is involved in acting. Dasein is already someone, because things matter to it in so far as it casts itself as someone by projecting itself onto a role. It is already someone by being attuned to the significances of the roles and options that confront it, by being attuned also to the significances of the world. And this is not straightforwardly a matter of already being in the midst of action. Again, Okrent "over-pragmatizes" Heidegger.

Heidegger describes this affectivity as my *finding* myself through my attunements. Why describe it this way? I do not *choose* or *press ahead into* my attunements; they *beset* me, or as Heidegger also says, I am *delivered over* to them. If I am sad, I cannot choose to be cheerful. What would it be to choose to be cheerful? How does one do that? What is the paraphernalia of cheerfulness? What are its sub-tasks? Being cheeful is not a possibility of being that is systematically linked up with tasks and equipment. But one might object, I certainly can choose to be cheerful in the sense that I can choose to make myself cheerful. Perhaps I know about myself that listening to Mozart makes me cheerful or at least well disposed, and for this reason I play Mozart as I drive on the treacherous streets of Washington. But when I do this, I do not choose to be cheerful.

> That through knowledge and will a Dasein can, should, and must become master of its attunements, may indicate a preeminence of willing and cognition in certain possibilities of existing. But that should not mislead one into denying that ontologically attunements are an originary way of being for Dasein, in which Dasein is disclosed to itself *before* all cognition and willing and *beyond* [*über hinaus*] their range of disclosure [*Erschließungstragweite*]. (*S&Z*, 136)

I can choose to play a Mozart tape, and I can hope or even know that this may very well make me cheerful. But in this case, becoming cheerful is a consequence of what I do choose to do.

Furthermore, even when one does choose to do things that typically alter one's attunement, one cannot step outside of one's attunements and, in an unattuned way, choose to make oneself attuned in some way. "And moreover, we never unattunedly [*stimmungslos*] become master of attunement, but rather always out of a counter-attunement," (*S&Z*, 136). If I choose to change my attunement from aggravation to cheerfulness by playing the Mozart tape, this choice is guided by my attunements. I cannot make any choice in an unattuned manner; being attuned makes me care about the possibilities and options I have. So, if I choose to make myself cheerful, I do so because making myself cheerful shows up for me as desirable in some way. *Making* myself cheerful is a task that can matter to me (in virtue of the way the roles in which it is involved matter to me); *being* cheerful is not an option for me, but an attunement that already structures the way things matter to me.

Heidegger identifies this aspect of care with the originary past: "being-already-in . . . announces in itself beenness" (*S&Z*, 327). I take him to mean by this that our attunements constitute the way things *already* matter to us. We saw that Heidegger calls our having attunements our being-*already*-in-a-world. When I fear the lion, the option of running seems urgent to me. Heidegger's point is that this option is *already* urgent for me. I don't see the lion, feel the fear, and then experience this option as urgent. It just shows up as urgent. Its urgency is *already constituted*.

Importantly, however, the "already" here is not an "already" of clock-time. It is not that I experience the option of running as *having been* urgent five minutes ago. Furthermore, understanding was never futurally directed toward the urgency of the option (but only toward the option itself, whose then way of mattering was then already constituted). But precisely these two things – the directedness of affectivity to the option's having been urgent back then in the past and the directedness of understanding to the option's being about to be urgent up then in the future – would follow from the idea that originary temporality is Dasein's ability to track its development (pragmatic whence and whither) through sequential (mundane) time. So, the "already" must derive its meaning from a different sort of temporal framework. Just as my possibilities are revealed as possible through my self-understanding, so they are revealed as mattering differentially by my affective attunement. Just as understanding propels us onward into possibilities that do not lie in the future of clock-time, so attunement reveals to us the ways in which these possibilities are already meaningful, though this does not mean that they were meaningful in this way in the past of clock-time. Thus, Heidegger links up attunement with an originary past in a fashion analogous with the way in which he links understanding with an originary future.

Interlude: The structure of being and time

Now, although Heidegger claims in chapter 5 of Division I that Dasein's possibilities are different in ontological kind from those of hammers and rocks, he does not pursue the point in great depth. That task is carried out by chapter 1 of Division II, on death. The non-actualizability of existential possibilities is not exactly what he calls "death," but rather one essential condition of the possibility for death. Very briefly, "death" is not an event that occurs at the end of Dasein's course of life, but rather a possible way to be (*S&Z*, 245). It is a condition in which existence is impossible ("the possibility of the absolute impossibility of Dasein"). Existence is being-ahead, constituting oneself as who one is by throwing oneself ahead into some possibility of being. Such being-ahead becomes impossible when all possibilities show up for Dasein as insignificant, as not in any way connected with who it is. (This way of mattering is anxiety.) There are several ways in which death would not be a possible condition for Dasein: if there were some possibilities that mattered by nature to Dasein; if socialization into a culture made Dasein care in some ways about some possibilities; or if Dasein could make itself be some way to be in the sense in which we have seen Heidegger deny above. It is, of course, the last possibility that is relevant here. If Dasein could make itself into a chef, that is, come to be already constituted as a chef, then death – as Heidegger defines it – would be a condition only of those cases of Dasein who have not accomplished any such possibility, a sort of loser's peril. But death is supposed to be a condition that threatens every Dasein at every moment. Thus, one condition of the possibility of death is that no way to be Dasein be accomplishable. It is for this reason that the unaccomplishability of Dasein becomes most prominent in chapter 1 of Division II. (And it is also for this reason that the unaccomplishability is typically covered up by Dasein – to help it cover up the anxiety that discloses the possibility of death – and thus why the temporal ontology Heidegger offers requires "doing violence" to common sense.)

The characteristic of Dasein that it must always be given to itself as already caring in some way, that is, that it cannot choose how things matter to it, is the "nullity" of its being the ground for its projections. Heidegger presents this feature of Dasein in detail in chapter 2 of Division II of *Being and Time*, on guilt. Heidegger writes,

> As *this entity*, delivered over to whom it can exist solely as the entity that it is, it *is existingly* the ground of its ability-to-be. Although it has *not itself* laid this ground, it rests in its weight, which attunement makes manifest as a burden. And how *is* it this thrown ground? Only such that it projects itself onto possibilities into which it is thrown. The self, which as such and of itself has to lay its own ground, can *never* become master of its ground and nevertheless has to take over being-the-ground .... Being-the-ground thus means *never* being master of one's ownmost being from the ground up. This *not* belongs to the existential sense of thrownness. In being-the-ground, it itself *is* a nullity of itself. (*S&Z*, 284)

Dasein is incapable of taking control of its being from the ground up, because the way things matter to it is always *already* constituted. The way things matter to it guides the way it projects itself onto possibilities. Thus, "care itself, in its essence, is shot through and through with nullity" (*S&Z*, 285). This nullity, this alreadiness of the way things matter to Dasein, characterizes Dasein's being. It is not a feature of what lies behind it in its past. It is an essential feature of care itself, just as death is.

Now, the pragmatist readers of Heidegger typically bracket the discussion of death, guilt, anxiety, authenticity and resoluteness (as Okrent and Olafson do); they thus implicitly argue that the " existentialist" dimension of *Being and Time* is separable from its ontological thrust. For this reason, they tend to pass from chapter 6 of Division I to s.65 on originary temporality. But if I am right, one cannot do this, for death and guilt are two of Dasein's crucial ontological features. Not surprisingly, they thus turn out to be indispensable to the account of temporality that begins to emerge in s.65. In fact, these two features are the source of Heidegger's argument for the necessity of a non-sequential manifold of originary temporality, for they are the features of Dasein that he argues cannot be assimilated to a sequential temporality. Importantly, moreover, this interpretive strategy does not force us to abandon the thesis that originary temporality is modally indifferent, because it does not identify death and guilt as features of authentic Dasein alone. Rather, they are modally indifferent features, the response to which tells the difference between authenticity and inauthenticity. In wedding the modal indifference of originary temporality to the centrality of death and guilt, this strategy is able to do justice to the structure of *Being and Time*, namely, that the discussion of death and guilt intervene between Division I and the account of originary temporality.

Pragmatic temporality

The form of temporality adumbrated by pragmatist interpreters of Heidegger is indeed a form that finds embodiment in Heidegger's account of temporality, but not where the pragmatists think it does. Recall that the pragmatist understanding of Dasein's temporality can be formulated thus: (1) humans make themselves who they are by throwing themselves into socially constituted projects that structure the way they encounter the future, viz. as teleologically organized; and (2) all human life is always situated *in medias res*, i.e., humans find themselves already caught up in projects which thus form the "initial conditions" from which all future projection must depart. For reasons that will become apparent shortly, let me render this description more abstract, so that it does not refer specifically to the temporality of self-constitution: Dasein tries to accomplish projects, and in doing so relies on the wherewithal provided by the past. Let me call that form of temporality "pragmatic temporality."

Now, compare this formulation of pragmatic temporality with Heidegger's statement of the "temporality of circumspective concern" in s.69a of *Being and Time*. Heidegger writes:

> In the simplest wielding of a piece of equipment there lies letting-be-involved [*Bewendenlassen*]. The in-which of letting-be-involved has the character of the for-which; with respect to the for-which the piece of equipment is usable, or better, in use. The understanding of the for-which,

that is of the in-which of involvement, has the temporal structure of expecting [*Gewärtigens*]. Only by expecting the for-which can concern at the same time come back to something with which there is an involvement. The *expecting* of the in-which in unity with the *retaining* [*Behalten*] of the with-which of involvement makes possible in its ecstatic unity the specifically manipulative enpresenting of the piece of equipment. (*S&Z*, 353)

In this passage Heidegger is describing, in temporal terms, the structure of Dasein's equipment use. This structure opens up for Dasein the Now with which it is primarily familiar in its everyday going about business in the world, even if, as he argues in chapter 6 of Division II, Dasein's explicit accounts of time overlook this Now in overlooking the world. His account is roughly this.

1   Dasein expects the "for-which." The for-which is the work that is to be accomplished in wielding a tool. Every tool is defined through the work that it is for accomplishing. Heidegger expresses this by saying that every piece of equipment is defined through its "in-order-to" relation, that is, by the tasks in which it serves. In wielding the piece of equipment, one does so in order to accomplish the work or task in question. Heidegger's point in the passage above is that Dasein's ability to grasp a piece of equipment in terms of its work or task requires a form of what he calls "expecting" (*gewärtigen*).[23] In driving the nail in with the hammer one expects or looks forward to the accomplishment of the task it serves, let's say building a bookshelf. One simply could not *use* the hammer *as a hammer* unless one did look forward to some accomplishment in this way.

2   Dasein retains the "with-which." The with-which is the wherewithal that one relies on in accomplishing the task by means of wielding the equipment one does.[24] In hammering I rely on the availability of nails, saw, vise, countersink, etc. If these bits of co-equipment were not already available along with the hammer that I use, then I would be unable to carry out the hammering. There is a form of givenness, alreadyness that characterizes the wherewithal on which I rely in using the hammer. To retain here is to grasp what is already given, to keep a handle on the supporting props and material that serve as accompanying bits of paraphernalia.

3   I enpresent the piece of equipment that I use. Both the expecting of the task and the retaining of the wherewithal make possible the use of the particular piece of equipment that I wield. What is the difference between the wherewithal that is on hand – say, the countersink and putty – and the piece of equipment that I use? Of course, the difference is that the wielded piece of equipment is *present* to my use, taken hold of. It is not just already available, supporting my use as a sort of backdrop and precondition, but rather is the very piece of equipment deployed. It has a kind of bodily presence or presence in person that the countersink does not (*S&Z*, 346).

Now, the pragmatists are right to find pragmatic temporality in *Being and Time*, just wrong to apply it to the temporality of Dasein's self-constitution. It does describe the temporality of Dasein's equipment use. Let us step back from the details of the account of the temporality of circumspective concern, and put it in a nutshell: in using equipment, Dasein tries to accomplish tasks, and in doing so relies on the wherewithal that is already available. This is just the general form of what above I called "pragmatic temporality". Heidegger employs it to describe equipment use, rather than the understanding of Dasein's self-constitution. The temporality of circumspective concern is a form of pragmatic temporality.

The dependence of pragmatic temporality on originary temporality

One of the central claims of chapter 4 of Division II of *Being and Time* is that pragmatic temporality is derivative of originary temporality. What is the relation of derivation that holds between pragmatic temporality and originary temporality? Heidegger lays down the basic claim in s.65 of *S&Z*: "So when we have shown that the 'time' that is accessible to Dasein's intelligibility is *not* originary and, what's more, that it arises out of originary temporality, then we are justified, in accordance with the propositon, *a potiori fit denominatio*, in labelling *temporality*, which has just been exhibited, *originary time*" (*S&Z*, 329). Heidegger's basic pattern of argument is that pragmatic temporality "arises out of" (*entspringt aus*) originary temporality. But what is the force of this claim? Perhaps that pragmatic temporality depends on originary temporality: there could be no pragmatic temporality without originary temporality, yet there could be originary temporality without pragmatic temporality. I shall call this putative relationship between pragmatic temporality and originary temporality, "simple dependence."[25]

Can the thesis of simple dependence be maintained? Let us consider the two future dimensions: the existential possibility (role, or for-the-sake-of-which) in originary temporality and the task (for-which) aimed at in pragmatic temporality. Can we maintain a relation of simple dependence between these two? Simple dependence in this case would entail that one could not expect tasks unless one pressed ahead into roles. Heidegger does argue vigorously for this claim. Tasks are in part defined teleologically by the roles in which they, in turn, serve. Hammering is a task that typically serves, *inter alia*, in the larger task of building bookshelves, which in turn serves in the role of being a carpenter, or homeowner, or whatever. It is through this complex network of roles that the task of building a bookshelf gets its place and meaning, and unless one were pursuing one of these roles, one would not be building a bookshelf. To build a bookshelf in part *is* to press ahead into one of these roles. So, it is true that there could be no pragmatic future without the originary future.

So, perhaps simple dependence is vindicated? No, for it is just as true that one could not press ahead into roles unless one were also aiming at tasks. I must look forward to the realization of some task if I am to take up and throw myself into some role, some possibility of human existence. One cannot throw oneself into being a teacher without taking up the tasks assigned to that role, either lecturing or grading or supervising or discussing or something that serves in that role. A person who does none of those things, who pursues none of the tasks that serves in being a teacher, is not a teacher, does not understand herself as a teacher. So, there could be no originary future without the pragmatic future. The dependence is symmetrical. *Simple dependence does not hold.*

This argument is so simple that one wonders how anyone could have attributed simple dependence to Heidegger. But the problem here lies with Heidegger's formulations. In the *Grundprobleme*, for example, he explains the originariness of the originary future thus: "If we expect any happening, we always comport ourselves in our Dasein in some way to our ownmost ability-to-be. That very thing that we expect may be any event, any process at all; even so, in the expecting of the process itself our own Dasein is always co-expected [*mitgewärtigt*]"[26] (*GP*, 374–5). Here he argues that the originary future is the "origin" of the pragmatic future *because* Dasein could not pragmatically expect without also, as he says here, "expecting itself," that is, without taking up roles. Thus here, Heidegger argues for the originariness of originary temporality by claiming that there could be no pragmatic temporality without it. But the "no *x* unless *y*" claim only grounds an *asymmetrical* relation of derivation, dependence, or originariness if the "no *x* unless *y*" pattern is also asymmetrical. But clearly it is not. So, Heidegger's claim here is at best misleading.

So what is the relationship that Heidegger calls "derivation" or "arising out of?" Although the pragmatic future and the originary future are mutually dependent upon one another, the originary future *explains* the pragmatic future. This relationship can rightly be called "dependence," though it is not simple dependence.[27] The upshot of the explanation is this. The pragmatic future is teleological in character: one is looking forward to, or aiming at the completion of, the task in which the equipment serves. The task is the for-which that anchors the other side of the in-order-to relation. Heidegger claims that the task has its teleological status in virtue of the teleological status of existential roles. The pragmatic future is futural because the originary future is futural. Why does Dasein aim at the completion of the task of building this bookshelf? Because Dasein is pressing ahead into the role of carpenter. Thus, the crux of Heidegger's claim turns on this thesis:

1   The teleology of the originary future explains the teleology of the pragmatic future. This is the first thesis that we can analyze out of Heidegger's claim that pragmatic temporality is derivative of originary temporality. The derivation is explanation, even though the two phenomena are mutually dependent with respect to existence. The specific nature of the derivation relation in the case of the future is that the originary future explains the teleology of the pragmatic future.

What are the derivation relations in the cases of the past and Present? Consider the past. The discoveredness of things as reliable is explained by the way things matter to Dasein:

Earlier we said: the world, which has already been disclosed beforehand, lets intraworldly entities encounter. This prior [*vorgängige*] disclosedness of the world, which belongs to being-in, is co-constituted through affectivity. Letting-encounter is primarily *circumspective*, not just a sensing or staring. As we can now more sharply see in terms of affectivity, letting-encounter, which is circumspectively concernful, has the character of being affected [*des Betroffenwerdens*]. Being affected by the unserviceability, resistance, threat of the available only becomes ontologically possible, if being-in as

such is existentially determined in advance [*vorgängig*] so that the intraworldly encountering beings can *matter* to being-in in this way [e.g., as
unserviceable]. This ability to have things matter to one is grounded in
affectivity, as which it has disclosed the world in terms of, for example,
endangerability.[28] Only what is in the affectivity of fearing, or fearlessness
for that matter, can discover an intraworldly available entity as threatening.
The attunedness of affectivity existentially constitutes Dasein's openness to
the world [*Weltoffenheit*]. (*S&Z*, 137)

Here Heidegger says that the disclosedness of the way things matter to Dasein
involves a discoveredness of wherewithal or equipment as (un)serviceable,
(un)reliable, (un)steady, etc., and that the latter discoveredness is necessarily an
aspect of the former disclosedness.

We cannot forget that Heidegger is here discussing discovering something as,
e.g., serviceable, *in pursuing a task*. One can stand back from what one is doing,
look a hammer over, determine that its head is loose, appeal to some experiential
generalization to the effect that loose hammer heads sometimes fly off and hurt
people, and then conclude that the hammer is not serviceable. But Heidegger is
interested in encountering a hammer as unserviceable in the midst of pursuing a
task. This is why Heidegger interjects into his discussion above, that "letting-
encounter is primarily *circumspective*, not just a sensing or staring" (*S&Z*, 137).
In order to be able to discover the hammer as serviceable or unserviceable,
reliable or unreliable, dangerous or safe in so far as I am pursuing a task, I must
be atuned to whether anything is amiss in what I'm doing. Frederick Olafson
articulates the point well:

> Once again, it is important to emphasize that what is uncovered in the
> modality of [attunement] is indivisibly a state of the self and a state of the
> world. . . . Dasein's being an entity for which things matter or make a
> difference is the ground of the world's being in a favorable or unfavorable
> configuration, for there is no way in which the concerns of the self can be
> separated by a distinction of reason from the world in which they are
> deployed. (Olafson, 1987, p. 107)

Only if I have a sense for whether things are going well or ill, whether the job is
getting done properly, can something show up,[29] in the midst of using equipment, as reliable, let's say. The hammer shows up as reliable, because in using it I
sense that my activity is going well. Thus, attunement is a kind of sensibility.

I can sense that things are going well or ill, only if features of the situation
make a difference to me. Here we must be a little careful, for we do say such
things as, "I'm playing this softball game, but I don't really care about it." This
"not really caring" is a way of letting things matter:[30] even while playing the game
and not really caring about it, I still see things in the situation as making a
difference, though that difference is not terribly important. When the opposition's clean-up hitter hits a line drive past me at third base, I see that as making a
difference. I don't just observe it going by, and register its path: I see it as a
success for her, and a failure for me. Since I "don't really care," though, this

failure does not "hit very deep," but it does affect me. It is only because it makes a difference to me as third baseman, that I can see it as a failure. In order for it to make a difference to me as third baseman, I must care about the role I am playing in the game, even if this caring is what Heidegger sometimes calls "pallid indifference."[31]

So, caring about my options and discovering things as reliable, for instance, are interdependent. Heidegger makes this concrete in his discussion of fear. He distinguishes what Dasein *fears* from what Dasein *fears for*.[32] The point is that I can fear a bear, for instance, only because I fear for myself, or another person, or whatever. Fearing a bear is not just judging that it can damage something. It is caring about my life, let us say, and so it is a fearing, because I care about my life. Thus, fearing the bear presupposes fearing for myself. And this can be generalized. The line drive, or the loose hammer head, or whatever, make a difference, because they are involved in roles (third baseman, amateur carpenter) that make a difference to me, that I care for. Heidegger: "That *for which* the fear fears is the fearful entity itself, Dasein. Only an entity, for whom its being is at issue, can fear" (*S&Z*, 141). So, things make a difference because my roles and options and even my life make a difference to me, i.e.,

2   The alreadyness of the way possibilities matter explains the givenness as, e.g., serviceable, of the wherewithal of equipment use.

This is to say that the fact that while I hammer I discover the nails as already there to be relied on is explained by the fact that I care about the roles I press ahead into. The wherewithal's being already constituted as mattering is explained by the possibilities' being already constituted as mattering.

Falling, being-amidst, and presence

Finally, what about the mode of the Present? Above, I omitted the discussion of the originary Present, though I did indicate the character of the pragmatic Present (the presence in person of the equipment in use). Shortly it will become apparent why. To understand the nature of the originary Present, and of the dependence of the pragmatic Present on it, let us look at s.68c, where Heidegger investigates the "temporality of falling," that is, the mode of originary temporality that structures falling and being-amidst. What does he say there about the originary Present? "Perceiving [*Vernehmen*] in a broader sense lets the available and occurrent encounter "in person" [33] in themselves with respect to their look [*hinsichtlich seines Aussehens*]. This letting-encounter is grounded in a Present.[34] It gives the ecstatic horizon within which entities can be *present* in person [*leibhaftig anwesend*]" (*S&Z*, 346). This matches pretty well the less informative statement he makes in s.65: "Resolved being-amidst what is available in the situation, that is, letting what is environmentally present encounter in action [*handelnde*], is only possible in an *enpresenting* of the entity" (*S&Z*, 326).[35] So the originary Present is

Dasein's practical, circumspective relation to equipment in so far as it uses it in action.

But this is curious. Recall Heidegger's statement of what the pragmatic Present is: "The *expecting* of the in-which in unity with the *retaining* of the with-which of involvement makes possible in its ecstatic unity the specifically manipulative enpresenting of the piece of equipment" (*S&Z*, 353). What is the difference? Both the originary Present and the pragmatic Present seem to be an enpresenting (letting be present in person) of equipment in so far as Dasein goes about business. This overlap in Heidegger's expositions of what we should expect to be two different notions of the Present, the originary and the pragmatic, is accompanied by an unparalleled overlap of terminology; he uses the same word ("enpresenting") to pick out the two modes of the Present, whereas (in *Being and Time*) he uses different terms for the differing forms of the two other modes ("coming-towards-itself" or "future" *vs.* "expecting," and "coming-back-to" or "beenness" *vs.* "retaining"). In fact, the identification is much stronger; in the two-page introduction to s.69, he writes,

> The Interpretation of the temporality of circumspective, as well as theoretically concernful being-amidst *intraworldly* entities, entities that are available and occurrent, at the same time shows how this same temporality is already in advance the condition for the possibility of being-in-the-world, in which being-amidst intra*worldly* entities is in general grounded. (*S&Z*, 351)

That is, the temporality of circumspective concern (pragmatic temporality) is the condition for the possibility (i.e., the temporal sense) of being-amidst. But the condition for the possibility of being-amidst should be the originary Present, shouldn't it? Why do Heidegger's descriptions and terminology overlap for the Present, indeed, why does Heidegger just about identify the two modes of the Present?

Our clue here is provided by Heidegger's discussion of the Present in s.69c: "Existing for the sake of itself in its abandonment to itself as thrown, Dasein is at the same time enpresenting as being-amidst . . . The horizonal schema of the *Present* is determined through the *in-order-to*" (*S&Z*, 365). The originary Present opens up the entire field of the in-order-to. That is, the in-order-to encompasses both the with-which (the wherewithal) and the for-which (the task), for the piece of equipment serves along with the wherewithal in the task. The in-order-to is the entire relational whole that binds together the with-which and the for-which and thereby structures an actual use of a piece of equipment. So according to the passage above, originary enpresenting is directed at this entire relational whole. Thus, the expecting and retaining that belong to pragmatic temporality are moments of enpresenting. Pragmatic temporality turns out to be an elaboration of enpresenting; pragmatic temporality is one aspect of originary temporality. I shall call this the "embeddedness" of pragmatic temporality in originary temporality.

Let me elaborate on this embeddedness. We saw that the originary Present is Dasein's being-amidst the intraworldly. Now, what is it to be originarily confronted by a piece of equipment? To wield it, to use it for getting a task done. This use of the equipment involves retaining the wherewithal of the activity and aiming for the realization of the task in which the equipment serves. Thus, the originary Present (enpresenting) is engagement with *all three dimensions* of pragmatic temporality. We have also seen that the future of pragmatic temporality borrows its teleological character from the future of originary temporality, and that the past of pragmatic temporality borrows its givenness as mattering from the past of originary temporality. But the past and the future of pragmatic temporality still belong inherently to the structure of the in-order-to, and this structure is revealed in the originary Present. Thus, the entire pragmatic framework belongs to the framework of the originary Present.

There is an additional level of complication here. The structure from the expecting to the retaining is the understanding of the Now. But it is essential to the Now that it is part of a sequence of Nows. An understanding of a sequence, however, is in no way represented in the structure depicted above. To get the understanding of a sequence, we must interpret the structural unit that ranges from the expecting to the retaining as iterable. We must understand the object of expecting, for instance, as a *terminus a quo* from which a new Now departs; we must understand the object of retaining as a *terminus ad quem* where a different Now ends. That is, we must apply the very same structure of expecting-using-retaining to what is expected and retained; we must understand the horizons of realization and retention as themselves being Nows. Another way of looking at the iterability point is this: Why can I say "when my task is done" but cannot say (according to Heidegger's account) "when I have projected myself onto my role?" The concept of *when*, of temporal position, is always the concept of an encountering of equipment (or something derived therefrom). The Now is always the Now when I use such-and-such a piece of equipment. I can say "when my task is done," because the expecting of the task iteratively applies the entire framework of the in-order-to to the expected and retained. The expecting is directed to another Now. And the same holds *mutatis mutandis* of the past.

It is this iterative application of the structure of pragmatic temporality to the expected and retained that is attested in Heidegger's doctrine that in pragmatic temporality enpresenting "leaps away from" (*entspringt*) and dominates the other modes of temporality. Heidegger writes, "Rather, [manipulative dealings] constitute themselves in unity with an expecting retaining, so much so, that the enpresenting that leaps away from them makes possible the characteristic "absorption" of concern" (*S&Z*, 354). In this passage Heidegger is playing with the word *entspringen*. It is hard to translate this word in these passages, for it can mean either (or both) "arise out of" or "leap away from." Heidegger's discussion of inauthentic temporality in s.68c exploits this double meaning. In his discussion of curiosity, for example, which Heidegger interprets as the relentless search to experience something new, he describes the *entspringen* of enpresenting from expecting:

> Curiosity is constituted [*konstituiert*] through an enpresenting that is not held, which by enpresenting only, thereby seeks to escape [*entlaufen*] the expecting in which it is "held" as unheld. The Present "leaps away from"

[*"entspringt"*] the expecting that belongs to it, and does so in the sense of escape that we have emphasized. (*S&Z*, 347)

He fills this in by interpreting the expecting that goes along with enpresenting as a "leaping after" (*nachspringen*) the Present. He concludes, "through the expecting that leaps after, enpresenting is more and more abandoned to itself" (*S&Z*, 347). In pragmatic temporality, expecting is understood as a kind of enpresenting. This makes the enpresenting dominant in such a way that Heidegger refers to pragmatic temporality as an expecting-retaining enpresenting (*gewärtigend-behaltendes Gegenwärtigen*). In pragmatic temporality expecting and retaining are understood as *also* having the form of enpresenting. They are directed at a not-yet and an already, but the not-yet is understood as a not-yet-*Now* and the already is understood as an already-*Now*, that is, a no-longer-*Now*.[36] So, the characteristic features of pragmatic temporality arise from the originary Present in so far as it applies the entire framework of expecting-retaining enpresenting to what is expected and what is retained, that is, in so far as expecting and retaining are understood as kinds of enpresenting.

Cashing out the dependence

What philosophical advantages are gained by endorsing the thesis that pragmatic temporality is derivative of originary temporality? Heidegger claims that there are several other features of our understanding of pragmatic temporality that can be explained if we view it as derivative of originary temporality. In chapter 6 of Division II of *Being and Time* Heidegger offers a phenomenological description of the time that we primarily and usually encounter in everyday going about business, the time made accessible through the expecting-retaining enpresenting of pragmatic temporality. He calls this time "world-time," and identifies four features that characterize it: datability, spannedness, significance, publicness. Although not regularly part of this list, he also exhibits this time as sequential (in contrast to what is unveiled by originary temporality). Datability is the phenomenon that the times of world-time show up for Dasein as times when such and such happens. Times are dated or filled by events. Spannedness is the characteristic of world-time times that they span from a before to an after, that they are characterized by a "during." Significance is the feature of times that they are always times in order to do or accomplish something.[37] Finally, world-time times are public in the sense that they are there for Dasein publicly; they are generally and publicly interpretable and available so that many cases of Dasein can each make reference to the Now, and do so in a way that is mutually intelligible.

Now, Heidegger's Division II, chapter 6 claim is that we can account for why time shows up for us in just this way by showing how the understanding of these features can be explained by pragmatic temporality's being derivative of originary temporality. He offers the following explanations for why world-time shows up as having the features it does. It is datable, because the originary Present is an enpresenting and thus necessarily involves encounter with things and events in the environment. It is spanned, because the ecstases (the originary future, Present, and past) form a unity. It is significant, because the originary Present is an enpresenting specifically of in-order-to relations. It is public, because originary temporality is outside-itself. Finally, world-time is sequential, because it is an iterable application of the originary Present. It is not possible to explore all five of these claims here. In order to exhibit the sort of reasoning that Heidegger pursues, let me focus on just one of them: the explanation of spannedness.

Heidegger presents, or rather hints at, the explanation of spannedness in both *Being and Time* and the *Grundprobleme*. In *Being and Time* he writes, "Expecting-retaining enpresenting only interprets [time in terms of] a spanned "during," because it is thereby disclosed to *itself* as the ecstatic *stretchedness* of historical [i.e., originary] temporality, even if this disclosedness is unknown to it" (*S&Z*, 409). In the *Grundprobleme* he explains this more thoroughly in a somewhat murky passage:

> In every spoken [*gesagtem*, i.e., world-time] Now spannedness is spoken too [*mitgesagt*], because in the Now and the other time-determinations an enpresenting expresses itself, which temporalizes itself in ecstatic unity with expecting and retaining. In the ecstatic character of temporality there originarily already lies a stretchedness, which also enters into expressed time. In so far as every expecting has the character of a towards-itself and every retaining has the character of a back-to . . . and in so far as every towards-itself is in itself a back-to, temporality is *in itself stretched* as ecstatic. (*GP*, 382)

How does the unity of originary temporality explain the spannedness of world-time? As we have seen, the three "ecstases" of originary temporality are necessarily united; they come as a package deal. We have also seen that the originary future (the not-yet of roles) explains the pragmatic future (the not-yet of tasks), and that the originary past (the alreadiness that characterizes the way things matter to Dasein) explains the pragmatic past (the alreadyness of the wherewithal's making a difference). Since the originary Present thus requires the originary future and originary past, and these in turn give rise to the pragmatic future and pragmatic past, in order to be what it is the originary Present requires the pragmatic future and pragmatic past. One cannot encounter equipment (in the Present) without retaining wherewithal as reliable and looking forward to the task. In other words, it is not just an accident or even a brute fact that the pragmatic Now shows up as spanning from a no-longer-Now to a not-yet-Now, and not just an accident that pragmatic temporality involves, along with the wielding of the quipment, a prospective anticipation of realizing a task and a retentional grasp on what is reliable and what not. Dasein must throw itself into a role in order to be anything, and it must pursue a task in order to throw itself into a role: the enpresenting of equipment requires that we pursue a task. Similarly, Dasein must find itself already caring about its options if it is to be anything, and caring about its options makes it sensitive to the hindering or promoting significance of equipment: the enpresenting of equipment requires that we be sensitive to its significance for our task. The threefold structure of the pragmatic

Now is entailed by the three-fold structure of originary temporality. As Heidegger would say, the Now is spanned because originary temporality is ecstatically unified.

Thus, Heidegger aims to make some progress in the phenomenological explanation of why it is that time, in the mundane sense of the before and after that shows up for Dasein in going about business, shows up in just the way it does. He thus seeks to argue that his account is powerful through its explanatory virtues. It is not just an account that we are forced to through recognition of the several forms of nullity that characterize care. It is also an attempt to bring together, to unify into one account the many features of mundane time that offer themselves unproblematically to phenomenological inquiry.

Conclusion

Originary temporality is the temporal structure of Dasein's eixstence, of care. It is neither authentic nor inauthentic, but rather characteristic of any case of Dasein at all. Nonetheless, originary temporality is non-sequential in a way that does violence to our ordinary understanding of time. Originary temporality is a manifold consisting of a future that will neither come to be nor fail to come to be, a past that was not, and a Present that is not soon to be past. This manifold is rather temporal in an allegedly deeper sense, temporal in being the source of our everyday understanding of time. Heidegger is driven to this position because he wants both to connect projection, thrownness, and enpresenting to time, and to identify structures within those phenomena that, he argues, are not compatible with sequentiality. These two features of Dasein – the precondition on death that Dasein not be able to become any of its possibilities, and the nullity of its being-the-ground – arise in the context of Heidegger's discussion of authenticity and inauthenticity, yet they themselves are essential aspects of care, not phenomena of authentic Dasein alone. Once revealed, they force Heidegger to do "violence" to our everyday understanding of time, just because they are incompatible with sequentiality. They lie beneath the level of time's showing up that forms Dasein's pursuit of tasks within the context of what has happened and what it has done; they lie beneath pragmatic temporality. In this way we can also see why Heidegger, in *Being and Time*, could not be a pragmatist. The very (temporal) structure of pragmatic action cannot fit the deeper level of description of Dasein's existence.

This interpretation leaves us with many questions.[38] How is originary temporality connected not just with Dasein's understanding of world-time, but with world-time itself? How is world-time connected with the "vulgar conception" of time, the pure succession of moments that bear no significance? What are the broader implications for Heidegger's ontology of his placement of originary temporality at the heart of Dasein's sort of being? How are we to understand the existentiell modalities of originary temporality that constitute authentic and inauthentic existence? How strong is the argument that we must view the non-sequential manifold that Heidegger calls "originary temporality" as a form of time? How is originary temporality related to Dasein's historicality, Dasein's peculiar way of being-in-time? All of these questions must be answered if we are to provide a comprehensive interpretation of the role of originary temporality in *Being and Time*.

REFERENCES

Works by Heidegger

B&T Heidegger, Martin (1962) *Being and Time*, translated by John Macquarrie and Edward Robinson, New York: Harper and Row.
GP Heidegger, Martin (1975) *Die Grundprobleme der Phänomenologie. Gesantausgabe*, vol. 24, edited by Friederich-Wilhelm von Herrmann, Frankfurt-am-Main: Vittorio Klostermann.
S&Z Heidegger, Martin (1979) *Being and Time*, 15th edn, Tübingen: Max Niemeyer Verlag.
GB Heidegger, Martin (1983) *Die Grundbegriffe der Metaphysik. Gesamtausgabe*, vol. 29/30, edited by Friedrich-Wilhelm von Herrmann, Frankfurt-am-Main: Vittorio Klostermann.

Other works

Aristotle (1963) *Categories*, translated by J. L. Ackrill. Oxford: Oxford University Press.
Barrett, William (1968) "The flow of time," in Richard M. Gale (ed.), *The Philosophy of Time*, New Jersey: The Humanities Press, pp. 355–77.
Blattner, William D. (1989) "Temporal synthesis and temporality in Kant and Heidegger," PhD dissertation, University of Pittsburgh.
Caputo, John D. (1986) "Husserl, Heidegger, and the question of a 'hermeneutic' phenomenology" in Joseph J. Kockelmans (ed.), *A Companion to Martin Heidegger's "Being and Time"*, Washington, DC: The Center for Advanced Research in Phenomenology and the University Press of America, pp. 104–26.
Dreyfus, Hubert L, and Rubin, Jane (1986) "You can't get something for nothing," *Inquiry* 30: pp. 33–75.
Dreyfus, Hubert L. (1990) *Being-in-the-World*, Cambridge, MA: MIT Press.
Guignon, Charles B. (1983) *Heidegger and the Problem of Knowledge*, Indianapolis: Hackett.
Haugeland, John (1982) "Heidegger on being a person," *Noûs* 16, pp. 15–26.
Heine, Stephen (19xx), *Existential Dimensions of Time in Heidegger and Dogen*, Albany, NY: SUNY Press.
Heinz, Marion (1986) "The concept of time in Heidegger's early works," translated by Joseph J. Kockelmans, in Joseph J. Kockelmans (ed.), *A Companion to Martin Heidegger's "Being and Time"*, Washington, DC: The Center for Advanced Research in Phenomenology and the University Press of America, pp. 183–207.
Herrmann, Friedrich-Wilhelm von (1974) *Subjekt und Dasein*, Frankfurt-am-Main: Vittorio Klostermann.
Hoffman, Piotr (1986) *Doubt, Time, Violence*, Chicago: University of Chicago Press.
Langan, Thomas (1983) *The Meaning of Heidegger*, Westport, CT: Greenwood Press.
Makkreel, Rudolf A. (1987) "The overcoming of linear time in Kant, Dilthey and Heidegger," in Rudolf A. Makkreel and John Scanlon (eds), *Dilthey and Phenomenology*, Washington, DC: University Press of America.
McInerney, Peter K. (1982) "Sartre's nihilations," *The Southern Journal of Philosophy* 20: pp. 97–110.
McInerney, Peter K. (1985) "The sources of experienced temporal features," in *Descriptions*, edited by Don Ihde and Hugh Silverman, Albany, NY: SUNY Press, pp. 91–107.

Marx, Werner (1971) *Heidegger and the Tradition*, translated by Theodore Kisiel and Murray Greene, Evanston, IU.: Northwestern University Press.

Millikan, James Dean (1966) "Heidegger, time, and self-transcendence," PhD dissertation, Yale University.

Okrent, Mark (1988) *Heidegger's Pragmatism*, New York: Columbia University Press.

Olafson, Frederick (1987) *Heidegger and the Philosophy of Mind*, New Haven, CT: Yale University Press.

Pöggeler, Otto (1982) "Temporal interpretation and hermeneutic philosophy," translated by Theodore Kisiel, in Ronald Bruzina and Bruce Wilshire (eds), *Phenomenology: Dialogues and Bridges*, Albany, NY: State University of New York Press, pp. 77–97.

Pöggeler, Otto (1983) *Der Denkweg Martin Heideggers*, Pfullingen: Verlag Günther Neske.

Starr, David E. (1975) *Entity and Existence*, New York: Burt Franklin and Co.

NOTES

I wish to thank Bert Dreyfus, John Haugeland, Mark Okrent, Arthur Ripstein, Ted Schatzki, and Steve Strange for their helpful comments on earlier drafts of this paper, as well as the Departments of Philosophy at Erindale College of the University of Toronto, the University of Pittsburgh, and Georgetown University, who heard earlier versions.

1 All translations of Heidegger's texts are my own, though I have of course relied heavily on existing translations when available.

2 Friedrich-Wilhelm von Herrmann is quite clear on this point (1974, p. 83). So are Otto Pöggeler (1982) and Mark Okrent (1988, ch. 6). Frederick Olafson seems to waffle a bit when he identifies the agent's active relation to time with the "*Augenblick*," he implies that originary temporality is authentic (1987, p. 91). (Unfortunately, this is not consistent with the view that originary temporality is the structure of agency (p. 90), for that appears to imply that inauthentic Dasein just looks at things and does not act.) For other examples of interpretations that take originary temporality to be authentic, see Heinz (1986), Marx (1971, Part II, ch. 2), and Hoffman (1986, ch. 2). (Note that Hoffman's interpretation is more complicated than just an identification of originary temporality with the temporal form of authentic existence, for he distinguishes three modes of temporality: authentic temporality, inauthentic temporality, and the temporality of anxiety.)

3 "*Wenn die Entschlossenheit den Modus der eigentlichen Sorge ausmacht, sie selbst aber nur durch die Zeitlichkeit möglich ist, dann muß das im Hinblick auf die Entschlossenheit gewonnene Phänomen selbst nur eine Modalität der Zeitlichkeit darstellen, die überhaupt Sorge als solche ermöglicht.*" The pronominal references in this passage are ambiguous: the "*sie*" in "*sie selbst*" could refer to either "*die Entschlossenheit*" or "*der eigentlichen Sorge*," and moreover, if to the latter, then to it either as "*der eigentlichen Sorge*" or as "*der Sorge*." This ambiguity can be handled by any interpretation, I suggest. The second ambiguity, however, is more crucial: the "*die*" in line 3 can refer to either "*die Entschlossenheit*," "*eine Modalität*," or "*der Zeitlichkeit*." "*Die Entschlossenheit*" is very unlikely as the antecedent, for then this sentence ends up changing subject midstream. However, the ambiguity between "*eine Modalität*" and "*der Zeitlichkeit*" is both much harder to decide and philosophically significant. What makes die "*Sorge als solche*" possible at all? Is it the *authentic modality* of temporality or *temporality as such*? If the former resolution of the reference is correct, then this passage supports the traditional way of understanding originary temporality as authentic; if the latter resolution is correct, then this passage supports my reading. I offer two reasons for

resolving the ambiguity in favor of my reading (as I do in my translation of the passage in the body of the text). (1) Reading it my way harmonizes it with the passage from p. 325 above, which otherwise would stand in a difficult tension with this passage. (2) If the other reading were right, then it would be unclear why Heidegger says here that authentic temporality must *only* represent a modality of temporality. On my reading, the rationale for this is that it is only a modality of care, and temporality as such makes care possible. (This also gives us reason to resolve the first ambiguity as a reference to "*der Sorge*.")

4   Heidegger distinguishes between the *disclosedness* of Dasein, the world, and being and the *discoveredness* of entities unlike Dasein. He groups together Dasein (and world, which Dasein is) and being, because the latter is supposed to be dependent on the former. Note also that discoveredness is dependent on disclosedness.

5   Here I make one crucial but highly controversial assumption: I have assumed that the middle element of disclosedness is falling, not telling. I do not have the space to justify this approach here. Let it be noted that although understanding and affectivity are always ascribed to the disclosedness-structure, Heidegger sometimes adds telling (e.g., *S&Z*, 296), sometimes falling (p. 316), and sometimes both (p. 335). In s.68, which makes the substantive connections between disclosedness and temporality, Heidegger associates understanding, affectivity, and falling with the three ecstases of originary temporality, and claims that telling is associated with them all. In effect, telling turns out to have no *specific* temporal sense, though it does receive a temporal interpretation in terms of all the ecstases.

6   "If we Interpret [understanding] as a fundamental existentiale, then we thereby indicte that this phenomenon is conceived as a fundamental mode [*Grundmodus*] of the *being* of Dasein. On the other hand, 'understanding', in the sense of *one* possible sort of cognition among others, perhaps distinguished from 'explaining', must thereby be Interpreted as an existential derivative of primary understanding, which co-constitutes the being of the There" (*S&Z*, 143).

7   The formulation in terms of coping is Dreyfus's (1990, ch. 10).

8   This is something of an oversimplification. One could distinguish between "originary" understanding, which is one's mastery of the activity or item in question, and "positive" understanding, which is one's ability to cope with its role among the paraphernalia and activities of our social world. In these senses, I (who do not play piano) do not have an originary understanding of pianos, though I do have a positive one.

9   Caputo offers "casting" as an interpretation of projection (1986).

10 This claim also depends upon Heidegger's thesis that playing a role is a necessary condition on being Dasein in some specific way, which in turn depends on his view that I am not essentially anything, independently of my self-understanding. This is what he means when he says that Dasein's essence is its existence.

11 This formulation is modeled upon Okrent's formulation (1988, p. 29).

12 Hoffman (1986) offers a valuable attempt to work these claims into his interpretation, although since he identifies originary temporality with authentic temporality, his attempts takes a fundamentally different direction from mine.

13 Some interpret Heidegger's claims as meaning that time is "dynamic" (Heine, 1985; Langan, 1983; Starr, 1975; Makkreel, 1987; Barrett, 1968). By "dynamic" one seems to mean either that time flows continuously (*dynamic* as opposed to *static*), or that it is an A-series rather than a B-series (*tensed* rather than *untensed*). Neither of these views captures Heidegger's arguments, I suggest. First, Heidegger clearly associates the "flow" of time with the vulgar conception of time, so-called, (*S&Z*, 422). More importantly, even a continuous (as opposed to discrete) sequence is a sequence; even if

sequential time is continuous, still the past is earlier than the present, and the future later than it. Secondly, an A-series (which Olafson (1987) and Barrett (1968) associate with originary temporality) is likewise a sequence; what makes it A, rather than B, is that it is a tensed sequence. Moreover, Heidegger's "world-time" (which contrasts with originary temporality) is clearly tensed (because indexical), if for no other reason than that it is a sequence of "Now's," relative to each of which earlier Now's are "back-then" (*Damals*) and later Now's are "up-then" (*Dann*).

14 Millikan makes a related point in emphasizing that Heidegger presents understanding as being directed towards "possibilities as possibilities" (1966, pp. 33–7).

15 For this reason, I am very uncomfortable with those interpreters who argue that Dasein's central characteristic is that it is a mode of "accomplishment" (*Vollzug*). This sounds too much like a kind of bringing-about, which I think Heidegger thinks can only really determine the being of things unlike Dasein. For interpretations of Heidegger in tems of modes of "accomplishment," see *inter alia*: Pöggeler (1983), Herrmann (1974), and Heinz (1986).

16 Thus, although I use the formulation of the for-the-sake-of-which as the "point" of my action, I do not think that this should in turn be glossed, as Okrent does, as Dasein's being an *end* or *purpose*.

17 It has been suggested to me by Steve Strange and Mark Okrent that one could construe Heidegger's point here to be that Dasein's projection of a role is like Aristotle's *energeia*: it has itself as its goal. This would additionally fit Heidegger's account of temporality into the larger picture one forms by studying the ways in which Heidegger's ontology is deeply influenced by Aristotle's. However, here this will not quite do, for Aristotelian *energeia* is complete in an instant; to be in act is to realize its end. But for Heidegger quite the opposite seems to be true: the goal is always "outstanding" (chapter 1 of Division II), and Dasein is never complete. See the discussion of death below.

18 This is a bit overly simple, though, for recall, Heidegger interprets understanding as competence (i.e., *skillful* mastery). So, when he says that Dasein *is* what it *can* be, he does not mean that if I cast myself as something, then *ipso facto* I am it skillfully. Rather, there is a sense of failure correlative with skillful mastery. I can cast myself as a lawyer clumsily, let's say, and this would be a sense in which I am *not* a lawyer, or better, am a lawyer *deficiently*.

19 In order to specify an ontology, one must specify the meanings of such modal language as "being something," "possible," "necessary," "not yet," etc.

20 "*Vorhandensein*" (which Macquarrie and Robinson translate as "presence-at-hand") is the sort of being of those entities that are independent of Dasein and its world. *Zuhandensein* (here, "being available," but in Macquarrie and Robinson, "ready-to-hand") is the sort of being of pieces of equipment and paraphernalia, which are essentially bound up with one another through a common (indeed, often joint) assignment to a task: they essentially serve in the tasks and activities of the social world.

21 Heidegger and Sartre have similar, yet crucially distinct, accounts of the futurity of human projection. In an article that helps, through contrast, to clarify Heidegger's account, Peter K. McInerney argues that Sartre held that the future is opened up to us through our having ends. "It is because the For-itself is 'ahead-of-itself' in having ends which are to be made to exist that consciousness can meaningfully refer to the future" (1982, p. 100). Using an argument similar to Heidegger's above, McInerney concludes, "Sartre maintains that the future *qua* future is not equivalent to what will become present" (1982, p. 105). The future *qua* future is a form of possibility, not what will become present, because it is not necessary that my ends be realized. Ends

are not what will become present, because I can fail to pursue them to completion; I am free. "If [ends were our future *simpliciter*], we would have to pursue these ends to their completion (which would limit our freedom to do otherwise), and 'the future of the For-itself' would be identical with the 'For-itself which is to-come'" (1982, p. 105). Thus, the issue for Sartre (according to McInerney) is my *freedom* not to make myself into what I once intended to become. For Heidegger, however, the issue is the *impossibility* of becoming anything. Sartre is still committed to projected ends being goals to be realized; this is especially clear in McInerney's later account, in which he states: "Having projects, conditions or states of acting consciousness that are to be attained, is one form of the futurity of consciousness" (1985, p. 101). Furthermore, Sartre wants to call what I project "my future," but does not want to assert the non-sequentiality of originary temporality. Thus, he is forced to the paradoxical assertion, in McInerney's words, of "a projected end['s] both being and not-being our future" (1982, p. 107). Heidegger avoids the paradox by distinguishing the differing sorts of futurity.

22 "Ground" should be read as "existential ground to stand on," so as to avoid the unfortunate co-optation of the word "ground" by those obsessed with reasoning. Note also the connection to Heidegger's term "being-the-ground" (*Grundsein*), which I shall draw out below.

23 The German word *gewärtigen*, has roughly two patterns of meaning: (1) a sense of resigned expectation, especially of untoward outcomes, as when we say in English, "You've got to expect that $300 sofas will fall apart in five years": (2) a sense of insistence or requirement, especially *vis-à vis* someone else's behavior, as when we say, "I expect better behavior of an esteemed professor of philosophy." Heidegger wants to draw on (2) rather than (1). So, we should hear "expect" in this context in an active way: the expectation in question is making deamnds of the world; it is trying to realize tasks and goals.

24 This is a controversial construal of the with-which. Heidegger seems to be of two minds about the with-which (*Womit*). On p. 84, where Heidegger originally introduces the with-which along with the language of involvement (*Bewandtnis*), he treats the with-which as the piece of equipment one wields. However, on p. 352 Heidegger indicates that the piece of equipment's "co-equipment" (i.e., the other pieces of equipment that are involved along with the one currently in use) are the with-which of involvement. Developing the second line of thought, I have taken up a suggestion first made to me by John Haugeland, that we understand the with-which as the "wherewithal," that is, as what Dasein relies on in accomplishing this task with this piece of equipment. This includes the co-equipment (when hammering, the saw, perhaps), materials, supporting props, and so on.

25 William Barrett objects to Heidegger at this point: "[I]t is just this derivative status accorded to the flow of time [pragmatic temporality] that we must now question. . . . It is the contention of this paper that the three tenses [Barrett's term for originary temporality] are the tenses they are because time does flow; and, conversely, that if time did not flow, there would not be the three tenses" (Barrett, 1968, pp. 363–4). For Barrett to respond to Heidegger's thesis of the derivativeness of pragmatic temporality by arguing that there couldn't be originary temporality without it, presupposes that what Heidegger means by that thesis is that there couldn't be pragmatic temporality without originary temporality, but not vice versa. Hoffman makes another well-worked-out attempt along these lines: "But, on the other hand, Dasein's coming face-to-face with the ultimate meaning of its Being – with finite temporality – demolishes the entire significance of the ordinary world and hence also the significance of commonsensical time" (1986, p. 78).

26 "Co-expecting oneself" is Heidegger's term in the *Grundprobleme* for the originary future.

27 In the *Categories*, chapter 12, Aristotle makes room for dependence by nature even when two phenomena mutually imply one another with respect of existence (14b9ff, 1963, pp. 39–40). The extra condition is that one phenomenon causes the other. Rather than causation, we have here explanation.

28 *Die Betroffenheit aber durch Undienlichkeit, Widerständigkeit, Bedrohlichkeit des Zuhandenen wird ontologisch nur so möglich, daß das In-Sein als solches vorgängig so bestimmt ist, daß in dieser Weise von innerweltlich Begegnendem angegangen werden kann. Diese Angänglichkeit gründet in der Befindlichkeit, als welche sie die Welt zum Beispiel auf Bedrohbarkeit hin erschlossen hat.*"

29 I am using "show up" to translate *Begegnen* instead of the more literal "encounter" in order to bring this more in line with ordinary English. Heidegger's usage is not ordinary German either. What he wants to indicate is that the thing is the subject of the process, not the passive object of some activity of ours.

30 "Primarily and usually we only meet up with specific attunements that tend to 'extremes': joy, sadness. A faint uneasiness or a gliding contentment are already less noticeable. But that *unattunedness [or,* not being in any mood], in which we are neither in a bad mood nor in a good mood, seems not to be there at all and yet is there. But all the same, in this 'neither-nor' we are never not attuned. . . . If we say that a well-disposed person brings spirits to a group, that only means that raised spirits or a boisterous mood is produced. It does not mean, however, that there was no attunement there beforehand. There was an unattunedness there, which apparently is difficult to ascertain and seems to be something indifferent, but which in no way is indifferent. We see anew: attunements do not suddenly emerge in the empty space of the soul and then disappear again; rather, Dasein as Dasein is from the ground up always already attuned. There is always only an alteration of attunements" (*Die Grundbegriffe der Metaphysik*, p. 103).

31 Heidegger goes further and argues that even "theoretical, pure discovery" requires attunement: "But even the purest *theoria* has not left all attunement behind it; what is merely occurrent shows itself in its pure look to *theoria's* looking, only if *theoria* lets the occurrent come towards it in its *calm* lingering amidst ["*ruhigem Verweilen bei*"] (*S&Z*, 138). Thus, since things make a difference to me, they *look* different to me when I do look at them, and so the features discovered by sense-perception are also dependent upon affectivity: "And the 'senses' can be 'touched' and 'have a taste for,' in such a way that the touching shows itself in affection [*Affektion*], only because they belong ontologically to an entity that has the sort of being of affective being-in-the-world" (*S&Z*, 137).

32 He invents some more technical vocabulary here, but I shall avoid it. He distinguishes the fearing itself from that *in the face of (vor)* which I fear and that *for (um)* which I fear. I fear for myself in the face of whatever is, in this case, fearsome.

33 The German word here is "*leibhaftig*" (the scare-quotes are Heidegger's). Macquarrie and Robinson translate it as "bodily" to try to get at the roots of the word, however, it means something more like "in person." Kersten translates it as "in person" in his translation of Husserl's *Ideas*. (See Edmund Husserl, *Ideas Pertaining to a Pure Phenomenology and Phenomenological Philosophy*, translated by F. Kersten, The Hague: Martinus Nijhoff, 1982, p. 327.) Husserl uses it to get at the nature of originary givenness, that the object is given as really and truly being there, in person, not as having been there, as seeming to be there, nor by way of a representative. Heidegger clearly intends to refer back to Husserl's discussion.

34 I follow Macquarrie and Robinson in translating "*anwesend*" as "present" and "*Gegenwart*" as "Present" (with a capital P).

35 This passage is somewhat complex, because Heidegger is here addressing the conditions of the possibility of *authentic* or *resolved* action. The point is, though, that such action is only possible in an enpresenting, which is the originary Present (see section 1 above). Thus, he continues: "Only as the *Present* in the sense of enpresenting can resoluteness be what it is: the undistorted letting-encounter of what it grasps in action." In other words, it cannot be this undistorted use of equipment unless it is that as the originary Present, i.e., enpresenting.

36 I have mixed the discussions of curiosity and circumspection, even though the former is clearly inauthentic and the latter is indifferent. I interpret inauthentic temporality as the attempt to understand myself in terms of the temporal framework of equipment, that is, in terms of pragmatic temporality. So, inauthentic temporality is Present-dominated, *because* pragmatic temporality is Present-dominated.

37 This is a characteristic only of world-time, and not of the stripped down form of time described by natural science and much traditional philosophy, which takes time not to be qualitative.

38 I make a start on these questions in Blattner (1989).

6
History and Commitment in the Early Heidegger

Charles Guignon

One common way of reading *Being and Time* is to see it as promoting a "decisionistic" view of human action. This is the interpretation found in Jürgen Habermas's claim that the language of *Being and Time* suggests "the decisionism of empty resoluteness."[1] And it is spelled out in an extreme form in Richard Wolin's recent book, *The Politics of Being*:

> A philosophy of existence such as Heidegger's presupposes that all traditional contents and truths have lost their substance; and thus all that remains is *naked facticity*, that is, the sheer fact of existence. Thus, unlike traditional hermeneutics, which believes that the past contains a store of semantic potentials that are inherently worthy of redemption, *Existenzphilosophie* in its Heideggerian variant tends to be inherently destructive of tradition.[2]

There is, of course, something right about this reading. Heidegger's discussions of anxiety and death present us with a picture of Dasein as, at a basic level, individualized, non-relational, and ultimately "not at home" anywhere. These passages support the idea that Heidegger regards choice and action as resting on a kind of "leap," in a "moment of vision," cut off from all bonds to traditional social standards and moral ideals.

But this way of looking at *Being and Time* ignores that work's emphasis on Dasein's embeddedness in a wider communal context. Heidegger explicitly rejects the idea of freedom as "a free-floating arbitrariness," insisting that we can understand "freedom in its finitude" only if we see that "proving boundedness" does not impair freedom.[3] To say that Dasein is "thrown possibility" is to say that our agency is always situated in a cultural context that provides the pool of possibilities from which we draw our concrete identities as agents of particular types. And, above all, it means that we are historical beings whose possibilities for self-interpretation are made accessible by our shared history. "Whatever the way of being it may have at the time," Heidegger says, "Dasein has grown up both into and in a traditional [*überkommene*] way of interpreting itself: in terms of this it understands itself proximally and, within a certain range, constantly."⁴ Thus, even authentic resolutions draw on the possibilities handed down to us by our historical culture: "The authentic existentiell understanding is so far from extricating itself from the way of interpreting Dasein which has come down to us [*überkommenen Ausgelegtheit*], that in each case it is in terms of this interpretation, against it, and yet again for it, that any possibility one has chosen is seized upon in one's resolution" (*BT*, 435).

Far from promoting an anything goes decisionism, then, *Being and Time* is working toward a notion of what Charles Taylor calls "situated freedom,"⁵ an understanding of action as nested in and guided by a range of meaningful, historically constituted possibilities, which are binding on us because they define who we are. In what follows, I shall sketch out Heidegger's conceptions of human existence, historicity, and authentic action, showing how these ideas seem to emerge out of a dialogue with Dilthey and Nietzsche. This sketch should help to clarify why Heidegger said that "his concept of historicity was the basis for his political engagement" with the Nazis in the thirties.⁶ But I hope to show also that this connection between *Being and Time* and Heidegger's actions does not entail that this early work is inherently fascist or proto-Nazi.

Human existence as temporality

Although the avowed aim of *Being and Time* is to pose the question of being, the published portions concentrate on working out the being of the entity which has some understanding of being, that is, of Dasein. It is important to keep in mind that the term "Dasein" does not refer simply to individual human beings. Heidegger tells us that Dasein's being a "self" is "'only' one way of being [*Weise des Seins*] of this entity" (*BT*, 163, 153). It is especially misleading to think of Dasein as a center of experiences or actions. As Heidegger says, "even one's *own* Dasein becomes something that it can itself proximally 'come across' only when it *looks away* from 'experiences' and the 'center of its action,' or does not as yet 'see' them at all. Dasein finds 'itself' proximally in *what* it *does*"(*BT*, 155). Because Dasein *is* what it *does*, human existence is portrayed not as an object or thing of any sort, but instead as a "happening" or "event" (*Geschehen*) in which Dasein *is* what it makes of itself in the course of living out its life.

This conception of Dasein as a self-constituting life-course reflects what might be called a "manifestationist" view of human existence.⁷ We can get a feel for what such a view involves by contrasting it with the standard view of human agency. According to the standard view, a person's actions are regarded as outer expressions or signs of some causally effective inner states – the agent's beliefs and desires, for instance. We can understand a person as an agent, then, only by reading backward from the outer behavior to the inner impetus. The standard view assumes that what is most "real" about the person is found in the inner sources and origins of behavior, and that the outer, physical movement is secondary and derivative. It also assumes that the mental exists and is identifiable independent of the outer bodily events it causes.

A manifestationist view drops this way of treating the mental as fundamental and action as derivative. To say that we *are* what we *do* is to say that our very identity as agents – our "being" as humans – is something that comes to be defined and realized only in our ways of "being manifest" in our active lives. Even one's own mental life is something that generally remains amorphous and inchoate until it is given shape in action. I find out how deeply I care for someone, for example, not through introspection, but through seeing how I respond when that person is hurt. Here my response gives form to the feelings; it does not merely vent a pregiven emotion.

On a manifestationist view, then, what we do is a *presentation* of who we are, not just a signifier which represents some inner reality. Because our deeds "let us be" the kinds of humans we are, we can think of a human as a "coming-into-presence" that comes to fulfillment throughout its life-time. Who a person *is* is defined by the entire story of his or her life – the total "emerging-into-presence" which is "stretched along between birth and death" (*BT*, 426). Thought of as an unfolding life-story, Dasein is described as a "movement" which binds together thrownness and being-toward-death into a "unity" (*BT*, 426–7). The unifying "connectedness of life" (*Zusammenhang des Lebens*), Dasein's "happening," is to be found in the "specific movement in which Dasein *is stretched along and stretches itself along*" (*BT*, 425, 427). The "*structure of happening*, and the existential-temporal conditions of its possibility," make up what Heidegger calls "historic-ity" (*Geschichtlichkeit*).

Heidegger's conception of existence as an ongoing happening is clearly indebted to Dilthey's conception of life. Dilthey also questions the idea of an introspectible mental element distinct from our expressions. The terror and the response are not two different things, he says. The "narrow limits of... an introspective method of self-knowledge" are revealed when a person "tries to hold fast and grasp his states of mind by turning attention upon himself."[8] Since the mental is ephemeral and shapeless until it is given form in concrete productions, we can understand humans – ourselves as well as others – only through what they do in the world. "Thus, humans come to know themselves only by the circuitous route of understanding" (*PM*, 71).

For Dilthey, human existence is a "perpetual movement," a temporal unfold-ing characterized by continuity and connectedness. Describing how any moment is tied to the past and future, he suggests that current experiences make sense because of the ways they are connected to "what has been lived and remembered or still lies in the future." These relationships to the past and future make possible the continuity "which constitutes the course of a life," the "connected-ness of life" through time (*PM*, 102–3). Life is bound together into a unified flow by "development," "formation" (*Gestaltung*), and "purposiveness" (though there is no pre-given purpose holding for all humans). The most fundamental characteristic of life, however, is captured by the category of "meaning": "the connectedness of a life can only be understood through the meaning the individual parts have for understanding the whole. . . . Meaning is the compre-hensive category through which life becomes comprehensible" (*PM*, 105). It is meaning which lets us grasp the parts of a life as counting or mattering in some way in the formation of the whole. A moment in a person's life is "significant for the individual," Dilthey says, "because, in it, an action or outer event committed him for the future, or a plan for the conduct of his life was made or carried forward to realization." (*PM*, 106).

It follows, then, that grasping any part of a life requires having some understanding of the whole. Dilthey compares understanding a life to construing a sentence. We can make sense of the words in a sentence only by working with come construal of the meaning of the whole sentence. In the same way, an event in a life must be grasped in terms of some anticipations about where that life is going overall. "We recognize this meaning as we do that of words in a sentence, through memory and the potentialities of the future" (*PM*, 107). This parts–whole circularity implies that our grasp of a life will be open-ended so long as the individual is still alive and capable of reinterpreting his or her life through future actions. "Our conception of the meaning of a life is constantly changing. . . . The purpose we set for the future conditions how we determine the meaning of the past" (*PM*, 106). For example, a religious conversion at the end of a life can totally recast the meaning of earlier years of cocky atheism. And so the meaning of a life "is never complete. One would have to wait for the end of a life and, in the hour of death, survey the whole to ascertain the relation between the whole and its parts. One would have to wait for the end of history to have all the material necessary to determine its meaning" (*PM*, 106). We can make sense of events in a life, therefore, only by projecting some vision of the final outcome of that life – what Gadamer calls an "anticipation of completion" – to serve as the basis for seeing events as part of a process with cumulativeness and direction in building toward the whole.

Dilthey's conception of the connectedness of life gives us a way of understanding Heidegger's account of the "existentials" or essential structures of Dasein's "happening." For Heidegger, any "existentiell" life is made possible by certain temporal structures. First of all, human existence is characterized by futurity in the sense that each of our actions is contributing to the realization of our being as a totality – our "being-*toward*-the-end" or "being-*toward*-death." If I just am what I do in my life, then my actions are composing my being as a person, regardless of what I might think of myself in my reflective moments. For this reason, Heidegger describes the being of Dasein as a "bringing itself to fruition" (*Sich-Zeitigung*, translated as "temporalizing") in which we "come toward" (the German word for the future, *Zu-kunft*) what we "finally" are to be as a totality. Since this culmination always stands before us, Heidegger says that Dasein's being is always impending and "not yet" realized so long as it still exists.

Second, we find outselves "already in" a world, bound up with a shared context and set on a track in life. This dimension of "thrownness" defines our being as "having-been." Yet, as for Dilthey, how our past involvements can *count* is something which is defined only through their relation to our commitments for the future. This is what Heidegger means when he says that Dasein's past "'happens' out of its future on each occasion" (*BT*, 41). The past counts for me in some determinate way only in the light of my sense of what my life is "coming to" as a whole. For example, my mid-life change of career makes my previous years in business, seemingly so important at the time, now appear largely a waste of time. Finally, the third dimension of Dasein's being, its "being-at-home" with entities in its everyday preoccupations, is made possible by the dynamic structure of its "thrown projection."

Both Dilthey and Heidegger emphasize the fact that the temporal unfolding of a life-happening is inseparable from the wider context of a public world. Dilthey describes how the child comes to be initiated into the "common life" of a historical culture, a shared background of significance which he calls (following Hegel) "objective mind."

> Every word, every sentence, every gesture or polite formula . . . is intelligible because the people who express themselves through them and those who understand them have something in common; the individual always experiences, thinks and acts in a common sphere. . . We live in this atmosphere, it surrounds us constantly. We are immersed in it. We are at home everywhere in this historical and understood world . . . . we ourselves are woven into this common sphere (*PM*, 123–4).

Because we are "crossing points" of historically shaped systems of social interaction, we embody history in ourselves and so always have some mastery of our "historicity" (*PM*, 124). For Dilthey, we only *become human* by becoming participants within a concrete historical culture.

Similarly, for Heidegger our identity as humans is given form through the ways we are tuned into the possibilities circulating in the "they" or the "one." Dasein's self-understanding is drawn from the public world into which it is thrown. "From this world," Heidegger says, "it takes its possibilities, and it does so first in accordance with the way things have been interpreted by the 'they.' This interpretation has already restricted the possible options of choice to what lies within the range of the familiar, the attainable, the respectable – that which is fitting and proper" (*BT*, 239). The understanding of being embodied in the practices of the "they" provides the medium from which we slip into familiar roles – being a teacher in the school system, a moderate in politics, a church-goer in the religious system, and so on. These possibilities for coherent action are deposited in our public language.

> In language . . . there is hidden a way in which the understanding of Dasein has been interpreted . . . . Proximally, and with certain limits, Dasein is constantly delivered over to this interpretedness, which controls and distributes the possibilities of average understanding and the situated-ness belonging to it . . . This everyday way in which things have been interpreted is one into which Dasein has grown in the first instance, with never a possibility of extrication. In it, out of it, and against it, all genuine understanding, interpreting and communicating, all re-discovering and appropriating anew, are performed. (*BT*, 211, 213)

It is because we are, at the deepest level, participants within the systems of interaction of the public world that Heidegger can say that Dasein just is the "they" (*BT*, 167). For this reason, authentic existence is only an "existentiell modification of the 'they'" (*BT*, 168, 312).[9]

Historicity, history, and historiography

In *Being and Time*, Heidegger is not merely cataloging facts about existentiell cases of Dasein. Instead, he wants to grasp the "existential-ontological" conditions for the possibility of humans and world in general. The idea that there is something more basic than humans (though always embodied in humans) is clear in such statements as: "*More primordial than humankind is the finitude of the Dasein in it.*"[10] The implication here is that it is because there is finite temporality of a particular sort that there can be a world with its diverse peoples and cultures. In line with this project of identifying the conditions for there being entities in general, Heidegger introduces, in chapter 5 of Division II, an "interpretation of Dasein's historicity" as "a more concrete working out of temporality" (*BT*, 434). This discussion aims at clarifying the possibility of "authentic historicity" as a way of existing for Dasein. Heidegger's view in this context seems to be that it is only because there is the ability-to-be (*Seinkönnen*) of authentic historicity that there can be the unified "temporalizing" that lets different types of entities show up at all.

Whatever one makes of these reflections on transcendental conditions, it is clear that the account of historicity introduces a number of important new concepts into Heidegger's description of Dasein. He points out that his central discussion of authentic existence in Division II has worked out the idea of anticipatory resoluteness in the face of one's finitude, that is, one's being-toward-death. But we now are told that this account of the authentic stance "toward the end" is "one-sided," in so far as it fails to account for Dasein's relation to its "beginning" (*Anfang*) – its "birth" (*BT*, 425). To grasp the unified movement or happening of authentic Dasein "from birth to death," Heidegger says, we must clarify the "sources" (*Ursprünge*) from which Dasein draws its possibilities of self-understanding (*BT*, 427). One's resolute stance in relation to death guarantees the continuity and constancy of a life-course. "But the factically disclosed possibilities of existence can not be gathered from death." And so the question remains "whence, *in general*, Dasein can draw those possibilities upon which it factically projects itself" (*BT*, 434).

The question of the source of our possibilities of self-interpretation has been answered already, in fact, in the discussion of our thrownness into the world of the "they." As thrown, Heidegger reiterates, Dasein "understands itself in terms of those possibilities which 'circulate' in the 'average' public away of interpreting Dasein today" (*BT*, 435). There is no exit from the understanding of things deposited in the public language and embodied in the practices of our current world. But, in the context of this discussion of historicity, Heidegger points to a different manner in which we might encounter those public possibilities. As authentic, he says, one can encounter them as a "heritage" (*Erbe*). Dasein's resoluteness "discloses current factical possibilities as *from the heritage* which resoluteness, as thrown, *takes over*" (*BT*, 435).

Combined with the notion of resoluteness, the concept of a "heritage" makes it possible to formulate an image of authentic historicity as a life combining both focus and rootedness. First, authentic Dasein clear-sightedly confronts its own finitude and faces up to the fact that not everything is possible. As resolute, Heidegger says, Dasein achieves "simplicity" as "every accidental and 'provisional' possibility [is] driven out." Facing death "gives Dasein its goal [*Ziel*] outright and pushes existence into its finitude" (*BT*, 435). The "goal," as I understand it, just is having focus and coherence in one's life. But second, Dasein encounters the possibilities of self-interpretation made accessible in the public world as "goods" (*Gute*) inherited from its heritage which provide assets for meaningful decisions about what is worth pursuing. In other words, we grasp the range of goals available to us as defined by our historical legacy.

Heidegger here re-emphasizes the fact that one's life is always indebted to and inseparable from the wider communal context. Dasein's own life-story is bound up with the "co-happening . . . of the community, of a people [*Volk*]" – what Heidegger refers to as our shared "destiny" or "mission" (*Geschick*). "Our fates have already been guided in advance in our being with one another in the same world. . . . Dasein's fateful destiny in and with its 'generation' goes to make up the full authentic happening of Dasein" (*BT*, 436). To say that our communal past is a "heritage" that points to a "destiny" is to say that we can find insights in our past as to what we should accomplish as a community. Thus, in an example made familiar by Robert Bellah and his colleagues, rediscovering the "second language" of civic humanist ideals buried in our culture can help us focus our aims as participants in a democracy.[11] It is because we have the resources of our shared past available to us that we have a basis for selecting the life-defining possibilities that help us "simplify" and focus our lives.

Authentic historicity lifts Dasein out of the dispersal and drifting of being a they-self, and provides it with guidelines for taking a coherent stance on the future. In so far as the past gains its sense from its possible ways of making a contribution to the future, Dasein's "own past – and this always means the past of its 'generation' – is not something that *follows along after* Dasein, but something which already goes ahead of it" (*BT*, 41). As in temporality generally, the future has priority in authentic historicity. Our commitments towards the future "destiny" of our community first let the past become manifest as counting or mattering in some determinate way.

Heidegger's account of authentic historicity expands the conception of authentic agency by (1) showing how we draw guidance from the past, and (2) providing an account of action as the transmission and realization of a tradition. First, the discussion of the individual's grounding in the past comes across in the description of authenticity as involving "repetition" or "retrieval." When Dasein "explicitly" grasps its indebtedness to "the way in which Dasein has been traditionally understood," according to Heidegger, it grasps its own actions as drawing on and making manifest the possibilities opened by a shared heritage. Authentic Dasein "chooses its hero" and is "free for the struggle of loyally following in the footsteps of that which can be repeated" (*BT*, 437). What is suggested here is that, when one understands oneself as relying on "the Dasein which has been there," one draws a role-model or exemplar from the heroes and heroines of the past and uses that model as a guide for orienting one's life. The paradigmatic stories of our predecessors provide plot-lines, so to speak, for articulating our own lives into coherent, focused happenings. This is most apparent, of course, in the way religious people draw on the lives of the saints or on Old Testament stories in defining their aims. But it is also true for people in professions (Socrates for philosophers, Florence Nightingale for nurses), for cultural groups (Sitting Bull for Native Americans, Martin Luther King for American blacks), and so on. Following the guidelines of the life of the Dasein who came before, the authentic individual finds a sense of direction and an awareness of his or her place in the wider drama of the historical culture. Only in this way, Heidegger claims, can one achieve genuine "self-constancy" and "connectedness" (*BT*, 439, 442).

Secondly, authentic historicity shows how our agency contributes to the transmission of a tradition. This aspect of historicity is worked out in the account of authentic historiography. Heidegger starts from the familiar observation that writing history always involves "selection," and that the ability to select what can count as historically relevant requires that we operate with some understanding of the overall outcome or impact of the unfolding course of events. For this reason, "Even the disclosure of *historiography* temporalizes itself *in terms of the future*" (*BT*, 447). Our ability to identify what genuinely matters in the events of the past depends on our ability to grasp history as a "context of effectiveness and development"[12] which is seen as adding up to something as a totality – as going somewhere or making sense overall.

Heidegger draws on Nietzsche's *The Use and Abuse of History for Life* in formulating his account of authentic historiography. Where Nietzsche had suggested that there are three distinct kinds of historiography – the monumental, the antiquarian, and the critical – Heidegger treats these as three elements, corresponding to the three temporal "ecstases," of a single form of historiography. The most fundamental moment of historiography, corresponding to the dimension of the future, is the "monumental." Nietzsche saw monumental history as needed by "the active and powerful person . . . who requires models, teachers and comforters, and cannot find them among his associates and contemporaries." The monumental view of the past shows that "the great which once existed was at least *possible* once and may well again be possible sometime"[13] Similarly for Heidegger, Dasein must project "monumental" possibilities for the future to provide a way of grasping the most meaningful possibilities for acting in the current situation: "Dasein exists authentically as futural," he claims, when, by coming "back resolutely to itself, it is, by repetition, open for the 'monumental' possibilities of human existence" (*BT*, 448). As monumental, authentic historiography is driven by a "utopian impulse": it projects an image of what history can and should accomplish in order to make sense of what should be done in the present.

When Dasein is thrown back onto its heritage, its understanding of the past is antiquarian. Nietzsche claimed that antiquarian history "belongs to the preserving and revering soul – to him who with loyalty and love looks back upon his origins . . . [trying] to preserve the conditions in which he grew up."[14] This notion of reverence for the past also appears in Heidegger's account of the antiquarian moment in authentic historiography. Since resoluteness involves "loyalty" in the sense of "revering the sole authority which a free existing can have, [i.e.,] the repeatable possibilities of existence," authentic historiography also calls for reverence, "the possibility of reverently preserving the existence that has been there, in which the possibility one is seizing upon [originally] became manifest" (*BT*, 443, 448). Monumentalization thus requires the antiquarian stance toward the past.

Finally, authentic historiography is critical. But it is critical not in Nietzsche's sense of "judging and annihilating a past."[15] Instead, for Heidegger, critique is aimed at the "today": authentic historiography becomes a way in which the 'today' gets deprived of its character as present; in other words, it becomes a way of painfully detaching oneself from the fallen publicness of the 'today'" (*BT*, 449). As critical, authentic historiography requires a "*disavowal* of that which in the 'today' is working itself out as the past," that is, a "destructuring" of the hardened interpretations circulating in the public world in order to recover "those primordial experiences in which we achieved our first ways of determining the nature of being – the ways which have guided us ever since" (*BT*, 438, 44). The critical stance "*deprives* the 'today' of its character *as present*, and weans one from the conventionalities of the 'they'" (*BT*, 444). Heidegger's claim here is that it is only on the basis of utopian ideals together with a sense of alternative ways of living discovered by antiquarian preservation that we can have a standpoint for criticizing calcified forms of life of the present. The present can be seen as deformed or defective only in contrast to an understanding of the potential built into our heritage and the truest aims definitive of our destiny.

The account of authentic historiography in *Being and Time* is clearly not just a recipe for writing better history books. Rather, historiography bcomes a model for authentic action. Authentic Dasein understands its fundamental task as the preservation and transmission of its historical culture for the purposes of realizing a shared destiny. As transmitters of a tradition, it is incumbent on us to seize on the defining possibilities of our common world, to creatively reinterpret them in the light of the demands of the present, and to take a stand on realizing the prospects for the future. As always, the future is primary. Just as the life of the individual is primarily defined by its "being-toward-the-end," so the community's being is defined by its directedness toward its "destiny," that is, the task of working out the basic experiences that define it.

According to this monumentalized picture of history, it is the understanding of history as a future-directed *quest* that lets the course of events show up as what is being "brought to fruition" in our actions. This understanding of our place in the stream of history provides the basis for Heidegger's description of "authentic temporality":

> Only an entity which, in its being, is essentially *futural* . . . and can let itself be thrown back upon its factical "there," . . . that is to say, only an entity which, as futural, is equiprimordially *having-been*, can, by handing down to itself the possibility it has inherited, take over its own thrownness and be *in the moment of vision* for "its time." (*BT*, 437)

This picture of authentic existence then provides the basis for the writings of the thirties. As Heidegger claims in his lectures of 1935, it is our task to retrieve "the beginning of our historical-spiritual existence in order to transform it into a new beginning." And this calls for taking "a creative view of [our] tradition," reinterpreting what came before in the light of a monumentalized vision of what we can be.[16] Because authentic historiography is the creative reinscription of what has been handed down to us for the purposes of the future, Heidegger says that "history . . . if it is anything at all, [is] mythology."[17]

3 Authenticity and taking action

Heidegger's account of authentic historicity answers Dilthey's "question of the 'connectedness' of life" by showing the possibility of "constancy" and "steadiness" in a life-course. As authentically historical, Dasein pulls itself away from the dispersal and inconstancy of the "they" and appropriates the possibilities it inherits in order to accomplish something for the future. This conception of authentic existence displays both the embeddedness and future-directedness of an authentic life. As a participant in the wider drama of history, Dasein is indebted for its possibilities of interpretation and aspiration to the historical context in which it finds itself. And, as a transmitter of the tradition, Dasein contributes to making manifest its community's potential by taking a coherent stand on its legacy. The "steadiness" of a life-course involves "the repetition of the heritage of possibilities by handing these down to oneself" so that Dasein is "in a moment of vision *for what is world-historical in its current Situation*" (*BT*, 442, my emphasis).

The idea of a "Situation" is crucial to understanding the account of authentic agency. Heidegger tries to clarify this notion by contrasting it with that of a "state of affairs" (*Lage*). A state of affairs is a context of action where what is called for on the part of an agent seems fairly straightforward. It is characteristic of a state of affairs that we feel it can be grasped in an objective way by any impartial observer. "Anyone" can see the opportunities that present themselves and can estimate the probable costs and benefits of different courses of action. That is why Heidegger says that the "'they' knows only the *general state of affairs*'" (*BT*, 346). The "they" treats things in this way because "the common sense of the 'they' knows only the satisfying of manipulable rules and public norms, or the failure to satisfy them" (*BT*, 334). As a result, it needs to see contexts of action as collections of intersubjectively specifiable facts that can be subsumed under universal principles or assigned precise values in standardized decision procedures.

The concept of a "Situation," in contrast, refers to a setting where a decisive, clear-sighted and creative stance is demanded from an individual. Heidegger seems to think of a Situation as a life-defining turning-point where failure to act would mean complete self-loss. Luther found himself to be in a Situation in this sense when he said, "Here I stand. I cannot do otherwise." These words suggest that everything in his life leads to this action, and that this action makes manifest and defines everything yet to come. Thus, a Situation is thought of as a unique conjuncture of a person's unfolding life-story, a crucial turning-point in the course of historical events, and a concrete context where action becomes unavoidable. It is by acting in a Situation that, in the words of Pindar quoted by Heidegger, you "become what you are" (*BT*, 186).

As Heidegger describes it, a Situation makes a demand on an individual which cannot be explicated to others in terms of objective features of the circumstances. Only someone who is already deeply committed and bound up with the flow of events can hear the call of the Situation. For this reason Heidegger says, "Resoluteness does not first take cognizance of a Situation and put that Situation before itself" (*BT*, 347). On the contrary, only a person who is already engaged in the world can grasp the weightiness and significance of the current setting. One must be authentic to encounter a Situation, for authentic existence is what first discloses "what is factically possible at the time" and so "calls us forth into the Situation" (*BT*, 345, 347). Thus, it is because authentic Dasein "is already *taking action*" that it "has put itself into the Situation already" (*BT*, 347). Far from being a factual state of affairs about which one adopts a pro or con attitude, a meaningful Situation can present itself only to someone whose involvements predefine what can *count* as the "facts" of the matter. General principles, designed as rules of thumb to guide the public through states of affairs, are worthless when one confronts a Situation.

It should be clear, then, that an authentic individual will have no access to fixed, objective criteria that determine which course of action is correct in dealing with a Situation. But what this indicates is not so much an anything-goes decisionism as a sense of the tenuousness of a life which is inescapably "thrown" into a world. For Heidegger, we are always caught in the position of an "insider," already up to our ears in the midst of things, underway in living out our lives, entangled with others in projects and concerns, and so having some prior fix on things. There is no exit from this "being-in-the-world." Only by resolutely grasping this complicity in the world can we fully realize the "primordial truth of existence" (*BT*, 355). This is why Heidegger's 1928 lectures take such pains to show that the need to start from a description of "neutral Dasein" does not entail that the existential analytic is describing a Dasein who is blandly indifferent about everything. On the contrary, Heidegger insists that the existential analytic starts from a "factical Situation" of "extreme existentiell involvement" – without, however, recommending one specific involvement over others.[18]

Heidegger's conception of authentic action might be clarified by contrasting it with the more clearly decisionistic view of the early Nietzsche. When Nietzsche says "All acting requires forgetting," he is claiming that there comes a time when all reflections, considerations, and estimations of outcomes must end. Action is impossible so long as it is "sicklied o'er with the pale cast of thought." Eventually the moment comes when one just has to *leap* in one direction or the other, regardless of all considerations and reflections. For action to be possible, one must "draw a horizon around oneself" and *forget*: a "clear conscience, the carefree deed, faith in the future, all this depends . . . on one's being able to forget at the right time."[19] Here action does indeed seem to spring from raw adventures of the will, with no guidelines or meaningful directions to point the way.

There are claims in *Being and Time* that seem to echo Nietzsche's views. Heidegger also suggests that action requires forgetting when he says, "The self must forget itself if, lost in the world of equipment, it is to be able 'actually' to go to work and manipulate something" (*BT*, 405). But note that in this context Heidegger is talking about the "making-present" of everyday dealings with equipment – that is, the busy-ness and preoccupations typical of our inauthentic distraction and dispersal in the "they." Authentic action, in contrast, requires a form of remembering. It calls for a clear-sighted sense both of one's indebtedness to the repeatable possibilities of history and of one's actions as woven into the "mission" shared with a wider community. In Heidegger's account of authentic action, there is the suggestion that such action involves a break or a rift – a severing of ties with that crowd in order to take a *leap* into the future. The idea of a leap seems to be part of what is meant by the statement, "Factually . . . any taking-action is necessarily 'conscienceless'" (*BT*, 334) – words which echo Goethe's well-known line, "The man of action is always without a conscience."[20] But it is important to keep in mind that, for Heidegger, authentic actions are still bound up with the shared undertakings of a historical community. The action is a response to "what is world-historical in [one's] current Situation."

Even if we grant that *Being and Time* is not decisionistic in any straightforward sense, however, we might still ask whether it is inherently fascist or proto-Nazi. My own view is that Heidegger's accounts of historicity and authenticity do not point to any particular political orientation, and that his actions in the thirties resulted solely from his own deeply held conservative beliefs. The early concepts of history and authentic action seem consistent with diverse political views because of their highly formal nature. Heidegger's ontology of human existence identifies a tripartite temporal structure according to which Dasein's "happening" springs from a projection onto future possibilities, draws on what is embodied in the past, and thereby acts in the present. The authentic mode of this temporal existence involves encountering a future as a "destiny," the past as a "heritage," and the present context as a "world-historical Situation." The clear-sighted recognition that we are always implicated in the undertakings of the shared "co-happening of a community" gives one some guidance in making choices. But it should be evident that this formalistic image of "temporalizing" and historicity *by itself* gives us no guidance as to which political stance we should adopt.

In fact, it appears that this picture of historical unfolding – this "metanarrative" or "narrative framework" – can be made to accommodate almost any political position. With its *mythos* of pristine beginnings, a time of "falling," and a final recovery of origins, it recapitulates the traditional Christian model of creation, sinfulness, and redemption. It is this soteriological model which also underlies the Marxist story-line of human species-beings currently deformed by capitalism but promised fulfillment in world communism. And it can be made to fit the liberal story of humans who are born to be free but now languish in the chains of ignorance and superstition, or the conservative story of a return to community after wandering in the wilderness of extreme individualism.

Heidegger's account of authentic historicity demanded that he take a stand on the situation in Germany in the thirties. This explains his comment to Löwith that "the concept of historicity was the basis for his political engagement." What we do know is that, faced with what most Germans at the time saw as the need for a decision between Bolshevism and Nazism, Heidegger sided with the Nazis. Yet ultimately it seems to be only a mix of opportunism and personal preference that directed his decision, not anything built into his fundamental ontology.

NOTES

1 *The Philosophical Discourse of Modernity: Twelve Lectures*, trans. F. Lawrence, Cambridge, MA: MIT Press, 1987, p. 141.
2 *The Politics of Being: The Political Thought of Martin Heidegger*, New York: Columbia University Press, 1990, p. 32.
3 *The Metaphysical Foundations of Logic*, trans. M. Heim, Bloomington: Indiana University Press, 1978, p. 196.
4 *Being and Time*, trans. John Macquarrie and Edward Robinson, New York: Harper & Row, 1962, p. 41. Future references to this work will be cited as *BT* in parentheses in the text. I frequently revise translations for the sake of clarity.
5 *Hegel and Modern Society*, Cambridge: Cambridge University Press, 1979, pp. 154–66. See also my "Existentialist ethics," in *New Directions in Ethics*, eds Joseph P. DeMarco and Richard M. Fox, New York: Routledge & Kegan Paul, 1986.
6 Reported by Karl Löwith in *Mein Leben in Deutschland vor und nach 1933*, Stuttgart: J. B. Metzler, 1986, p. 57. An excerpt has been translated as "My last meeting with Heidegger in Rome, 1936," in *New German Critique*, Fall 1988: 115–16.
7 "Emanationist" would be the more apt term were it not so loaded down with theological connotations. Elsewhere I have called this an "expressivist" view, a term which has only created confusion. See "Truth as disclosure: art, language, history," in *Heidegger and Praxis*, ed. Thomas J. Nenon, supplement to *The Southern Journal of Philosophy* 28 (1989), 105–20.
8 Wilhelm Dilthey, *Pattern and Meaning in History: Thoughts on History and Society*, ed. H.P. Rickman, New York: Harper and Row, 1961, p. 71 (henceforth cited parenthetically as *PM*).
9 I discuss these claims in detail in "Heidegger's 'authenticity' revisited," *The Review of Metaphysics*, December 1984: 321–39.
10 *Kant and the Problem of Metaphysics*, trans. James S. Churchill, Bloomington: Indiana University Press, 1962, p. 237.
11 Robert Bellah, Robert Madsen, William M. Sullivan, Ann Swidler, and Steven M. Tipton, *Habits of the Heart: Individualism and Commitment in American Life*, New York: Harper & Row, 1985.
12 *Frühe Schriften*, Frankfurt: Klostermann, 1972, p. 369.
13 *On the Advantage and Disadvantage of History for Life*, trans. Peter Preuss, Indianapolis: Hackett Publishing Co., 1980, pp. 14, 16.
14 Ibid., p. 19.
15 *Advantage and Disadvantage*, p. 22.
16 *An Introduction to Metaphysics*, trans. Ralph Manheim, New Haven, CT: Yale University Press, 1980, pp. 38–9.
17 Ibid., p. 155.
18 *Metaphysical Foundations of Logic*, pp. 139–41.
19 *Advantage and Disadvantage*, p. 10.
20 The words of Goethe, from his "Sprüche in Prosa," are quoted in Nietzsche's *Advantage and Disadvantage*, p. 12.

7

The Truth of Being and the History of Philosophy

Mark B. Okrent

Introduction

In a recent article, Richard Rorty has attempted to juxtapose Heidegger and Dewey. While finding significant points of agreement between the two, and by implication praising much of Heidegger's work, Rorty also suggests a series of criticisms of Heidegger. The problems which Rorty finds with Heidegger can, I think, all be reduced to one basic criticism, which has two main sides. In Rorty's view Heidegger cannot really differentiate between Being and beings in the way that he wants, and thus can give no sense to the word 'Being' other than the old metaphysical one. That is, Being and the ontological difference are metaphysical remnants, the last evaporating presence of the Platonic distinction of the real world and the apparent world. This is indicated in two ways. First, Rorty feels that Heidegger can make no real distinction between philosophy, which they both agree has ended, and "thinking" in the specifically Heideggerian sense. Second, Rorty claims that it is impossible to distinguish ontic from ontological becoming. That is, the various epochs of Being which Heidegger distinguishes are, for Rorty, parasitic upon and reducible to the ordinary history of man's activity in relation to things, material and social. As such Heidegger's account of ontological epochs is a species of idealistic reflection upon the history of man's activity upon things.

This paper attempts to reflect upon the adequacy of both main parts of Rorty's criticism of Heidegger. Is it possible to differentiate Being and beings in such a way as to allow for epochs of Being which are not simply reducible to ordinary historical periods? If not, then we will have reason to accept Rorty's criticism of the ontological difference, and hence of Heidegger's formulation in regard to Being. If this distinction can be maintained then one major element of Rorty's pragmatist criticism of Heidegger will need to be abandoned. Is it possible to distinguish the matter of Heidegger's thought from the concerns of philosophy in such a way as to preserve this thought given the end of philosophy? If not, then Heidegger's thinking is just another attempt to keep alive a bankrupt tradition. If this distinction can be maintained, then the other major element of Rorty's criticism must be abandoned.

2   Varieties of difference

Rorty thinks that Heidegger is necessarily impaled on the horns of a dilemma in regard to the history and historicity of Being. *Either* Being is radically different and distinct from beings, in which case "Being" can be nothing other than the old Platonic "real" world, a "real" which is impossibly vague, abstract, and lacks content and historical determinacy, *or* in order to give the historical becoming of Being definiteness, the history of "Being" can be seen as utterly dependent on the history of beings. If Heidegger accepts the first alternative then he is committed to, in words Rorty quotes from Versenyi, "an all too empty and formal, though often emotionally charged and mystically-religious, thinking of absolute unity."[1] On the other hand, if Heidegger admitted that the history of Being must be seen in terms of the history of beings, then he would see that Philosophy (or Heidegger's own alternative, "thought"), as a discipline or even a distinct activity, is obsolete. That is, his concern with Being would be replaced by concrete attention to beings. In fact Rorty feels that Heidegger wants it both ways. While maintaining that he is giving us a history of Being, Heidegger necessarily has recourse to the ordinary history of nations, persons, and their relation to beings in order to give concreteness and definiteness to his ontological history.

It seems clear that before we can evaluate this criticism we need a better notion of just what Heidegger means by 'Being' and how it is supposed to be different from beings. Rorty, of course, denies that Heidegger can give any other than a negative account.

> All we are told about Being, Thought, and the ontological difference is by negation . . . Heidegger thinks that the historical picture which has been sketched offers a glimpse of something else. Yet nothing further can be said about this something else, and so the negative way to Being, through the destruction of ontology, leaves us facing beings-without-Being, with no hint about what Thought might be of.[2]

But Rorty himself inadvertently indicates Heidegger's attempt to hint at the matter to be thought, although he doesn't discuss it. In the first quote from Heidegger in the paper, from the "Letter on Humanism," Heidegger clearly distinguishes the truth of Being from Being itself. "Ontology, whether transcendental or pre-critical, is subject to criticism not because it thinks the Being of beings and thereby subjugates Being to a concept, but because it does not think the truth of Being."[3] Often Heidegger commentary does not recognize that in all of his periods Heidegger focuses not so much upon Being as on the *sense* of Being, or the *truth* of Being, or the *place* of Being.[4] The distinction between Being and the truth of Being is swallowed, as it were, by the distinction between Being and beings. This failure to note the distinction between Being and the truth of Being is perhaps not surprising, given that Heidegger himself is often unclear in regard to it. In the *Introduction to Metaphysics* for example, which Rorty cites extensively, this distinction barely makes an appearance as the distinction between the inquiry into Being as such and the inquiry into the Being of beings.[5] Nevertheless, this distinction is both present in Heidegger's texts and the hidden light which illuminates those texts. Heidegger "knows with full clarity the difference between Being as the Being of beings and Being as 'Being' in respect of its proper sense, that is, in respect of its truth (the clearing)."[6]

"Being" then is used by Heidegger in two different, indeed opposed, senses. First, "Being" is the Being of beings, what each being is thought to need so that it is, rather than nothing. That is, "Being" in this first sense refers to that which each being involves simply and solely in so far as it *is* at all. The science which studies Being in this sense is metaphysics, the science of Being *qua* Being. Equally, metaphysics, as the science of Being *qua* Being, increasingly comes to see Being in this sense, i.e., the Being of beings, as the ground of beings and itself. "The Being of beings reveals itself as the ground that gives itself ground and accounts for itself."[7] Metaphysics thus comes to see Being in this first sense as both what is most general, that which every being possesses in that it is, and as that which supplies the ground for all such beings. "Metaphysics thinks of the Being of beings both in the ground-giving unity of what is most general, what is indifferently valid everywhere, and also in the unity of the all that accounts for the general, that is, of the All-Highest."[8] As such, such views of Being as pure act, as absolute concept, or even Heidegger's own view of the Greek notion of Being as the presence of the presencing, all speak to this first sense of Being.

The question of Being also concerns the *aletheia* of Being, that which allows for the possibility of *any* answer to the question of Being in the first sense.

> The question of Being, on the other hand, can also be understood in the following sense: Wherein is each answer to the question of Being based i.e., wherein, after all, is the unconcealment of Being grounded? For example: It is said that the Greeks defined Being as the presence of the presencing. In presence speaks the present, in the present is a moment of time; therefore, the manifestation of Being as presence is related to time.[9]

In this second sense "Being" is sometimes used, unfortunately, as a shorthand expression standing for the "sense of Being," or the unconcealment (truth) of Being, or, more simply, the clearing or opening in which Being, in the first sense as presence, occurs. This "Being," as the sense of Being, time, is the concern of Heidegger's thought from *Being and Time* onward.

What then does Heidegger mean by "the truth of Being?" (Although there are serious differences among Heidegger's successive formulations, the sense of Being, the truth of Being, and the place of Being, for the sake of brevity I will speak mainly of the truth of Being, the formulation from his "middle" period.) Abstractly, the truth of being is thought as the opening or clearing which allows Being as presencing to appear and manifest itself. In order to think this it is necessary to explicate the sense in which Heidegger uses the term "truth."

Beginning with *Being and Time* and continuing until very late in his career Heidegger interprets "truth" with the aid of an idiosyncratic and etymological translation of the Greek *aletheia*. Etymologically *"aletheia"* is a privative of *"lethe,"* it is the not-hidden, the uncovered. "'Being-true' ('truth') means Being-uncovering."[10] Yet equally essential to Heidegger's thinking on truth is the claim that unconcealment also involves concealment, hiddenness.

> The nature of truth, that is, of unconcealment, is dominated throughout by a denial. Yet this denial is not a defect or a fault, as though truth were an unalloyed unconcealment that has rid itself of everything concealed. If truth could accomplish this, it would no longer be itself . . . Truth, in its nature, is untruth. We put the matter this way in order to serve notice . . . that denial in the manner of concealment belongs to unconcealedness as clearing.[11]

The initial motivation for this interpretation of truth is clear enough. In order for there to be truth in either of the traditional senses, as correspondence or coherence, there must be evidence. That is, the object referred to in the true statement must be manifest, must show itself, it must be uncovered. But that the being disclosed can be uncovered depends upon the possibility of such uncovering. In *Being and Time* this possibility is supplied by the being whose Being consists in Being-in-the-world, Dasein. Thus the early Heidegger distinguishes two senses of "true," the Being-uncovered of beings and the Being-uncovering of Dasein.

> Circumspective concern, or even that concern in which we tarry and look at something, uncovers entities within-the-world. These entities become that which has been uncovered. They are "true" in a second sense. What is primarily "true" – that is, uncovering – is Dasein. "Truth" in the second sense does not mean Being-uncovering, but Being-uncovered.[12]

When the later Heidegger speaks of truth as unconcealedness he is speaking on analogy with the Being-uncovering of *Being and Time*, without the subjectivist bias of the latter. That is, "truth" is that which allows beings to show themselves through providing an area of showing. As such Heidegger's "truth" is analogous with the horizon of earlier phenomenology, but with Heidegger the horizon allows for the possibility of focus, or being manifest, and in that sense is primary truth. As such however it itself is that which is ordinarily *not* manifest, not present. "Only what *aletheia* as opening grants is experienced and thought, not what it is as such. This remains concealed."[13] The concealedness and hiddenness which is fundamental to truth is primarily the essential non-presence (in the sense of not being in the present) of the opening which allows beings to be present. Only secondarily is it the perspectival hiddenness native to those beings themselves.

After 1964 Heidegger gives up the translation of *aletheia* as truth, without giving up the matter thought by *aletheia*. This matter, the clearing or opening in which both beings and Being can appear, remains the primary "object" of

Heidegger's thought. In *On Time and Being* Heidegger returns to his earliest treatment of the clearing, in terms of temporality. The ecstatic temporality which is the meaning of the Being of Dasein in *Being and Time* is now thought as "time-space." Time-space is introduced during a discussion of presence in terms of the present and absence. As opposed to the traditional understanding of the present as a now point in a sequence of now points, Heidegger interprets the present as that which concerns human being, the matter illuminated in concern. "What is present concerns us, the present, that is: what, lasting, comes toward us, us human beings." "Presence means: the constant abiding that approaches man, reaches him, is extended to him"[14] Presence, understood in this way as that which lasts in concern, involves more than the present ordinarily so called. It necessarily also involves absence, the absence of that which has been, and of that which is coming toward us. That which is "past" and "future" for Heidegger, is equally present, but *only* in the sense of being of concern, not in the sense of being in the temporal now. There is a presence of "past" and "future" precisely in so far as they are absent from the now, i.e., as having been and coming toward.

> But we have to do with absence just as often, that is, constantly. For one thing, there is much that is no longer present in the way we know presencing in the sense of the present. And yet, even that which is no longer present presences immediately in its absence – in the manner of what has been, and still concerns us.
>   . . . absence, as the presencing of what is not yet present, always in some way concerns us, is present no less immediately than what has been.[15]

Thus not every presencing involves the present. But the present too is itself a mode of presence.

Heidegger's concern, however, is not with that which is present, past, or future. Reverting to a distinction which is focal in *Kant and the Problem of Metaphysics*, he is rather interested in temporality itself or the opening in which that which is temporal can be so. "For time itself is nothing temporal, no more than it is something that is." "Time-space now is the name for the openness which opens up in the mutual self-extending of futural approach, past, and present."[16] Time-space supplies this openness in which present and absent beings can be, however, only in that the dimensions of time, past, present, and future, are both related to one another and distinct. Within this distinction lies a withholding of the present. The past and future are present *only* through their absence.

> we call the first, original, literally incipient extending in which the unity of true time consists "nearing nearness", "nearhood". . . . But it brings future, past, and present near to one another by distancing them. For it keeps what has been open by denying its advent as present . . . . Nearing nearness has the character of denial and withholding.[17]

It is both possible and helpful to distinguish Heidegger's truth of Being, as we have just interpreted it, from certain other contemporary notions which seem to be similar to it. First, the truth of Being should not be seen as analogous to a conceptual scheme. Aside from the obvious fact that Heidegger associates the truth of Being with temporality, rather than concepts, there is a deeper difference between these notions. As Donald Davidson pointed out in his paper "On the Very Idea of a Conceptual Scheme," the idea of a conceptual scheme depends ultimately upon something like the hard Kantian distinction between sensibility and understanding. But Heidegger rejects this distinction as fully as do Davidson, Sellars, and Rorty. As early as *Being and Time*, Heidegger held that we never have merely "raw feelings."[18] Rather, for Heidegger, all human "experience" is only possible within a *world*, a world which is always already linguistically articulated. But then, perhaps the truth of Being should be seen as similar to the analytic notion of a set of linguistic rules which allow for the possibility of language use? There is more to be said in favor of this analogy, as Heidegger frequently remarks on the connection between the truth of Being and the pre-thematic articulation of a world by language. We must be careful here with the concept of a rule. The word "rule" suggests a situation in which a person acting according to a rule must either be obeying the rule (i.e., the rule is a principle which is explicit *for* the agent) or merely acting in conformity to a rule (i.e., the agent's acts fall into a regular, perhaps causal, pattern, although the agent is not aware of this).[19] Heidegger wishes to avoid both of these alternatives, which he sees as metaphysical. In both cases we are seen as capable, in principle, of giving a single correct interpretation and explication of what is involved in acting according to any particular rule. That is, every rule can be made explicit and focal, either by the agent (in the case of obeying a rule) or by a scientist observing the behavior (in the case of conforming to a rule). For Heidegger, the necessity of the hermeneutic circle, which precludes the possibility of any fully grounded interpretation, points to the *necessarily* nonfocal character of both language and the truth of Being. Thus Heidegger's truth of Being must also be distinguished from the notion of a set of linguistic rules. Put bluntly, Heidegger's position is that "rules" cannot be successfully used to account for the possibility and actuality of language use.

The matter of Heidegger's thought, then, is the truth of Being, the clearing in which beings can appear and in which Being, as the presencing of presence, can manifest itself. The clearing is analogous with the phenomenological horizon. As such it is the concealed possibility of unconcealment, the "truth" of Being. Further, the opening is temporality, the ecstatic extendedness and distinction of past, present and future. All of this is different from Being, or presencing as such. But how is any of this relevant to Heidegger's insistence on the epochal history of Being, and his distinction of thought and philosophy, and Rorty's criticism of these?

3   The truth of Being and the history of philosophy

The thrust of Rorty's criticism of Heidegger is aimed at the supposed vacuity of Heidegger's thought of Being without beings. In order to overcome this vacuity,

Rorty thinks that Heidegger has recourse to the history of beings. But the form ordinary history takes for Rorty's Heidegger is the alienated form of the history of philosophy. "If he [Heidegger] were true to his own dictum that we should 'cease all overcoming, and leave metaphysics to itself,' he would have nothing to say, nowhere to point. *The whole force of Heidegger's thought lies in his account of the history of philosophy.*"[20] For Rorty's Heidegger, therefore, the content of the history of Being arises out of the history of philosophy. But the history of Being can be subsumed under the history of philosophy, for Rorty, only if philosophy is *of* Being. Thus Rorty's Heidegger is necessarily committed to the view that metaphysics was always about Being, and that his own thought is tied to this tradition. "The only thing which links him with the tradition is his claim that the tradition, though persistently sidetracked onto beings, was really concerned with Being all the time – and, indeed, constituted the history of Being.[21] But if Heidegger's "thought" is really different from the tradition as Heidegger claims, then he is committed to the odd view that his thought is essentially a continuation of the *same* thinking as metaphysics, although at the same time he utterly rejects everything in that tradition. The criticism thus has three steps. First, Being without being is a vacuous notion. Second, this vacuity is overcome through a consideration of the history of philosophy. This in turn commits Heidegger to the absurd position that his thought is both entirely different from the tradition and also a continuation of the tradition which is about the very same thing as that tradition. Heidegger needs the tradition in order to identify the matter of his thinking, but then turns around and denies that the tradition tells us anything about that matter.

The criticism is dominated throughout by the reading of Heidegger which sees his primary distinction in the difference between Being and beings. Rorty's initial claim, that Being without beings is a vacuous notion, is motivated by this reading. We have argued in the previous section that this understanding of Heidegger is inadequate. Nevertheless, this fact, by itself, is not sufficient to show that the criticism is not cogent. It still may be the case that this other matter of Heidegger's thought, the truth of Being, may also prove to be vacuous. That is, Heidegger might be equally unable to determine the truth of Being without recourse to his version of the history of philosophy. As Heidegger rejects that tradition as, at least, inadequate, he would once again be in the position of identifying the matter of his thinking through ontology, while denying that ontology has anything positive to say about that matter.

Although Heidegger's truth of Being is in no sense the same as is thought in Kant's thing in itself (the truth of Being is not a "real world" or beings as they are independent of experience), there does seem to be a certain formal analogy between them. The truth of Being cannot successfully be made into an object of experience. This is because it is not an object at all, whether of experience or in itself. It *is* not. Rather it is meant as the concealed space in which objects can be. But if the truth of Being can never be an object of experience, how can it be indicated, "pointed to"? It can't be ostensively determined, it cannot be distinguished as this as opposed to that, and it cannot be defined in terms of some being. The reference to Kant, however, suggests a transcendental procedure for the determination of the truth of Being. But, even though Heidegger often uses transcendental sounding language, even in his late writings, he specifically precludes the option of considering the truth of Being as merely the necessary condition for the possibility of experience, as this would be overly subjectivistic. Nonetheless Heidegger often *does* use quasi-transcendental arguments in order to identify the place and role of the truth of Being. Indeed, the characterizations we have already given to the truth of Being in the last section all arise out of such transcendental considerations. On the other hand, the base step for these procedures is not the certainty of experience. When the truth of Being is discussed as the clearing, that which it supplies the condition of the possibility of is not experience, but Being. Similarly, when *aletheia* or temporality are under consideration it is Being in the sense of present evidence or presencing as such which is the basis for the transcendental discussion.[22]

It is clear that Heidegger thinks there can be no direct access to the truth of Being, no uncovering of the truth of Being such as occurs in regard to beings. I am suggesting that Heidegger substitutes a quasi-transcendental approach. The foundation for this transcendental access is not experience, however, but rather Being. But how is Being itself to be determined and characterized? It seems that we are back to Rorty's problem. If the truth of Being can only be identified in and through Being, then Being itself must be available to us. But Being as presencing is not. It, Being, is not in the open to be viewed. Where then does Heidegger get the determination of Being as presencing? Heidegger explicitly addresses this question in "On Time and Being." He suggests two answers, one of which is a blatant statement of Rorty's contention that Heidegger can only determine Being from out of the tradition of ontology.

> But what gives us the right to characterize Being as presencing? This question comes too late. For this character of Being has long since been decided without our contribution . . . Thus we are bound to the characterization of Being as presencing. It derives its binding force from the beginning of the unconcealment of Being as something that can be said . . . Ever since the beginning of Western thinking with the Greeks, all saying of "Being" and "Is" is held in remembrance of the determination of Being as presencing which is binding for thinking.[23]

In this same passage Heidegger also suggests a second mode of access to Being or presencing. Harkening back to *Being and Time* he asserts that a phenomenological approach to *Zuhandenheit* and *Vorhandenheit* will also yield a characterization of Being as presencing. We will leave aside this second answer to the question concerning the determination of being as presencing and concentrate on the adequacy of the first answer, given Rorty's criticism of it.[24]

Heidegger explicitly asserts that Being has already been characterized as presencing, and that this has been done at the beginning of the Western philosophical traditon.[25] It would thus seem that Rorty is right in regard to the first two steps of his argument. Even though Heidegger is not primarily concerned with Being, but rather with the truth of Being, the characterization of the truth of Being depends upon the determination of Being. Apart from the phenomenological arguments developed in *Being and Time* and then mostly ignored by Heidegger, there is no way to determine Being except through the supposedly already established determination given by the tradition. Rorty is thus apparently correct in his contention that Being is a vacuous notion which is only given content in and through the history of philosophy.

The third step in Rorty's argument is accomplished through the juxtaposition of Heidegger's dependence upon the tradition with his rejection of that tradition. But Heidegger *never* simply rejects or refutes the tradition of Western thinking as wrong. In speaking specifically of Hegel, he makes the general point that it is impossible ever to give such a refutation or to hazard such a rejection. "Whatever stems from it [absolute metaphysics] cannot be countered or even cast aside by refutations. It can only be taken up in such a way that its truth is more primordially sheltered in Being itself and removed from the domain of mere human opinion. All refutation in the field of essential thinking is foolish."[26] But if Heidegger does not see himself as refuting or rejecting the history of ontology as wrong, then what is the character of his rejection of the traditon? For reject it he does. The answer has already been given. The tradition is inadequate because it never thinks the truth of Being. This, necessarily, remains hidden from metaphysics " . . . the truth of Being as the lighting itself remains concealed from metaphysics. However, this concealment is not a defect of metaphysics but a treasure withheld from it yet held before it, the treasure of its own proper wealth."[27]

> In the history of Western thinking . . . what is, is thought, in reference to Being; yet the truth of Being remains unthought, and not only is that truth denied to thinking as a possible experience, but Western thinking itself, and indeed in the form of metaphysics, expressly, but nevertheless unknowingly, veils the happening of that denial.[28]

The tradition of ontology, for Heidegger, is not wrong in regard to its continuous thinking of Being as presencing. It is inadequate and incomplete in that it fails to think the clearing, or truth of Being, in which there can be both present beings and presencing itself, Being.

Two crucial conclusions rest upon the character of Heidegger's rejection of the tradition. First, the fact that Heidegger rejects metaphysics in the way he does, does not commit him to the position that metaphysics is wrong in regard to its characterization of Being. Quite the contrary appears to be the case. It is not even possible for us to "give up" the content of Being as presencing, we necessarily live in terms of it. We can no longer *do* metaphysics not because it is wrong, but rather because it has ended in, and been continued by, technology and the positive sciences. Second, Heidegger's thinking is *not* about the very same thing metaphysics was about. Rorty is just wrong in his contention that it is. Rather, Heidegger's thinking is distinguished from metaphysics precisely in so far as it is not concerned with Being, but is concerned with the truth of Being. It is in this sense that we must read his dictum that we need to leave metaphysics to itself. Heidegger would seem to agree with Rorty that the proper "end" to philosophy is in the sciences, natural and social, and in practical, technological activity. But there is something left unthought in philosophy, the clearing in which philosophy happens, the truth of Being.

Indicating the nature of Heidegger's rejection of metaphysics does not yet, however, decide the issue between him and Rorty. One additional step is necessary. We have already seen that there is a sense in which Heidegger cannot "leave metaphysics to itself." Even though he is not directly determining the matter of his thinking through the characterization of Being in the history of philosophy, Rorty is right in thinking that Heidegger does need the tradition in order to identify that matter. The truth of Being is identified by asking how Being as presencing is possible. Only through rethinking the tradition as the successive revelation of Being as presencing does it become possible to ask this question. But *this* relation between Heidegger and the tradition is not open to the criticism Rorty levels. There is nothing odd, contradictory, or impossible about rejecting ontology as incomplete because it does not think the truth of Being, which is necessary for its own possibility, and then determining the truth of Being through a quasi-transcendental discussion of the possibility of the ontological tradition. On the contrary, this is the "method" which is adequate and appropriate to the task.

4   The truth of Being and epochs of Being

Rorty's criticism of Heidegger in regard to the possibility for thinking at the end of philosophy is co-ordinated with a second criticism. This criticism concerns the relation among Heidegger's account of Being, the history of Being, and ordinary history. Heidegger's account of Being is, admittedly, dependent for its determination upon his understanding of the history of Being. Rorty claims that this history of Being is reducible to history in the usual sense. At best it is a history of ideas, which itself is parasitic upon the social, political, and economic history of peoples. At worst it is vacuous.

There are two distinct though related claims involved in Rorty's criticism of Heidegger on the history of Being. For most of his paper Rorty asserts that Heidegger's history of Being must be seen as simply a version of the history of philosophy. "Heidegger's sense of the vulgarity of the age . . . is strongest when what is trivialized is the history of metaphysics. For this history is the history of Being."[29] On this account, the history of Being is both constituted by and manifest in the writings of the great philosophers. As such, ordinary history is seen as secondary to metaphysical history – a period is characterized as a failure or a success in terms of its ability to actualize the thought of its philosophers. On the other hand, Rorty also claims that the history of Being must be seen in terms of, and gets its content from, the ordinary history of "ages, cultures," etc. "Unless Heidegger connected the history of Being with that of men and nations through such phrases as 'a nation's relation to Being' and thus connected the history of philosophy with just plain history, he would be able to say only what Kierkegaard said,"[30] i.e., his history of Being would be vacuous. These two claims do not, of course, contradict one another. Rather, together they amount to a single assertion concerning Heidegger's history of Being. For Rorty, Heidegger sees the history of Being *as* the history of philosophy. But, for Rorty, following Marx and Dewey, the history of philosophy itself is composed of a series of *Weltanschauung*, which in turn are determined in and through ordinary history. Rorty emphasizes those passages in Heidegger which connect the history of Being with ordinary history because for Rorty it is ultimately through this reference that the history of philosophy is made definite.

There are thus two relations in question in Rorty's discussion of Heidegger's history of Being – the relation between the history of Being and the history of philosophy, and the relation between the history of philosophy and ordinary history. We have already seen that there is a sense in which the history of metaphysics *is* a history of Being for Heidegger. The various metaphysical determinations of Being as presencing do constitute something like a history of Being. "The development of the abundance of transformations of Being [in metaphysics] looks at first like a history of Being."[31] It is also the case that whatever genuinely characterizes the history of Being for Heidegger, the indications for the concrete stages of this history are taken almost exclusively from the thinking of philosophers. But these metaphysical systems are not *themselves* the epochs of Being which compose the history of Being, for Heidegger. Rather, Heidegger attempts to differentiate the epochs of Being, which are the stages of his history of Being, from the metaphysical systems, which are merely the concrete indicators for discovering the content of this history. This differentiation can be seen clearly in Heidegger's use of the term "epoch" to stand for the stages of the history of Being. For the word "epoch" has a specific technical sense in Heidegger's thought which goes beyond and is different from its ordinary sense.

> To hold back is, in Greek, *epoche*. Hence we speak of the epochs of the destiny of Being. Epoch does not mean here a span of time in occurrence, but rather the fundamental characteristic of sending, the actual holding-back of itself in favor of the discernability of the gift, that is of Being with regard to the grounding of beings.[32]

An epoch of Being, then, is not characterized by what is positive in any metaphysical thesis in regard to Being. Rather, it is determined by what is absent, held back, in that position. The history of Being is a history of hiddenness, not of presence. It is a history of the specific ways in which the place and truth of Being have been forgotten, not of Being in the ontological sense, itself.

At this point an apparent, but only apparent, similarity between Heidegger and Hegel suggests itself and is instructive. Hegel's history of philosophy is also a history of absence, of holding back. For Hegel, each successive stage in philosophical development (corresponding roughly to moments in the Logic) is, as finite, determined by its limit. A philosophical system is as it is because it fails to incorporate within its own thought something which is nonetheless necessary for itself. This other, its limit, is both the determination of the philosophy, and, ultimately, its *Aufhebung*. But in Hegel's "history of Being" this holding back is itself limited. That is, thought progressively overcomes each of its successive limits until limitation itself is finally incorporated into philosophy in the *Science of Logic*. In this culmination the form of finitude, temporality, is also *Aufgehoben*. In Heidegger's history of Being, on the other hand, there is not and can not be any such final reappropriation of the hidden. At best there can be only a simple recognition of the hidden, non-present limit of all philosophical discourse.

Returning to the main problem, however, how does the epochal character of Heidegger's history of Being affect the relation between that history and the history of philosophy? The history of Being is obviously dependent upon Heidegger's critical rethinking of the history of philosophy, but only in a negative way. The actual content that Heidegger gives to his history of Being is both discovered through and different from the actual content of the history of philosophy. It is discovered through the tradition in that it traces what is forgotten by but necessary for each specific moment in the history of philosophy. It is different from the content of the tradition in that no particular stage in the tradition, or even that tradition taken as a whole, thinks what is at issue in the history of Being. For what is at issue in the history of Being is *not* Being, but the truth of Being. The history of Being includes, for example, a history of the ways in which temporality functions but is passed over, and must be passed over, in ontology, But if this is the case then it is clear that the history of Being is not simply reducible to the history of metaphysics. Rorty's claim that "this history [the history of metaphysics] is the history of Being" is just false. As was the case in regard to the relation of thinking and philosophy, Rorty has confused an admitted *dependence* of Heidegger on the tradition with the false proposition that the matter of Heidegger's thinking must be *identical* with the content of the tradition.

If Heidegger is not committed to the view that the history of Being is reducible to the history of metaphysics, then what are we to make of the relation between the history of Being and ordinary history? A simple transitive relation like the one implied by Rorty will not do. That is, if the history of Being is *not* the history of philosophy, then the determination of the content of the history of philosophy by ordinary history does not necessitate, by itself, an equal determination of the content of the history of Being by ordinary history. But *we* can *discover* the actual content of the history of Being only through recourse to the actual content of philosophical thought. Doesn't this imply the dependence in question? Not really. As the history of philosophy and the history of Being are correlative, and the history of philosophy and ordinary history are also, at least, correlative, there must be some correlation between ordinary history and the history of Being. But this correlation would allow for a criticism of Heidegger only if it made it impossible to differentiate Being or (more accurately) the truth of Being, from beings. That is, if the history of Being were a function of ordinary history, and ordinary history was not reciprocally a function of the history of Being, then the truth of Being would also be a simple function of the actual history of beings. In that case the investigation of the history of Being, in Heidegger's sense, could only be an alienated and unselfconscious study of the ordinary history of beings. Being and the truth of Being would not be radically different from beings, but only abstract and alienated ways in which a tradition of scholars had indirectly encountered beings. Rorty accepts this inference because he thinks of the history of Being as identical with the history of metaphysics and further thinks of the history of metaphysics as a function of ordinary history. We have already seen, however, that the history of Being is *not* identical with the history of metaphysics, for Heidegger. Given this lack of identity, Rorty's argument could work only if he showed that the history of Being were a function of the history of metaphysics. This relationship between the history of Being and the history of metaphysics he does not show, and Heidegger would deny. Although there is a correlation between an epoch of Being and a positive metaphysical assertion in regard to Being itself, which allows for the possibility of discovering the content of an epoch of Being, the metaphysical assertion does not *determine*, causally or otherwise, the holding back which is definitive for an epoch. Rather, Heidegger suggests, the reverse is more likely. Thus, even if the history of philosophy is a function of ordinary history, it does not follow that the history of Being is a function of ordinary history. An epoch of Being is defined by the field of openness in which both beings and Being can be manifest in the particular way they are in that epoch. This "clearing", as the truth or place of Being, is itself hidden from the period. The correlation between ordinary history and the history of Being can be accounted for and is necessitated by the fact that the truth of Being opens a field or world of possibility in which the life of peoples, nations, etc., occurs. This implies no priority to either the ordinary historical events and structures or to the particular character of the open during a particular temporal period. Nor does this correlation make it impossible to distinguish and differentiate beings from the truth of Being.

The history of Being, although discoverable for Heidegger in and through the history of metaphysics, is not the history of metaphysics. Equally, the history of Being, although correlated with ordinary history, need not be for Heidegger simply a function of ordinary history. We then see that the second main aspect of Rorty's criticism of Heidegger fails to be conclusive. As was the case with the first main aspect of his criticism (in regard to the relation of thinking and philosophy), Rorty's failure to identify the difference between Being and the truth of Being in Heidegger's thought is crucial here. If this distinction is ignored, then the history of Being can only be identified with the history of metaphysics. If this were the case, Rorty's criticism would be correct and cogent. But as the history of Being is not simply a new version of the history of metaphysics, Rorty's criticism must be rejected.

5 Conclusion: Heidegger, Rorty, and appropriation

Although the aims of this paper have now been reached, there is still a matter involved in the paper that needs further elucidation. I have somehow managed to write a paper which is primarily concerned with Heidegger but which never once speaks of *Ereignis*, or "appropriation."

It has been suggested throughout this paper that the real "matter" of Heidegger's thinking is not Being, but rather the truth of Being. This is not entirely accurate. The ultimate concern of Heidegger's thought is neither Being nor the truth of Being. It is appropriation. "What lets the two matters [Being and time] belong together, what brings the two into their own and, even more, maintains and holds them in their belonging together – the way the two matters stand, the matter at stake – is Appropriation."[33]

Why then have I intentionally suggested that the matter is temporality, or the truth of Being? This has been done for the sake of simplicity. Appropriation itself can only be grasped in terms of the relation between Being and the truth of Being. As such, it is almost totally incomprehensible without a prior thinking of the truth of Being, a thinking which Rorty's paper lacks. For appropriation operates for Heidegger precisely in the relation, the belonging together, of the two. "The matter at stake [appropriation] first appropriates Being and time into their own in virtue of their relation."[34] Heidegger often speaks of appropriation as the "It" which gives both time and Being. This suggests that appropriation is some third thing, a Being over and beyond Being and time. But this substantialization of appropriation is a mistake. "Appropriation neither *is*, nor *is* Appropriation there."[35] Rather, the mutual opening up and belonging together of Being and the truth of Being is at issue in appropriation, and only that. In appropriation Heidegger is suggesting an entirely "formal" feature of all historical worlds, the difference and relation of Being as presencing and the truth of Being as temporality. A preliminary attention to the truth of Being is thus necessary to open the way to Heidegger's appropriation. Since Rorty's article fails to give this attention to the truth of Being, this paper has attempted to remedy this lack. To have brought up *Ereignis* prematurely would only have muddied the waters.

Then does this paper assert that Heidegger is right and Rorty is wrong, that "thinking" is possible at the end of philosophy, and that there is indeed a history of Being independent of ordinary history? No, it remains uncommitted in regard to these issues. Neither does it suggest that there is no significant difference between Rorty and Heidegger. There is indeed such a difference. But Rorty has misidentified it. Rorty thinks that the difference between Heidegger and himself lies in Heidegger's insistent consideration of "Being." This amounts, for Rorty, to the "hope" that even after the end of ontology there might still be philosophy, as thought, which searches for the "holy," which while rejecting the tradition, still looks for something analogous to the "real world." In an odd way Rorty's interpretation and criticism of Heidegger mirrors Derrida's reading and criticism of Heidegger. For Derrida, "Being" is used by Heidegger as a "unique name," signifying a "transcendental signified." That is, the verb "to be" is thought of by Derrida's Heidegger as having a "lexical" as well as a grammatical function, a lexical use which signifies a transcendental "Being" in a unique way. This supposed Heideggerian meaning of "Being" amounts, for Derrida, to a certain "nostalgia" for presence. In fact, as we have seen, neither of these interpretations can be justified in Heidegger's texts. The truth of Being is not Being as presencing, and *Ereignis* is nothing outside of the open field in which beings and meanings occur. Heidegger does not "hope" for a "real world," nor is he nostalgic concerning presence. Dominique Janicaud has made this point persuasively in regard to Derrida's criticism.

I do not think it right to claim that there is nostalgia in Heidegger's works . . . The Heideggerian *Ereignis* does not mean any self-closure or self-achievement, but rather an *ek-statikon*. My last words on this point will be taken from "Time and Being": *"Zum Ereignis als solchem gehort die Enteignung,"* which one might translate as follows: disappropriation belongs to appropriation as such. I thus do not see how one could assimilate the Heideggerian *Ereignis* to the appropriation of presence.[36]

But if "Being" in Heidegger is not a "transcendental signified," if Heidegger does not hold out any "hope" for a "holy" real world, what then does oppose Heidegger and Rorty? It is precisely the same thing which really distinguishes Rorty from Derrida. Both Heidegger and Derrida consider the field in which presencing can occur, in Heidegger's language the open and appropriation, in Derrida's language *"différance,"* as worthy of thought. Heidegger is claiming that there is a "formal" necessity involved in any actual world of activity and meaning, the opposition and belonging together of Being and time. This clearing and belonging together is approachable for Heidegger through something like transcendental argumentation. These arguments do not get us outside of our world, however, only into it in a different way. It is this claim and this "hope" which Rorty is really denying. "Overcoming the Tradition: Heidegger and Dewey" unfortunately does not address this issue.

NOTES

1 R. Rorty, "Overcoming the tradition: Heidegger and Dewey," in *Review of Metaphysics*, Vol. XXX, No. 2, December 1976, p. 297 (cited hereafter as OTT).

2 OTT, p. 297.

3 OTT, p. 280.

4 Otto Pöggeler and Thomas Sheehan are among those who *have* recognized the importance of the meaning or truth of Being in Heidegger's thought. For example, cf. Pöggeler's "Heidegger's Topology of Being," in Joseph J. Kockelmans (ed.), *On Heidegger and Language*, Evanston, IU.: Northwestern University Press, 1972; and Sheehan's "Heidegger's interpretation of Aristotle: *Dynamis and Ereignis,*" in *Philosophy Research Archives*.

5 This distinction itself appears mostly in an interpolation into the text which was written after 1935. Cf. Heidegger, *Introduction to Metaphysics*, Garden City, NY: Doubleday, 1961, p. 14ff.

6 Heidegger, *On the Way to Language*, New York: Harper & Row, 1971, p. 20.

7 Heidegger, "The Onto-theo-logical Constitution of Metaphysics," in Stambaugh (ed.), *Identity and Difference*, New York: Harper & Row, 1969, p. 57.

8 Ibid., p. 58.

9 Heidegger, ed. R. Wisser, *Martin Heidegger in Conversation*, New Delhi, India: Arnold Hinneman Publishers, 1977, p. 45.

10 Heidegger, *Being and Time*, New York: Harper & Row, 1962, p. 262, H. 219.

11 Heidegger, "The origin of the work of art," in Hofstadter (ed.), *Poetry, Language, Thought*, New York: Harper & Row, 1971, p. 54.

12 Heidegger, *Being and Time*, p. 263, H, 220.

13 Heidegger, "The end of philosophy and the task of thinking," in Stambaugh (ed.), *On Time and Being*, New York: Harper & Row, 1972, p. 71.
14 Heidegger, "On time and being," in Stambaugh (ed.), *On Time and Being*, p. 12 (cited hereafter as *OTB*).
15 *OTB*, p. 13.
16 *OTB*, p. 14.
17 *OTB*, p. 15. At this point Heidegger's discussion of time bears a striking resemblance to Hegel's treatment of time in the *Philosophy of Nature*. What distinguishes Heidegger's treatment from Hegel's, however, is his insistence that temporality is irreducible to a mode of thought.
18 Cf., *Being and Time*, s.34, etc.
19 This tendency can be seen in Sellars' article, "Some reflections on language games," in *Science, Perception, and Reality*. As I understand it, Sellars' own attempt to avoid these poles ultimately depends on a simple conformity, perhaps causal, to metarules.
20 OTT, pp. 302–3.
21 OTT, p. 303.
22 I describe Heidegger's procedure for identifying the truth of Being as "quasi-transcendental." This term needs some explication. For Heidegger, there *is* a sense in which the truth of Being is phenomenal, roughly the same sense in which a phenomenological horizon is phenomenal. (As opposed to a Husserlian horizon, however, the truth of Being can *never* be made focal.) It is this that leads Heidegger to assert, in the Introduction to *Being and Time*, that both the sense of Being and the Kantian forms of intuition are 'phenomena'. So, if a transcendental argument is seen as one which necessarily argues to a conclusion which asserts the being of a non-phenomenal condition, Heidegger's procedure can not be termed transcendental. Nevertheless, Heidegger's method for identifying and determining the truth of Being does have a transcendental form. That is, he moves from that which is admitted to be the case, beings and their Being, to the necessary condition for the possibility of beings, the truth of Being. For this reason I have called his procedure quasi-transcendental. I have no objection, however, to calling this method "transcendental," as long as it is remembered that: (1) the argument does not start from experience and (2) the condition argued to is neither an existent nor non-phenomenal.
23 *OTB*, pp. 6–7.
24 But cf. section 4 of this paper.
25 *OTB*, p. 8.
26 Heidegger, "Letter on humanism," in *Basic Writings*, ed. David Krell, New York: Harper & Row, 1977, pp. 215–16.
27 Heidegger, "Letter on humanism," p. 213.
28 Heidegger, "The word of Nietzsche," in Lovitt, (ed.), *The Qeustion Concerning Technology*," New York: Harper & Row, 1977, p. 56.
19 OTT, p. 299.
30 OTT, p. 296.
31 *OTB*, p. 8
32 *OTB*, p. 9
33 *OTB*, p. 19
34 *OTB*, p. 19.
35 *OTB*, p. 24.
36 D. Janicaud, "Presence and appropriation," in *Research in Phenomenology*, vol. VIII, 1978, p. 73.

8
Attunement and Thinking

Michel Haar

From the well-known descriptions of primordial affectivity or "affectedness" (*Befindlichkeit*)[1] in *Being and Time*, to the recognition of the historical import[2] of mood (*Stimmung*), it would seem that the power imparted to *mood to disclose the world most primordially* has been consolidated and amplified. After anxiety and boredom, other moods also seen as "fundamental" ones (*Grundstimmungen*) were discovered and analyzed in the 1930s. Their newest and most general characteristic – especially in the case of Hölderlinian "sacred grief,"[3] or of the moods of wonder and terror[4] – is to furnish the basis and ground for epochs in the history of being. But as early as the first analyses of *Being and Time*, mood sets forth, or rather has always already unfolded, being-in-the-world in its totality: the totality made up of projection, being with others, and all the possibilities of praxis, starting from a given situation. "It [*Stimmung*] is an existential and fundamental mode of *opening, equally primordial* [with], the world, being-with, and existence . . ."[5] Our moods reveal the co-presence of all things in a way more comprehensive than any comprehension, more immediate than any perception. As a way of access to a preconceptual totality which, as *What is Metaphysics?* shows, precedes and makes possible all metaphysical surpassing of being as a whole, mood not only exposes for the first time a secret – and so already unthought – basis of all metaphysics, but prefigures the mutation of seeing thanks to which the theme of an attunement of man *by* being will be developed. That being, understood as destining, sending, history, "tunes man in," then means, among other things, that all *Stimmung* is *Bestimmung*, or determination of an epochal climate. Already in *On the Essence of Truth*, a transitional text if ever there was one,[6] we can read this phrase: "All the behavior of *historical man* is, whether he expressly feels it or not, whether he conceives it or not, attuned in a mood and transported by this mood into the totality of beings."[7] I have italicized the expression *historical man*. Since mood is relative to history or to the epochness of being (in a relationship that is, moreover, ambiguous and difficult to clarify, since moods, especially if fundamental, are at once determined by and determining of the epoch), Heidegger's position here marks a *turning* with respect to that of *Being and Time*. For the later Heidegger, all action and all thought, all works are at once "borne ekstatically" and inscribed by some mood or other in the totality of an epoch. All mood, even individual, escapes reduction to subjective sentiment as well as to background or general climate. It is not reduced to an historical given, but is rather the very style in which an historical unit presents itself and so is thoroughly diffused.

In *Being and Time*, just as all projecting is "thrown," all comprehension is certainly "attuned" (*gestimmt*). And the "affective situation" is without doubt the way in which the irretrievable anteriority or the putative "natural" already-there of being-in-the-world is discovered or felt as a totality. But affectedness or mood is not placed explicitly in relation to an epochal horizon. Before Heidegger's lecture on Hölderlin, the concept of "world" is quasi ahistorical. In the later thought, being disposed is interpreted as the first resonance in man of the *Anspruch* (demanding address) of being, the first hearing of its sending. *Stimmung* is understood as *Entsprechung*, that is, response and "correspondence"[8] to the *Stimme* (voice) of being: a "voice" not to be made into a subject, since it plays or constitutes merely the counterpart of mood, its other face, its non-human origin. That mood is "called" by the "voice" means only in fact that its origin is not human subjectivity, but the world, or rather being itself as time and history.

But if it is true that mood is the hearing of being, how is it to be distinguished from thought, which is also defined as response? Precisely in that mood is of itself *Sprachlos*, speechless: the silent tonality whose very muteness calls and demands words all the more strongly. Thought is the accomplishment in language of a giving of being to man, who is first attuned in the silence of mood. In *What is Metaphysics?*, we recall, the fundamental mood of anxiety, in producing a distance from being as a whole, in suspending the significant involvement of *Dasein* in the world, makes *Dasein* temporarily mute, unable to utter the least discourse on being, and thus incapable of thought! "Anxiety leaves us speechless. . . . Any sentence formed by the word 'is' falls quiet in its presence."[9] Yet Heidegger emphasizes in the lecture, "What is Philosophy?" that if philosophy is the "correspondence" with being through speech (*Entsprechung* means etymologically, "speech in response"), this speech only finds its *precise* articulation against the background of a *mood*: "all precision in saying is based on a disposition of correspondence" (*Jede Prazision des Sagens in eine Disposition des Entsprechens gründet*).[10] While substituting the word *Disposition* for *Stimmung*,[11] perhaps to be better understood by the French audience at this lecture, Heidegger twice reaffirms, by playing on the root word *stimmen*, that all conceptual determination depends upon a certain mood. It is only from *Gestimmtheit* (being disposed, disposition, mood) that the philosophical utterance receives its *Bestimmtheit*, which is to say its determined, precise, situated character. There can be no *Bestimmtheit*, or determination of the philosophical utterance, without a mood opening to the being of beings as a whole. Such a mood is not a vague sentiment or a simple atmosphere, but always a *Grundstimmung*, a fundamental attunement, at once determined and determining *for the epoch*.

Rapidly, Heidegger evokes three of these epoch-making *Grundstimmungen* which organize thought and give it its original thrust: astonishment[12] for the Greeks; doubt and its corollary certainty in Modern Times (the mood proper to

Richtigkeit, exactitude of rationality); finally a mood of the age of completed metaphysics, difficult to embrace under a single label in as much as today "fear and anxiety mingle with hope and confidence." This ambiguous contemporary mood, which does not touch calculating thought – still always marked by doubt and certainty – is principally defined, as we shall see, by fright. This dread or terror seizes thought in the face of the abyss of being whose history is on its way to completion and which awaits a new beginning. It would seem that there are only a very few *Grundstimmungen,* only one apparently, in each great epoch of Being.

In the face of these major historical moods – variations of which are the "sacred grief" which Hölderlin celebrates or, more recently, the "absence of distress" which marks the double face of technology, a mixture of extreme security and the presentiment of disaster – what rank should then be given to the nonhistorical moods, principally anxiety and boredom, which are analyzed in the context of *Sein und Zeit*? Should they simply be subsumed under the contemporary historical moods of dread and the absence of distress? Do they keep their specific truth unchanged, as moods which do not give access in any degree whatsoever to "thought" or to utterance concerning being, but rather effect a silent ontological modification of *Dasein,* by allowing a view on the whole of finite temporality? Anxiety and boredom both lead to a narrowing of time, a decisive instant where Dasein, squarely facing the repeatable character of its past and anticipating its future to the extreme limit, finds itself able to assume its own temporality. Now the silence of anxiety – which makes possible the silence of the resolution by which *Dasein* projects itself authentically, temporalizes itself – is situated, it would seem, outside all epochal continuity, outside the "universal" history of being. Is there a place in the later Heidegger for nonhistorical moods? What then about individual anxiety?

1 The ahistorical relation between mood and metaphysics

To return to the first of the questions just formulated, what structural, phenomenological relation – at first glance improbable and yet necessary – can we discover between affectedness and conceptual language, between mood and philosophy? There would seem to be, in the early Heidegger, an irreconcilable heterogeneity, a hiatus between mood on the one hand, which silently reveals thrownness (individual facticity as well as the obscure factical base of the world), and on the other hand, philosophy, which names the being of beings or thought, which tries to approach unconcealment (*aletheia*).

The link between the two is explicitly established as early as *What is Metaphysics?* (1929). The logic of understanding, the traditional metaphysical rationality in its various forms, can never conceive a totality in which questioning is in fact implicated and situated, or more exactly, it is not the totality in itself, but being *situated in the totality* that escapes rational conceptualization. "There remains finally an essential difference between *seizing* conceptually the totality of being in itself, and finding oneself amidst being in totality. The former is fundamentally impossible. The latter happens continually to our Dasein."[14] This event which lays hold of Dasein is brought about by a primordial relationship between mood and thought.

One must start from this notion of factical totality or of totality given beforehand in mood. Mood reveals that the whole of beings is *given before* any judgement that affirms or negates it. By pretending to *deduce* totality as objective, (starting, for example, from the principle of reason), traditional metaphysics forgets the prerequisite self-giving of the open. Now this opening as entirety springs from both facticity and transcendence. On the one hand, Dasein "is found" in mood in the *already-there* of itself, of others, and of the world. The particular meaning of this already-there is that some possibilities of being-thrown are *determined*. Three times Heidegger repeats the word *determined* in the very definition of thrownness. Thrownness discloses, he says, "the fact that Dasein is always already as mine and as such, in a *determined* world, and in relation to a *determined* sphere of *determined* intra-worldly beings."[15] But on the other hand, this factical determination concerns *possibilities*. Dasein "sees" its project through such and such a mood.[16] There is a circle here: the project is thrown, but inversely being-thrown is possibilized, projected in the possible, and this is done by mood itself. Mood is the reciprocal implication of the fact of being with being as project. This is why it shows a sort of universality and apparent objectivity. It emanates phenomenologically from the world or from things taken in their entirety, as that which touches, strikes, or surprises us. All mood is phenomenologically, preconceptually universal and total. It is the whole of being-in-the-world that reveals itself with such and such a coloring or climate of joy or sadness, and never a thing taken in isolation. There is also totality inasmuch as the subject subject and the object are indissociable within it. One is implicated in a situation experienced from the first without any need for recourse to the self-enclosed interiority of a feeling or judgement. This non-objectifiable whole is at once a given and a possible totality within which projects of action or thought can develop. "The moods," writes Heidegger in his 1929–30 lecture, "are the presupposition and milieu of thought and action."[17] This had already been clear in *Being and Time*. Were we not to experience the moods of security and fear, we would not come to know what there is. The pure perception of the occurrent, even if it delved to the core of being, would leave us eternally at a distance; in order for *Dasein* to desire to know, it has to have been at least implicated, "concerned" in some fashion, if not theatened.[18]

Whence the criticism, from the point of view of mood, of theoretical thought, or of representation. "Theoretical thought has always already dulled the world, by reducing it to the uniformity of purely subsistent being."[19] However, while in *Being and Time* Heidegger shows that knowledge, *theoria*, constitutes a more limited opening than the original opening of mood (derived, however, not from the latter but from the practical utensilary relationship in some way suspended), seven years later, in the 1934–35 lecture on Hölderlin, he goes so far as to define representation in general as issuing from a certain repression or "stifling" of mood produced in order to veil this very repression. This notion of repression of mood was already present in *Being and Time*: "Mood is ordinarily repressed"[20] Here is the text of the lecture on Hölderlin:

It is only on the basis of a certain belittling and stifling of mood, an apparent attempt to forget it, that one arrives at what we call the simple representation of things and objects. For representation is not first, as if it were so to speak by a piling up or grouping of represented objects that something like a world is constructed in strata. A world never allows itself to be opened and then stuck back together beginning from a multitude of perceived objects reassembled after the fact; rather it is that which in advance is most originally and inherently manifest, within which alone such and such a thing may come to meet us. The world's opening movement *comes about* in the fundamental mood. The power to transport, integrate, and thus open, that a fundamental mood possesses is therefore a power to found, for it places *Dasein* upon its foundations facing its abysses. The basic mood determines for our Dasein the place and time that are inherently open to its being (place being not understood spatially nor time temporally in its habitual sense)."[21]

Mood does not *think* the totality, but rather makes it *come about*, emerge more originarily than representation, which proceeding by construction or assemblage, can only think after the fact. Mood makes thought possible as an event of being. When anxiety results in the negation of beings as a whole, the negation is not a thought in the sense of a representation, but rather an experience. Mood initiates into the very principle of thought as the experience of being, an experience which is that of a dispossession or a decentering of Dasein. By itself, thought is incapable of producing essential negation, that is, the principle of all negation, the Nothing. Mood is a prelude to thought as a setting in motion and as a condition given by being. It allows us to feel that, in anxiety, the essence of thought is not to posit being, but to be posited by being. Mood leads into thought, as it were, overtaken (surprised) by being.

The second relation established between mood and thought is engendered from their common correspondence to the Nothing, this Nothing "belonging originarily to being," without which there would be no manifestation of beings as such.[22] All mood, says Heidegger, refers us back to a situation of *distress-and-constraint*. Or, conversely, distress constrains in the mode of mood.[23] As a new figure of thrownness, distress does not refer to any material poverty, or any situation that would give alarm by virtue of an objective lack; it refers to a radical powerlessness, a fundamental absence, negation, or rather negativity. All distress implies: first a not being able to "escape," practically speaking, but also an incapacity to *think* this very negation, an ignorance, a not knowing. All distress – and Heidegger uses this expression several times in the last part of the 1937–38 lecture (vol. 45) – is a "knowing neither the way out nor the way in." [24] In other words, being without access to being as such, being disarmed, without recourse: being "out(side) of proportion," Pascal would have said. And this disarray resembles Pascalian dread. Distress is the inverse of *Techné* and of assurance. Not knowing how to get along, to get one's bearings, to manage, not with respect to this or that, but *in the face of everything*. The true distress of thought is not a localized, ephemeral aporia, but the collapse of established signposts, indetermination taking hold of being in its entirety. This indetermination, says Heidegger, if it is *sustained* as "determining distress", if it reaches from mood to thought, is then richer than all knowledge possessed and all certainty. It is "the contrary of a lack": a "surplus," a "superabundance."[25] For not knowing and disarray stretch out then to the limits of being. There is no way out or in because the whole becomes problematic. In astonishment, it can be said, everything is in question and in doubt. Everything is still more in question in the dread of the bottomless abyss.

Mood each time translates the degree of negativity of the fundamental climate, a degree varying with its historical modality. For the not knowing and the not being able of distress must be understood according to the history of being and not as a psychological dimension of man. To be astonished is a very precise way of not being able to explain. We shall return to this point. Astonishment does not yet know the why, but moves toward it almost immediately. Here there enters no fear of the void, no threat of the absence of ground. Whence the question which appears towards the end of metaphysics, "Why is there being rather than Nothing?", where the nothing is present in a quasi-rhetorical way. The question contains "the answer left blank." In fact, there is already no more astonishment here, but the mood is already that of certainty. Little negativity enters into the marveling of the Greeks; negativity is expelled and set fixedly on the "impassible way" of Parmenides' *Poem*. On the contrary, the mood of doubt, voluntary and calculated, leaves almost no portion to nothingness. As for dread, it allows the Nothing to show through in all its power.

A third possible correlation between mood and thought is formed beginning with a common transport, transposition, or "exposition."[26] The transport, says Heidegger, is "the essential feature of what we know by the name of mood or feeling."[27] The transport is another ekstatic movement of transcendence toward the totality of the world. This ekstatic movement transports while being implicated with the world, specifies Heidegger, in his 1934–35 lecture:[28] it joins Dasein simultaneously to history and to the Sacred, but also to the nocturnal seat of the world: the Earth.

Even if mood is transportative, however, it does not discover these relations as *already extant* ones. It doubtless founds the space-time of a whole new relation to the world, but with an *indetermination* as to the essence of this relation and, likewise, the essence of encountered beings. To think is to let oneself first be carried by this ekstatic movement, to gain access by mood to this moving opening of being, but then immediately to grasp in language the determination of the relation thus revealed. Mood is transport, exposition in being; it allows being to be, but thought alone *names* being. "Thought," writes Heidegger, in his 1937–38 lecture, "here means letting what is emerge in its being . . . grasping it as such and by that fact naming it initially in its beingness."[29]

Thought *completes* transport by articulation. This determination by the thought of the indetermination of mood is not a break with it. Yet mood is more than a simple *inclination* or a penchant which would continue harmoniously in thought. There is a *leap*. By revealing such and such an uncovering and/or recovering of the world, mood "constrains," that is to say, pushes thought strongly on to the path of a "decision" as to the radical limits of being. "This transport puts mankind originally in a position to decide the most decisive relations with being and non-being."[30]

2   The double historical turning of fundamental attunement

With terror, the *historical* dimension of anxiety is uncovered. The word terror appears for the first time (in a published text) in 1943, in the Afterword to *What is Metaphysics?*, but it is present both in the winter semester lecture of 1937–38, *Grundfragen der Philosophie* (*GA* 45), and in the *Beiträge*, the large, recently published manuscript dating from the same years. It is in the Afterword that metaphysics receives its first historical definition. Metaphysics is not only the truth of being as such, the conceptualizing of the beingness of being; metaphysics is the *history* of that truth, that conceptualization. As we know, the Afterword defends the lecture against certain accusations (nihilism, scorn of logic, philosophy of sentiment), but above all it specifies the meaning of anxiety relative to that period of history in which the will to will and universal calculability mark Being. Terror is anxiety in the face of the disquieting abyss (*Abgrund*), which escapes calculating thought. The hidden abyss upon which the assurance of technology is projected is more terrorizing than anxiety producing. Terror is as it were *anxiety about being*, "essential anxiety." Now this anxiety comes from being itself as abyss, which is to say as unfounded, incalculable, withdrawn from any goal. The "devouring essence of calculation" rests upon the Nothing, the wholly other than being. "Anxiety grants an experience of being as the other of all beings . . . supposing we do not hide from the silent voice which disposes us to the terror of the abyss".[31] Terror itself is related to a feeling Heidegger calls modesty, *Scheu*, which is to say a fear mingled with respect, which can very well be understood as "horror," provided it be understood more or less as sacred horror. The evocation of horror is close in fact to that of marveling at being. Horror appears linked to the extreme distress of thought in the face of completed metaphysics and the prodigious wandering that it foretells. In the climate of horror, there appears with brutal clarity the strangeness of being, still not yet thought, "horribly" forgotten: the terrible desert of a long transition.

Anxiety with respect to being, terror, requires to be sustained, even sharpened, and not to be experienced in a merely passive way. Whence the necessity of another mood, valor. "Valor recognizes in the abyss of terror the barely trodden field of being."[32] This valor is not a heroism of action, but a disposition of thought with respect to the history of being. It is the courage to recognize and confront the historical event of the absence of metaphysics, its collapse, which leaves no other fulcrum than anxiety. Anxiety is called "the permanent fulcrum" of valor as a capacity to withstand Nothingness. Another name for valor is *Verhaltenheit*, restraint: the capacity to refrain from rushing to blot out the experience of Nothingness, restraint from immediately giving a new name to being. "Restraint" is precisely, says the 1937–38 lecture, the blending of terror and modesty, which corresponds to the tonality of the thought that is to come.[33] The dominant tonality of the previous philosophy would be rather melancholy: the sadness attendant on the break between the sensible and the intelligible, or at last, in Nietzsche, the joy of cancelling that break.

According to these divers tonalities, thought is always that which is disposed and determined by being, and which, beyond any calculation and any logic, responds to the unmasterable riddle. This response is first defined by Heidegger in the first version of the Afterword (1943) as *silent response* to the silent speech of being, implying "thanks" and offering, which is to say sacrifice (the word is resonant of piety), and gift in return. This flush of thankful acceptance, profoundly free, would be the "origin" of all human speech, and thus the silence of a mood composed of calm gratitude and anxious courage would be at the origin of thought. In the Afterword the most primordial thought remains close to the silence of being. Terror is the disposition which retains for the longest possible time the benefit, so to speak, of that muteness proper to anxiety. In terror, the relation to the abyss is maintained, without total muteness, in the form of "concern for the usage of language," "care given to speech," a "poverty" and a spareness of words. Only this obedience to the pre-verbal silence guarantees that thought thinks in proximity to being.

One may wonder, however, whether this tonality of terror and of valor is not more Nietzschean than Heideggerian, recalling Nietzsche's evocation of the terrifying fall into the void, into the abyss. For the terror that lays hold of the *foolish one* in paragraph 125 of *The Joyful Wisdom* concerns not only the murder of God, but the caving in of the ground, the loss of the land. "Woe to thee, if homesickness for the land overcome thee . . . when there is no longer any land!" (end of paragraph 124). "What have we done, in unchaining this earth from its sun? Whence is it rolling now? . . . Have we not thrown ourselves into a continuous fall? . . . Are we not straying as across an infinite nothingness? Do we not feel the breath of the void?" Anxiety and distress in the face of the absent ground, the withdrawal not only of the metaphysical foundation but of the earthly seat do not refer in Heidegger to a crime or taint on the part of man, but to an epochal destiny. The age of the "night of the world" is that in which the base of the world has crumbled into the abyss. This abyss is much more fearful than the bottom of a precipice lurking before us or the threat of the gaping gulf, says Heidegger; it is rather to be understood more radically as "the total absence of the foundation." The foundation is not only the principle, the *arche*, the logical and metaphysical basis, but *the Earth*.

> The foundation is the soil for a putting down of roots and a bringing to a stand. The age in which the foundation is missing is suspended in the abyss. Supposing that for this time of distress a turning be still in store, that turning can only come about if the world veers from bottom to top, and this clearly means if it turns, starting from the abyss. In the age of the night of the world, the abyss of the world must be experienced and endured.[34]

Again we find this tone of dread and courage. Terror gives courage.

Ultimately, it is not the abyss that is most to be dreaded, but the possibility that the abyss itself be covered over, and distress changed into an infinitely durable absence of distress, from which no essential mutation could any longer issue. "Long is the time of distress of the night of the world. . . . Then the indigent age no longer feels even its indigence."[35] The abyss and dread are still conforting and encouraging in comparison to the greater danger: a mood of complete insensitivity to or forgetting of distress, a world in which the night would be hidden forever by the day of technology and its artificial light, permanently burning. The turning, which remains unaccomplished for lack of a mutation in the essence of technology; the coexistence of calculated distance and of the non-calculable proximity of things; the simultaneity of devastating Enframing and the saving Event, all these traits of the thought of the later Heidegger accord uneasily with a *unique* tonality of terror. It seems that the expectation of an "other history," even if its coming is uncertain, implies other moods than terror which is turned principally towards that which in the present has collapsed, obstructing the future.

Indeed, it is expectation, and more exactly "presentiment" which is designated in the later texts as belonging to divers fundamental climates of present and future thought. This plurality is essential in order to characterize the climate of a transitional period. In *What is Philosophy?* Heidegger emphasizes this: "What we are encountering [today] is uniquely this: different types of moods of thought."[36] Among the forms of contemporary moods he classifies not only hope and despair, but blind confidence in outworn principles and the coldness of planning rationality. As for releasement, the well-known "serenity" (*Gelassenheit*), it is not understood as a mood, but as *the very essence of thought*: letting being be.

How can thought come to itself, detach itself from calculating reason, free itself from the grasp of the will to will? Again, under the impetus and in the context of another fundamental climate which itself has several facets. The transmutation of the will into a resting from will comes only by waiting and patience, but more precisely by "patient nobility of heart" (*die langmutige Edelmut*). Thought is noble when it knows gratitude, knows how to give back to being what being has given to it; thought is patient when it knows how to await change in being and how to accompany it. In the word *Mut* there is at once heart, patience, and courage. The moods of thought are courageous in the sense of a nonheroic courage, but patient, "grateful," full of generosity. In a poem entitled *Instance* (*Instandigkeit*), published first in the dialogue that follows *Discourse on Thinking* and in the collection *Winke*, Heidegger links thought to the "heart" (*das denkende Herz*) and again subjects the very possibility of thought to these two conjoining moods, "patience" and "nobility", adding a third, "generosity": "Assign to your thinking heart the simple patience/of the one generosity/of a noble remembrance."[37]

The most enigmatic of these moods is "nobility." Nobility no doubt is the capacity to recognize provenance, ascendancy, place in the destiny of being. "What has provenance is noble," says the same text. But what is truly noble, as Nietzsche says, is what distinguishes itself in the self-affirming of itself, which does not need to be compared or call upon its letters of nobility. True nobility of thought sets itself beyond terror, for it has learned to "leave metaphysics to itself." Can we not see here a very clear turning of that purely historical mood, terror, towards one or more nonhistorical moods, such as "patient nobility" as the attunement to the region (*Gegnet*), gathered around the thing in its particularity. "All of the hisorical," says Heidegger, "rests in the region."[38]

3 History opens upon wonder and closes upon terror

Nevertheless, it is to the fundamental historical moods – notably that of the beginning of thought, astonishment, and that of the present period or of the transition to that possible "other beginning," terror, that Heidegger pays most attention in his last texts. Of individual anxiety, which in *Being and Time* seemed a necessary condition of access to authenticity for all Dasein of all periods, there is no longer any question in a text such as *What is Philosophy?* Does this mean that there is no longer any individual anxiety at the end of the history of being? Is it entirely reabsorbed into terror? But in that case it would seem that it could no longer fulfill the role of individuating power, which it played in *Being and Time*. Is it in the age of technology a sort of survival from the previous age, the age of the metaphysics of subjectivity? And is it thus perhaps destined to disappear, in as much as in Enframing there is no longer subject nor object? In other words, does anxiety belong only to one period, which would open with Pascalian *effroi* and go by way of Kierkegaard up to *Being and Time* and its Sartrian offshoots? The Greeks certainly did not experience anxiety, but only fright, the first affect of the tragic, for they did not think in terms of reflexivity and self-consciousness.

So let us return to the fundamental historical moods. In the lectures of 1937–38, we find fairly long expositions of these moods, without any allusion to anxiety. One passage sums up these expositions: "In astonishment, the fundamental mood of the first beginning, being comes for the first time to stand in its own form. In terror the basic tonality of the other beginning, there is unveiled, underneath all progressivism and all domination of being, the somber void of goallessness and flight from the first and ultimate decisions."[39]

Marveling at the unveiling of being, held in suspense, in visual stasis by the *eidos*, the *Gestalt*, the figure or visage of being, the Greeks for the first time named the as-such of all beings. That beings *might be*, in the constancy and disclosedness of form, ceaselessly escaping engulfment in non-being, this struck and dazzled them. In volume 45, Heidegger analyzes at length the multiple and complex aspects of that apparently simple mood (he finds thirteen of them!) and shows how the *astonishment*, the maintaining of the wonder in looking, contains the seed of the passing on to metaphysics. Suffice it here to retain three essential points in this description of wonder:

1 Wonder is an unsustainable seesawing back and forth between the habitual and the inhabitual;
2 it reaches its achievement in the specification of the questioning of being as such; and
3 corresponding to such a fundamental mood is a kind of suffering.

1 In wonder, the most familiar becomes the strangest. This strangeness leaves one disarmed. There is no explanation. Wonder makes one *experience* an aporia, an absence of way out, without there being any formulated aporia. Unable to dwell either in the most familiar, or see one's way through the strangest, wonder remains in a swinging back and forth "between two." This movement is

not a contented floating, but reveals a distress as well as a requirement to stop, to be stable. The very space of the swinging back and forth sketches out the total space of the opening. Thought emerges from mood when the latter reveals the *as such* : that it is being as a whole as such that is taken up in the seesawing.

2   From the requirement that the seesawing and the confusion between habitual and inhabitual cease, thought is brought to a *decision*. It must ask about the most habitual, so that this may appear as strange. It must seize and fix that which is accessible or inaccessible, manifest or not, in the open. Thought is *forced* to question (man is only astonished because he is amazed by being as such). The decision as to the limits of being, and questioning in general are events of thought *determined* by mood. The articulation of the question, says Heidegger, is the achievement of wonder. Philosophy, on the other hand, deals with this distress of not-having a way out *by repressing it*.

3   The "fulfillment of distress" means that the answer to astonishment is not itself a sort of indecisive floating or affective fusion with being, but a firm and decided position with respect to being as such. Whence the suffering, for one must be able to *sustain* the fundamental mood and answer it by an appropriate questioning. "Every meditation on being-as-such is essentially a suffering."[40] The undergoing of this suffering is situated "beyond" activity and passivity. It consists in taking onto oneself that overwhelming totality in which questioning is caught up. It consists in the capacity to be transformed by these questions. To suffer is to have the courage to seize that which is given, while being at the same time seized by it. To suffer is also to be able to await the opportune time for this seizing. To quote Hölderlin:

> For every thing needs to be seized,
> By a demi-god or by
> A man, according to the suffering . . .

> For he hates,
> That god who meditates,
> A premature upspringing.[41]

Under the heading of astonishment, does not Heidegger describe his own mood of expectation? For the Greek philosopher, he says, hardly knew how to "suffer." He quickly replaced wonder with curiosity, or the hunger to know. When philosophy is conceived of as a reign (the philosopher-kings), this is the sign that the original distress of wonder is lost, that the beginning has started to decline. The initial wonder has become alien to us. Heidegger seems no longer to believe, as he wrote at the end of *What is Metaphysics?*, that wonder and metaphysics itself are derived from anxiety and founded on the revelation of Nothingness in anxiety. The Greeks' wonder doubtless continues to determine us first through metaphysics, then science. But at the same time as these have been developing a knowledge of beings in their being, they have accustomed us to the exactness and certainty of forms and essences. The fundamental attunement has changed: the surprise and wonder of the Greeks has reversed itself to become Cartesian evidence and assurance. For us, the permanence of forms has become the habitual. Technology goes beyond even certainty. The will to will masters too well the essence of a world totally *produced* to be able to experience its enigmatic emergence. How could it surprise itself? But there is more: the levelling of differences, notably between the near and the far, introduces a new tonality which is a new form of indifference or insensitivity, (the contemporary equivalent, says Heidegger, in *The Seven Hundred Years of Messkirch*, of boredom): the refusal of distress, technological security, whose postulated limit is *the absence of all mood*.

Would terror therefore, rather than horror of the abyss, be the supreme panic that seizes thought in the face of the growing insensitivity of our age? And yet terror is not – and still less is the panic of thought – the dominant tonality. It is as rare as anxiety, but just as crucial. *Terror slumbers*. Thus we must return ceaselessly to the profound analogy between terror and anxiety. Terror is anxiety about the caving in or the eclipse of epochal principles. Just as anxiety happens not as metamorphosis of the subject, but as the sudden placing of the world at a remove – the unreality of intra-world relations which until then had been taken for granted – just so, terror appears as the eclipse of the metaphysical truth which had been reigning until now, the onto-theological truth. Terror emerges from the return to the unsoundable and indeterminable character of being. Again deprived of an essential name that would be imposed, being becomes once more entirely enigmatic. Beings appear very rich, but they are "abandoned to what there is," given over to the emptiness of goal-less fabrications, to the nothingness of power or *Machenschaft*, of technological "machinery," whose nihilistic structure has the circularity of an eternal return.

Thus terror and distress, the distress of a possible "other beginning," are far from being universally perceived by the age itself. The distress in which we find ourselves is most often powerless to make itself heard as a *fundamental* attunement. Of course, there is always a vague, median tonality, but from this mood no thought can emerge. In fact, this mood is no more than the neutralized anxiety that reigns beneath the mask of security-making; it is the "distress of the absence of distress," the false certainty that one has the real "well in hand," that there is not on the whole any need for great disquiet.

Thus it appears that a fundamental attenement like astonishment or terror means at once a mood which calls one to think, and one which does not merely characterize an epoch, but which founds both an epoch and history itself. Nor does this mood merely respond to an epochal situation; far from it, it allows there to be an epoch and is the very source of epochality. "It is called a fundamental disposition or mood, because it transports the one it disposes into a domain upon and within which word, work, and action can be founded as things which come about and which history may initiate," writes Heidegger, apropos of astonishment.[42] Such a mood is temporalization of time and source of thought as well as source of history. This mood is not radically caught in history or floating above history as a "spirit of the times," but is the matrix in which being becomes epoch. As such, it seems to be situated both within and outside of history?

Is there not by this fact a "trans-epochal" privilege attached to anxiety, and that in several respects? If as terror (of the abyss of being), it remains – even if it does not pierce through – the background tonality of our age and of the thought of passage, it is the sole mood which, although it may be experienced in a wholly subjective manner by its capacity to reveal the "self," does not reinstate the self-assurance of subjectivity. Nor is it the simple reflexive self-grasping of consciousness nor the dilution of subjectivity in the world. "In anxiety, 'we are in suspense'. . . . This is why it is not, finally, 'you' nor 'I' who is overtaken by a malaise, but a 'we.' Alone still present in the upsettingness of this suspense where one can hold onto nothing is the pure being 'there'."[43] The "we" translates the German *einem*: "someone." In anxiety the subject no longer knows who he is. He attends at his own deconstruction, so to speak. He is no longer a subject, but an indeterminate being who feels himself invaded by a disquieting strangeness. Anxiety makes manifest the dispossession of the transcendental faculties of man, because it marks a pause in the metaphysical race toward the ceaseless reinforcement of the human subject's powers. This experience of radical fragility and powerlessness forever leaves the human presence exposed to the breath of the abyss. No assurance given by logic or science can forearm us against this dispossession which means that "the deepest finitude is inaccessible to our freedom."[44]

The thought of mood marks the end of the philosophy of will and opens the era of expectation. Expectation of events not measurable, not chronologically nor even epochally situatable and perhaps already outside the history of being: "Original anxiety can at any moment awaken in being-there. For this it does not need an unheard-of event to awaken it. To the depth of its reign corresponds the meaninglessness of what may evoke it."[45] All anxiety is outside memory, outside sequence, outside tradition, and yet it is *transition*.

Mood gives birth to thought because it is the first experience of being, the first hearing of its voice. All thought begins by the test of a putting into situation, responds to a silent vocation. Now anxiety is *par excellence* this test of withdrawal from speech. Does not this withdrawal from speech place not only daily forgetting but also history itself in parentheses? Does not anxiety make us lose our foothold in the epochal world? This placing in parentheses of history causes the self as well as the totality of the age – and of ages and situations – to be seen as suspended possibles. "Anxiety will not suffer being opposed to joy, or to the privileged pleasure of a peaceful activity. It stands this side of such oppositions, in a secret alliance with the serenity and sweetness of creative aspiring."[46] Far from being contrary to serenity, far from being linked with subjectivist willfulness, anxiety maintains a profound affinity with letting-be. Revealing what metaphysics has forgotten, the Nothing, it sets upon the path of a post-metaphysical, hence post-historical relation with being, where thought is reborn, so to speak, from its zero degree.

NOTES

1 In paragraphs 29 and 50 of *Sein und Zeit*, hereafter *SZ*.
2 Notably in the lecture at Cerisy, *Was ist das die Philosophie?* (1955). Hereafter *W.Phil.*
3 Cf. *GA* 39, lecture of 1934–35, *Hölderlins Hymnen "Germanien" un "der Rhein."*
4 Cf. *GA* 45, lecture of 1937–38, *Grundfragen der Philosophie.*
5 *SZ*, p. 137

6   Its elaboration dates from 1930 to 1943.
7   *Vom Wesen der Wahrheit*, chapter V, *Wegmarken* 2, p. 189, *Wegmarken* is hereafter *W*. (= *G.A.*)
8   *Entsprechung* is different from an *adequation*, or *homoiôsis*, for although it implies accord, it does not imply any mimesis. *Entsprechen* means speaking beginning with. With what? With a silence in language, a solicitation that leads to saying what until then had remained to be said.
9   *W*, p. 111.
10 *Was ist das die Philosophie?*, p. 37.
11 In German; but Heidegger advises elsewhere to translate *Stimmung*, in French at least, as "disposition."
12 Astonishment too subsists in our age, but no longer as fundamental or original disposition or mood.
14 *W*, p. 109 (my emphasis).
15 *SZ*, p. 221.
16 *SZ*, p. 248.
17 *GA*, 29/30, p. 102
18 See *SZ*, p. 138.
19 Ibid
20 Ibid, p. 135.
21 *GA*, 39, pp. 140–41 (my emphasis of *comes about*).
22 *WiM*, *W* p. 114.
23 *GA*, 45, p. 159.
24 Op.cit., pp. 152–4.
25 Op.cit., p. 160, cf. also p. 153: "the excess of a gift doubtless more difficult to bear than any loss."
26 *GA* 39, p. 141.
27 *GA* 45, p. 161.
28 Cf. *GA* 39, p. 223.
29 *GA* 45, p. 153.
30 Op.cit., p. 160.
31 *W*, pp. 306–7.
32 Ibid., p. 305.
33 *GA* 45, p. 2.
34 *HW*, pp. 248–9.
35 *HW.*, p. 249.
36 *W i Ph*, p. 43.
37 *GA* 13, p. 65.
38 *GA* 13, p. 62.
39 Ibid., p. 197.
40 Ibid., p. 175
41 Hölderlin, *Aus dem Motivkreis der Titanen*, *SW* IV, p. 215.
42 *GA* 45, p. 170.
43 *W.*, p. 111.
44 *W.*, p. 117.
45 Ibid.
46 Ibid.

9
Heidegger's History of the Being of Equipment

Hubert Dreyfus

1 Introduction

Heidegger's occasional retrospective remarks on *Being and Time* are mostly
limited to pointing out the way *Being and Time* is already on the way to
overcoming metaphysics by reawakening concern with Being,[1] or to acknowledg-
ing *Being and Time*'s transcendental neglect of the history of Being.[2] But one
looks in vain through Heidegger's occasional references to his most celebrated
work for an indication of how we are to fit *Being and Time* into the history of
Being which later Heidegger elaborated. To what extent is *Being and Time* itself
metaphysical? To what extent is it nihilistic? As a step toward answering these
difficult questions, one might well begin by asking a more manageable question:
To what extent is the account of the being of equipment in *Being and Time* a
critique of the ontology of technology and to what extent is it a contribution to
the development of a technological understanding of Being?

In his reflections on Nietzsche, Heidegger singles out the subject/object
distinction as the philosophical development which makes possible modern
technology:

> In this revolutionary objectifying of everything that is, the earth, that
> which first of all must be put at the disposal of representing and setting
> forth, moves into the midst of human positing and analyzing. The earth
> itself can show itself only as the object of assault, an assault that, in human
> willing, establishes itself as unconditional objectification. Nature appears
> everywhere – because willed from out of the essence of Being – as the
> object of technology.[3]

In so far, then, as the analysis of Dasein as Being-in-the-world offers a
phenomenological critique of the subject/object relation, *Being and Time* would
seem to stand in direct opposition to the technological understanding of Being.

Likewise, the central theme of Division I of *Being and Time*, that ready-to-hand equipment is ontologically more fundamental than present-at-hand objects, in that present-at-hand objects can be made intelligible as privative (i.e., decontextualized) modes of equipment, whereas equipmental relations can never be built up by adding value predicates to present-at-hand objects, is directly opposed to the implicit ontology of objective thought. Calculating, logistic intelligibility is criticized by showing its dependence upon the nonformalizable everyday intelligibility of the primordial way human beings encounter entities within the world.[4]

The phenomenological description of our primordial way of encountering entities purports to light up a way of being which has not changed since the beginning of our history. In his lectures from the period of *Being and Time*, Heidegger does not hesitate to read this everyday understanding of beings as equipment back into the meaning of *ousia*.

> That which first of all constantly lies-before in the closest circle of human activity and accordingly is constantly disposable is the whole of all *things of use* with which we constantly have to do, the whole of all those existent things which are themselves meant to be used on one another, *the implement that is employed* and constantly used products of nature: house and yard, forest and field, sun, light and heat. What is thus tangibly present for dealing with is reckoned by everyday experience as that which is, as a being, in the primary sense . . . [T]he pre-philosophical proper meaning of *ousia* . . . Accordingly *a being* is synonymous with the present-at-hand.[5]

It is precisely the loss of the everyday understanding of the priority of things of use, reflected in Descartes' subject/object metaphysics, which provides the conditions for the rise of modern science:

> We first arrive at science as research when and only when truth has been transformed into the certainty of representation.

> What it is to be is for the first time defined as the objectiveness of representing, and truth is first defined as the certainty of representing, in the metaphysics of Descartes. (*QCT*, 127)

Being and Time, then, sets out to rescue beings from objectivity and representation by returning to a pre-philosophical, ahistorical understanding of equipment.

So it might have seemed in 1927, but Heidegger's later understanding of the history of Western thought reveals that things may not be so simple. Indeed, there are hints scattered throughout Heidegger's later works that in opposing the subject/object ontology by an appeal to the primacy of equipment, *Being and Time* was itself a formulation of the penultimate stage of technology.

As early as *The Origin of the Work of Art* – the only sustained treatment of equipmentality after *Being and Time* – Heidegger notes "the possibility . . . that differences relating to the history of Being may also be present in the way equipment *is*."[6] This immediately casts suspicion on the ahistorical transcendental priority given to equipment in *Being and Time*. And, indeed, at this same point in the text Heidegger cautions against "making thing and work prematurely into subspecies of equipment" (*PLT*, 32).

Heidegger, however, never works out a history of the being of equipment, so we will have to construct it from hints. The most important of these hints are Heidegger's discussion of the Greek notion of *techné* at the beginning of our history and his remark in "Science and Reflection" that, in the technological understanding of the being, subject and object no longer stand in a relation of representation but are both absorbed into a total systematic ordering. ("Both subject and object are sucked up as standing-reserve") (*QCT*, 173). It follows that opposing the Cartesian subject/object distinction in terms of an account of Dasein as a user of equipment becomes an ambiguous form of opposition, for it is no longer clear whether such an analysis offers a critique of technology in the form of a transcendental account of the pre-technological everyday understanding of equipment, or whether, under the guise of a transcendental account of everyday activity, such an analysis reflects a transition in the history of the way equipment *is* which prepares the way for technology. In other words, it is not clear whether *Being and Time* opposes technology or promotes it.

The answer to this question can only be found in a detailed analysis of the phenomenology of equipment and worldhood offered in *Being and Time*. As we turn to *Being and Time* our *Vorgriff* will be the hypothesis that the analysis of equipment in *Being and Time* is neither pre-technological nor fully technological, but rather, that *Being and Time* plays a transitional role in the history of the being of equipment. That, far from resisting the modern tendency to transform everything into standing-reserve, the understanding of the being of the ready-to-hand in *Being and Time* leaves equipment available for the assault of technology, the way the Cartesian understanding of the being of the present-at-hand made nature available for the assault of scientific research. Thus, early Heidegger might be said to have a privileged place in the transition from *techné* to technology, which corresponds to Descartes' privileged place in the transition from *theorea* to modern science.

2   Sketch of a history of the being of equipment

The way equipment *is* no doubt goes through as many stages as there are epochs in the history of Being. For our purposes, however, it will suffice to distinguish three stages. Sociologically we might equate these three periods with craftsmanship, industrialization, and cybernetic control, which find expression, respectively, in the Greek notion of *techné*, pragmatism, and systems theory as the basis of global planning.

Distinguishing three stages in the history of the being of equipment enables us to avoid two simple interpretations of the place of equipment in *Being and Time* which at first seem attractive. One reading notes the similarity between Heidegger's remark in *Being and Time* that "the wood is a forest of timber; the mountain a quarry of rock, the river is water-power" (*BT*, 100), and his later observations that in the clearing opened up by technology "the river is a . . . water power supplier" (*QCT*, 16) and "nature becomes a gigantic gasoline station."[7] This interpretation concludes that the identification of Nature in *Being and Time* as "an entity within-the-world which is proximally ready-to-hand" (BT, 128) shows that the understanding of equipment in *Being and Time* is already fully technological. The opposite interpretation, on the other hand, sees no step-wise history of the being of equipment but only a total opposition between the pre-technological and the technological. Since, according to Heidegger, "calculated being makes beings into what can be mastered by modern, mathematically structured technology, which is something *essentially* different from every other hitherto known use of tools,"[8] and since *Being and Time* explicitly denies the possibility of a "mathematical functionalization" (*BT*, 122) of the ready-to-hand, this interpretation concludes that *Being and Time* presents an account of man's perennial tool using stance which is radically opposed to the technological understanding of equipment.

The very possibility of these two readings suggests that *Being and Time* offers an understanding of the being of equipment which hovers ambiguously between that of craftsmanship and technology and so temps readers to identify *Being and Time* with one or the other, while at the same time resisting either assimilation. We will now attempt to bring the intermediate position of *Being and Time* into focus by comparing what later Heidegger says about the Greek and the technological understanding of use, equipment, and nature, with the account of these phenomena in *Being and Time*. Only then will we be in a position to move from these ontic considerations to an ontological account of the difference between the world of the craftsman, worldhood in *Being and Time*, and the way of revealing of technology.

The essential characteristic of equipment at any period is that it is used, but usefulness itself turns out to have a history. In *What is Called Thinking?* Heidegger attempts to recover Parmenides' understanding of *chré* by discussing the early Greek understanding of "the useful."

> "To use" means, first, to let a thing be what it is and how it is. To let it be this way requires that the used thing be cared for in its essential nature – we do so by responding to the demands which the used thing makes manifest in the given instance.[9]

> "Using" does not mean the mere utilizing, using up, exploiting. Utilization is only the degenerate and debauched form of use. When we handle a thing, for example, our hand must fit itself to the thing. Use implies fitting response. (*WCT*, 187)

The degenerate form of use – exploiting – clearly corresponds to the technological attitude in which equipment is only insofar as it is at our disposal – otherwise it is to be ignored or disposed of. To describe this "debauched" form Heidegger paraphrases Rilke on the *Ersatz*:

> [O]bjects are produced to be used up. The more quickly they are used up, the greater becomes the necessity to replace them even more quickly and

more readily . . . What is constant in things produced as objects merely for consumption is: the substitute – *Ersatz*. (*PLT*, 130)

Equipment in *Being and Time* is not assimilable to either of the above extremes. It is characterized by disposability: "Equipment . . . is manipulable in the broadest sense and at our disposal" (*BT*, 98). A hammer, for example, is defined in *Being and Time* in terms of its function – its in-order-to. On this view it makes no sense to speak of equipment's essential nature, and, in spite of the manual implications of *Zuhandenheit*, in all the discussions of hammering there is no mention of hands. There is, in fact, no place for a "fitting response." Yet the hammer is not something standing by to be used-up and disposed of like a styrofoam cup, a ballpoint pen, or the latest type of fever thermometer. Rather, there is still talk of taking care of equipment – not the way the craftsman takes care of his personal tools, but the way the foreman takes care of industrial equipment. Thus, when manipulation ceases, care "can take on a more precise kind of circumspection, such as 'inspecting', checking up on what has been attained, or looking over the 'operations'" (*BT*, 409). This seems to suggest a three-stage progression, or better a degeneration, in the history of equipment, from use, to utility as fulfilling a function, to using-up as exploitation.

The above decline from craftsmanship to industrial production to technology can be seen even more clearly if we turn from the equipment the craftsman uses to the equipment he produces. The craftsman, Heidegger tells us, must be understood as responding to his materials:

[A] true cabinetmaker . . . makes himself answer and respond above all to the different kinds of wood and to the shapes slumbering within wood – to wood as it enters into man's dwelling with all the hidden riches of its nature. In fact, this relatedness to wood is what maintains the whole craft.

Without that relatedness, the craft will never be anything but empty busywork, any occupation with it will be determined exclusively by business concerns. (*WCT*, 21, 22)

Indeed, without concern for the nature of its materials, craftsmanship turns into industrial production:

[W]hat maintains and sustains even this handicraft is not the mere manipulation of tools, but the relatedness to wood. But where in the manipulations of the industrial worker is there any relatedness to such things as the shapes slumbering within wood? (*WCT*, 23)

In *Being and Time* we find no place for the resistance and the reliability of equipment – only its on-going functioning or its breakdown. There is no mention of "the hidden riches of nature." In the language of the later Heidegger, *Being and Time* has no place for the withdrawal and resistance of the Earth. As Heidegger remarks in discussing Van Gogh's painting of the peasant's shoes, as if he were repudiating the simple pragmatism of *Being and Time*:

The equipmental quality of the equipment consists indeed in its usefulness. But this usefulness itself rests in the abundance of an essential being of the equipment. We call it reliability. By virtue of this reliability the peasant woman is made privy to the silent call of the earth . . .

The usefulness of equipment is . . . the essential consequence of reliability. (PLT, 34, 35)

If equipmentality is equated merely with usefulness as utility without resistance or reliability, the stage is set for technology. Everything becomes available for cost/benefit analysis.

[T]he setting-upon that challenges forth the energies of nature is an expediting. . . . [E]xpediting is always itself directed from the beginning toward furthering something else, i.e., toward driving on to the maximum yield at the minimum expense. (*QCT*, 15)

Having no nature of its own, industrialized equipment is ready to be absorbed into the constant restructuring which is the final form of technological organization – beyond objectification, and even beyond the fixed functions of the ready-to-hand.

Everywhere everything is ordered to stand by, to be immediately at hand, indeed to stand there just so that it may be on call for a further ordering. Whatever is ordered about in this way has its own standing. We call it the standing-reserve [*Bestand*] . . . Whatever stands by in the sense of standing-reserve no longer stands over against us as object. (*WCT*, 17)

Heidegger's notion of *Bestand* enables us to distinguish three ways that nature can be understood. For the first thinkers, according to Heidegger, nature was self-contained.

For the Greeks, *physis* is the first and the essential name for beings themselves and as a whole. For them the being is what flourishes on its own, in no way compelled, what rises and comes forward, and what goes back into itself and passes away.[10]

In *Being and Time* nature is encountered as a source of raw material.

In the environment certain entities become accessible which are always ready-to-hand, but which, in themselves, do not need to be produced. Hammer, tongs, and needle, refer in themselves to steel, iron, metal, mineral, wood, in that they consist of these. In equipment that is used, 'Nature' is discovered along with it by that use . . . (*BT*, 100)

In advanced technology, nature is attacked and transformed to insure that it will always be available for use and further development.

[A] tract of land is challenged into the putting out of coal and ore. The earth now reveals itself as a coal mining district, the soil as a mineral deposit. (*QCT*, 14)

"Challenging forth into revealing . . . concerns nature, above all, as the chief storehouse of the standing energy reserve."(*QCT*, 21)

With respect to the being of nature, then, *Being and Time* shows itself to be again transitional. When *Being and Time* describes the river as waterpower, there is no suggestion that this power is a gift, but neither is there talk of a hydroelectric powerstation which dams up the river in order to convert it into a pure energy reservoir. But to understand fully the significance of *Being and Time*'s transitional position we must ask: Does *Being and Time* contend that the river is, *among other things*, a source of energy, or does it hold that the use of the river as water-power is *the primordial way* the river is encountered?

Here *Being and Time* reveals its profound ambiguity. At first it seems that approaching nature in terms of its utility – what one might call the pragmatism of *Being and Time* – is only one ontic way of encountering it. Indeed, according to a puzzling passage early in *Being and Time*, there are at least three ways of encountering nature. Nature can be encountered as ready-to-hand, present-at-hand, or as the Nature which "stirs and strives":

As the "environment" is discovered, the "Nature" thus discovered is encountered too. If its kind of Being as ready-to-hand is disregarded, this "Nature" itself can be discovered and defined simply in its pure presence-at-hand. But when this happens, the Nature which 'stirs and strives', which assails us and enthralls us as landscape, remains hidden. (*BT*, 100)

Yet, the rest of *Being and Time* concentrates on showing that the way of being of nature, presence-at-hand, must be a privative mode of readiness-to-hand: "The entity which Descartes is trying to grasp ontologically and in principle with his '*extensio*', is rather such as to become discoverable first of all by going through an entity within-the-world which is proximally ready-to-hand – Nature" (*BT*, 128). The nature that stirs and strives (*physis*) is never mentioned again.

These hesitations and contradictions regarding the place of nature, must finally be settled on the level of ontology. Thus Heidegger's pragmatic view of Nature only becomes clear in the discussion of reality at the end of Division I:

The "Nature" by which we are "surrounded" is, of course, an entity within-the-world; but the kind of Being which it shows belongs neither to the ready-to-hand nor to what is present-at-hand as "Things of Nature." No matter how this Being of "Nature" may be interpreted, *all* the modes of Being of entities within-the-world are founded ontologically upon the worldhood of the world, and accordingly upon the phenomenon of Being-in-the-world. (*BT*, 254)

Nature is neither present-at-hand nor ready-to-hand, yet the being of nature must be understood as founded upon worldhood. To understand worldhood, however, Heidegger tells us, we must begin with an account of equipment. Now the primary point which distinguishes equipment from "mere things" is its thoroughgoing interrelatedness: "To the being of any equipment there always belongs a totality of equipment, in which it can be this equipment that it is" (*BT*, 97). What it is to be a hammer is just to be involved in appropriate ways with nails, carpenters, furniture, houses, families, and so on. In other words, what an item of equipment *is* is entirely dependent on how it is incorporated into a total equipment context. Thus:

> As the Being of something ready-to-hand, an involvement is itself disco-vered only on the basis of the prior discovery of a totality of involvements. So in any involvement that has been discovered (that is, in anything ready-to-hand which we encounter), what we have called the "worldly character" of the ready-to-hand has been discovered beforehand. (*BT*, 118)

At this point, in a move whose full implications only become apparent later, Heidegger passes from speaking of a totality of involvements as prior to any *equipment*, to the same totality as the "primordial totality," i.e., the structure of the world.

> The "for-the-sake-of-which" signifies an "in-order-to"; this in turn, a "towards-this"; the latter, an "in-which" of letting something be involved; and that in turn, the "with-which" of an involvement. These relationships are bound up with one another as a primordial totality . . . The relational totality of this signifying we call "*significance*." This is what makes up the structure of the world. (*BT*, 120)

Thus, in spite of Heidegger's acknowledgement that nature is not ready-to-hand, it follows that *all* beings including those of nature are founded ontologically, i.e., get their intelligibility from the structure of the equipmental totality.

Heidegger clearly wished to resist this conclusion. In a torturous footnote discussing Nature in *The Essence of Reasons*, he protests that "a study of the ontological structure of 'environmental' being (in so far as it is discovered as tool)" is a "*preliminary characterization*" of the phenomenon of world." Such an account, Heidegger assures us, only "prepares the way for the transcendental problem of world."[11] Yet in *Being and Time*, Division II, chapter 4, when the temporal schema is introduced in its transcendental role as "the existential-temporal condition for the possibility of the world" (*BT*, 416), the "present" dimension of the horizontal schema is still the in-order-to and Heidegger repeats on this transcendental level the claim of Division I that "significance-relationships . . . determine the structure of the world" (*BT*, 417). Thus, even on the transcendental level, the world is equated with the totality of involve-ments, and all entities, including Nature, can only be encountered as they show up in the equipmental world.

In spite of Heidegger's published disclaimers, the dangerous consequences of the ontological priority given to Dasein's practical activity are everywhere evident in *Being and Time*. Even language is ontologically grounded in the totality of equipment: "[I]n significance . . . there lies the ontological condition which makes it possible for Dasein, as something which understands and interprets, to disclose such things as 'significations'; upon these, in turn, is founded the Being of words and of language" (*BT*, 121).

Here the pragmatic implications are so unacceptable that, rather than try to retroactively reinterpret *Being and Time*, Heidegger is obliged to repudiate the priority of the equipmental context. In his own copy of *Being and Time* he wrote at this point: "Untrue. Language is not layered, but rather *is* the primordial essence of truth as there."[12]

The full technological tendency implied in the ontological priority granted to the structure of the totality of involvement as the structure of the world only becomes apparent, however, when we investigate in slow motion Heidegger's sleight of hand with the notion of totality. When introducing the notion of equipment, Heidegger tells us that a condition of the possibility of equipment is that it functions within a relatively autonomous local context (the workshop, the room, etc). In *Being and Time* Heidegger calls these contexts "regions." "Something like a region must first be discovered if there is to be any possibility of allotting or coming across places for a totality of equipment that is circumspectively at one's disposal" (*BT*, 136). But, to complete the ontological project of *Being and Time*, Heidegger must show "how the aroundness of the environment, the specific spatiality of entities encountered within the environment, is founded upon the worldhood of the world" (*BT*, 136). He thus expands the local context to a single overarching totality. He recognizes that this tendency to totalize is a specifically modern phenomenon whose full meaning he realizes has not yet been revealed:

> *In Dasein there lies an essential tendency towards closeness.* All the ways in which we speed things up, as we are more or less compelled to do today, push us on towards the conquest of remoteness. (*BT*, 140)[13]

It is as if in *Being and Time* Dasein is uprooted from the dwelling in nearness which is illustrated by later Heidegger in his description of "the bridge which *gathers* the earth as landscape around the stream" (*PLT*, 152). Indeed, the totality of equipment more closely resembles "the highway bridge . . . tied into the network of long-distance traffic" (*PLT*, 152), for equipment in *Being and Time* is finally taken to be dependent on one total network in which it is a node. This is a complete reversal of the ancient understanding evoked by Heidegger, in which the thing is not a slot in a global system but rather that which organizes a local region around itself. "[T]he bridge does not first come to a location to stand in it; rather, a location comes into existence only by virtue of the bridge . . . *Accordingly, spaces receive their being from locations and not from 'space'*" (*PLT*, 154). The failure to realise "the origin of space in the properties peculiar to site"[14], plus the ontologizing of the pragmatic structure of temporality, enables

Heidegger in *Being and Time* to treat spatiality as a mode of temporality – a form of metaphysical violence he later retracts. ("The attempt in *Being and Time*, section 70, to derive human spatiality from temporality is untenable" (*OTB*, 23)).

The idea that in the technological world equipment more and more comes to fit together in one single system is already a step from the relatively autonomous and autochthonous workshop of the craftsman towards the uprooted interconnectedness of industrial mass production. Its final achievement would be a world system under the feedback control of cybernetics. Heidegger makes a similar point in *The Question Concerning Technology*, when he criticizes Hegel's definition of the machine as an autonomous tool and contrasts the autonomous tools of the craftsman with the total ordering characteristic of technology.

> When applied to the tools of the craftsman, [Hegel's] characterization is correct. Characterized in this way, however, the machine is not thought at all from out of the essence of technology within which it belongs. Seen in terms of the standing-reserve, the machine is completely unautonomous, for it has its standing only from the ordering of the orderable. (*QCT*, 17)

In *The Question Concerning Technology* the total system of ordering in which all beings are caught up, stored, and endlessly switched around is called the *Gestell*. This technological kind of revealing is contrasted with the world of the craftsman. In fact, according to later Heidegger the technological totality is no world at all. "[I]n the ordering of the standing-reserve, the truth of Being remains denied as world." (*QCT*, 48).

Heidegger's identification of the "phenomenon of world" (with its structure, worldhood) with one interconnected referential totality in *Being and Time* can thus be seen as a transitional stage. By highlighting the interrelationship between all items of equipment and by defining equipment by its position in this referential totality, *Being and Time* denies localness, thus removing the last barrier to global totalization, and preparing the way for the "total mobilization of all beings" which, according to later Heidegger, makes up the essence of technology.[15]

3   Conclusion

Seen in the light of the relation of nature and technology revealed by later Heidegger, *Being and Time* appears in the history of the being of equipment not just as a transition but as *the* decisive step towards technology. (A step later Heidegger tries, unconvincingly, to read back into Nietzsche.) As later Heidegger sees it, at the beginning of our history *techné* was subordinated to nature or *physis*:

> If man tries to win a foothold and establish himself among the beings (*physis*) to which he is exposed, if he proceeds to master beings in this way or that way, then his advance against beings is borne and guided by a

knowledge of them. Such knowledge is called *techné* . . . (*NI*, 81) [T]he bringing forth of artworks as well as utensils is an irruption by the man who knows and who goes forward in the midst of *physis* and upon its basis (*NI*, 82)

In *Being and Time*, however, the relation between *physis* and *techné* is transposed: Nature can be encountered only as it fits, or fails to fit, into the referential totality. This is a crucial reversal of the Greek understanding, for the "going-forward" of *techné* "thought in Greek fashion, is no kind of attack; it lets what is already coming to presence arrive" (*NI*, 82).[16] In *Being and Time* there is no outright attack but no openness to arrival either. But it is precisely this lack of receptivity to "the nature that stirs and strives" which leaves open, indeed, encourages, the kind of attack and reordering of nature which encounters natural objects as standing reserve.

This can be seen even more clearly if we look at the role assigned to care by the early Greeks, *Being and Time*, and technology. According to later Heidegger we must "conceive of the innermost essence of *techné* . . . as . . . care" (*NI*, 164). For the Greeks "such carefulness is more than practiced dilligence; it is the mastery of a composed resolute *openness to beings*" (*NI*, 164). This sounds at first exactly like the characterization of authentic care in *Being and Time*. But Heidegger hastens to add: "The unity of *melete* and *techné* . . . characterizes the basic posture of the forward-reaching disclosure of Dasein, which seeks to ground beings *on their own terms*" (*NI*, 165). This qualification shows again that in *Being and Time* the relationship between Dasein and beings is the reverse of that laid out by later Heidegger. In *Being and Time* beings are discovered in terms of Dasein's concerns. The care structure is definitive of Dasein, the being whose being is an issue for it, and beings are disclosed in terms of Dasein's possibilities. The interconnection between significance, the totality of involvements, world-hood, and Dasein's possibilities as conditions for encountering beings is laid out in Division II.

> Any discovering of a totality of involvements goes back to a "for-the-sake-of-which"; and on the understanding of such a "for-the-sake-of-which" is based in turn the understanding of significance as the disclosedness of the current world. In seeking shelter, sustenance, livelihood, we do so "for-the-sake-of" constant possibilities of Dasein which are very close to it; upon these the entity for which its own Being is an issue, has already projected itself. (BT, 344)

To be sure, Dasein is not a subject and the for-the-sake-of-which is not a goal. But this only shows that in *Being and Time* Heidegger already left behind the understanding of care as individual self-assertion which gradually becomes explicit in the development of objectivity from Descartes to Nietzsche, and finds expression in early industrialization. For Rilke, Heidegger tells us, modern "'caring' has the character of purposeful self-assertion by the ways and means of unconditional production" (*PLT*, 120). Such willful self-assertion still resists impersonal, global technology. The account of worldhood in *Being and Time*, however, removes every vestige of resistance – that of *physis* and earth, as well as that of will and subjectivity – to the technological tendency to treat all beings (even man) as resources. Nothing stands in the way of the final possibility that for Dasein the only issue left becomes ordering for the sake of order itself. This is the understanding of Being definitive of technological nihilism, an understanding prepared but not consummated by the account of equipment in *Being and Time*.

NOTES

1 See Martin Heidegger, "Letter on humanism," *Basic Writings*, ed. David Farrell Krell, New York: Harper & Row, 1977.

2 Martin Heidegger, *The end of philosophy*, New York: Harper & Row, 1954, p. 15, where Heidegger speaks of the questions of *Being and Time* as "transcendental-hermeneutic questions not yet thought in terms of the history of Being."

3 Martin Heidegger, "The Word of Nietzsche: 'God is Dead'," in *The Question Concerning Technology and Other Essays*, trans. William Lovitt, New York: Harper & Row, 1977, p. 100. Hereafter, cited in text as *QCT*.

4 For an elaboration and application of Heidegger's argument, see Hubert Dreyfus, *What Computers Can't Do*, Cambridge: MIT Press, 1992.

5 Martin Heidegger, Basic Problems of Phenomenology, Bloomington: Indiana University Press, 1982, pp. 108, 109. Heidegger would, however, be reluctant to read our everyday understanding of equipment back into prehistory. As he notes in *Being and Time*, trans. John Macquarrie and Edward Robinson, New York: Harper & Row, 1962, p. 113: "Perhaps even readiness-to-hand and equipment have nothing to contribute as ontological clues in interpreting the primitive world . . . " *Being and Time* cited hereafter in text as *BT*.

6 Martin Heidegger, "The origin of the work of art," in *Poetry, Language, Thought*, trans. Albert Hofstadter, New York: Harper & Row, 1971, p. 32. Hereafter, *PLT*.

7 Martin Heidegger, *Discourse on Thinking*, trans. by John Anderson and E. Hans Freund, New York: Harper & Row, 1959, p. 50.

8 Martin Heidegger, *An Introduction to Metaphysics*, trans. Ralph Manheim, Garden City, New York: Anchor Books, 1969, p. 162.

9 Martin Heidegger, *What is Called Thinking?*, trans. Fred D. Wieck and J. Glenn Gray, New York: Harper & Row, 1968, p. 191. Hereafter, cited in text as *WCT*.

10 Martin Heidegger, *Nietzsche*, Vol. 1, New York: Harper & Row, 1979, p. 81, hereafter cited in text as *NI*.

11 Martin Heidegger, *The Essence of Reasons*, trans. Terrence Malick, Evanston: Northwestern University Press, 1969, p. 81.

12 *"Unwarhr. Sprache ist nicht aufgestockt, sondern* ist *ursprüngliche Wesen der Wahrheit als Da."*. Martin Heidegger, *Sein und Zeit*, Tübingen: Niemeyer Verlag, 1977, p. 442.

13 From the point of view of the account of Falling in *Being and Time*, it might seem that this tendency to bring everything close is the result of curiosity (BT, p. 216), and so would be overcome by authentic resoluteness as described in Division II. Indeed, we are told in Division II that resolute Dasein is plunged into its own concrete, local situation. ("Resoluteness brings the Being of the 'there' into the existence of its Situation." *BT*, p. 347). But it is also clear in Division II that this characteristic of resolute Dasein does not change the fact that the only clearing for encountering entities conceivable within the framework of *Being and Time* remains the public referential totality laid out by the one (das Man). ("The one itself articulates the referential context of significance," *BT*, p. 167.) In Division II, Heidegger states explicity: "As phenomena which are examples of Being among, we have chosen the

using, manipulation, and producing of the ready-to-hand . . . In this kind of concern Dasein's authentic existence too maintains itself, even when for such existence this concern is 'a matter of indifference'." (*BT*, p. 403)

14 Martin Heidegger, *On Time and Being*, trans. Joan Stambaugh, New York: Harper & Row, 1972, p. 23. Hereafter, cited in text as *OTB*.

15 Martin Heidegger, *The Question of Being*, trans. Jean T. Wilde and William Kluback, New Haven: College & University Press, 1958.

16 That this is, indeed, a reversal of the traditional ontological view inherited from the Greeks, is clear in Heidegger's lectures from the Summer Semester of 1925, *History of the Concept of Time*, tr. T. Kisiel, Bloomington: Indiana University Press, 1985, p. 199. "It will perhaps be said that just this present-at-hand, environmental nature, is the most real, the authentic reality of the world. The work-world bears within itself references to an entity which in the end makes it clear that it – the work-world, what is of concern – is not the primary entity after all . . . This conclusion, it seems, cannot be avoided. But what does it mean to say that the world of nature is the most real? The environmental references, in which nature is present primarily in a worldly way, tell us rather the reverse: nature as reality can only be understood on the basis of worldhood. The entitative relationships of dependence of worldly entities among themselves do not coincide with the founding relationships in being. . . For the time being, it can only be said that even the presence-at-hand of nature as environing world, that is, as it is experienced quite implicitly and naturally, that just this presence is first discovered in its sense and is there upon and in the world of concern."

10
Work and *Weltanschauung*: The Heidegger Controversy from a German Perspective

Jürgen Habermas

Prefatory note

This text was originally written as the foreword to the German edition of Victor Farias' book, *Heidegger et le Nazisme* (1988). I believe a separate publication is warranted because certain aspects of the general issue have not been sufficiently distinguished in previous discussion. The moral judgment of a later generation, which in any case is called forth more strongly by Heidegger's behavior after 1945 than by his political engagement during the Nazi period, must not be allowed to cloud our view of the substantial content of his philosophical work. But just as little should the legitimate distinction between person and work cut off the question of whether – and, if so, to what extent – that work itself may be affected, in its philosophical substance, by the intrusion of elements from what we Germans call "*Weltanschauung*" – an ideologically tinged worldview. This question takes a clearer shape in light of the historical investigations of Farias and Hugo Ott. But it cannot be answered with the methods of historical analysis alone.

1 In his excellent critical bibliography of Heidegger's writings, Winfried Franzen introduces the section on "Heidegger and Nazism" with these words: "Meanwhile, the Federal Republic has also produced a whole series of pertinent discussions of the 'case of Heidegger'; . . . A genuinely open and unhindered discussion, however, has not yet taken place in Germany, notably not in the 'camp' of the Heidegger school itself." That was in 1976.[1] The situation has since changed. Discussion has been sparked by, among other things, the publication in 1983 of notes in which Heidegger sought to vindicate, from the point of view of 1945, his political conduct in 1933–34. (A reprint of the "Rektoratsrede," Heidegger's inaugural address as Rector of the University of Freiburg, is also included.)[2] Most important, the work of the Freiburg historian Hugo Ott[3] and of

the philosopher Otto Pöggeler, himself associated with Heidegger for decades,[4] have brought new facts to light, as did Karl Löwith's report (set down in 1940) of a 1936 meeting with Heidegger in Rome.[5] In addition, the ongoing publication of the *Gesamtausgabe*, the complete edition of Heidegger's works, has shed light on the lectures and writing from the thirties and forties, themselves still not published in their entirety.[6] It required, however, the efforts of a Chilean professor in Berlin to make, at last, a political biography of Heidegger available in Germany – by way of its French translation, however, and with recourse to the Spanish original. This detour through the viewpoint of a foreigner may provide the most appropriate response to the cramped discussion Franzen noted in Germany; the resulting distance of Farias' work, which must ultimately speak for itself, from the current German context may justify my attempt to relate the two.

From the perspective of a contemporary German reader, one consideration is particularly important from the start. Illumination of the political conduct of Martin Heidegger cannot and should not serve the purpose of a global deprecia- tion of his thought. As a personality of recent history, Heidegger comes, like every other such personality, under the judgment of the historian. In Farias' book as well, actions and courses of conduct are presented that suggest a detached evaluation of Heidegger's character. But in general, as members of a later generation who cannot know how *we* would have acted under conditions of a political dictatorship, we do well to refrain from moral judgments on actions and omissions from the Nazi era. Karl Jaspers, a friend and contemporary of Heidegger, was in a different position. In a report that the denazification committee of the University of Freiburg requested at the end of 1945, he passed judgment on Heidegger's "mode of thinking": it seemed to him "in its essence unfree, dictatorial, uncommunicative."[7] This judgment is itself no less informat- ive about Jaspers than about Heidegger. In making evaluations of this sort Jaspers, as can be seen from his book on Friedrich Schelling, was guided by the strict maxim that whatever truth a philosophical doctrine contains must be mirrored in the mentality and lifestyle of the philosopher. This rigorous conception of the unity of work and person seems to me inadequate to the autonomy of thought and, indeed, to the general history of the reception and influence of philosophical thought.[8] I do not mean by this to deny all internal connection between philosophical works and the biographical contexts from which they come – or to limit the responsibility attached to an author, who during his lifetime can always react to unintended consequences of his utte- rances.

But Heidegger's work has long since detached itself from his person. Herbert Schnädelbach is right to begin his presentation of philosophy in Germany with the comment that our "contemporary philosophy has been decisively shaped by . . . Ludwig Wittgenstein's *Tractatus logico-philosophicus* (1921), Georg Lukács' *Geschichte und Klassenbewusstsein* [*History and Class-Consciousness*] (1923) and Martin Heidegger's *Sein und Zeit* [*Being and Time*] (1926)."[9] With *Being and Time*, Heidegger proved himself, almost overnight, to be a thinker of the first rank. Even philosophers at some remove, such as Georg Misch, immediately recognized the "indefatigability" and "craftsmanship" of a leading philosopher. In *Being and Time*, Heidegger did nothing less than meld and recast,

in an original way, the competing intellectual movements of Diltheyan hermeneutics and Husserlian phenomenology, so as to take up the pragmatic themes of
Max Scheler and bring them into a postmetaphysical, historicizing overcoming of
the philosophy of subjectivity.[10] This new venture in thought was all the more
amazing because it seemed to allow the impassioned themes of the Kierkegaardian dialectic of existence to engage the classical Aristotelian philosophical
problematic. From today's standpoint, Heidegger's new beginning still presents
probably the most profound turning point in German philosophy since Hegel.

While the *detranscendentalizing* of the world-constituting ego carried through in
Being and Time was unprecedented, the *critique of reason* that set in later and built
on Nietzsche was the idealist counterpart – somewhat delayed – to a materialist
critique of instrumental reason that was itself indebted to Hegel while productively combining Marx with Weber. Heidegger paid for the wealth of his later
insights, which among other things revealed the ontological premises of modern
thought, with a narrowing of his view to the dimension of a resolutely stylized
history of metaphysics. This abstraction from the contexts of social life may be
one reason for Heidegger's reliance on whatever interpretations of the age
happened by, unfiltered by any knowledge of the social sciences. The more real
history disappeared behind Heideggerian "historicity," the easier it was for
Heidegger to adopt a naive, yet pretentious, appeal to "diagnoses of the present"
taken up *ad hoc*.

With his detranscendentalizing mode of thought and his critique of metaphysics, Heidegger, whose work was of course criticized but whose position
remained uncontested during the thirties and forties, had an *uninterrupted* impact
on German universities. This academic, school-founding impact continued until
the late sixties. Its importance is well documented in a collection of essays keyed
to "perspectives on the interpretation of his work," which Pöggeler edited for
Heidegger's eightieth birthday.[11] The Heideggerian school retained its dominant
position during the long incubation of the Federal Republic, to the beginning of
the sixties; when analytical philosophy of language (with Wittgenstein, Rudolf
Carnap, and Karl Popper) and Western Marxism (with Max Horkheimer,
Theodor Adorno, and Ernst Bloch) then regained footing in the universities, that
was really only a delayed return to normalcy.

Still more significant than its academic influence on several generations of
scholars and students is the inspirational glow of Heidegger's work on independent minds who selected particular themes and made them fruitful in systematic
contexts of their own. The early Heidegger, to begin with, had influence on the
existentialism and phenomenological anthropology of Jean-Paul Sartre and
Maurice Merleau-Ponty. In Germany something similar holds for the philosophical hermeneutics of Hans-Georg Gadamer. Productive developments continue
into my generation as well, for example, with Karl-Otto Apel, Michael Theunissen, and Ernst Tugendhat.[12] Heidegger's critique of reason has been taken up
more strongly in France and the United States, for example, by Jacques Derrida,
Richard Rorty, and Hubert Dreyfus.

Questionable political conduct on the part of a thinker certainly throws a
shadow on his work. But the Heideggerian *oeuvre*, especially the thought in *Being
and Time*, has attained a position of such eminence among the philosophical ideas

of our century that it is simply foolish to think that the substance of the work could be discredited, more than five decades later, by political assessments of Heidegger's fascist commitments.

So what interest, apart from the detached one of historical and scientific concern, can examination of Heidegger's political past claim today – especially in the Federal Republic? I think that these matters deserve our attention primarily from two points of view. *On the one hand*, Heidegger's attitude to his own past *after* 1945 exemplifies a state of mind that persistently characterized the history of the Federal Republic until well into the sixties. It is a mentality that survives up to the present day, as in the so-called historian's debate about revisionistic interpretations of German war crimes.[13] In order to ferret out what is symptomatic of deeper matters in Heidegger's refusal to change his mind and in his unwavering practice of denial,[14] we must inform ourselves of what Heidegger, to his death, repressed, glossed over and falsified. *On the other hand*, in Germany *every* tradition that served to make us blind to the Nazi regime needs a critical, indeed a distrustful, appropriation. That certainly holds for a philosophy that, even in its rhetorical means of expression, absorbed impulses from the ideologies of its epoch. One cannot bring the truth-content of a philosophy into discredit by associating it with something external to it; but no more can – or may – one make a complex, traditon-shaping form of objective spirit into an object of conservation like a national park, immunizing it against the question of whether issues of substance have been confused with those of ideology.[15] What was always acceptable in Germany with respect to Stalinism must also be acceptable with regard to fascism.

Manfred Frank has recently expressed the opinion, with reference to the variations on the Heideggerian critique of reason currently disseminated in France, that the question of refurbishing a constellation of *Weltanschauungen* of German (that is, Young-Conservative) origin has not yet been laid to rest in Germany: "The new French theories are taken up by many of our students like an evangel . . . It seems to me that young Germans are here eagerly sucking back in, under the pretense of opening up to what is French and international, their own irrationalist tradition, which had been broken off after the Third Reich."[16] I would like here to supplement Farias' investigation with a few remarks, taking up a question I previously broached in another place:[17] whether there was an *internal* connection between Heidegger's philosophy and his political perception of the world-historical situation.[18]

2   In 1963, Otto Pöggeler presented the "path of thought of Martin Heidegger" in a version that, authorized by Heidegger himself, mirrored Heidegger's own self-understanding. It is this faithful collaborator to whom, twenty years later, doubts came: "Was it not through a definite orientation of his thinking that Heidegger fell – and not merely accidentally – into the proximity of National Socialism without ever truly emerging from this proximity?"(*HPT*, 272). Pöggeler has since presented a point of view that brings the history of Heidegger's works closer together with that of his life than was previously done.

He distinguishes, in the first instance, the religious crisis into which Heidegger personally fell around 1917 from the general mood of crisis of 1929, into which

Heidegger was drawn politically. As Heidegger, in 1919, withdrew at his own request from the philosophical training for Catholic theologians, he explained the step by saying that for him "epistemological insights . . . have made the system of Catholicism problematic and unacceptable to me – but not Christianity and metaphysics (these, of course, in a new sense)" (*HPT*, 265). When we connect this with Heidegger's growing interest in Martin Luther and in Søren Kierkegaard, as well as with his intense communication with Rudolf Bultmann in Marburg, we can understand the point of view from which the problem of mediating historical thought and metaphysics must have posed itself for Heidegger: the attitude of methodical atheism did not yet require closing off the authentically Christian domain of experience. Heidegger pursued at that time a "phenomenology of life" that was grounded in boundary experience of personal existence. The experience of history, therefore, arose in contexts of self-reassurance on the part of concrete individuals in their current situations. This (1) suggested a hermeneutical interpretation of Husserl's phenomenological method, (2) required an interpretation of the metaphysical question of Being from the horizon of the experience of time, and (3) called forth the path-breaking transformation of the generative achievements of the transcendental ego into the historically situated life-projection of a factical being that finds itself in the world – Dasein. The connection between (2) and (3) explains, finally, why Heidegger's interest *remained* fixed on the constitution of human existence as such, and required a clear differentiation of existential ontology from the then contemporary enterprise of existentialism (Jaspers). The "analytic of Dasein" carried through in *Being and Time* remained, however, rooted in concrete experiences, a *theory* of Being-in-the-world as such. This explains the contrast, remarked many times, between a pretension of radical historical thinking and the fact that Heidegger rigidly maintained the abstraction of historicity (as the condition of historical existence itself) from actual historical processes.

The path-breaking achievement of *Being and Time* consists in Heidegger's decisive argumentative step towards overcoming the philosophy of consciousness.[19] This achievement may be *illuminated* by the motivational background of a personal life-crisis, but is not *impeached* by it. Naturally the spirit of the times, with which our author was already imbued, shows itself in this central work. The prevailing critique of mass civilization finds expression particularly in the connotations of his analysis of "das Man"; elitist complaints about the "dictatorship of public opinion" were common currency to the German mandarins of the twenties, and similar versions are to be found in Jaspers, E. R. Curtius, and many others. Indeed, the ideology inscribed in the "hidden curriculum" of the German Gymnasium has affected entire generations – on the Left as well as the Right. To this ideology belong an elitist self-understanding of academics, a fetishizing of *Geist*, idolatry for the mother tongue, contempt for everything social, a complete absence of sociological approaches long developed in France and the United States, a polarization between natural science and the *Geisteswissenschaften*, and so forth. All these themes are unreflectively perpetuated by Heidegger. More specific to him are the remarkable connotations with which he already at that time loaded terms like "fate" [*Schicksal*] and "destiny" [*Geschick*]. The pathos of heroic nihilism binds Heidegger to Young Conservatives, such as

Osdwald Spengler, the Jünger brothers, Carl Schmitt, and the circle connected with the journal *Die Tat*. But Pöggeler correctly dates the real invasion of such ideological motifs into Heidegger's self-understanding and, in fact, into the heart of his philosophical thought only from 1929 – the time of the world economic crisis and the downfall of the Weimar republic.

If we understand the ideology of the German mandarins in the sense of Fritz Ringer,[20] we may see connections between the mandarin consciousness of the German professor Heidegger and certain *limitations* from which the argumentation of *Being and Time* cannot free itself. But even from the point of view of the sociology of knowledge one would hardly discover more than what immanent critique has already shown anyway. To put it in a nutshell: with his steady focus on the invariant structures of Dasein, Heidegger from the start cuts off the road from historicity to real history.[21] Attributing a merely derivative status to *Mitsein* (Being-with others) he also misses the dimension of socialization and intersubjectivity.[22] With the interpretation of truth as disclosure, Heiddegger further ignores the aspect of unconditionality that attaches to a validity-claim, which, *as a chain*, transcends all merely local standards.[23]. Heidegger's methodical solipsism prevents him, finally, from taking seriously normative validity-claims and the meaning of moral obligations.[24] From all this it is already apparent why "the philosophy of *Being and Time* obviously cannot, whether for Heidegger or for a whole series of colleagues and students who stand near him, possess critical potential *vis-à-vis* Fascism."[25] Franzen, too, comes to the judgment that "much of what Heidegger said and wrote in 1933–34, if it did not necessarily follow from what was in *Being and Time*, was at least not incompatible with it" (*E*, 80).

I would like to close the gaps this negative explanation leaves open with the thesis that from around 1929 on, Heidegger's thought exhibits a *conflation* of philosophical theory with ideological motifs. From then on themes of an unclear, Young-Conservative diagnosis of the time enter into the heart of Heidegger's philosophy itself. Only then does he wholly open up to the antidemocratic thought that had found prominent right-wing advocates in the Weimar Republic and had attracted even original minds.[26] The defects that immanent textual criticism can detect in *Being and Time* could not be seen *as* defects by Heidegger because he shared the widespread anti-Western sentiments of his intellectual environment and held metaphysical thinking to be more primordial than the vapid universalism of the Englightenment. Concrete history remained for him a mere "ontical" happening, social contexts of life a dimension of the inauthentic, propositional truth a derivative phenomenon, and morality merely another way of expressing reified values. Blind spots in Heidegger's innovative *Being and Time* can be explained in this way. But only after *Being and Time* would the "anti-civilizational" undercurrent of German tradition (Adorno) erode that approach itself.[27]

3   Pöggeler is surely correct to emphasize the biographical turning-point of 1929. Three things came together at that time. First, Friedrich Hölderlin and Nietzsche came into view as the authors who were to dominate the following decades. This paved the way for the *neopagan turn* that pushed Christian themes into the background in favor of a mythologizing recourse to the archaic; even at

the end of his life, Heidegger placed his hopes in "a" god who can save us. Pöggeler asks himself:

> Was there not . . . a road from Nietzsche to Hitler? Did not Heidegger attempt, from 1929 on, with Nietzsche, to find his path, by way of the creativeness of the great creators, back to the tragic experience of life and thus to an historical greatness, in order then to win back for the Germans the beginnings of Greek thought and a horizon transposed by myth?[28]

Second, Heidegger's understanding of his role as a philosopher changed. During his encounter with Ernst Cassirer at Davos (March 1929), he expressed brusque dismissals of the world of Goethe and German Idealism. A few months later, after his July inaugural address as a professor in Freiburg, Heidegger completed the break with his teacher Husserl. At the same time, he returned to a theme he had last engaged ten years previously: he lectured on the "essence of the university and on academic studies." He seems at that point to have carried out a conscious break with academic philosophy, in order thenceforth to philosophize in another, nonprofessional way – in immediate confrontation with problems of the time perceived as urgent. As can be shown from the "Rektoratsrede" of 1933, Heidegger perceived the university as the preferred institutional locus for a spiritual renewal, to be brought about with unconventional means.

Third, Heidegger also opened himself up to Young-Conservative diagnoses of the times, even in his classroom.[29] In his lectures for the 1929–30 winter semester on "Basic Concepts of Metaphysics," he relates himself to writers such as Spengler, Ludwig Klages, and Leopold Ziegler, and swears by the heroism of audacious Dasein against the despised normality of bourgeois misery: "Mystery is lacking in our Dasein, and with it the inner horror which every mystery bears with it and which gives Dasein its greatness."[30] In the following years Heidegger studied the writings of Ernst Jünger: *War and Warrior* (1930) and *The Worker* (1932).

The invasion of the philosophy of *Being and Time* by ideology is not merely to be explained, however, by an awareness of the contemporary crisis that made Heidegger receptive to Nietzsche's critique of metaphysics: that also suggested the role of a savior in the moment of highest necessity for a philosophy freed from academic chains and for its site, the university; and that, finally, opened the doors to pickup critiques of civilization. The invading forces came together with a problematic that arose from the uncompleted opus itself, *Being and Time*.

Existential ontology had followed the transcendental approach so far that the structures it laid bare had to be attributed to Dasein *as such*: they had retained the character of being above history. This was not consistent with Heidegger's aim of subjecting the basic concepts of metaphysics to a radically temporalized analysis. Two works from 1930–31 (which are however available only in a later revised version) attempt to make good on that claim.

In the lectures "On the Essence of Truth" and "Plato's Doctrine of Truth," the existentials change from basic constitutional features of Dasein into the products of a process coming from afar. They come forth from an idealistically deified history, which is supposed to have completed itself in the medium of changes in ontological frames, metaphysics, *behind* or *above* real history. The dialectic of revelation and concealment is no longer conceived as an interplay of invariant possibilities of Being that continually holds open to the individual the perspective of authenticity, but as the story of a fall, which begins with Plato's metaphysical thought and proceeds in epochal fashion through different "peoples." With this shift, Heidegger gains a dimension within which the analytic of Dasein can illuminate the conditions under which it itself arose. Theory becomes reflexive in a way similar to that of the Hegelian Marxism of Lukács – though with the essential difference that Lukács' social theory conceives of its own genesis in terms of a concrete historical context that is accessible to social-scientific research, while existential-ontological thought transcends itself towards a sublime, primordially operative domain that is removed from all empirical (and ultimately all argumentative) grasp. In this domain, philosophy rules alone; it can therefore contract a dark alliance with scientifically unexamined diagnoses of the times. Heidegger's reconstruction of an unfolding of metaphysics that lies before all history is guided by the consciousness of crisis of the present moment to which he continually appeals, that is, by a conservative/ revolutionary interpretation of the German situation at the beginning of the thirties.

Interpreters of his thought today follow Heidegger's retrospective self-interpretation in holding that he completed his turn from existential ontology to the thinking of the history of Being with the two texts from 1930–31. But this is not wholly correct, for those essays merely open up a path that ultimately leads, in several stages, to the "Letter on Humanism" of 1947. The pathos of bondage and letting-be, the quietistic understanding of man as the shepherd of Being, the thesis that "language is the house of Being in which man ek-sists by dwelling, in that he belongs to the truth of Being, guarding it"[31] – all this is only the later result of the deliverance of philosophical thinking over to a "World-destiny" that, between 1930 and 1945, prescribed various twists and turns to a philosopher who was quite ready to go along.

At the beginning of the thirties, not only the word but the very concept of the "history of Being" is missing. What changes at that time in Heidegger's philosophical conception is not the activist demand for resoluteness and projection, but rather Heidegger's way of taking authenticity as the standard for the responsible acceptance of one's own life history. This standard is liquidated and along with it the critical moment of *Being and Time* provided by the *individualistic* heritage of existential philosophy. The concept of truth is then transformed so that historical challenge through a collective fate takes over. Now it is a "people" and no longer the individual, which ek-sists. Not we as individuals, but *We* with a capital *W* see ourselves exposed to the "need of turning" and the "prevailing of the mystery." But this does not yet free us from decision: "By leading him astray, errancy dominates man through and through. But, as leading astray, errancy at the same time contributes to a possibility that man is capable of drawing up from his ek-sistence – the possibility that, by experiencing errancy itself and by not mistaking the mystery of Da-sein, he *not* let himself be led astray."[32]

After 1929 we see a "turning" only in the sense that Heidegger (1) relates the analytic of Dasein reflectively to a movement of metaphysical thought conceived in terms of a history of the Fall (from Being); in that (2) he allows ideological motifs from a scientifically unfiltered diagnosis of crisis to filter into his present-oriented reconstruction; and in that (3) he dissociates the dialectic of truth and untruth from the individual's care for his own Dasein and interprets it as happening, which challenges the people to a resolute confrontation with a common historical fate.[33] With this, the switches are set for a national/ revolutionary interpretation of what in *Being and Time* was a self-heeding and self-assertion sketched in existential terms. Thus Heidegger, who had opted for the Nazi Party before 1933, could explain Hitler's successful power-grab in terms of concepts *retained* from his own analytic of Dasein.[34] But he adds something: the nationalistic privileging of the *German* fate, the conflation of the collectivistically interpreted category of "Dasein" with the Dasein of the German people, and those mediating figures, the "guides and guardians of the German destiny," who can shape necessity and create the new, if only their followers keep themselves in hand.

The leaders [*Führer*] are, then, the great creators, who put truth to work.[35] But the relation of leader to followers only concretizes the decision, as formal now as it was previously, "whether the entire people chooses its own Dasein, or whether it rejects it." In Heidegger's agitation for the Führer and "the complete transformation of our German Dasein," the old semantics of *Being and Time* can still be recognized – though it is now obscenely recolored. For example, in the speech Heidegger gave to the election rally of German scholars and scientists held at Leipzig on 11 November 1933, we hear that from "a coordinated readiness to follow in regard to the unconditional demand of responsibility-for-self, there first arises the possibility of mutually taking each other seriously . . . What sort of event is this? The people win back the truth of its will to exist, for truth is the manifestation of that which makes a people secure, lucid, and strong in its knowing and acting. From such truth stems the real desire to know."[36]

With *this* as background, the acceptance of the rectorship at Freiburg and the "Rektoratsrede" are not only compatible with Heidegger's earlier work but result from his dismissal of academic philosophy, from his elitist understanding of the German university, from his unbounded fetishizing of *Geist*, and from the missionary view of himself that allowed him to see the role of his own philosophy only in contexts of an eschatological world destiny. It is doubtless a specifically German *deformation professionelle* that gave Heidegger the idea of leading the Leader, Hitler. There is today no longer any controversy over the details of Heidegger's behavior at that time.

4   The lectures and writings that mark Heidegger's philosophical development during the Nazi period have not yet been completely published. Nonetheless, a careful reading of the two volumes on Nietzsche could teach us that Heidegger did not rid himself, even to the end of the war, of his original political option for the Nazis. The work of Franzen (1975–76) and Pöggeler (1983, 1985 and 1988) confirms the impression "that in the thirties, Heidegger himself placed the decision about the truth of Being as he sought it in a political context" (*HPT*, 278). The orientation of his thought, through which he "fell into the proximity of National Socialism," kept him from "ever truly emerging from this proximity" (*HPT*, 272).[37] Heidegger's philosophical trajectory between 1935 and 1945 shows

itself to be a process of working through a series of disappointments, without any real insight, so as to *continue* the "turn" introduced with the texts of 1930–31. Three aspects must here be distinguished: (1) the development of the critique of reason through the history of metaphysics; (2) the essentially unchanged, nationalistic estimation of the Germans as the "heart of all peoples", and (3) the position with regard to National Socialism. Only from this third aspect is the significant reconfiguration revealed, through which the concept of a "history of Being" first gains its definitive form.

(1) Instigated by an increasingly intense confrontation with Nietzsche – also the authoritative point of reference for official Nazi philosophy – Heidegger works up an approach under which the "destruction of metaphysics," which he had in view early on, merges completely with the known themes of his critique of the times. The thought of Plato – forgetful of Being, theoretically objectifying – hardens (in several stages) into the modern thought of subjectivity. Heidegger's analyses of "representational thought," though enlightening on several matters, now have as their target the ontological premises on which the determining spiritual powers of modernity, natural science and technology, rely. In the context of a history of metaphysics, "technology" is the expression for a will to will, which in practice makes itself felt in the phenomena of positivistic science, technological development, industrial labor, the bureaucratized state, mechanized warfare, the management of culture, the dictatorship of public opinion, and generally of urbanized mass civilization. Traits of totalitarian politics find their way into this template for the age of the masses, Nazi racial politics included. In spite of Heidegger's sustained relationship with one of the leading Nazi theoreticians of race, he was himself no racist; his anti-Semitism, so far as it can be confirmed at all, was rather of the usual, culturalistic breed. However that may be, *after* 1935 Heidegger subsumed political and social practice hastily under a few stereotypical code words without even an attempt at nuanced description, to say nothing of empirical analysis. His ontologizing talk of "technology" itself as a destiny that is at once mystery, security, and danger reaches globally, and with strongly essentialistic conceptions, through the foreground domains of the ontical. Even within the frame of this *Weltanschauung*, Heidegger pursues critical insights about reason that have not been superseded even today.

(2) The crude nationalism Heidegger openly sustained even after 1933 remains, in a form more or less sublimated through Hölderlin, an invariant feature of his thought. The basic schema of interpretation is established by 1935. In the *Introduction to Metaphysics* the German people, heir to the Greeks, is privileged as the metaphysical people from which alone a turning of the planetary fate can be expected. In the wake of an ideology of the "country of the middle," itself developed long ago, the Germans' Central European location is the key to their world-historical vocation: Heidegger expects "the peril of world darkening . . . to be forestalled" only "if our nation in the center of the Western world is to take on its historical mission" (*IM*, 50). Thus Heidegger relates "the question of being to the destiny of Europe, where the destiny of the earth is being decided – while our own historic being-there proves to be the center for Europe itself" (*IM*, 42). And further: "Europe lies in a pincers between Russia and America, which are metaphysically the same, namely in regard to their world

character and their relation to the spirit" (*IM*, 45). Because Bolshevism stems from Western Marxism, Heidegger sees in it only a variation on something worse – Americanism. Pöggeler reports a passage in a lecture manuscript that Heidegger, tastefully, did not actually deliver. It relates to Carnap, who had emigrated in the meantime: "his philosophy manifests 'the most extreme flattening and uprooting of the traditional theory of judgement under the guise of mathematical-scientific method' . . . It is no accident that this kind of 'philosophy' is both 'internally and externally connected' with 'Russian communism' and celebrates its triumph in America" (*HPT*, 276). Heidegger repeats his interpretation again in the Parmenides lecutures of 1942–43 and the Heraclitus lectures of the 1943 summer semester, when he sees the planet already "in flames," the "world slipping its moorings": "Only from the Germans can world historical meditation come – provided that they find and defend what is German."[38]

(3) After leaving the rectorate in April 1934, Heidegger is disillusioned. He is convinced that this historical moment was as if intended for himself and his philosophy; and he remains convinced of the world-historical importance and of the metaphysical meaning of Nazism to the bitter end. In the summer of 1942, he again speaks unmistakably, in a lecture on Hölderlin, of the "historical uniqueness of National Socialism,"[39] For Nazism is privileged by its particularly intimate relation to the nihilism of the time – and it remains so, even after Heidegger, apparently under the impact of the events of the war, learned to re-evaluate the *position* of Nazism with respect to the history of Being.

In the first instance – in 1935 – Heidegger's talk of the "inner truth and greatness" of the Nazi movement (*IM*, 199) betrays a distancing from certain phenomena and practices that are supposed to have nothing to do with the spirit of the thing itself. The philosopher, anyhow, knows better: *he* knows the metaphysical status of the national revolution. All is not yet lost, though the political leaders are allowing themselves to be deceived about their *true* mission by false philosophers such as Ernst Krieck and Alfred Bäumler. Walter Bröcker, who heard that lecture, recalls that Heidegger actually spoke of the inner truth and greatness of "the" movement, and not – as the published text has it – of "this" movement: "With the term 'the movement' the Nazis, and *only* they, meant their own party. That is why Heidegger's 'the' was for me unforgettable."[40] If that is right, then Heidegger's identification with the Nazis cannot exactly have been broken by 1935. Pöggeler reports as well on a passage in the Schelling lecture of the summer of 1936, which was struck from the published version of 1971 (supposedly without Heidegger's knowledge): "the two men who, each in his own way, have begun a countermovement to nihilism, Mussolini and Hitler, have both learned from Nietzsche, in essentially different ways. This does not mean, however, that Nietzsche's true metaphysical domain has come into its own."[41] The same image thus comes again, and is also consonant with Löwith's report of an encounter in Rome at the same time: the leaders of fascism know their own calling; but they must heed the philosopher in order to know its exact meaning. Only he could explain to them what it means, in terms of the history of metaphysics, to overcome nihilism and put truth to work. He at least sees the goal clearly before him: how the fascist leaders, if only they succeed in awakening the heroic will to Dasein of their peoples, could overcome the "bleak frenzy of unleashed technology and the rootless organization of the normal human being."

(4) I do not know exactly when the next stage of working through his disillusionment began: perhaps after the beginning of the war, perhaps only after the depressing knowledge of inevitable defeat. In the notes on "Overcoming Metaphysics" (from the years after 1936, especially from the wartime), Heidegger is increasingly impressed by the totalitarian traits of an age that ruthlessly mobilizes all reserves of strength. Only now does the messianic mood of basic change of 1933 become an *apocalyptic* hope of salvation: now, *only* in the greatest need does the saving force also grow. World-historical tragedy alone sounds the hour for overcoming metaphysics: "Only after this decline does the abrupt dwelling of the Origin [*Anfangs*] take place for a long span of time."[42] With this change of mood, the evaluation of National Socialism changes again. Heidegger's working through his disillusionment after 1934 had led to a differentiation between the unfortunate superficial forms of Nazi practice and its essential content. Now he undertakes a more radical revaluation, which has to do with the "inner truth" itself ot the Nazi movement. He resolves on a recasting of the roles in the history of Being. Whereas previously national revolutions with their leaders at the head represented a *countermovement* to nihilism, now Heidegger thinks that they are a particularly characteristic *expression* of it, and thus are a mere symptom of that fateful destiny of technology against which they were formerly supposed to be working. Technology, now the signature of the epoch, expresses itself in the totalitarian "circularity of consumption for the sake of consumption," and

"leader natures" are those who allow themselves to be put in the service of this procedure as its directive organs on account of their assured instincts. They are the first employees within the course of business of the unconditional consumption of beings in the service of the guarantee of the vacuum of the abandonment of Being (OM, 107)

Untouched by this is the nationalistic privileging of the Germans as that "humanity" that is suited to bring about unconditional nihilism in a historical manner" (OM, 103). It is in this that the "uniqueness" of National Socialism consists, while "the Nazi power holders are in a way stylized into chief functionaries of the abandonment of Being" (*E*, 99).

For the *internal* connection between Heidegger's political engagement and his philosophy, it seems to me of the greatest importance that only his hesitant – indeed in comparison with other intellectual fellow travelers of the regime astonishingly *protracted* – detachment from and re-evaluation of the Nazi movement leads to a revision, which Heidegger's postwar concept of the history of Being finally grounds. As long as Heidegger could imagine that national revolution could, with its projection of a new German Dasein, find an answer to the objective challenge of technology, the dialectic of claim [of Being] and correspondence [to that claim] could still be conceived in harmony with the basically activist tendency of *Being and Time*, precisely in terms of national revolution. Only after Heidegger gave up this hope and had to demote fascism and its leaders into symptoms of the disease they were originally supposed to heal – only after this change of attitude did the overcoming of modern subjectivity take on the meaning of an event that is *only* to be undergone. Until then, the decisionism of self-assertive Dasein, not only in the existential version of *Being and Time* but also (with certain changes of accent) in the national/revolutionary version of the writings from the thirties, had retained a role in disclosing Being. Only in the final phase of working though his disillusionment does the concept of the history of Being take on a fatalistic form.[43]

(5)   The fatalism of the history of Being already exhibited clear countours in, for example, the 1943 afterword to "What is Metaphysics?" After the end of the war, Heidegger's apocalyptically darkened mood changes yet again. An "apocalypse" is conditioned by the expectation of coming catastrophe. That was averted for the moment by the entry of French troops into Freiburg, but this was only a postponement for the time being. The victors were America and Russia, alike in their essence, who now divided up world hegemony. So the Second World War, in Heidegger's view, had decided nothing *essential*. That is why the philosopher prepared, after the war, to persevere *quietistically* in the shadows of a still unconquered destiny. In 1945 there remained for him only retreat from the disappointing history of the world. But this only underscores his continuing conviction that the history of Being is articulated in the words of essential thinkers – and that this thinking is eventuated by Being itself. Heidegger had allowed his thought to be engaged for over a decade and a half by political events. The "Letter on Humanism" of 1947 reflects this development, but only in such a way as to obscure its context of origin and – once historically displaced – to detach it from all relation to surface historical reality.

In the "Letter on Humanism," the traces of nationalism are effaced. The *Daseinsraum* of the people is sublimated into the *Heimat*, the natural home: "the word is thought here in an essential sense, not patriotically or nationalistically but in terms of the history of Being" (LH, 217). The world-historical mission of the people in the heart of Europe is retained only on a grammatical level: it lives on in the metaphysical privileging of the German language, in which Heidegger (now as before) sees the only legitimate successor to Greek. In his late interview with the German magazine *Der Spiegel* it is still clear: one must speak German in order to understand Hölderlin. The middle realm of the "demigods," of the creative leaders, disappears without a trace. The leaders are sublimated into poets and thinkers: the philosopher achieves an immediate relation to Being. What once held for political adherence is now generalized for all into obedience to the destiny of Being: only such submission "is capable of supporting and obligating" (LH, 238)

With the help of an operation that we might call "abstraction via essentialization," the history of Being is thus disconnected from political and historical events. This, again, allows for a remarkable self-stylization by Heidegger of his own philosophical development. From now on he emphasizes the continuity of his problematic and takes care to cleanse his concept of the history of Being from telltale ideological elements by projecting it back onto the never completed *Being and Time*. Heidegger's "turn," supposedly completed by 1930, "is not a change of standpoint from *Being and Time*" (LH, 208).[44]

Heidegger dealt with the theme of humanism at a time when the images of the horror that the arriving Allies encountered in Auschwitz and elsewhere had made their way into the smallest German village. If his talk of an "essential happening" had any meaning at all, the singular event of the attempted annihilation of the Jews would have drawn the philosopher's attention (if not already that of the concerned contemporary). But Heidegger dwells, as always, in the Universal. His concern is to show that man is the "neighbor of Being" – not the neighbor of man. He directs himself, undisturbed, against "the humanistic interpretations of man as *animal rationale*, as 'person,' as spiritual-ensouled-bodily being," because "the highest determinations of the essence of man in humanism still do not realize the proper dignity of man" (LH, 210). The "Letter on Humanism" also explains why moral judgements in general must remain beneath the level of essential thinking proper. Hölderlin had already left behind "the mere cosmopolitanism of Goethe." Heidegger's philosophizing, now become commemorative, strikes right through "ethics" and reaches, instead, the "destined": "Whenever thinking, in historical recollection, attends to the destiny of Being, it has already bound itself to what is fitting for it, in accord with its destiny." In writing this sentence, the memory of the "unfittingness" of the National Socialist movement must have struck the philosopher, for he immediately adds: "To risk discord in order to say the Same" – Being is always only itself – "is the danger. Ambiguity threatens, and mere quarreling" (LH, 241).

Heidegger has nothing more than this to say about his own error. That is hardly inconsistent. For the place of all essential thinking with respect to the eventuating of Being transposes the thinker into error. He is absolved from all personal responsibility, because error itself objectively befalls him. A mistake could be ascribed only to an intellectual, an unessential thinker. In the "case of the rectorate [in] 1933/34," which "in itself" was "unimportant," Heidegger sees, even after the war, only "a sign of the metaphysical state of the essence of science" (R. 497). For him, "it is as unimportant as the barren rooting in past attempts and measures taken, which in the context of the entire movement of the planetary will to power are so insignificant that they may not even be called tiny" (R, 498–9).

Some insight into Heidegger's retrospective assessment of his own conduct is given by the "Facts and Thoughts" that he noted down in 1945, and the interview with *Der Spiegel*, also published only posthumously, in which he essentially repeats the testimony of 1945.[45] It is precisely under the premises of the objective irresponsibility of essential thinking, and of the moral indifference of personal entanglements, that the palliative character of this self-presentation is so astounding. Instead of giving a sober account of the facts, Heidegger simply whitewashes himself. The "Rektoratsrede" he understands as already an "opposition," his entrance into the Nazi party under spectacular circumstances as a "matter of form" (R, 490, 493). For the following years, he claims, "the opposition that had begun in 1933 had continued and grown more vigorous" (R. 500). Silenced in his own country, he saw himself as sacrificed to a "witch hunt."

True, he mentions a "Clean Up Drive"[46] during his rectorship, "which often threatened to exceed its goals and limits" (R, 492). But there is only one mention of guilt – the guilt of others, "who even then were so endowed with the gift of prophecy that they foresaw all that came" yet nevertheless waited "almost ten years before opposing the threatening disaster" (R, 486). For the rest, Heidegger resists those who today wrongly understand his words of that time: "'Armed Service,' however, I mentioned neither in a militaristic, nor in an aggressive sense, but understood it as defense in self-defense" (R, 487).[47] The investigations of Hugo Ott and Victor Farias do not leave many details of these excuses standing. But it was not only in his posthumously published self-justifications that Heidegger resorted to falsification.

In 1953 Heidegger published his lectures from 1935 on the *Introduction to Metaphysics*. I was, as a student, at that time so impressed with *Being and Time* that reading these lectures, fascist right down to their stylistic details, actually shocked me. I discussed this impression in a newspaper article – mentioning especially the sentence about the "inner tuth and greatness of the Nazi movement." What shocked me most was that Heidegger had published in 1953, without explanation or comment, what I had to assume was an unchanged lecture from 1935. Even the foreword made no reference to what had happened in between. So I directed to Heidegger the question: "Can even the planned mass murder of millions of people, about which all of us know today, be made understandable in terms of the history of Being, as a fateful error? Is it not the factual crime of those who were responsible for carrying it out – and the bad conscience of an entire people?"[48] It was not Heidegger, but Christian E. Lewalter who answered.[49] He read the lecture with eyes completely different from mine. He understood it as documenting that Heidegger had in 1935 seen the Hitler regime, not as an "indication of new well-being" but as a "further symptom of decline" in the whole story of the decline of metaphysics. In this, Lewalter relied on an addition to the text, in parentheses, which characterized the Nazi movement as "the encounter between global technology and modern man" (*IM*, 199). Lewalter read this as saying that "the Nazi movement is a symptom for the tragic collision of man and technology, and as such a symptom it has its 'greatness,' because it affects the entirety of the West and threatens to pull it into destruction."[50] Surprisingly, Heidegger then expressed himself in a letter to the editor concening Lewalter's article: "Christian E. Lewalter's interpretation of the sentence taken from my lecture is accurate in every respect . . . It would have been easy to remove that sentence, along with the others you have mentioned, from the printed version. I have not done this, and will not do it in the future. On the one hand, the sentence historically belongs to the lecture; on the other, I am convinced, that the lecture itself can clarify it to a reader who has learned the craft of thinking"[51]

We may well suspect that Heidegger did not keep to this later, but struck politically offensive passages without indicating the omissions. (Or did Heidegger know nothing of this publication procedure?). More notable is the circumstance that Lewalter's interpretation, which falsely projected a later self-understanding back to 1935, was explicity condoned by Heidegger even though it rested solely on a clause that Heidegger himself had added to the manuscript in 1953. In fact, Heidegger had, in the "Prefatory Note" of the book, explicitly declared that this clause was part of the original lecture, and he maintained this deception even in the interview with *Der Spiegel*: but, little by little, the truth has come to light. In 1975, Franzen, after a careful examination of the text, substantiated doubts that "Heidegger really meant, what in 1953 he claimed he had" (*E*, 93). In 1983, Pöggeler reported that the page of the manuscript with the controversial passage was missing from the Heidegger archives. He too considered the parenthetical remark to be a later addition, but did not consider the possibility of an intentional minipulation (*HPT*, 277–8). After publication of the French version of Farias' book, Rainer Marten, a close associate of Heidegger, protrayed the incident as follows: Heidegger, in 1953, had refused the advice of his three collaborators that the insidious sentence be struck out and had added in parentheses the contentious commentary, on which Lewalter's interpretation and Heidegger's chronologically misleading self-presentation were then based.[52]

Interestingly enough, in 1953 the real issue was lost in the conflict of philosophical opinions. On the question of his position with regard to the Nazi mass crimes, Heidegger never, then or later, gave an answer. We may suspect, with solid grounds, that the answer as usual would have been very general. In the shadow of the "universal rule of the will to power within history, now understood to embrace the planet," everything becomes one and the same: "today everything stands in this historical reality, no matter whether it is called communism, or fascism, or world democracy" (R, 485). That is how it was in 1945, and that is how Heidegger always repeated it: abstraction by essentialization. Under the levelling gaze of the philosopher of Being even the extermination of the Jews seems merely an event equivalent to many others. Annihilation of Jews, expulsion of Germans – they amount to the same. On 13 May 1948, Herbert Marcuse answered a letter in which Heidegger had maintained just that:

You write that everything I say about the extermination of the Jews holds equally for the Allies, if instead of "Jew" we write "Eastern German." With this sentence, do you not place yourself outside the realm in which a conversation among humans is possible at all – outside the logos? For only from fully beyond this "logical" dimension is it possible to explain, adjust, "comprehend" a crime by saying that others did the same thing too. More: how is it possible to place the torture, mutilation, and annihilation of millions of people on the same level as the forcible resettlement of groups in which none of these misdeeds has occurred (save perhaps in a few exceptional cases)?[53]

(6) Heidegger's entanglement with National Socialism is one thing, which we can safely leave to the morally sober historical judgment of later generations. Quite another is Heidegger's apologetic conduct after the war, his retouchings and manipulations, his refusal publicly to detach himself from the regime to which he had publicly adhered. That affects us as his contemporaries. In so far as we share a life-context and a history with others, we have the right to call one

another to account. Heidegger's letter to Marcuse, in which he takes up a manner of settling accounts that even today is widespread in academic circles, was his reply to the following challenge from Marcuse, a former student: "Many of us have long waited for a word from you, a statement that you would clearly and definitively free yourself from this identification, a statement that expresses your real current attitude to what has happened. You have made no such state-ment – at least none has escaped the private sphere."[54] In this regard, Heidegger remained bound by his generation and his time, the milieu of the Adenauer era of repression and silence. He acted no differently from others, was one of many. The excuses that came from his circle are hardly convincing: that Heidegger had to defend himself against slander, that any new admission would be taken for a further adaptation, that Heidegger was struck dumb by the inadequacy of any possible explanation, and so on. The image of his character that is gradually coming to the fore makes most plausible the report of a friend that Heidegger saw no occasion for a "trip to Canossa" because he had not been a Nazi; and because he feared that such a move would deter young people from reading his books.[55]

A self-critical attitude, an open and scrupulous comportment to his own past, would have demanded from Heidegger something that would surely have been difficult for him: the revision of his self-understanding as a thinker with a privileged access to truth. After 1929, Heidegger veered farther and farther away from the circle of academic philosophy; after the war he actually strayed into the regions of a thinking *beyond* philosophy, *beyond* argumentation itself. This was no longer the elitist self-understanding of an academic corporate guild. It was the consciousness of a mission cut to the form of one's own person, with which the admission of a few mistakes, to say nothing of guilt, was incompatible.

As a contemporary, Heidegger is thrown into an ambiguous light, overtaken by his own past because when everything was finished and done he could not adequately relate to it. His behavior remained, even according to the standards of *Being and Time*, ahistorical. But what makes Heidegger into a manifestation, typical for his time, of a widely influential postwar mentality concerns his person – not his work. The conditions of reception for an *oeuvre* are largely independent of the behavior of its author. That holds, at least, for the writings up to 1929. Up to *Kant and the Problem of Metaphysics*, Heidegger's philosophical work is faithful enough to the stubborn logic of his problematic that those portions of it explainable in terms of the sociology of knowledge and relating to the context in which it arose do not prejudice the context of justification. One does Heidegger a favor when one emphasizes the autonomy of his thought during this most productive phase – in 1929 he was already forty years old – particularly against Heidegger's later self-stylizations, against his overemphasis on continu-ity.

Even after the beginning of the process of ideological infiltration – a process that, at first insidious, eventually burst forth so spectacularly – Heidegger remained the productive philosopher he had previously been. Even his critique of reason, which begins with the Plato interpretation of 1931 and is developed between 1935 and 1945, especially in his confrontation with Nietzsche,[56] is responsible for *lasting* insights. These insights, which reach a high point in the influential Descartes interpretation, became points of departure for interesting developments and inspired extremely productive new approaches. An example of this is the philosophical hermeneutics of Hans-Georg Gadamer, one of the most important philosophical innovations of the postwar period. Further visible testimony to the effect of the Heideggerian critique of reason, undistorted by his worldview, are, in France, the phenomenology of the late Merleau-Ponty and Michel Foucault's analysis of forms of knowledge; in America, Rorty's critique of representational thought and Dreyfus' investigation of life-world practice.[57]

No shortcircuit can be set up between work and person. Heidegger's philosophical work owes its autonomy, as does every other such work, to the strength of its arguments. But then a productive relation to his thinking can be gained only when one engages those *arguments* – and *takes them out* of their ideological context. The further the argumentative substance sinks into the unchallengeable morass of ideology, the greater is the demand on the critical force of an alert and perceptive appropriation. This hermeneutical commonplace loses its triviality especially when the later generations appropriating a work stand in the same tradition from which it has drawn its themes. In Germany, therefore, the critical appropriation of a thought that has been supportive of Nazism can only succeed when we learn from Heidegger to take into account the *internal* relations that exist between his political engagement and the changes in his attitude towards fascism, on the one hand, and the arguments of his critique of reason, which was also politically motivated, on the other.

The indignant tabooing of this set of problems is counterproductive. We must divest ourselves of the self-understanding, the postures, and the claims that Heidegger connected with his *role* before we can get to the substance of the matter. Hedging the authority of the great thinker – only he who thinks greatly can err greatly[58]–can only inhibit the critical appropriation of his arguments in favor of merely socializing people into an unclarified language game. The conditions under which *we* can learn from Heidegger are incompatible with the anti-Occidental frame of mind deeply rooted in Germany. Fortunately, we broke with this after 1945. It should not be resurrected with a mimetically assimilated Heidegger. I refer above all to Heidegger's pretension that "there is a thinking more rigorous than the conceptual" (LH, 235). This attitude is connected, first, to the claim that a few people have privileged access to truth, may dispose of an infallible knowledge, and may withdraw from open argument. Further, connected with the same attitude are concepts of morality and truth that detach the validity of knowledge from inter-subjective examination and recognition. The same attitude suggests, finally, detaching philosophical thinking from the egalitarian business of science, severing the emphatically extraordinary from its roots in ordinary, everyday experience and practice, and destroying the principle of equal respect for all.

Response to the French publication of the present book was lively. In Germany, professionl philosophers held back from taking positions. With some justification, it was pointed out that the topic of "Heidegger and Nazism" has been treated often in the Federal Republic, from Georg Lukács and Karl Löwith via Paul Hühnerfeld, Christian Von Krockow, Theodor Adorno, and Alexander

Schwan, to Hugo Ott – while in France Heidegger was instantly denazified and even given the status of a resister.[59] But in Germany also, the effect of the critique was minor. Neither Franzen's critical presentation of Heidegger's philosophical development nor the newer points established by Ott and Pöggeler on Heidegger's political engagement have become anything more than specialists' affairs.

NOTES

First Published in *Critical Inquiry* 15 (Winter 1989). English translation by J. McCumber ©/1989 by The University of Chicago. 0093–18961 89/1502–003$01.00. All rights reserved.

1　Winfried Franzen, *Martin Heidegger*, Stuttgart, 1976. p. 78: all translations from German texts are mine unless a previous English translation could be found – TRANS.

2　Heidegger, *Die Selbstbehauptung der deutschen Universität. Rede, genaltern bei der feierlichen Übernahme des Rektorats der Universität Freiburg i. Br. am 27. 5 .1933*, and *Das Rektorat 1933–34. Tatsachen und Gedanken*, Frankfurt-am-Main, 1983; trans. Karsten Harries, under the title "The Self-Assertion of the German University: Address, Delivered on the Solemn Assumption of the Rectorate of the University Freiburg," and "The Rectorate 1933/34: Facts and Thoughts," *Review of Metaphysics* 38 (March 1985): 467–502: quotations from "The Rectorate" are hereafter abbreviated "R."

3　Hugo Ott,"Martin Heidegger und die Universität Freiburg nach 1945," *Historisches Jahrbuch* 105 (1985): 95–128. See also Ott, "Martin Heidegger und der Nationalsozialismus," in *Heidegger und die praktische Philosophie*, ed. Annemarie Gethmann-Siefert and Otto Pöggeler, Frankfurt-am-Main, 1988, pp. 64–77.

4　See Pöggeler, "Den Führer führen? Heidegger und kein Ende," *Philosophische Rundschau* 32 (1985): 26–67, and Pöggeler "Heideggers politisches Selbstverständnis," in *Heidegger und die praktische Philosophie*, pp. 17–63.

5　Karl Löwith, *Mein Leben in Deutschland vor und nach 1933. Ein Bericht*, Stuttgart, 1986, p. 57.

6　See Nicolas Tertulian, "Heidegger – oder: die Bestätigung der Politik durch Seinsgeschichte. Ein Gang zu den Quellen. Was aus den Texten des Philosophen alles sprudelt," *Frankfurter Rundschau*, 2 February 1988.

7　Ott, "Martin Heidegger und der Nationalsozialismus," p. 65.

8　Refraining from political and moral evaluation of Heidegger's conduct from that time ought to include renouncing comparisons that are only too easily set up in an endeavor to balance accounts. We can learn this lesson even from the circumspect Pöggeler, who not only compares Heidegger's engagement with Hitler to Ernst Bloch's and Georg Lukács' option for Stalin, but adduces as well a review in which Theodor Adorno, completely misunderstanding the situation in 1934, thought himself able to survive the nightmare in Germany. See Pöggeler, "Den Führer führen? Heidegger und kein Ende," p. 28. When in 1963 Adorno was confronted (in the pages of the Frankfurt student newspaper *Diskus*) with that review from 1934, he responded with a completely open letter; his words could not contrast more impressively with the shameful silence of Heidegger. See Adorno, *Gesammelte Schriften*, ed. Rolf Tiedemann, 22 vols, Frankfurt-am-Main, 1973–78, 19: 635–9. In these pages, one will find Tiedemann's editorial afterword, Adorno's letter, and a statement by Max Horkheimer.

9　Herbert Schnädelbach, *Philosophie in Deutschland 1831–1933*, Frankfurt-am-Main, 1983; trans. Eric Matthews, under the title *Philosophy in Germany 1831–1933*, Cambridge, 1984, p. 1.

10 For pragmatic themes in Heidegger, see C. F. Gethmann, "Vom Bewußtsein zum Handeln. Pragmatische Tendenzen in der Deutschen Philosophie der ersten Jahrzehnte des 20. Jahrhunderts," in *Pragmatik: Handbuch pragmatischen Denkens*, ed. Herbert Stachowiak, 2 vols, Hamburg, 1986–87, 2: 202–32.

11 See *Heidegger: Perspektiven zur Deutung seines Werks*, ed. Pöggeler, Cologne, 1969.

12 An intensive engagement with the early Heidegger left its marks on my own work as well, up to *Knowledge and Human Interests*, trans. Jeremy J. Shapiro, Boston, 1971. See also the bibliographical references in Franzen, *Martin Heidegger*, p. 127. The Heideggerian Marxism of the young Herbert Marcuse fascinated me: see Alfred Schmidt, "Existential Ontologie und historischer Materialismus bei Herbert Marcuse," in *Antworten auf Herbert Marcuse*, ed. Habermas, Frankfurt, 1968, pp. 17ff.

13 Hans-Ulrich Wehler, *Entsorgung der deutschen Vergangenheit? ein polemischer Essay zum "Historikerstreit"*, Munich, 1988. Even in the work of the historian Andreas Hillgruber, one could find in 1986 the same comparison of the German crimes with the expulsion of Germans from the Eastern territories, a comparison that Marcuse objected to in an open letter to Heidegger in 1949; on this correspondence, see pp. 201–202 of this essay.

14 Jaspers and Archbishop Gröber even demanded, or expected, from their friend Heidegger in 1945 a "genuine rebirth" and a "spiritual reversal" (Ott, "Martin Heidegger und der Nationalsozialismus," p. 65).

15 Even Richard Rorty misses the point that the problem is not the relation between person and work, but the amalgamation of work and worldview. See Rorty, "Taking philosophy seriously," a review of *Heidegger et le Nazisme*, by Victor Farias. *The New Republic*, 11 April 1988, pp. 31–4.

16 Manfred Frank, "Philosophie heute und jetzt," *Frankfurter Rundschau*, 5 March 1988.

17 Habermas, *The Philosophical Discourse of Modernity: Twelve Lectures*, trans. Frederick Lawrence, Cambridge, Mass., 1987, pp. 155–60.

18 Unfortunately, I was at that time unacquainted with the pertinent investigation by Franzen, *Von der Existentialontologie zur Seinsgeschichte*, Meisenheim am Glan, 1975, part 3, pp. 63–101 (hereafter abbreviated *E*), and with the afterword to the second edition of Pöggeler, *Der Denkweg Martin Heideggers* (Pfullingen, 1983), pp. 319–55: trans. Daniel Magurshak and Sigmund Barber, under the title *Martin Heidegger's Path of Thinking*, Atlantic Highlands, N.J., 1987; hereafter abbreviated *HPT*.

19 Habermas, *The Philosophical Discourse of Modernity*, pp. 141ff. On the controversial prehistory of *Being and Time*, see the following contributions in *Dilthey-Jahrbuch für Philosophie und Geschichte der Geisteswissenshaften* 4 (1986–87): Hans-Georg Gadamer, "Erinnerungen an Heideggers Anfänge," pp. 13–26; Gethmann, "Philosophie als Vollzug und als Begriff. Heideggers Identitäts-philosophie des Lebens in der Vorlesung vom Wintersemester 1921/22 und ihr Verhaltnis zu *Sein und Zeit*," pp. 27–53: and Theodor Kisiel, "Das Entstehen des Begriffsfeldes 'Faktizität' im Frühwerk Heideggers," pp. 91–120.

20 Fritz K. Ringer, *The Decline of the German Mandarins: The German Academic Community 1890–1933*, Cambridge, Mass., 1969; see my review of this book in Habermas, *Philosophisch politische Profile*, Frankfurt-am-Main, 1971, pp. 239–51. See also H. Brunkhorst, *Der Intellektuelle im Land der Mandarine*, Frankfurt-am-Main, 1987.

21 See *E*, 47ff. Adorno, by the way, had already noted this in his inaugural lecture of 1931. See Adorno, "The actuality of philosophy," *Telos* 31 (Spring 1977): 120–33.

22 See Michael Theunissen, *Der Andere: Studien zur Sozialontologie der Gegenwart*, Berlin, 1977, p. 182: trans. Christoper Macann, under the title *The Other: Studies in the Social Ontology of Husserl, Heidegger, Sartre, and Buber*, Cambridge, Mass., 1984.

23 See Ernst Tugendhat, "Heideggers Idee von Wahrheit," in *Heidegger: Perspektiven*

zur Deutung seines Werks, pp. 286–97. See also Karl-Otto Apel, *Transformation der Philosophie*, 2 vols, Frankfurt-am-Main, 1973, vol. 1, part 2.

24 Gethmann, "Heideggers Konzeption des Handelns in *Sein und Zeit*," in *Heidegger und die praktische Philosophie*, pp. 140–76.

25 Ibid., p. 142.

26 Kurt Sontheimer, *Antidemokratisches Denken in der Wiemarer Republik: die politischen Idee der deutschen Nationalismus zwischen 1918 und 1933*, Munich, 1962. See also Christian von Krockow, *Die Entscheidung: eine Untersuchung über Ernst Jünger, Carl Schmitt, Martin Heidegger*, Stuttgart, 1958.

27 Heidegger's French apologists get things backwards when they seek to explain his commitment to National Socialism by saying that the thought of *Being and Time* is still too rooted in "metaphysical thinking" and still too bound up with the fate of nihilism. See Philippe Lacoue-Labarthe, *La Fiction du politique: Heidegger, l'art et la politique*, Paris, 1987. For a critical treatment see Luc Ferry and Alain Renaut, *Heidegger et les modernes*, Paris 1988.

28 Pöggeler, "Den Führer führen? Heidegger und kein Ende," p. 47.

29 See the early essay by Marcuse – still one of the keenest analyses of this relationship – "The struggle against liberalism in the totalitarian view of the state," *Negations: Essays in Critical Theory*, Boston, 1968, pp. 3–42. See especially p. 41 for references to Heidegger's article in the Freiburg student newspaper, *freiburger Studentenzeitung*, 10 November 1933.

30 Heidegger, *Die Grundbegriffe der Metaphysik*, ed. Friedrich-Wilhelm von Herrmann, vol. 29/30 of *Gesamtausgabe*, Frankfurt-am-Main, 1983, p. 244. For an analysis of the whole of section 38 of this work, see Franzen, "Die Sehnsucht nach Härte und Schwere," in *Heidegger und die praktische Philosophie*, pp. 78–92.

31 Heidegger, Letter on humanism," trans. Frank A. Capuzzi, J. Glenn Gray, and David Farrell Krell, *Basic Writings*, ed. Krell, New York, 1977, p. 213: hereafter abbreviated *LH*.

32 Heidegger, "On the Essence of Truth," trans. John Sallis, *Basic Writings*, p. 136.

33 Some interpreters of Heidegger are inclined to view the final chapters of *Being and Time*, especially the talk of "fate" and "destiny," in a collectivistic sense. This way of reading, however, only repeats Heidegger's own retrospective self-portrait. See my remarks in *The Philosophical Discourse of Modernity*, pp. 403–4, n. 41.

34 Johannes Gross, a trustworthy witness, has communicated, in the sixty-second installment of the new series of his "Notizbuch" in the magazine of the *Frankfurter Allgemeine Zeitung*, the content of a letter from Heidegger to Carl Schmitt of 22 August 1932(!). The last paragraph runs: "Today I would just like to say that I am very much counting on your resolute collaboration in rebuilding the entire faculty of law from the inside out, both as to research and as to teaching. Everything is unfortunately very gloomy here. It becomes ever more urgent to gather together the spiritual forces that can bring about what is to come. For today I close with friendly greetings. Heil Hitler. Yours, Heidegger."

35 This figure of thought stands in the center of Heidegger's lectures on the "Introduction to Metaphysics" of 1935. See *Einführung in die Metaphysik*, Tübingen, 1953; trans. Ralph Manheim, under the title *An Introduction to Metaphysics*, New Haven, CT, 1979: hereafter abbreviated *IM*. See also Alexander Schwan, *Politische Philosophie im Denken Heideggers*, Opladen, 1965.

36 Quoted in *Nachlese zu Heidegger, Dokumente zu seinem Leben und Denken*, ed. Guido Schneeberger, Bern, 1962, pp. 149–50. Connections between the "Rektoratsrede" and *Being and Time* are explored in Harries, "Heidegger as a Political Thinker," in *Heidegger and Modern Philosophy: Critical Essays*, ed. Michael Murray, New Haven,

CT, 1978, pp. 304–28.

37 Pöggeler formulates this as a question – though certainly a rhetorical one.
38 Heidegger, *Heraklit*, ed. Manfred S. Frings, vol. 55 of *Gesamtausgabe*, p. 123. For references to similar passages, see *HPT*, 279.
39 Heidegger, *Hölderlins Hymne "Der ister,"* ed. Walter Biemel, vol. 53 of *Gesamtausgabe*, p. 106.
40 Pöggeler, "Heideggers politisches Selbstverständnis," p. 59, n. 11.
41 Pöggeler, "Den Führer führen? Heidegger und kein Ende," p. 56.
42 Heidegger. "Überwindung der Metaphysik," *Vortrage und Autsätze* (1954: Pfullingen, 1978): trans. Joan Stambaugh, under the title "Overcoming Metaphysics." *The End of Philosophy*, New York, 1973, p. 84: hereafter abbreviated *OM*.
43 See Habermas, *The Philosophical Discourse of Modernity*, pp. 159–60.
44 On this discussion, which I cannot take up here, see *E* 152ff.
45 See "Nur noch ein Gott kann uns retten," interview with Heidegger, *Der Spiegel* 23 (1976): 193–219: trans. William J. Richardson, under the title "Only a God Can Save Us: *Der Spiegel's* Interview with Martin Heidegger," in *Heidegger: The Man and the Thinker*, ed. Thomas Sheehan, Chicago, 1981, pp. 45–67.
46 "Säuberungsaktion" might also be translated as "purging action" – TRANS.
47 To capture the wordplay in Heidegger's sentence, one could translate it as follows: "'defense service' I understood neither in a militaristic nor an aggressive sense, but in the sense of self-defense" – TRANS.
48 Habermas, "Zur Veröffentlichung von Vorlesungen aus dem Jahre 1935," *Frankfurter Allgemeine Zeitung*, 25 July 1953; reprinted in Habermas, *Philosophisch-politische Profile*, pp. 65–72.
49 Christian E. Lewalter, *Die Zeit*, 13 August, 1953.
50 Another of Lewalter's sentences deserves to be recorded here:

> The extent to which Heidegger's accusers have fallen victim to the passion for persecution is shown by a particularly venomous remark of the present critic. "A Fascist intelligentsia as such," says Habermas, "did not exist only because the mediocrity of the Fascist leadership could not accept the offer of the intellectuals. The forces were indeed there. Only the inferior stature of the political functionaries pressed those intellectual forces into the oppositon." In other words: Heidegger offered himself to Hitler but Hitler, in his "mediocrity," rejected the offer and forced Heidegger into opposition. So Habermas presents it. (ibid.)

> Lewalter could have had no idea that Heidegger would eventually confirm my remark, which was rather more clairvoyant than venomous: "National Socialism did, indeed, go in this [correct – J. H.] direction. Those people, however, were far much too poorly equipped for thought to arrive at a really explicit relationship to what is happening today and has been underway for the past 300 years" ("Nur noch ein Gott kann uns retten," p. 214; "Only a God Can Save Us," p. 61).

51 Heidegger, letter to the editor, *Die Zeit*, 24 September 1953.
52 Rainer Marten, "Ein rassistisches Konzept von Humanität," *Badische Zeitung*, 19–20 December 1987. Upon my inquiry, Marten confirmed the matter in a letter of 28 January 1988: "At that time we were reading corrections for Heidegger, for the preparation of the new edition of *Being and Time* (Tübingen, 1953) and the first publication of the lectures from 1935. The passage stood out, to the best of my memory, not because of any explanatory parenthesis, but only through the monstrous nature of its content, which struck all three of us."

53 Herbert Marcuse, *Pflasterstrand* (January 1988): 48–9
54 Ibid., p. 46.
55 See Heinrich Wiegand Petzet, *Auf einen Stern zugehen. Begegnungen und Gespräche mit Martin Heidegger, 1926–76*, Frankfurt-am-Main, 1983, p. 101.
56 See Heidegger, *Nietzche*, 2 vols (Tübingen, 1961).
57 See Hubert L. Dreyfus, "Holism and hermeneutics," *Review of Metaphysics* 34 (September 1980): 3–23.
58 Ernst Nolte concludes his essay on philosophy and National Socialism with this sentence: "I believe that Heidegger's engagement of 1933 *and* the insight of 1934 into his errors were both more philosophical than the correctness of the consistently distanced and extremely respectable conduct of Nicolai Hartmann" ("Philosophie und Nationalsozialismus," in *Heidegger und die praktische Philosophie*, p. 355).
59 On this see Ott, "Wege und Abwege," *Neue Zürcher Zeitung* 27 (28–29 November 1987): 67. This essay also includes an expert's critical comments on Farias' book.

11
Heidegger, Contingency, and Pragmatism

Richard Rorty

One of the most intriguing features of Heidegger's later thought is his claim that if you begin with Plato's motives and assumptions you will end up with some form of pragmatism. I think that this claim is, when suitably interpreted, right. But, unlike Heidegger, I think pragmatism is a *good* place to end up. In this paper, I shall try to say how far a pragmatist can play along with Heidegger, and then try to locate the point at which he or she must break off.

A suitable interpretation of Heidegger's claim requires defining Platonism as the claim that the point of inquiry is to get in touch with something like Being, or the Good, or Truth, or Reality – something large and powerful which we have a duty to apprehend correctly. By contrast, pragmatism must be defined as the claim that the function of inquiry is, in Bacon's words, to "relieve and benefit the condition of man" – to make us happier by enabling us to cope more successfully with the physical environment and with each other. Heidegger is arguing that if you start with Plato's account of inquiry you will eventually wind up with Bacon's.

The story Heidegger tells about the transition from the one set of goals to the other is summarized in his "Sketches for a History of Being as Metaphysics" in the second volume of his *Nietzsche*.[1] Here is one such sketch, entitled "Being" (*Das Sein*):

Alétheia (*apeiron, logos, ben – arche*).
Revealing as the order at the start.
Physis, emergence (going back to itself).
Idea, perceivability (*agathon*), causality.
Energeia, workness, assembly, *en-echesia to telos*
Hypokeimenon, lie present (from *ousia, ergon*).
(presence – stability – constancy – *aet*).
Hyparchein, presencing which rules from what is already present.
Subiectum.
Actualitas, beings – the real – reality

Creator – ens creatum
causa prima (ens a se).
Certituido–res cogitans.
Vis – *monas (perceptio – appetitus), exigentia essentiae.*
Objectivity
Freedom
   will-representation
   practical reason
will – as absolute knowledge: Hegel.
As will of love: Schelling.
Will to power: eternal recurrence: Nietzsche.
Action and Organization – pragmatism
The will to will.
Machination (Enfaming)[2]

This potted history of Western philosophy stretches from the Greek conviction
that the point of inquiry is apprehension of *archai*, principles, things greater and
more powerful than everyday human existence, to the American conviction that
its point is technological contrivance, getting things under control. Heidegger
sees this chronological list of abbreviations for philosophers' "understandings of
Being" as a downward escalator. Once you have gotten on you cannot get off until
you have reached the bottom. If you start off with Plato you will wind up with
Nietzsche and, worse yet, Dewey.

Heidegger claims that to understand what is going on here at the bottom of the
escalator, in the twentieth century, the age in which philosophy has exhausted its
possibilities, "we must free ourselves from the technical interpretation of
thinking." The beginnings of that interpretation, he says, "reach back to Plato
and Aristotle."[3] As I read him, his point here is the same as Dewey's: that Plato
and Aristotle built what Dewey called "the quest for certainty" into our sense of
what thinking is for. They taught us that unless we can make the object of our
inquiry *evident* – get it clear and distinct, directly present to the eye of the mind,
and get agreement about it from all those qualified to discuss it – we are falling
short of our goal.

As Heidegger says, "All metaphysics, including its opponent, positivism,
speaks the language of Plato."[4] That is, ever since Plato we have been asking
ourselves the question: what must we and the universe be like if we are going to
get the sort of certainty, clarity, and evidence Plato told us we ought to have?
Each stage in the history of metaphysics – and in particular the Cartesian turn
toward subjectivity, from exterior to interior objects of inquiry – has been an
attempt to redescribe things so that this certainty might become possible. But,
after many fits and starts, it has turned out that the only thing we can be certain
about is what we want. The only things that are really evident to us are own own
desires.

This means that the only way we can press on with Plato's enterprise is to
become pragmatists – to identify the meaning of life with getting what we want,
and imposing our will. The only cosmology we can affirm with the certainty Plato
recommended is our own (communal or individual) world picture, our own way

of setting things up for manipulation, the way dictated by our desires. As Heidegger says:

> world picture, when understood essentially, does not mean a picture of the world but the world conceived and grasped as picture. What is, in its entirety, is now taken in such a way that it first is in being and only is in being to the extent that it is set up by man, who represents and sets forth.[6]

To see how the quest of certainty took us down this road, think of Plato as having built the need to overcome epistemological skepticism – the need to answer questions like "What is your evidence?" "How do you know?" "How can you be sure?" – into Western thinking. Then think of the skeptic as having pressed the philosopher back from a more ambitious notion of truth as accurate representation to the more modest notion of truth as coherence among our beliefs. Think of Spinoza and Leibniz as having elaborated proto-coherence theories of truth. Think of the coherence theory of truth becoming philosophical common sense after Kant explained why a "transcendental realist" account of knowledge would always succumb to skeptical attack. Think of Kant as completing the Cartesian turn toward interior objects by replacing the realist story about inner representations of outer originals with a story about the relation between privileged representations (such as his twelve categories) and less privileged, more contingent representations.

As soon as we adopt this Kantian story, however, we begin to drift toward Nietzsche's view that "the categories of reason" are just "means toward the adjustment of the world for utilitarian ends."[7] We begin to see the attractions of Deweyan redefinitions of terms like "truth" and "rationality" in terms of contributions to "satisfaction" and "growth." We move from Kant to pragmatism when we realize that a coherence theory of truth must be a theory about the harmony not just of beliefs, but rather of beliefs *and desires*. This realization leads us to the common element in Nietzsche's perspectivalism and C. I. Lewis's "conceptual pragmatism" – the doctrine that Kantian categories, the forms in which we think, the stuctures of our inquiries, are malleable. We change them (as, for example, we changed from an Aristotelian to a Newtonian understanding of space and time) whenever such a change enables us better to fulfill our desires by making things more readily manipulable.

Once we take this final step, once human desires are admitted into the criterion of "truth," the last remnants of the Platonic idea of knowledge as contact with an underlying nonhuman order disappear. We have become pragmatists. But we only took the path that leads to pragmatism because Plato told us that we had to take evidence and certainty, and therefore skepticism, seriously. We only became pragmatists because Plato and Aristotle already gave us a technical, instrumental account of what thinking was good for.

Heidegger thinks of himself as having tracked down the assumption common to Plato, the skeptic, and the pragmatists – the assumption that truth has something to do with evidence, with being clear and convincing, with being in possession of *powerful, penetrating, deep* insights or arguments – insights or arguments which will put you in a commanding position *vis-à-vis* something or somebody else (or *vis-à-vis* your own old, bad, false self). The West, Heidegger thinks, has been on a power trip ever since, with the Greeks, it invented itself. A metaphysics of the Will to Power (the metaphysics Heidegger ascribed to Nietzsche by taking some of Nietzsche's posthumous fragments to be the "real" Nietzsche) and an antimetaphysical technocratic pragmatism are the destined lost stages of Western thought. This is the ironic result of Plato's attempt to rise above the pragmatism of the marketplace, to find a world elsewhere.

A familiar way to see Plato as power freak – as an example of what Derrida calls "phallogocentrism" – is to emphasize his conviction that mathematical demonstration is the paradigm of inquiry, his awe at the geometers' ability to offer knockdown arguments. But another way is to think of him as convinced that all human beings have the truth within them, that they are already in possession of the key to the ultimate secrets – that they merely need to know themselves in order to attain their goal. This is the basic assumption of what Kierkegaard, in his *Philosophical Fragments*, called "Socratism." To make this assumption is to believe that we have a built-in affinity for the truth, a built-in way of tracking it once we glimpse it, a built-in tendency to get into the right relation to a more powerful Other. In Plato, this assumption was expressed as in the doctrine that the soul is itself a sort of *arché* because it is somehow connate with the Forms. Down here at the bottom of the escalator, it is expressed in the pragmatist's claim that to know your desires (not your deeply buried "inmost," "true" desires, but your ordinary everyday desires) is to know the criterion of truth, to understand what it would take for a belief to "work."

For Kierkegaard, the opposite of Socratism was Christianity – the claim that man is not complete, is not in the truth, but rather can attain truth only by being recreated, by being made into a New Being by Grace. Kierkegaard thought that Socratism was Sin, and that Sin was the attempt by Man to assume the role of God, an attempt which found its *reductio* in Hegel's System. A lot of Heidegger can profitably be read as a reflection on the possibility that Kierkegaard was right to reject Socratism but wrong to accept Christianity – or, more generally, on the possibility that humanism and Pauline Christianity are alternative forms of a single temptation. Suppose that both are expressions of the need to be overwhelmed by something, to have beliefs forced upon you (by conclusive evidence, rational conviction, in the one case, or by Omnipotence recreating you, in the other). Suppose that this desire to be overwhelmed is itself just a sublimated form of the urge to share in the power of anything strong enough to overwhelm you. One form such sharing might take would be to become identical with this power, through a purificatory askesis. Another would be to become the favored child of this power.

The result of thinking through these suppositions was Heidegger's attempt to struggle free from what he came to think of as the underlying assumption of the West – the assumption that truth is somehow a matter of the stronger overcoming the weaker. This notion of overcoming is what is common to suggestions that intellect can overcome sensual desire, that Grace can overcome Sin, that rational evidence can overcome irrational prejudice, and that the human will can overcome the nonhuman environment. This assumption that power relations are of the essence of human life is, Heidegger thinks, fundamental to what he sometimes calls "the ontotheological tradition."

I take Heidegger to be saying that if one is going to stay within this tradition, then one might as well be a pragmatist. One might as well be a self-conscious, rather than a repressed and self-deceived, power freak. Pragmatism has, so to speak, turned out to be all that the West could hope for, all we had a right to expect once we adopted a "technical" interpretation of thinking. Plato set things up so that epistemological skepticism would become the recurrent theme of philosophical reflection, and pragmatism is, in fact, the only way to answer the skeptic. So if the only choice is between Platonism and pragmatism, Heidegger would wryly and ironically opt for pragmatism.

This qualified sympathy for pragmatism is clearest in *Being and Time*, the book which Dewey described as "sounding like a description of 'the situation' in transcendental German." In Part I of his *Heidegger's Pragmatism*, Mark Okrent has shown, very carefully and lucidly, how to read *Being and Time* as a pragmatist treatise.[8] The crucial point is the one Okrent puts as follows: "it is built into Heidegger's view of understanding that beliefs and desires must be ascribed together."[9] Once understanding is de-intellectualized in the way in which both Dewey and Heidegger wanted to de-intellectualize it – by viewing the so-called "quest for disinterested theoretical truth" as a continuation of practice by other means – most of the standard pragmatist doctrines follow.[10] In particular, it follows that, as Heidegger puts it, Dasein's Being-in-the-world is "the *foundation* for the primordial phenomenon of truth."[11] It also follows that "Being (not entities) is something which 'there is' only in so far as truth is. And truth is only in so far and as long as Dasein is. Being and truth 'are' equiprimordially."[12] That is to say: Being, which Plato thought of as something larger and stronger than us, is there only as long as we are here. The relations between it and us are not power relations. Rather, they are relations of fragile and tentative codependence. The relations between *Sein* and *Dasein* is like the relation between hesitant lovers; questions of relative strength and weakness do not arise.[13]

With Okrent, I read Division I of *Being and Time* as a recapitulation of the standard pragmatist arguments against Plato and Descartes. I read Division II, and in particular the discussion of Hegelian historicism, as recapitulating Nietzsche's criticism of Hegel's attempt to escape finitude by losing himself in the dramas of history. Hegel hoped to find in history the evidence and certainty that Plato hoped to find in a sort of super-mathematics called "dialectic," and that positivism hoped to find in a unified science. But from Heidegger's point of view, Plato, Descartes, Hegel, and positivism are just so many power plays. They are so many claims to have read the script of the drama we are acting out, thus relieving us of the need to make up this drama as we go along. Every such power play is, for Heidegger as for Dewey, an expression of the hope that truth may become *evident*, undeniable, clearly present to the mind. The result of such presence would be that we should no longer have to have projects, no longer have to create ourselves by inventing and carrying out these projects.

This quest for certainty, clarity, and direction from outside can also be viewed as an attempt to escape from time, to view *Sein* as something that has little to do with *Zeit*. Heidegger would like to recapture a sense of what time was like before it fell under the spell of eternity, what we were like before we became obsessed by the need for an overarching context which would subsume and explain us – before we came to think of our relation to Being in terms of power. To put it another way: he would like to recapture a sense of *contingency*, of the fragility and riskiness of any human project – a sense which the ontotheological tradition has made it hard to attain. For that tradition tends to identify the contingent with the merely apparent. By contrasting powerful reality with relatively impotent appearance, and claiming that it is all-important to make contact with the former, our tradition has suggested that the fragile and transitory can safely be neglected.

In particular, the tradition has suggested that the particular *words* we use are unimportant. Ever since philosophy won its quarrel with poetry, it has been the thought that counts – the proposition, something which many sentences in many languages express equally well. Whether a sentence is spoken or written, whether it contains Greek words or German words or English words, does not, on the traditional philosophical gview, greatly matter. For the words are mere vehicles for something less fragile and transitory than marks and noises. Philosophers know that what matters is literal truth, not a choice of phonemes and certainly not metaphors. The literal lasts and empowers. The metaphorical – that which you can neither argue about nor justify, that for which you can find no uncontroversial paraphrase – is impotent. It passes and leaves no trace.

One way to describe what Heidegger does in his later work is to see him as defending the poets against the philosophers. More particularly, we should take him at his word when, in the middle of *Being and Time*, he says: "In the end, the business of philosophy is to preserve the *force of the most elemental words* in which Dasein expresses itself, and to keep the common understanding from levelling them off to that unintelligibility which functions as a source of pseudo-problems."[14] I think that we should read "unintelligibility" here as "the inability to attend to a word which is common currency."[15] When a word is used frequently and easily, when it is a familiar, ready-to-hand instrument for achieving our purpose, we can no longer *hear* it. Heidegger is saying that we need to be able to hear the "most elemental" words which we use – presumably the sort of words which make up the little "Sketch of the History of Being" I quoted above – rather than simply using these words as tools. We need to hear them in the way in which a poet hears them when deciding whether to put one of them at a certain place in a certain poem. By so hearing them we shall preserve what Heidegger calls their "force." We shall hear them in the way in which we hear a metaphor for the first time. Reversing Hobbes, Heidegger thinks that words are the counters of everyday existence, but the money of Thinkers.[16]

Another way of describing Heidegger's later work is to emphasize a line in his own quasi-poem, *Aus der Erfahrung des Denkens*: "Being's poem, just begun, is man."[17] Think of the list of words cited above as a sort of abstract of the first stanza of that poem. Then think of the stanza being abstracted as *us*, the dwellers in the West.[18] To think of that poem that way, we have to think of ourselves as, first and foremost, the people who used – who *just happened* to use – those words. This is hard for us to do, because our tradition keeps trying to tell us that it isn't the words that matter, but the realities which they signify. Heidegger, by contrast, is telling us that the words do matter: that we are, above all, the people who have used those words. We of the West are the people whose project consisted in running down that particular list, in riding that particular escalator. There was no more *necessity* about getting on that escalator than there is about a poet's use of a given metaphor. But once the metaphor is used, the fate of the poet's audience is, Heidegger thinks, determined.

It is important to emphasize at this point that there is no hidden power called Being which designed or operated the escalator. Nobody whispered in the ears of the early Greeks, the poets of the West. There is just us, in the grip of no power save those of the words we happen to speak, the dead metaphors which we have internalized. There is no way, and no need, to tell the dancer from the dance, nor is there any point in looking around for a hidden choreographer. To see that there is *just us* would be simultaneously to see ourselves – to see the West – as a contingency and to see that there is no refuge from contingency. In particular, it would be to accept Heidegger's claim that "Only as long as Dasein is (that is, only as long as an understanding of Being is ontically possible) 'is there' Being."[19] If we could only see *that* Heidegger thinks, then we might shake off the will to power which is implicit in Plato and Christianity and which becomes explicit in pragmatism.

But if Being is not a hidden choreographer, not a source of empowerment, what is it? So far I have tossed "Being" around insouciantly, spoken Heideg-gerese. Now, in a brief excursus from my main topic – the relation between Heidegger and pragmatism – I shall try to say something about why Heidegger uses this term, and to offer a quasi-definition of it.

I think that Heidegger goes on and on about "the question about Being" without ever answering it because Being is a good example of something we have no criteria for answering questions about. It is a good example of something we have no handle on, no tools for manipulating – something which resists "the technical interpretation of thinking." The reason Heidegger talks about Being is not that he wants to direct our attention to an unfortunately neglected topic of inquiry, but that he wants to direct our attention to the difference between inquiry and poetry, between struggling for power and accepting contingency. He wants to suggest what a culture might be like in which poetry rather than philosophy-cum-science was the paradigmatic human activity. The question "What is Being?" is no more to be *answered correctly* than the question "What is a cherry blossom?" But the latter question is, nevertheless, one you might use to set the theme of a poetry competition. The former question is, so to speak, what the Greeks happened to come up with when they set the theme upon which the West has been a set of variations.

But doesn't Heidegger's use of "Being" immerse him in the tradition which he wants to wriggle free of: the ontotheological tradition, the history of metaphy-sics? Yes, but he wants to get free of that tradition not by turning his back on it but by attending to it and redescribing it.[20] The crucial move in this redescrip-tion, as I read Heidegger, is his suggestion that we see the metaphysician's will to truth as a self-concealing form of the poetic urge. He wants us to see metaphysics as an inauthentic form of poetry, poetry which thinks of itself as antipoetry, a sequence of metaphors whose authors thought of them as escapes from metaphoricity. He wants us to recapture the force of the most elementary words of Being – the words on the list above, the words of the various Thinkers who mark the stages of our descent from Plato – by ceasing to think of these words as the natural and obvious words to use. We should instead think of this list as as contingent as the contours of an individual cherry blossom.

To do this, we have to think of the West not as the place where human beings finally got clear on what was really going on, but as just one cherry blossom alongside actual and possible others, one cluster of "understandings of Being" alongside other clusters. But we also have to think of it as the blossom which *we* are. We can neither leap out of our blossom into the next one down the bough, nor rise above the tree and look down at a cloud of blossoms (in the way in which we imagine God looking down on a cloud of galaxies). For Heidegger's purposes, we are nothing save the words we use, nothing but an (early) stanza of Being's poem. Only a metaphysician, a power freak, would think we were more.

So is Being the leaf, the blossom, the bole, or what? I think the best answer is that it is what elementary words of Being refer to.1 But since such words of Being – words like *physis* or *subiectum* or *Wille zur Macht* – are just abbreviations for whole vocabularies, whole chains of interlocked metaphors, it is better to say that *Being is what vocabularies are about*. Being's poem is the poem about Being, not the poem Being writes. For Being cannot move a finger unless Dasein does, even though there is nothing more to Dasein than Being's poem.

More precisely, Being is what *final* vocabularies are about. A final vocabulary is one which we cannot help using, for when we reach it our spade is turned. We cannot undercut it because we have no metavocabulary in which to phrase criticisms of it.[21] Nor can we compare it with what it is about, test it for "adequacy" – for there is no nonlinguistic access to Being. To put the point in slightly more Heideggerian language: all we know of Being is that it is what understandings of Being are understandings of. But that is also all we need to know. We do not need to ask which understandings of Being are better understandings. To ask that question would be to begin replacing love with power.

To see the point of this quasi-definition of "Being," it is essential to realize that Being is not the same thing under all descriptions, but is something different under each. That is why the line between Being and Language is so thin, and why Heidegger applies many of the same phrases to both. Heidegger insists that he is writing a History *of Being*, not just a History of Human Understandings of Being. An imperfect analogy is that every description of space given by the definitions and axioms of a geometry is a description of a different space (Euclidean space, Riemannian space, etc.), so there is no point in asking whether the space was there before the geometry, nor in asking which geometry gets space-in-itself right. A History of Geometry would also be a History of Space. The analogy is imperfect because we construct geometries for particular purposes, but we do not *construct* final vocabularies. They are always already there; we find outselves thrown into them. Final vocabularies are not tools, for we cannot specify the *purpose* of a final vocabulary without futilely twisting around inside the circle of that very vocabulary.

The metaphysical thinker thinks that if you can just get the right understanding of Being – the one that gets Being right – then you are home. Heidegger thinks that the notion of "the right understanding of Being" is a confusion of Being with beings. You can relate beings to other beings (e.g., points in space to other points in space) in more or less useful ways – indeed, such relating is what Being-in-the-world consists of. But you cannot relate some beings – and in particular, some words – to Being any more than they are already related by the wimpy, impotent relation of "aboutness." In particular, Being is not the sort of thing which one can master, or which masters one. It is not related by the power relationships, the means-end relationships, which relate *beings* to one another.

The metaphysician, as Heidegger tells us in "On the Essence of Truth," regularly confuses truth with correctness. He confuses the relation of a vocabulary to Being with the relation of a sentence like "the sky is blue" to the color of the sky. There are criteria of correctness for deciding when to use that sentence to make a statement, but there are no criteria of correctness for final vocabularies.[22] If I am right in interpreting *Seinsverständnis* as "final vocabulary" and *Sein* as what final vocabularies are about, then one would expect Heidegger to say that no understanding of Being is more or less an understanding of Being, more or less true (in the sense of truth-as-disclosedness – *aletheia, Erschlossenheit, Unverborgenheit, Ereignis*) than any other. No petal on a cherry blossom is more or less a petal than any other.

Sometimes Heidegger does say things like this. For example: "Each epoch of philosophy has its own necessity. We simply have to acknowledge that philosophy is the way it is. It is not for us to prefer one to the other, as is the case with regard to various *Weltanschauungen*."[23] But often, as his use of the term "Forgetfulness of Being" suggests, he seems to be saying the opposite. For he makes all sorts of invidious comparisons between the less forgetful people at the top of the escalator – the Greeks – and the more forgetful ones at the bottom, us. The question of whether he has any business making such comparisons is the question of whether he has any business disliking pragmatism as much as he does. So now I return from my excursus on Being to the main topic of this paper.

The question of Heidegger's relation to pragmatism can be seen as the question: does Heidegger have any right to nostalgia? Any right to regret the golden time before Platonism turned out to be simply implicit pragmatism? Is there any room in his story for the notion of belatedness, for the notion of a *downward* escalator? To put it another way, should we read him as telling a story about the contingency of vocabularies or about the belatedness of our age? Or rather: since he is obviously telling both stories, can they be fitted together? I do not think they can.

To get this issue about contingency and belatedness in focus, consider the preliminary problem of whether Heidegger's early "ontological" enterprise can be fitted together with his later attempt to sketch the "history of Being." The reader of *Being and Time* is led to believe that the Greeks enjoyed a special relationship to Being which the moderns have lost, that they had less touble being ontological than we do, whereas we moderns have a terrible time keeping the difference between the ontological and the ontic in mind. The reader of the later work, however, is often told the Descartes and Nietzsche were as adequate expressions of what Being was at their times as Parmenides was of what Being was at his time. This makes it hard to see what advantage the Greeks might have enjoyed over the moderns, nor how Parmenides and Nietzsche could be compared in respect of the "elementariness" of the "words of Being" with which they are associated. Since there is no more to Being than its understanding by Dasein, since Being is not a power over and against Dasein, it is not clear how there could be anything more authentic or primal about the top of the escalator than the bottom. So it is not clear why we should think in terms of an escalator rather than of a level moving walkway.

Although *Being and Time* starts off with what looks like a firm distinction between the ontological and the ontic, by the end of the book the analytic of Dasein has revealed Dasein's historicity. This historicity makes it hard to see how ontological knowledge can be more than knowledge of a particular historical position. In the later work, the term "ontology" drops out, and we are told that what the Greeks did was to invent something called "metaphysics" by construing Being as "presence." What *Being and Time* had called "ontological knowledge," and had made sound desirable, now looks very like the confusion between Being and beings which the later work says is at the heart of the metaphysical tradition. Something seems to have changed, and yet the more one rereads Heidegger's writings of the 1920s in the light of his later essays the more one realizes that the historical story which he told in the 1930s was already in his mind when he wrote *Being and Time*. One's view about what, if anything, has changed, will determine what one makes of the idea that, for example, *logos* is *more* primordial than *Wille zur Macht* (in some honorific sense of "primordial").

Heidegger's own later glosses on *Being and Time* are of little help when it comes to the question of whether "the average vague understanding of Being" which is supposed to be the datum of the "analytic of Dasein" is itself an historical phenomenon, rather than something ahistorical which provides a neutral background against which to portray the differences between the Greeks and ourselves. My own guess is that in the 1920s Heidegger thought that it is ahistorical and that in the 1930s he came to think of it as historically situated.[24] If this guess is right, then the later Heidegger abjures the quest for ahistorical ontological knowledge and thinks that philosophical reflection is historical all the way down. But if it is, then we confront the problem of contingency and belatedness I sketched above. We face the question: is coming to an understanding of what Heidegger calls "what in the fullest sense of Being now is"[25] *simply* a matter of recapturing our historical contingency, of helping us see ourselves *as* contingent by seeing ourselves as historical, or is it, for example, learning that this is a particularly dark and dangerous time?[26]

The $32 question of whether the later Heidegger still believes there is an ahistorical discipline called "ontology" leads fairly quickly to the $64 question of whether he has a right to the nostalgia for which Derrida and others have criticized him, and to the hostility he displays towards pragmatism. Returning now to the former question, I would argue that the "analytic of Dasein" in *Being and Time* is most charitably and easily interpreted as an analytic of *Western Dasein*, rather than as an account of the ahistorical conditions for the occurrence of history.[27] There are passages in *Being and Time* itself, and especially in the roughly contemporary lecture course *The Basic Problems of Phenomenology*, which support this interpretation. These passages seem to make it clear that Heidegger comes down on the historicist side of the dilemma I have sketched. Thus towards the end of *Being and Time* he approvingly quotes Count von Yorck as saying: "it seems to me methodologically like a residue from metaphysics not to historicize one's philosophizing."[28] At the very end of that book he reminds us that the analytic of Dasein was merely preparatory and that it may turn out not have been the right way to go;[29] he hints that it might be what it later turned out to be; a disposable ladder.

In *Basic Problems of Phenomenology* he says that "even the ontological investigation that we are now conducting is determined by its historical situation." He goes on to say that

> These three components of phenomenological method – reduction, construction, destruction – belong together in their content and must receive grounding in their mutual pertinence. Construction in philosophy is necessarily destruction, that is to say, a de-constructing [Abbau] of traditional concepts carried out in a historical recursion to the tradition . . . Because destruction belongs to construction, philosophical cognition is essentially at the same time, historical cognition.[30]

This seems a proto-Derridean line of thought, in which philosophy becomes identical with historicist ironism, and in which there can be no room for nostalgia.

But there are plenty of passages in which the other horn of the dilemma, the ontological horn, seems to be grasped. In the "Introduction" to *Basic Problems*, from which I have just been quoting, Heidegger says that in our time, as perhaps never before, philosophizing has become "barbarous, like a St Vitus' dance." This has happened because contemporary philosophy is no longer ontology, but simply the quest for a "world-view." Heidegger defines the latter by contrast with "rheoretical knowledge." The definition of "world-view" which he quotes from Jaspers sounds a good deal like my definition of "final vocabulary." Something is equally a world-view whether it is based on "superstitions and prejudice" or on "scientific knowledge and experience."

However, after seeming to contrast ontology and world-view, Heidegger goes on to say the following:

> It is just because this positivity – that is, the relatedness to beings, to world that *is*, Dasein that *is* – belongs to the essence of the world-view, and thus in general to the formation of the world-view, that the formation of a world-view cannot be the task of philosophy. To say this is not to exclude but to include the idea that philosophy itself is a distinctive primal form [*eine ausgezeichnete Urform*] of world-view. Philosophy can and perhaps must show, among many other things, that something like a world-view belongs to the essential nature of Dasein. Philosophy can and must define what in general constitutes the structure of a world-view. But it can never

develop and posit some specific world-view *qua* just this or that particular one.[31]

But there is an obvious tension in this passage between the claim that philosophy "is a distinctive primal form of world-view" and that "philosophy . . . can never develop and posit some specific world-view." Heidegger never tells us how we can be historical through and through and yet ahistorical enough to step outside our world-view and say something neutral about the "structure" of all actual and possible world-views. To put the point in my own jargon, he never explains how we could possibly do more than create a new, historically situated, final vocabulary in the course of reacting against the one we found in place. To do something more – something ontological – would be to find a vocabulary which would have what he calls "an elementary and fundamental relation to all world-view formation" – the sort of relation which all the vocabularies of the metaphysical tradition have tried and failed to have. To possess such a vocabulary would, indeed, be to have a "distinctive primal form of world-view." Yet the very *attempt* at such a vocabulary looks like what Yorck called "a residue of metaphysics."

I read this confusing passage about philosophy and world-view as an early expression of the tension between saying that each epoch in the "history of Being" – each stage in the transition from the Greeks to the moderns – is on an ontological par, and saying that the Greeks' relation to Being was somehow closer than ours, that our "forgetfulness of Being" and lack of "primordiality" is responsible for the barbaric and frenzied character of the modern world. In other words, I see the difficulty about the historicity of ontology as a manifestation of the more basic difficulty about whether it can make sense to *criticize* the "understanding of Being" characteristic of one's own age. The early work suggests that the present age can be criticized for its lack of ontological knowledge. The later work continues to criticize the present age but seems to offer no account of the standpoint from which the criticism is made.

In the later work, as I have said, the term "ontology" drops out, as does "Dasein." The pejorative work done by ontic–ontological distinction in *Being and Time* is now done by the distinction between the nonprimordial and the primordial. Yet we are never told what makes for primordiality, any more than we were told how to step outside of our facticity long enough to be ontological. "Primordial" (*ursprünglich*) in the later work has all the resonance and all the obscurity which "ontological" had in the earlier.

This point can be put in other words by saying that Heidegger has two quite different things to say about the way the West is now: that it is contingent and that it is belated. To say that it is contingent it is enough to show how self-deceptive it is to think that things *had* to be as they are, how provincial it is to think that the final vocabulary of the present day is "obvious" and "inescapable." But to say that this vocabulary is belated, to contrast it with something more primordial, one has to give "primordial" some kind of normative sense, so that it means something more than just "earlier."

The only candidate for this normative sense which I can find in Heidegger is the following: an understanding of Being is more primordial than another if it makes it easier to grasp its own contingency. So to say that we in the twentieth century are belated, by comparison with the Greeks, is to say that their understanding of Being in terms of notions like *arche* and *physis* was less self-certain, more hesitant, more fragile, than our own supreme confidence in our own ability to manipulate beings in order to satisfy our own desires. The Greek thinkers presumably did not think of their "most elementary words" as "simply common sense," but we do. As you go down the list of words for "Being" in the West, the people using those words become less and less able to hear their own words, more and more thoughtless – where "thoughtless" means something like "unable to imagine alternatives to themselves." Something in these words themselves makes it increasingly easy not to hear them.

The importance of appreciating contingency appears most clearly, I think, in a passage from "On the Essence of Truth" in which Heidegger seems to be saying that history, Being's poem, begins when the first ironist has doubts about the final vocabulary he finds in place. It begins when somebody says "maybe we don't have to talk the way we do," meaning not just "maybe we should call this *Y* rather than *X*" but "maybe the language-game in which '*X*' and '*Y*' occur is the wrong one to be playing – not for any particular reason, not because it fails to live up to some familiar criterion, but just because it is, after all, only one among others. Here is the passage:

> History only begins when beings themselves are expressly drawn up in their unconcealment and conversed in it, only when this conservation is conceived on the basis of questioning regarding beings as such. The primordial disclosure of being as a whole, the question concerning beings as such, and the beginning of Western history are the same.[32]

I interpret this as saying that prehistorical people living in the West may have played sophisticated language-games, written epics, built temples, and predicted planetary motions, but they didn't count either as "thinking" or as "historical" until somebody asked "Are we doing the right things?" "Are our social practices the right ones to engage in?"

Thought, in Heidegger's honorific sense of the term, begins with a willing suspension of varificationism. it begins when somebody starts asking questions such that nobody, including himself or herself, can verify the answers for corectness. These are questions like "What is Being?" or "What is a cherry blossom?" Only when we escape from the verificationist impulse to ask "How can we tell a right answer when we hear one?" are we asking questions which Heidegger thinks worth asking. Only then are we Dasein, because only then do we have the possibility of being *authentic* Dasein, Dasein which knows itself to be "thrown." For, at least in the West, "Dasein . . . is ontically distinguished by the fact that, in its very Being, that Being is an *issue* for it."[33] So only then is there a *Da*, a clearing, a lighting-up. Before that, we were just animals that had developed complicated practices, practices we explained and commended to one another in the words of a final vocabulary which nobody dreamt of questioning. Afterward, we are divided into inauthentic Dasein, which is still just a complexly behaving animal in so far as it hasn't yet realized that its Being is an issue for it, and authentic Dasein, made up of Thinkers and Poets who know that there is an open space surrounding present-day social practices.

In Heidegger's mind, the attitude of questioning which he thinks begins historical existence, and thus makes Dasein out of an animal, is associated with an ability to do what he calls "letting beings be." This, in turn, is associated with freedom. In "Letter on Humanism" he says that there is a kind of nonontological thinking which is "more rigorous [*strenger*] than the conceptual"[34] – a phrase which I take to mean "more difficult to achieve than the kind of 'technical', verificationist thinking which submits to criteria implicit in social practices." "The material relevance [*sachhaltige Verbindlichkeit*]" of such thinking, Heidegger says, is "essentially higher than the validity of the sciences, because it is freer. For it lets Being – be."[35] In "On the Essence of Truth" he says "The essence of truth reveals itself as freedom. The latter is ek-sistent, disclosive letting beings be [*das ek-sistente, entbergende Seinlassen des Seienden*]."[36]

You let beings be when you disclose them, and you disclose thekm when you speak a language. So how can any language-user be less free, less open, less able to let Being and beings be, than any other? This is a reformulation of my previous question – how can any understanding of Being be preferable to any other, in the mysterious sense of being "more primordial"? The beginning of Heidegger's answer is that "because truth is in essence freedom, historical man can, in letting being be, also *not* let beings be the beings which they are and as they are. Then beings are covered up and distorted. Semblance [*der Schein*] comes to power." Further, Heidegger claims, this ability to *not* let beings be increases as technical mastery increases. As he says:

> where beings are not very familiar to man and are scarcely and only roughly known by science, the openedness of beings as a whole can prevail more essentially than it can where the familiar and well-known has become boundless, and nothing is any longer able to withstand the business of knowing, since technical mastery over things bears itself without limit. Precisely in the leveling and planning of this omniscience, this mere knowing, the openedness of beings gets flattened out into the apparent nothingness of what is no longer even a matter of indifference but rather is simply forgotten.[37]

But *what* is forgotten when we forget the "openedness of beings"? Heidegger's familiar and unhelpful answer is "Being." A slightly more complex and helpful answer is: that it was Dasein using language which let beings be in the first place. The greater the ease with which we use that language, the less able we are to *hear* the words of that language, and so the less able we are to think of language as such. To think of language as such, in this sense, is to think of the fact that no language is fated or necessitated. So to forget the openedness of beings is to forget about the possibility of alternative languages, and thus of alternative beings to those we know. It is, in the terms I was using before, to be so immersed in inquiry as to forget the possibility of poetry. This means forgetting that there have been other beings around, beings which are covering up by playing the language-games we do, having the practices we have. (The quarks were covered up by the Olympian deities, so to speak, and then later the quarks covered up the deities.) This forgetfulness is why we Westerners tend to think of poets referring to the same old beings under fuzzy new metaphorical descriptions, instead of thinking of poetic acts as the original openings up of the world, the acts which let new sorts of beings be.

In "On the Essence of Truth" the sections on freedom as the essence of truth are followed by a section called "untruth as concealing." This section is rather difficult to interpret, and I am by no means certain that I have caught Heidegger's intent. But I would suggest that the heart of Heidegger's claim that "Letting-be is intrinsically at the same time a concealing"[38] is just that you cannot let all possible beings be at once. That is, you cannot let all possible languages be spoken at once. The quarks and the Olympians, for example, would get in each other's way. The result would be chaos. So the best you can do is to remember that you are not speaking the only possible language – that around the openness provided by your understandings of Being there is a larger openness of other understandings of Being as yet unhad. Beyond the world made available by *your* elementary words there is the silence of other, equally elementary, words, as yet unspoken.

If I understand him, Heidegger is saying that the ability to *hear* your own elementary words is the ability to hear them against the background of that silence, to be aware of that silence. To be primordial is thus to have the ability to know that when you seize upon an understanding of Being, when you build a house for Being by speaking a language, you are automatically giving up a lot of other possible understandings of Being, and leaving a lot of differently designed houses unbuilt.

Assuming this interpretation is on the right track, I return to the question of why the Greeks are supposed to have been so good at knowing this, and why we are supposed to be so bad. Heidegger says

> However, in the same period in which the beginning of philosophy takes place, the *marked* domination of common sense (sophistry) [*Herrschaft des gemeinen Verstandes (die Sophistik)*] also begins.
>
> Sophistry appeals to the unquestionable character of the beings that are opened up and interprets all thoughtful questioning as an attack on, an unfortunate irritation of, common sense.[39]

I take this to say that right after we ceased to be animals, as a result of some Thinker having questioned whether the beings which our practices had opened up were the right beings, we divided up into sophistic and thoughtful Dasein. Sophistic, inauthentic Dasein could not see the point of questioning common sense, whereas thoughtful and authentic Dasein could. But, somehow, sophistry has become easier here in the twentieth century than it was back then. Somehow the beings that have been opened up by the languages *we* are speaking have become more unquestionable than those which the early Greeks opened up.

But is it in fact the case that we in the twentieth century are less able to question common sense than the Greeks were? Offhand, one can think of a lot of reasons why we might be *more* able to do so: we are constantly reminded of cultural diversity, constantly witnessing attempts at novelty in the arts, more and more aware of the possibility of scientific and political revolutions, and so on. If one wants complacent acceptance of common sense, one might think, the place to go is a fairly insular society, one which did not know much about what went on beyond its borders, one in which historiography had barely been invented and in which the arts were just getting started – some place like Greece in the 5th century BC.

Heidegger, of course, would dismiss this suggestion. For him, the very diversity and business of the modern world is proof that it is unable to sit still long enough to hear "elementary words." For Heidegger, cosmopolitanism, technology, and polymathy are enemies of Thinking. But why? Here we face the $64 question in all its starkness, a question which may be rephrased as follows: can we pragmatists appropriate all of Heidegger except his nostalgia, or is the nostalgia integral to the story he is telling? Can we agree with him both about the dialectical necessity of the transition from Plato to Dewey, and about the need to restore force to the most elementary words of Being, while nevertheless insisting that we in the twentieth century are in an exceptionally *good* position to do the latter? Can pragmatism do justice to poetry as well as to inquiry? Can it let us hear as well as use?

Predictably, my own answer to these last two questions is "yes indeed." I see Dewey's pragmatism – considered now not simply as an antirepresentationalist account of experience and an antiessentialist account of nature, but in its wholeness, as a project for a social democratic utopia – as putting technology in its proper place, as a way of making possible social practices (linguistic and other) which will form the next stanza of Being's poem. That utopia will come, as Dewey put it, when "philosophy shall have co-operated with the course of events and made clear and coherent the meaning of the daily detail, [and so] science and emotion will interpenetate, practice and imagination will embrace. Poetry and religious feeling will be the unforced flowers of life."[40]

I cannot, without writing several more papers, back up this claim that Dewey was as aware as Heidegger of the danger that we might lose the ability to hear in the technological din, though more optimistic about avoiding that danger. But I think that anybody who reads, for example, the section of Dewey's *A Common Faith* called "The Human Abode," or the concluding chapter ("Art and Civilization") of *Art as Experience*, will see the sort of case that might be made for my claim.[41]

If one asks what is so important about the ability to hear, the ability to have a sense of the contingency of one's words and practices, and thus of the possibility of alternatives to them, I think Dewey's and Heidegger's answers would overlap. They both might say that this ability, and only this ability, makes it possible to feel *gratitude* for and to those words, those practices, and the beings they disclose.

The gratitude in question is not the sort which the Christian has when he or she thanks Omnipotence for the stars and the trees. It is rather a matter of being grateful to the stars and trees themselves – to the beings that were disclosed by our linguistic practices. Or, if you prefer, it means being grateful for the existence of *ourselves*, for our ability to disclose the beings we have disclosed, for the embodied languages we are, but not grateful *to* anybody or anything. If you can see yourself-in-the-midst-of-beings as a *gift* rather than as an occasion for the exercise of power, then, in Heidegger's terms, you will cease to be "humanistic" and begin to "let beings be." You will combine the humility of the scientific realist with the spiritual freedom of the Romantic.

That combination was just what Dewey wanted to achieve. He wanted to combine the vision of a social democratic utopia with the knowledge that only a lot of hard work and blind luck, unaided by any large nonhuman power called Reason or History, could bring that utopia into existence. He combines reminders that only attention to the daily detail, to the obstinacy of particular circumstance, can create a utopia with reminders that all things are possible, that there are no *a priori* or destined limits to our imagination or our achievement. His "humanism" was not the power mania which Heidegger thought to be the only remaining possibility open to the West. On the contrary, it put power in the service of love – technocratic manipulation in the service of a Whitmanesque sense that our democratic community is held together by nothing less fragile than social hope.

My preference for Dewey over Heidegger is based on the conviction that what Heidegger wanted – something that was not a calculation of means to ends, not power madness – was under his nose all the time. It was the new world which began to emerge with the French Revolution – a world in which future-oriented politics, romantic poetry, and irreligious art made social practices possible in which Heidegger never joined. He never joined them because he never really looked outside of philosophy books. His sense of the drama of European history was confined to the drama of his own "Sketches for a History of Being as Metaphysics." He was never able to see politics or art as more than epiphenomenal – never able to shake off the philosophy professor's conviction that everything else stands to philosophy as superstructure to base. Like Leo Strauss and Alexandre Kojève, he thought that if you understood the history of Western philosophy you understood the history of the West.[42] Like Hegel and Marx, he thought of philosophy as somehow geared into something larger than philosophy. So when he decided that Western philosophy had exhausted its possibilities, he decided that the West had exhausted its. Dewey, by contrast, never lost the sense of contingency, and thus the sense of gratitude, which Heidegger thought only an unimaginably new sort of Thinking might reintroduce. Because he took pragmatism not as a switch from love to power, but as a switch from philosophy to politics as the appropriate vehicle for love, he was able to combine skill at manipulation and contrivance with a sense of the fragility of human hopes.

In this paper I have been reading Heidegger by my own, Deweyan lights. But to read Heidegger in this way is just to do to him what he did to everybody else, and to do that what no reader of anybody can help doing. There is no point in feeling guilty or ungrateful about it. Heidegger cheerfully ignores, or violently reinterprets, lots of Plato and Nietzsche while presenting himself as respectfully listening to the voice of Being as it is heard in their words. But Heidegger knew what he wanted to hear in advance. He wanted to hear something which would make his own historical position decisive, by making his own historical epoch terminal.

As Derrida brilliantly put it, Heideggerian hope is the reverse side of Heideggerian nostalgia. Heideggerian hope is the hope that Heidegger himself, his Thinking, will be a decisive event in the History of Being.[43] Dewey had no similar hope for his own thought. The very idea of a "decisive event" is foreign to Dewey. Pragmatists like Dewey hope that things may turn out well in the end, but their sense of contingency does not permit them to write dramatic narratives about upward or downward escalators. They exemplify a virtue which Heidegger preached, but was not himself able to practice.

NOTES

1 Martin Heidegger, "Entwurfe zur Geschichte des Seins als Metaphysik," *Nietzsche* II, Pfullingen: Neske, 1961, pp. 455ff. This and the preceding section "Die Metaphysik als Geschichte des Seins," have been translated by Joan Stambaugh and appear in Heidegger, *The End of Philosophy*, New York: Harper & Row, 1973.

2 *The End of Philosophy*, pp. 65–6 (*Nietzsche* II, pp. 470–1). Stambaugh leaves words untranslated because, as I shall be saying later, Heidegger insists that the sounds of words matter, not just what they have in common with their translations into other languages. (In particular, he thinks that Cicero's translation into Latin of Plato's and Aristotle's Greek was a decisive turn in Western thought.) Nevertheless, I shall list the most common English translations of the Greek and Latin terms here. *Alétheia*-truth, *apeiron*-infinite; *logos*-word, reason, thought, *hen*-one; *arche*-principle; *physis*-nature (derived from *phyein*, to grow, to emerge); *idea*-idea in the Platonic sense of "Idea" or "Form," deriving from *idein*-to see, to perceive; *agathon*-the good; *energeia*-actuality (as opposed to potentiality); *en-echeta to telos*-having the end within it, having achieved its purpose (*entelechia* is a word sometimes used synonymously with *energeia* by Aristotle; it too is frequently translated as "actuality"); *hypokeimenon*-substrate (a term applied to matter when Aristotle is discussing metaphysics, and to the subject of predication when he is discussing logic), *ousia*-substance (but also a participle of the verb *einai*, "to be"); *ergon*-work, activity; *aet*-eternity; *hyparchein*-to possess, or (in Aristotle's logic) to have as a property; *subiectum*-Latin translation of, and etymologically equivalent to, *hypokeimenon*, "substrate" – but also, after Descartes, a word for "subject" in both senses – the subject of a sentence and the ego as subject of experience; *actualitas*-Latin translation of *energeia*, "actuality"; *creator*-creator; *ens creatum*-created being; *causa prima*-first cause; *ens a se*-being capable of existing by itself (i.e., God); *certitudo*-certitude; *res cogitans*-thinking thing (Descartes's term for the mind); *vis*-force, power; *monas*-monad (Leibniz's term for the ultimate components of the universe, nonspatiotemporal loci of force, of perception [*perceptio*], of appetite [*appetitus*], and of a need to exist in order to express themselves [*exigentia essentiae*]). Heidegger offers, in one place or another in his writings, alternative translations of each of these terms, designed to restore their force by stripping them of their familiar connotations.

3 Heidegger, "Letter on humanism," in *Basic Writings* (hereafter abbreviated as *BW*), ed. David Krell, New York: Harper & Row, 1977, p. 194. The original is at Heidegger, *Wegmarken* (hereafter *WM*), 2nd edition, Frankfurt: Klostermann, 1978, p. 312.

4 Heidegger. "The end of philosophy and the task of thinking," *BW*, p. 386. The original is at Heidegger, *Zur Sache des Denkens*, Tubingen: Niemeyer, 1976, p. 74. See also Heidegger, *Nietzsche*, vol. 4, trans. Frank Capuzzi, New York: Harper & Row,

1982, p. 205; *"Metaphysics as metaphysics is nihilism proper.* The essence of nihilism *is* historically as metaphysics, and the metaphysics of Plato is no less nihilistic than that of Nietzsche.*"* The original is at *Nietzsche* II, Pfullingen: Neske, 1961, p. 343.

5   "In the subjectness of the subject, will comes to appearance as the essence of subjectness. Modern metaphysics, as the metaphysics of subjectness, thinks the Being of that which is in the sense of will." Heidegger, "The word of Nietzsche," in *The Question Concerning Technology and Other Essays* (hereafter *QT*), trans. William Lovitt, New York: Harper & Row, 1977, p. 88. The original is at Heidegger, *Holzwege*, Frankfurt: Klostermann, 1972, p. 225. This quotation summarizes the transition, on the list above, from Being as Cartesian *subiectum* to Being as the Leibnizian *exigentia essentiae* within the monad, and thence to the Kantian conception of the nonphenomenal self as will under the aspect of practical reason. The notion of "will" is then reinterpreted by Hegel and Schelling in a way which quickly brings one to Nietzsche and Dewey. The same transition is formulated at *QT*, p. 128, by saying that with "man becoming subject", gradually "man becomes the relational center of all that is."

6   *QT*, pp. 129–30. *Holzwege*, p. 81.

7   Nietzsche, *The Will to Power*, trans. Kaufmann, New York: Random House, 1967, s. 584, p. 314.

8   I first learned how much of *Being and Time* can be read as a pragmatist tract from Robert Brandom's seminal "Heidegger's Categories in Being and Time," *Monist* 60 (1983).

9   Mark Okrent, *Heidegger's Pragmatism*, Ithaca, N.Y.: Cornell University Press, 1988, p. 64. See also p. 123: "Husserl conceives of the fundamental form of intentionality as cognitive; Heidegger conceives of it as practical. As a result, Husserl thinks of the horizons in which beings are presented on the model of sensuous fields in which objects are placed before us for our intuitive apprehension, whereas Heidegger thinks of these horizons as fields of activity." One can substitute "the early Russell" or "the early Wittgenstein" for "Husserl," and "Dewey" or "the later Wittgenstein" for "Heidegger," in these sentences *salva veritate*.
On Heidegger's conception of the relation between cognition and action, see Brandom, "Heidegger's Categories," pp. 405–6. Brandom notes that on the traditional, Platonic account "the only appropriate response to something present-at-hand is an assertion, the only use which can be made of assertion is inference, and inference is restricted to theoretical inference" whereas on the Heideggerian and pragmatist accounts "the only way in which the present-at-hand can affect Dasein's projects is by being the subject of an assertion which ultimately plays some role in practical inference."

10 The difference between pragmatists and nonpragmatists on this point comes out very clearly in an early criticism of Bradley by Dewey. ("The Intellectualist Criterion for Truth," in *Middle Works*, vol. 4, pp. 50–75; the quotations that follow are from pp. 58–9) After quoting Bradley as saying "You may call the intellect, if you like, a mere tendency to a movement, but you must remember that it is a movement of a very special kind . . . Thinking is the attempt to satisfy a special impulse." Dewey comments: "The unquestioned presupposition of Mr. Bradley is that thinking is such a wholly separate activity . . . that to give it autonomy is to say that it, and its criterion, having nothing to do with other activities . . . " Dewey argues that "intellectual discontent is the practical conflict becoming deliberately aware of itself as the most effective means of its own rectification." Compare Heidegger, *Being and Time* (hereafter *BT*), trans. Macquarrie and Robinson, New Hork: Harper & Row, 1962, p. 95: "The kind of dealing which is closest to us is . . . not a bare perceptual cognition, but rather that kind of concern which manipulates things and puts them to

use." (The original is at *Sein und Zeit* (hereafter *SZ*), Tubingen: Niemeyer, 1963, p. 67.

In Part I of the first volume of these papers, I criticize Bernard Williams for agreeing with Bradley about the autonomy of truth-seeking, about the distinction between theoretical inquiry and practical deliberation. The assumption of such autonomy is, I think, essential to the intelligibility of Williams's notion of "the absolute conception of reality." The Heideggerian-Deweyan reply to Descartes and Williams on this topic is put by Brandom ("Heidegger's Categories," p. 403) as follows: "the move from equipment, ready-to-hand, fraught with socially instituted significances, to objective things present-at-hand, is not one of decontextualization but of *re*contextualization".

11 Heidegger, *BT*. p. 261, *SZ*. p. 219.

12 *BT*, p. 272; *SZ*, p. 230.

13 To be fair to Kierkegaard, he too realized that something other than power relations were needed to make sense of Christianity. See his claim that "the form of the servant was not something put on" in his discussion of the Incarnation as a solution to a loving God's need not to overwhelm the beloved sinner. *Philosophical Fragments*, trans. Howard and Edna Hong, Princeton: Princeton University Press, 1985, p. 32.

14 *BT*, p. 262; *SZ*, p. 220 Emphasis in the original

15 This interpretation coheres with Heidegger's remark at *BT*, p. 23 (*SZ*, p. 41) about the easy intelligibility of "is" in "the sky is blue." He says that "here we have an average kind of intelligibility, which merely demonstates that this is unintelligible."

16 On hearing, see *BT*, p. 228 (*SZ*, p. 183) "But Being 'is' only in the understanding of those entities to whose Being something like an understanding of Being belongs." Heidegger added a marginal note here which reads, "Understanding is to be taken here in the sense of 'hearing.' That does not mean that 'Being' is only 'subjective' but that Being (as the Being of beings) is 'in' Dasein as the thrown is in the throwing" (*SZ*, 15th edition, p. 443) I construe this passage in the light of the passage I quoted earlier about "the force of the most elementary words." See also *BT*, p. 209 (*SZ*, 163); "Hearing constitutes the primary and authentic way in which Dasein is open for its ownmost potentiality-for-Being – as in hearing the voice of the friend whom every Dasein carries with it."

17 Heidegger, *Poetry, Language, Thought*, trans. Albert Hotstader, New York: Harper & Row, 1971, p. 4. The original is *Wir kommen für die Gotter zu spät und zu früh für das Seyn. Dessen angefangenes Gedicht ist der Mensch.* Heidegger, *Aus der Erfahrung des Denkens*, Pfullingen: Neske, 1954, p. 7.

18 Heidegger often refuses to make a distinction between Dasein, the "Da" of Dasein, and the lighting-up of beings by Dasein's use of language to describe beings. See *BT*, p. 171 (*SZ*, p. 133): "To say that it [Dasein] is illuminated [*erleuchtet*] means that *as* Being-in-the-world it is cleared [*gelichtet*] in itself, not through any other entity, but in such a way that it *is* itself the clearing [*die Lichtung*]." But he also, especially in the later works, refuses to make a distinction between Dasein and Sein. Note the use of *Lichtung*, in "Letter on Humanism" (*BW*, p. 216; *WM*, p. 333) where Heidegger says that "Being is essentially broader than all beings because it is the lighting [*Luchtung*] itself." When Heidegger says, at the beginning of "Letter on Humanism," that "Language is the house of Being. In its home man dwells" (*BW*, p. 193; *WM*, p. 145), the suggestion that the two dwellers cannot be distinguished from one another is deliberate. The more you read later Heidegger, the more you realize that the distinctions between language, human beings, and Being are being deliberately and systematically blurred. I read this blurring as a warning, analogous to Wittgenstein's, against trying to get between language and its object, plus a further warning against trying to get between language and its user. In Heidegger's version, the warning says: if you try to come between them – if you try to make the user more than his or her

words, and the object described more than its description in words, you risk winding up with some version of the Subject–Object or Human–Superhuman dualisms, and thus being condemned to think in terms of power relations between the terms of these dualisms. Though for purposes of *manipulating* them you may *have* to separate subject and object from each other and from language, remember that there are other purposes than manipulation.

19   *BT*, p. 255.

20   In 1962 Heidegger suggests that he may have done too much redescribing, and needs to start ignoring: "a regard for metaphysics still prevails even in the intending to overcome metaphysics. Therefore our task is to cease all overcoming, and leave metaphysics to itself." *Of Time and Being*, trans. Joan Stambaugh, New York: Harper & Row, 1972, p. 24; *Zur Sache des Denkens*, p. 25. But by 1962 he had put in thirty years struggling to overcome – the years in which he wrote his most intriguing and provocative works.

21   For a fuller explicit definition of "final vocabulary" see my *Contingency, Irony, and Solidarity*, Cambridge: Cambridge University Press, 1989, p. 73. Chapter 4 of that book is a sort of long contextual definition of this term.

22   See Okrent, *Heidegger's Pragmatism*, p. 286: "It seems possible to raise the question of which language, which vocabulary, which intentional horizon is the right or correct one. In fact, this is the very question that metaphysics in Heidegger's sense was designed to raise and answer . . . But according to both American neopragmatism and Heidegger as we have interpreted him, there is no determinate answer to this question, because being cannot be seen as grounding and justifying a particular intentional horizon." I agree with what Okrent says in this passage, but disagree with much of what he goes on to say at pp. 289–97 about the status of pragmatism as a doctrine. Okrent thinks that one should avoid "Heidegger's own desperate recourse to the view that assertions concerning the truth of being are not really assertions at all" (p. 292). I am not sure that one should; if pragmatism is to be viewed as saying something about the "truth of Being" (a phrase which Okrent finds more intelligible than I do), then I should like it to take the form of a proposal ("Let's try it this way, and see what happens") rather than an assertion. My disagreement with Okrent here is connected with my doubts about Okrent's claim that "all prgamatism either must be based on a transcendental semantics or be self-contradictory" (p. 280). See Okrent's "The metaphilosophical consequences of pragmatism", in *The Institution of Philosophy*, ed. Avner Cohen and Marcello Dascal, Totowa, N.J.: Rowan and Littlefield, 1988, for his defense of this latter claim and for criticism of some of my own views.

23   *BW*, p. 375; *Zur Sache des Denkens*, pp. 62–3.

24   Heidegger would of course deny this. But, as Okrent (*Heidegger's Pragmatism*, p. 223) notes, Heidegger "stubbornly refused to admit that he had changed his mind, made any crucial mistakes in earlier works, or significantly altered terminology over time."

25   "Letter on Humanism," *BW*, p. 221. The original is just as obscure as the English: *was in einem erfüllten Sinn von Sein fetzt ist* (*WM*, p. 338).

26   One should be clear that for Heidegger things like the danger of a nuclear holocaust, mass starvation because of overpopulation, and the like, are not indications that the time is particularly dark and dangerous. These merely ontic matters are not the sort of thing Heidegger has in mind when he says that "the wasteland spreads."

27   The ambiguity between these two alternatives is nicely expressed by a note which Heidegger inserted in the margin at *BT*, p. 28 (*SZ*, p. 8). Having said "This guiding activity of taking a look at Being arises from the average understanding of Being in which we always operate and *which in the end belongs to the essential constitution of Dasein itself [und das am Ende zur Wesensverfassung des Daseins selbst gehort]*," he glosses "in the end [*am Ende*]" with "that is, from the beginning [*d.h. von Anfang*

an]". *"Am Ende"* would naturally have been read as meaning "in the nature of Dasein," but *"von Anfang an"* can be read as reminding us that Dasein does not have a nature, but only an historical existence. The question remains whether Heidegger earlier, at the time of writing *Being and Time*, did think that Dasein – not just Western Dasein – had a nature which Daseinsanalytik could expose, or whether he meant the indexical "Da" to express historicity even back then.

28 *BT*, p. 453; *SZ*, p. 402.
29 *BT*, p. 487; *SZ*, pp. 436–7.
30 Heidegger, *The Basic Problems of Phenomenology* (hereafter *BP*), trans. Albert Hofstadter, Bloomington: Indiana University Press, 1982, p. 23. The original is at Heidegger, *Gesamtausgabe*, vol. 24: *Die Grundprobleme der Phänomenologie* Frankfurt: Klostermann 1975, p. 31.
31 *BP*, p. 10 *Die Grundprobleme*, pp. 12–13.
32 *BW*, p. 129; *WM*, p. 187.
33 See *BW*, p. 32; *SZ*, p. 12. I take it that for *das Man*, for the ordinary person-in-the-street, for inauthentic Dasein, Being is *not* an issue. If Heidegger means that it is an issue even for inauthentic Dasein, then I have no grasp of what "being an issue" is, what it is *um dieses Sein selbst gehen*.
34 *BW*, p. 235; *WM*, p. 353.
35 *BW*, p. 236; *WM*, p. 354.
36 *BW*, p. 30; *WM*, p. 189.
37 *BW*, p. 131; *WM*, 190.
38 *BW*, p. 132; *WM*, p. 190.
39 *BW*; p. 138, *WM*, p. 196.
40 Dewey, *Reconstruction in Philosophy*, Boston: Beacon, 1957, pp. 212–13.
41 The latter book is full of the kinds of criticisms of aestheticism which Heidegger himself makes. Heidegger would heartily agree with Dewey that "As long as art is the beauty parlor of civilization neither art nor civilization is secure". *Art as Experience*, New York: Putnam, 1958, p. 344. But Heidegger would not agree "that there is nothing in the nature of machine production *per se* that is an insuperable obstacle in the way of worker' consciousness of the meaning of what they do and work well done" (p. 343). Heidegger thought it in principle impossible that assembly line workers could have what Schwarzwald peasants had. Dewey had some ideas for arranging things so that they might.
In *A Common Faith*, New Haven, CT.: Yale University Press, 1934, Dewey praises "natural piety" for much the same reasons as Heidegger criticizes "humanism." See, for example, p. 53, in which both "supernaturalism" and "militant atheism" are condemned for lack of such piety, and for conceiving of "this earth as the moral center of the universe and of man as the apex of the whole scheme of things."
42 This preoccupation with philosophy made Heidegger ungrateful to the time in which he lived, unable to realize that it was thanks to living at a certain historical moment (after Wordsworth, Marx, Delacroix, and Rodin) – living in what he sneeringly called the age of the world picture – that he could paint his own picture, and find an appreciative audience for it.
43 See Derrida, "Différance." in *Margins of Philosophy*, trans. Alan Bass, Chicago: University of Chicago Press, 1982, p. 27. "From the vantage of this laughter and this dance, from the vantage of the affirmation foreign to all dialectics, the other side of nostalgia [cette autre face de la nostalgie], what I will call Heideggerian hope [espérance], comes into question."

12
Who is Heidegger's Nietzsche?
(On the Very Idea of the Present Age)

Randall E. Havas

Heidegger's overall account of life in the present age depends essentially upon his reading of Nietzsche. Approaching Nietzsche in the right way provides insight, Heidegger insists, into what it means to be modern. But an adequate grasp of the insight Heidegger promises depends upon a proper appreciation of the specific kind of reading he offers, and understanding that, in turn, depends upon coming to terms with his claim that Nietzsche's thinking fails to overcome metaphysics.

The question Heidegger raises about what reading Nietzsche can teach about belonging to the present age – about being modern – is, I believe, importantly continuous with certain central aspects of the question of authenticity as it is raised in *Being and Time*.[1] We may think of authenticity as a response to or an expression of a proper understanding of what Heideggerian anxiety tries to pass off as an experience of the groundlessness or contingency of human convention. Anxiety expresses a confused recognition of what we might call "the constraints of intelligibility," a recognition that if we are to go on with our ordinary dealings with the world, then we must let *these* things – hammers and so on – count as the things they are. It is a recognition that interpretation bottoms out in understanding. And while the constraints of intelligibility are not rooted in the world's nature – in what he calls "the present-at-hand" – Heidegger thinks it is simply philosophical confusion to say that the world's intelligibility is somehow "up to us." That there *is* anything to recognize here is something Heidegger later expresses by talking of letting beings be. That, on the other hand, there is nothing special to recognize here – that we all "let being be," most of the time anyway – is what gives the lie to the idea of authenticity as an attitude Heidegger thinks we may adopt toward the intelligibility of the world.

I think, then, that we should give up the idea that the authentic individual knows something of which the inauthentic individual remains ignorant. The world is, as I shall say, *authoritative* for the authentic individual, and she is not in the grip of certain philosophical pictures of that authority (say, by seeing it as either natural or conventional). But she does not *know* something about the world's intelligibility that the inauthentic person does not.

The parallel between Heidegger's early discussion of authenticity and his later concern to show what it means to belong to the present age – to accept the essence of technology as a "gift," or to hear in the right way what Nietzsche says about the death of God – is simply that belonging to the present age is not, like finding the world to be an intelligible place is not, a matter of knowing or believing something special about it. We should understand in this way Heidegger's repeated claims not to be trying to reveal some deeply hidden secret about the present age. Thinking, in the special Heideggerian sense, is not thinking *about* anything; it is not, in particular, thinking about something that mere "representation" cannot represent.

The argument of this essay tries, then, to show that the familiar difficulties in understanding Heidegger's critical assessment of modern life – and in particular his claim that Nietzsche's account of life in the present age is itself fundamentally metaphysical and nihilistic – stem from a mistaken idea of how the notion of modernity functions in his work. More specifically, I argue, these difficulties depend on the mistaken idea that Heidegger treats the present age as the object of an interpretation. In fact, Heidegger is better read as offering us a diagnosis of our tendency to think that it could be. He wants to show us how our ways of encountering the world in the present age are fateful for us, to show us what it means to be obedient to their authority. And he maintains that obedience to such authority cannot be a matter of adopting an interpretation of modern life.

Rather than address the question concerning technology and the present age head-on, however, I shall take what I find to be the necessary detour through Heidegger's reading of Nietzsche. The force of Heidegger's reading cannot be properly appreciated until it is understood why he scrupulously avoids referring to that reading as an interpretation. He says he wants to prepare what he calls a "confrontation" ["*Auseinandersetzung*"] with Nietzsche. In section 1 of this essay, then, I shall show how the notion of the present age functions in Heidegger's reading of Nietzsche. In section 2, I shall suggest how I think we should conceive Nietzsche's critical standpoint on the present age, and propose a way of assessing Heidegger's criticism of it.

1   The marketplace

In section 125 of *The Gay Science*, Nietzsche tells a story of a madman who lights a lantern "in the bright morning hours" and announces to a disinterested, even derisive marketplace crowd that "God is dead."[2] Talking about the death of God is Nietzsche's way of talking about what it makes sense to believe. The setting here suggests that Nietzsche thinks we may have some trouble making sense of what it makes sense to believe. In particular, he says, belief in the Christian god has become *un*believable. And the fact that the madman fails to make this development seem significant to those who, as Nietzsche says, already do not believe in God suggests that we have not yet really come to grips with what he says.

According to Heidegger, the death of God means, roughly, that the fact that we are increasingly unable to believe that our highest values have any other than a purely human origin is in some way definitive of who we are in the present age. On this reading, the fact that this or that is or has been most highly esteemed by us can only be the result of purely human – that is, historical, political, and psychological – influences. Recognition of this fact leads some individuals to become disenchanted with life. Such disenchantment is one form of nihilism. Nietzsche seems to think that a possible solution to this kind of nihilism lies in a proper understanding of the character of our responsibility for the value and significance of life: what he calls a revaluation of all values. Such revaluation may be necessary before we can truly appreciate the significance of what the madman says.

Most generally, then, Nietzsche's talk of the death of God refers to the question of how, in the wake of the Enlightenment, we are to understand our relation to the world and to each other. Nietzsche wants to understand the significance of our growing freedom from externally imposed authority, whether the authority in question be that of religion, tradition, institution, or custom. He takes the growth of such freedom more or less for granted; it is not something that he wishes to or even thinks it makes good sense to try to oppose. But it is something the status of which he thinks we are inclined to misunderstand, and it is important to see why this is so.

The death of God means that we can no longer make sense of the idea that the value of life is imposed upon it from without. This suggests in turn that we ourselves must in some way be responsible for it. But this very conclusion seems to leave us without a philosophically workable picture of what such responsibility comes to. That is to say, while the world remains an intelligible place in the wake of the death of God, that intelligibility, it now appears, can neither merely be imposed upon the world by us, nor be found simply written onto the surface of things, somehow inherent in the world's nature. The death of God suggests, then, that just when we think we are finally becoming most transparent to ourselves – most fully human – we are in fact confronted with an intrinsic difficulty in understanding ourselves. The death of God, that is to say, is inherently difficult to understand.

So it is important to see that the reason that the news of the death of God seems in section 125 to fall on deaf ears is *not* that it is too profound or too unsettling, that this is difficult news to bear. The laughter of the people in the marketplace is not *obviously* anxious laughter, as though they could not face up to some painful truth being revealed to them. The problem with the madman's audience – and hence, I think, with us – is not that they care too much about the significance of their lives, but that they – and we – care too little.

The part of this aphorism that is most important for understanding *Heidegger's* confrontation with Nietzsche is, therefore, the *third* of the madman's three speeches. The people in the marketplace understand what the madman says; his questions are clear enough. But they do not seem to the madman to hear his announcement in the right way. In response to the astonishment and silence with which those in the marketplace greet his account of the death of God, the madman says, "I have come too early . . . my time is not yet. This tremendous

event is still on its way, still wandering; it has not yet reached the ears of men."
The "not yet" guides Heidegger's reading of Nietzsche, early and late. Quite
generally, he wants to know what *sort* of event the death of God is that its
announcement should be so hard for us – in the marketplace – to hear properly,
and why it should be a madman who makes this announcement.

The Heideggerian exposition of Nietzsche's metaphysics is meant to grant us
insight into the nature of nihilism:

> The attempt to elucidate Nietzsche's word "God is dead" has the same
> significance as does the task of setting forth what Nietzsche understands by
> "nihilism" and of thus showing how Nietzsche himself stands in relation to
> nihilism.[3]

The suggestion here is that when we understand what Nietzsche means by
"nihilism", we will appreciate the extent to which his own account of the death of
God is itself nihilistic. Heidegger explains this claim by means of an analysis of
what he calls the metaphysics of the will to power. Heidegger's reading of the will
to power is elaborate, but its specific details need not occupy us here. The basic
idea behind his account of Nietzsche's doctrine is simply that the death of God
means that we must somehow make sense of the idea that life itself – *human* life
in the first instance – is the only conceivable standard of its own value. And the
doctrine of will to power, in turn, suggests how to represent to ourselves our own
responsibility for the significance and value of life.

Not surprisingly, that responsibility is analyzed, on Nietzsche's account, in
terms of a certain notion of freedom or autonomy. To see how such an analysis
might go, consider the account of nihilism itself as it appears in *The Will to
Power*. Nihilism, Nietzsche says there, is a crisis in our *values*. Values are the
conditions of what might, loosely following Aristotle, be called "human flourishing"; Nietzsche calls them life's "preservation-enhancement conditions." On
Heidegger's reading, the will to power "wills" or posits these conditions for itself.
The *autonomy* of the will to power consists precisely in the fact that it itself is the
source of its own value. Life is, in short, the unconditioned condition of itself.
Nihilism is the result of our unwillingness to acknowledge this fact.

Heidegger's analysis of the Nietzschean notion of self-overcoming serves to
show in two ways how his reading of the doctrine of will to power differs
essentially from a traditional "irrationalist" interpretation. On the one hand, "the
will to power" is a name for the three-part structure of willing: the willing itself,
the one who wills, and that which is willed in the willing. The will to power is
thus to be distinguished from a Schopenhauerian notion of will as mere striving.
On the other hand, what is willed and the one who wills it must be connected to
willing in an entirely intrinsic manner; that is, in such a way that both only are
what they are in the act of willing and no further. It is this latter fact that
expresses the autonomy or freedom of the will to power. Heidegger writes,

> The *decisive question* is this: how, and on what grounds, do the willed and
> the one who wills belong to the willing to will? Answer: on the grounds of

willing and by means of willing. Willing wills the one who wills, as such a one; and willing posits the willed as such . . . In each case will itself furnishes thoroughgoing determinateness to its willing.[4]

Nietzsche might, then, be thought of as a nihilist, on this reading, precisely because, on his view, none of our projects, aims, or goals in life has any independent content, nothing that we do has any meaning or significance *outside of its mere achievement.* Nothing is any more worthwhile than anything else. And we as "agents" – that is, as the ones who will – have no identity outside the willing of what is willed. The will to power is thus – from both ends, as it were – completely formal and empty. Life is, in *this* sense anyway, meaningless. The will to power can, in this sense, will only its own overcoming.

We might think that this purely formal and empty character of life understood as will to power means that in order for human actions to have significance for a human agent, such significance must in some way be *attributed* to those actions by the agent in so far as they do not have it of themselves. But on Nietzsche's view, any such significance we may attribute to our lives is itself just more will to power. It does not matter in the least *what* we do; and it does not matter how we may *feel* about what we do. All of this is simply more will to power. This is why Heidegger often refers to the will to power as the will to will. The "overcoming" of any given configuration of will to power is all that power comes to on this reading.

The connection between will to power and nihilism should, in outline anyway, be clear. The death of God requires a fundamental change in the way we think of what it means to be human. The activity definitive of us as human agents is to posit – to "will" – values. This basic shift in the meaning of being human means that life must now be thought of as the source of its own significance. Heidegger thinks that *the interpretation of life as will to power tells us what it means for life to be its own ground and justification.* The autonomy of willing – of value-positing – must therefore be complete and absolute: if everything is life, then anything that conditions life can only be more life.

But this means for Heidegger that the metaphysics of will to power represents the final turn on the circle of philosophical questions about what our relationship to the world might be. We now see what this idea comes to. The way Nietzsche's doctrine of will to power articulates the notion of life as the standard of its own value is the basis of Heidegger's claim. And that doctrine expresses a vision of complete autonomy. Heidegger understands this conception of absolute human freedom to express something like an accurate description of what we have become in the present age. But if all thinking is a matter of the autonomous positing of values, then *philosophical* thinking – the sort of thinking which would question the possibility and significance of just such autonomous reason – becomes itself just more valuation; that is to say, it becomes impossible. And for this reason, apparently, Heidegger concludes that by thinking of the death of God in terms of values, Nietzsche's own philosophy remains metaphysical and nihilistic.

What Heidegger thinks is expressed in Nietzsche's doctrine of will to power is thus a vision of human thought – of what we can think – as the absolute measure of what it means to be at all. On his reading, "to be" means "to be thinkable." Moreover, in the context of the doctrine of will to power, there is nothing that is not thinkable. It is in this sense that Heidegger says that, according to Nietzsche's metaphysics, "man is the measure of all things."

Heidegger's "confrontation" with Nietzsche is not meant, I said, to offer us some further piece of information about the present age, to show us something about who we are or have become that Nietzsche leaves out of account. On the contrary, it is meant to show us how that account is binding on us, to make live its authority for us. In as much as that authority in some sense depends upon our obedience to it, such obedience is therefore not something for which Nietzsche himself can be held accountable. He can have no *argument*, that is, for his own authority.

Now one important way of expressing our obedience to Nietzsche's authority – of not misunderstanding the way in which Nietzsche's account of the death of God is binding on us – is, Heidegger thinks, not to treat what he says about the present age as an interpretation of who we have become. That is to say, the advent of nihilism is not just one more way of describing ourselves, not just one more world-picture. Thus, it is essential to recognize that Heidegger thinks Nietzsche's account of nihilism is correct – true of us – and that it does not make sense to try to deny it. He wants us, however, to understand in the right way what Nietzsche says about who we have become.

Heidegger is convinced that the way in which the triumph of human freedom is expressed by Nietzsche's thought – and in particular by the metaphysics of will to power – rules out the possibility of seeing this development as a problem. This seems to be the case because the complete naturalization of human reason called for by the death of God appears to leave us with no *standpoint* from which to conceive of such a development as a problem. Expressed in more Nietzschean terms, the point is that the death of God rules out the possibility of seeing its own significance. This blindness is the *essence* of nihilism, as Heidegger conceives it. It is the lack of vision of those in the marketplace – the last men who blink.

Now Heidegger apparently thinks that such blindness afflicts *Nietzsche's* thought as well. This is why he stresses repeatedly that while Nietzsche was essentially right about the present age he nevertheless remained bound to the philosophical tradition he rejected. Heidegger seems to think, that is, that while Nietzsche was right about what it means to be human in the present age, in principle he could not *understand* what his thinking uncovered about who we have become.[5] One of Heidegger's names for what Nietzsche's thinking uncovers but cannot properly comprehend is "the withdrawal of Being." What sort of criticism – if, indeed, it *is* criticism – does this claim represent?

Heidegger wants to understand in what sense the rise of the modern conception of human freedom represents progress. But because he believes that Nietzsche is in essence *right* about the present age – that is, because he agrees that God is dead, that the idea of an external standard of value for life no longer makes sense – when Heidegger claims that the rise of absolute human freedom signifies the total withdrawal of Being, he cannot understand himself to be offering any intelligible alternative to such autonomy as the standard by means of which to assess the latter.

The temptation is therefore to think that when Heidegger apparently condemns Nietzsche's thinking for remaining bound to traditional philosophy, he must somehow be trying to criticize Nietzsche from *within* the picture of the present age Nietzsche presents. But because he denies the intelligibility of a standpoint outside that picture, it is unclear what this talk of "internal criticism" comes to. Indeed, this is why there is a *probnlem* for Heidegger about nihilism in the first place.

On the one hand, then, Heidegger wants to say that Nietzsche is essentially right about the present age: God *is* dead. On the other hand, however, he wants to say that Nietzsche does not understand the significance of God's death. But what exactly is Nietzsche not supposed to comprehend? The death of God means that we can make no sense of the idea of the value of life as imposed upon it from without. We ourselves must accept responsibility for whatever value we may find. In other words, that we take any given quality, institution, or practice to be of the highest value is only a contingent historical fact about *us*. The metaphysics of will to power serves to express this vision of our absolute autonomy. But in so far as Heidegger insists that Nietzsche is right about all of this, what does he think Nietzsche's account of life in the present age has left out? What, if anything, does Nietzsche not understand about the present age?

The solution to this puzzle lies, to say it again, in seeing that Heidegger does *not* think that Nietzsche *has* left anything out. What Nietzsche cannot see, according to Heidegger, is *that* this is who we have become. In Heidegger's own jargon, Nietzsche cannot see that the will to power is the final stage in the withdrawal of Being. But seeing this is not something that it makes sense to accuse Nietzsche of failing to do. It is rather *we* – as Nietzsche's readers – who are to see that this is who we have become. To see this is to grant authority to Nietzsche. This is the *"confrontation"* with Nietzsche that Heidegger is trying to prepare.

We may think of Heidegger's point in this way. Nietzsche is exactly right about the present age: there are no deep metaphysical truths, only purely human ones. But while neither Heidegger nor Nietzsche can claim without contradiction that it is a deep truth that there are no deep truths, the confrontation between them *is* meant to show *that* it is true and to show just what sort of truth it is. It is ment to show us what it means to belong to the present age. Like Nietzsche, Heidegger is calling on us to become what we are, to recognize who we have become; he thinks this recognition is essential to our being who we are. But like Nietzsche, Heidegger rejects the notion that such recognition requires an independent standpoint on who we are.

To see better what this conception of self-recognition comes to, it may help to situate it within the broader context of Heidegger's overall conception of modern life. The picture of absolute human freedom that Heidegger finds articulated in Nietzsche's philosophy crucially prefigures the rise of what he calls the modern "technological" experience of the world. According to Heidegger's conception of the essence of modern technology, we encounter the world solely as a resource to be manipulated and organized in terms of our goals and purposes, rather than – as Heidegger seems to think was formerly the case – encountering what we find in our environment as reflections of divine Forms or as God's creation or as substance with mathematically determinable attributes. It is the idea – as expressed in the will to power – of human life as the standard of its own value that provides the philosophical background for this conception of the essence of modern technology.

On an initial reading, what seems to make the modern experience of technology troubling to Heidegger is that these goals and purposes lack, in his view, any independent content. Human actions on this picture have no significance outside their mere accomplishment. Pure efficiency seems to be the only end pursued. The real problem here, however, is that as we lose our grip on the idea of the independent content of human action, it becomes increasingly difficult to make sense of the idea that anything other than being posited as such by a human agent is what confers worth on any given course of action. Heidegger believes that the elucidation of Nietzsche's metaphysics allows us to explore the nature of this development. And the confrontation with Nietzsche, Heidegger hopes, will show us in what sense it *is* a development.

Heidegger likes to say that anyone in the grip of the modern technological understanding of Being tends to resist the idea that it represents anything other than human progress. That is, it is difficult to give much content to our impression that something important is left out of the experience of the world as resource or "standing reserve." We may find this experience of the world disheartening, but Heidegger insists that we have no choice but to face up to and acknowledge it. Indeed, the only development it seems sensible to speak of here is that of the desirable evolution of human freedom, and questioning *that* can only seem dangerously reactionary. Any distress we may feel at the modern technological character of the world can, it seems, best be remedied by technological means: better education, better psychotherapy, better medical care, better laws, better economic management, better appliances, and so forth.

Now Heidegger *does* want to call this progress into question. His reading of Nietzsche is meant to do so, but not to *deny* that there has been progress. To see this, it is helpful to contrast Heidegger's interrogation of what I have called human freedom with a critique leveled at it from a different direction. It is natural to feel that advocating absolute human freedom denies the possibility of large-scale social agreement on the nature of the good, and that it is this lack of agreement as to what is worthwhile that produces our distinctively modern sense of distress. That is, the sort of freedom that Heidegger finds in modern technology may seem dangerously empty precisely in so far as it denies the tenability of either deeply shared values or the possibility of meaningful differences between ways of life which might otherwise serve to give our freedom some content.

From this point of view, we can say either that Heidegger has mischaracterized the present age by *ignoring* such deep agreement as there is, or that the *lack* of such agreement is the problem to which his analysis – his claims to the contrary notwithstanding – really points.[6] But Heidegger thinks that this criticism, in either form, sidesteps the most important issue by remaining attached to what he believes Nietzsche has effectively *shown* to be untenable notions of authority and tradition.

His reading of Nietzsche is meant to assess in a different way the rise of human freedom. He thinks that the characterization of freedom articulated by the doctrine of will to power accurately represents modern humanity, and that nothing *intelligible* has been left out of this description. But to represent what Nietzsche called the death of God *simply* as progress – which is the attitude of those in the marketplace – is ultimately to accept the philosophical terms of the debate and to close an issue about the relation between our practices and our lives that Heidegger thinks is better left open. Thus, while he thinks that Nietzsche's diagnosis of the present age is correct, and though he thinks that effective resistance to the technology for which it provides the ground is impossible, Heidegger would like us to express our obedience to it in a form other than blind acceptance.

What does Heidegger have to say to the unconverted about the "attitude" toward technology he apparently advocates? Indeed what, if anything, is supposed to be *wrong* with technology? After all, it seems quite plausible to think of technology – as would the very modern people in Nietzsche's marketplace – as representing positive human progress, and to view charges of emptiness and nihilism as little more than lingering nostalgia for authority. Heidegger's reading of Nietzsche is meant to respond to this charge of nostalgia.

The shape of that response should by now be clear. To accuse Heidegger of nostalgia is to accuse him of thinking that Nietzsche has left something out of his account of life in the present age. But Heidegger's point is that nothing *is* left out of Nietzsche's account. To be modern *does* represent progress over the past, and to belong to the present age is not to have one among many possible ways of viewing the world. To belong to the present age is not to be stuck within one particular conceptual scheme. Precisely *this* is the very modern picture of modernity Heidegger is trying to undercut.

To belong to the present age is to become human, to begin to grow up. To borrow Kant's term, it is to become mature. The charge of nostalgia leveled at Heidegger seems to demand that we conceive of our maturity *simply* as progress. But this demand seems to Heidegger to register an uncanny naiveté about both child- and adulthood. Maturity is not simply the result of a rejection of authority. The revaluation of all values demands a reconception of authority, not its outright rejection. In the terms with which we began, to belong to the present age is to be a member of the marketplace, to see that there is nowhere else to live. Nietzsche's thought might then be said to be nihilistic in the sense that, as I claimed, our recognition of ourselves in his work is not something for which he can be held responsible. It is something which seems to depend in some way on us as readers. To deny the appeal to authority *here* is to remain within the grip of the picture of the present age that Heidegger wants to avoid. Ultimately, it is to express the nihilist's wish for absolute and empty autonomy. And this, Heidegger would say, is the truest expression of nostalgia.

But all of this suggests that we give up the idea that Heidegger means to offer an interpretation of Nietzsche. To become what we are is to be conditioned by what we have become. My suggestion has been that a confrontation with Nietzsche is meant to show us what neither Nietzsche nor Heidegger can simply come out and say: what it means to belong to the present age – that is, to be conditioned by what we have become. The doctrine of will to power is the metaphysics of the marketplace; it shows us what it makes sense to say there. But it also tempts us to think that we are confined *within* the marketplace, unable to hear any voices from outside. And this is just the picture of the present age which, while seemingly forced upon us by the present age, prevents us from understanding who we are.

Now it seems that Nietzsche's madman is the voice from *outside* the marketplace, that his position outside the present age is what drives him mad. We will see, however, that this is exactly the picture of madness that Nietzsche rejects. This rejection, in turn, will show us how Nietzsche conceives his own relation to the present age. It will also point up some of the shortcomings of Heidegger's own confrontation with Nietzsche.

2 The madman

If Heidegger's claim about Nietzsche's account of the present age is that there is no standpoint outside the present age, and if the significance of this claim is to suggest that we give up the dichotomy of internal and external perspectives, then how *should* we conceive of the position Nietzsche adopts toward the present age? One of the most intriguing of his many names for this position is "exception." In section 26 of *Beyond Good and Evil*, Nietzsche refers to himself as the exception to "the crowd, the many, the great majority . . . [to] the rule 'man'"[7] But, he insists, "the rule is more interesting than the exception – than myself, the exception."[8]

Coming to terms with Nietzsche's diagnosis of the ills of modern life as well as understanding the special character of that diagnosis are a matter of correctly appreciating how he understands the relationship between rule and exception. Schematically put, life in the present age is the rule whose exception Nietzsche is. One of the principal virtues of this picture is that it expresses well the idea of being constrained by the conditions of intelligibility at any historical juncture. Both Nietzsche and Heidegger are concerned to understand the charcter of such constraint. The central idea here is that being an exception is not a matter of adopting an independent and external standpoint with respect to the rule. The intelligibility of the exception depends upon the intelligibility of the rule. Nietzsche hopes as well to show, however, that what it means to follow a rule, to be constrained by the rule, is illuminated by the possibility of the exception.

One of the ways in which he explores the possibility of the exception is in terms of the figure of the madman. If the parallel between madness and exceptionality which I am drawing is appropriate, then we should not expect madness to represent a distinct point of view on the marketplace, or a radically different way of thinking of the world. Indeed, as Nietzsche conceives of it, madness is rather a particular way of adopting that very same point of view. And if this is all that *can* be done, then we have some reason to suppose that nothing is expressed by speaking here of "points of view." It is in these terms that we should try to understand what makes the madman exceptional. For the exception is merely a version of the rule.

Those who do not believe in God find it difficult to take to heart the madman's announcement of the death of God. They laugh and shout at him, but they are not obviously threatened by his madness. And I have suggested that Nietzsche means us to find their reaction to be both an intelligible and a reasonable one. The madman does not confront them with anything they did not already know. But how shall we understand his madness? He is, evidently, not *simply* insane. In *Daybreak* Nietzsche writes that in the history of morality, madness prepares the way for every new idea. But this is *not* because truly new ideas drive one mad, nor because by definition one will appear to be mad if one strays outside the bounds of accepted morality. Nietzsche means to question both the notion of a "truly new idea" and that of "the bounds of morality" on which this notion of madness rests. Indeed, as we saw, what the madman actually *says* – the questions he asks – are perfectly intelligible, and the people in the marketplace *understand* what he says.

The death of God does not *drive* one mad. On the contrary, Nietzsche seems to think of madness as a curious sort of *precondition* for – rather than a consequence of – the announcement of anything new. He writes:

all superior men who were irresistibly drawn to throw off the yoke of any kind of morality and to frame new laws had, *if they were not actually mad*, no alternative but to make themselves or pretend to be mad – and this indeed applies to innovators in every domain and not only in the domain of priestly and political dogma.[9]

Nietzsche goes on to claim that such individuals drive themselves mad as a way of *believing in themselves*. The conditions of what is intelligible are always provided by the one's set of values. There simply is nowhere else to go. Nietzsche is not proposing some radically different way of looking at things: he can't have *that* kind of self-confidence. But the appearance of madness is a way of at least *feigning* such confidence.

To listen to the sighs of these solitary and agitated minds: "Ah, give me madness, you heavenly powers! Madness, that I may at last believe in myself! Give deliriums and convulsions, sudden lights and darkness, terrify me with frost and fire such as no mortal has ever felt, with deafening din and prowling figures, make me howl and whine and crawl like a beast: so that I may only come to believe in myself! I am consumed by doubt, I have killed the law, the law anguishes me as a corpse does a living man: if I am not *more* than the law I am the vilest of all men. The new spirit which is in me, whence is it if it is not from you? Prove to me that I am yours; madness alone can prove it." And only too often this fervour achieved its goal all too well: in that age in which Christianity proved most fruitful in saints and desert solitaries, and thought it was proving itself by this fruitfulness, there were in Jerusalem vast madhouses for abortive saints, for those who had surrendered to it their last grain of salt.[10]

At the end of *On the Genealogy of Morals* Nietzsche says that the genealogist stands on the threshold of the event of the demise of Christian morality. He lives on the trailing edge of a given way of looking at things. This edge provides Nietzsche's critical standpoint on the present age, but it is, as he says, little more than an exception to a rule. "We ourselves dwell," Nietzsche writes parenthetically, "in the little world of the exceptions and, so to speak, in the evil zone."[11] Writing from *this* standpoint, we have seen, removes the plausibility of his appealing to any external measure or standard for his denunciations of the present age. It denies his authority; or rather it *establishes* it as *his* authority – whereas beforehand shared standards and impartial reasoned argument had been the final court of appeal. This is why, I think, one often has the impression one cannot *argue* with Nietzsche; it is also one of the reasons that he calls *On the Genealogy of Morals* a polemic. Establishing the grounds for his apparent condemnation of the present age as *his* authority makes that condemnation a *matter* of authority. But, as such, it can and should, I think, seem to loosen the hold Nietzsche might have on us. For, after all, who *is* he to say these things?

What distinguishes the madman from the people in the marketplace – and hence Nietzsche from us – is that he *suffers* in some way from the present age, from the death of God. If I am right, this is suffering of an exceedingly curious sort, as there is no general way for Nietzsche to designate intelligibly the cause or significance of such suffering.

According to the view of communication Nietzsche articulates in *The Gay Science*,[12] there can be no "private" experience. Or perhaps better, the "privacy" of certain experiences cannot be a matter of knowledge, strictly so called. That is, either there are shared terms for shared experiences, or there are no experiences (nothing identifiable as an experience, much less as an experience of *mine* or of *Nietzsche's*). The ability to communicate, Nietzsche says, is a condition of any awareness of what is to be communicated. We do not first become aware of what we are going to say, and then figure out a way to express it to others.

If, then, there were an experience for which one did not yet have a common language, by Nietzsche's lights this would not – not *yet* anyway – *be* an experience in the strict sense of the word. As Nietzsche understands it, *nihilism* is just such an experience, one which is as yet without words, and therefore not yet an experience. A certain profound suffering affords knowledge of the advent of nihilism, but this is not yet an experience until it is held in common. What one would like to know is what Nietzsche thinks is necessary for it to be held in common, and thus for it to count as an experience. This is yet another way of asking the question of the death of God. The people of the marketplace do not recognize themselves in what the madman says. And yet all the madman offers them are their own words.

One might think that it was somehow Nietzsche's personal tragedy that he experienced a painful incapacity to feel himself understood in the terms of his community. But Nietzsche's claim is, on the contrary, that it is *our* tragedy that *he* cannot make himself understood in the shared terms of our community. The profound suffering that makes noble by separating is, I suggest, supposed to make *us* noble as well. But he could have no proper grounds for such a claim at all; it is an expression of the pure arrogance of suffering. Such suffering affords Nietzsche the curious perspective he takes on the present age: the "type of man that is also on a height and also has free vision – but looks *down*"[13] is the type of the sufferer. In such a condtion, Nietzsche says, "we experience downright convulsions of arrogance."[14] Again, this is no *argument*. Indeed, the first effect of "*convalescence*" from such suffering is

> that we fend off the dominance of this arrogance: we call ourselves vain and foolish to have felt it – as though we have experienced something out of the ordinary! [*als ob wir Etwas erlebt hätten, das einzig wäre!*] We humiliate our almighty pride, which has enabled us to endure our pain, without gratitude, and vehemently desire an antidote to it: we want to become estranged from ourselves and depersonalized after pain has for too long and too forcibly made us *personal*.[15]

Nietzsche's famous criticism of what he called "the morality of pity" should be understood along these lines. What he objects to in the attitude of pity is the pretense that suffering confers profound and profoundly hidden knowledge, knowledge that would be pity's proper object.

Neitzsche *did* want readers, and he *did* bemoan the lack of them. But he felt they had to be readers of a particular sort: pitiless ones, readers who resist the idea that he knew some secret to which they were forbidden access.

> Our personal and profoundest suffering is incomprehensible and inaccessible to almost everyone; here we remain hidden from our neighbor, even if we eat from one pot. But whenever people *notice* that we suffer, they interpret our suffering superficially. It is the very essence of the emotion of pity that it strips away from the suffering of others whatever is distinctly personal.[16]

Seen in this light, Heidegger might be considered to be one of Nietzsche's most pitiless readers. At his best, Heidegger resists the temptation to *interpret* Nietzsche. This resistance is what is expressed by his gesture of reading primarily *The Will to Power* to the exclusion of the works Nietzsche actually prepared for publication. It is in this way that Heidegger proposes to acknowledge Nietzsche's authority as the philosopher of the present age.

If this account of nihilism, suffering, and the madman is correct, then Heidegger seems to be approaching Nietzsche in the right way. In closing, however, let me suggest one reason that his *Auseinandersetzung* nonetheless failed – at least in part. Nietzsche writes, famously, "Whoever fights monsters should see to it that in the process he does not become a monster. And when you look into an abyss, the abyss also looks into you."[17] I think we would not be going far wrong if we understood Nietzsche's fascination with what he knew his readers would find to be abominable characters as posing such a danger for him. He seems to have been quite conscious that the twentieth century stood a very good chance of being horrendous, that the soil in which he saw himself rooted could produce history's greatest monsters. This is, I think, something like a standing possibility of nihilism: not that because God is dead, everything is permitted, but rather that because God is dead, some will find *these* things required.

Neitzsche did not think that this possibility was something connected solely with his personal suffering. If it has any significance at all, such suffering could ultimately only be our own. This suggests, I think, that a confrontation with Nietzsche must take the possibility of the reader's own monstrosity seriously. There is nothing in the present age to rule out this possibility, but Heidegger does *not* seem to have taken it to heart.

We might begin to account for Heidegger's more obvious ambivalence toward Nietzsche along these lines. For he does often seem to think that Nietzsche can be accused of *not* knowing something special about the present age. He often seems to think, that is, that there *is* something special to know about the present age. And at times Heidegger fails to come to terms with his fear that this might not be so. The most he seems concerned with is that the impressionm will arise that he is a mystic. But as Nietzsche says in the aphorism immediately following *The Madman*: "Mystical explanations are considered deep. The truth is that they are not even superficial."

NOTES

1 In drawing this parallel, I am making what might be called "genealogical" use of *Being and Time*. But some will object that Heidegger's early account of authentic Dasein is much more complex than I seem to suggest. This is, of course, true. I wish to focus attention here only on the idea of inauthenticity as the source of traditional ontology; but clearly not every form of inauthenticity in *Being and Time* leads Dasein down the path to traditional philosophy. In fact, Heidegger often describes inauthenticity in terms that speak of Dasein's *flight* from its "groundlessness": seeking to cover up its own character as disclosive of beings, Dasein flees into "curiosity," "idle talk," and "ambiguity." Authentic Dasein, on the other hand, resolutely acknowledges its "responsibility" for the character of the world it encounters.

Thus, when reading *Being and Time*, it is natural to ask Heidegger what distinguishes authentic from inauthentic forms of human existence. Yet a major problem with this very natural reading is that anything we might identify as a necessary mark or feature of authenticity *could* in principle be possessed by inauthentic Dasein. A distorted recognition of this fact is sometimes expressed by readers' concerns that Heidegger might not have ruled out the possibility of an authentic *Nazism*.

My reply is that the original question about what distinguishes authenticity from inauthenticity is badly posed. This becomes clear in Heidegger's later work: abandoning talk of authenticity as an "attitude" difficult to adopt toward the practical and conventional character of human understanding, he eschews talk of Dasein's flight from difficult truths about itself. But throughout his writings, Heidegger seeks to understand how something like *in*authenticity is possible; we are side-tracked from the real problem if we focus exclusively upon authenticity.

In terms of *Being and Time*, this means that Heidegger wants to know how the deformation of intelligibility expressed by traditional ontology is possible. He is, in short, looking there for the conditions of the possibility of *philosophy*. This represents, I freely admit, a relatively small part of his concern with authenticity in his early work, but it is this part of his discussion that he retains. In his later work, Heidegger comes to ask how it is that we fail to understand the essence of technology. The account – such as it is – of this *failure* is not meant to give us a *positive* explanation of what understanding the essence of technology really comes to; this is simply not where the problem lies. While this is obviously a selective reading of Heidegger's early work, it is, I think, a good way to get at Heidegger's overarching concerns with what he called "the oblivion of Being." *Being and Time begins* with the forgottenness of Being. My reading here suggests that the book as a whole is an extended commentary upon the passage from Plato's *Sophist* with which that work begins. We are not compelled by the letter of the text to read Heidegger's early work in this way, but I think it is the direction in which his later work points us.

2   In section 343 of *The Gay Science* Nietzsche writes, "The greatest recent event – that 'God is dead,' that belief in the Christian god has become unbelievable – is already beginning to cast its first shadows over Europe." See Heidegger's "The Word of Nietzsche: 'God is dead'," in *The Question Concerning Technology and Other Essays*, trans. William Lovitt, New York: Harper & Row, 1977. This essay sums up the conclusions of Heidegger's very long series of lectures delivered between 1936 and 1940 at Freiburg. Heidegger articulates this summary around the aphorism we are considering here.

3   Martin Heidegger, "The Word of Nietzsche: 'God is dead'," in *The Question Concerning Technology and Other Essays*, p. 62.

4   Martin Heidegger, *Nietzsche*. Vol. I: *The Will to Power as Art*, pp. 40–41.

5   Charles Taylor has been perhaps the most articulate exponent of this first sort of objection. His generally sympathetic attitude toward Heidegger's work is tempered by his distrust of what he takes to be Heidegger's overly monolithic descriptions of the present age. He raises this same sort of objection to Foucault in his "Foucault on Freedom and Truth," in *Philosophical Papers*, vol. 2, Cambridge: Cambridge University Press, 1985.

6   Put in more overtly "Heideggerian" terms, the point I mean here to be arguing for is this. Heidegger insists that Nietzsche cannot understand what his own thought uncovers about the present age: namely, that the rise of the modern technological understanding of being signals the total withdrawal of Being. My goal has been to understand this claim. It *looks* like a criticism of Nietzsche, and it is usually understood as such by readers who take upon themselves the fruitless and, I think, largely empty task of defending Nietzsche against Heidegger's perceived assault. But I have tried to show why this particular appearance is deceiving. Heidegger, I believe, wants to show *us* what it means – at the end of the metaphysical tradition that runs from Plato to Nietzsche – to respond thoughtfully to the total withdrawal of Being. And his claim about Nietzsche's apparent inability properly to understand what his thinking uncovers about the present age only functions in this context. Heidegger insists that to grant Nietzsche authority as the philosopher of the present age *is* to respond thoughtfully – to become "receptive" – to Being's withdrawal. And granting Nietzsche such authority is not a matter of believing something about the present age. On this reading, then, the claim that Nietzsche himself was not receptive to – did not appreciate how his philosophy gave voice to – the withdrawal of being hardly represents a criticism of his work, for to be so receptive Nietzsche would have to grant *himself* authority. And, as I argue in the second part of this paper, this is not something he can do. One cannot, Nietzsche believes, be one's own best reader.

7   Friedrich Nietzsche, *Beyond Good and Evil*, s. 26, p. 37, translation modified.

8   Ibid.

9   Friedrich Nietzsche, *Daybreak*, s. 14, trans. R. J. Hollingdale, Cambridge: Cambridge University Press, 1982, p. 14.

10   Ibid.

11   Ibid., s. 14, p. 13.

12 Friedrich Nietzsche, *The Gay Science*, s. 354, trans. Walter Kaufmann, New York: Vintage Books, 1974, pp. 297–300.
13 Neitzsche, *Beyond Good and Evil*, s. 286, p. 227.
14 Neitzsche, *Daybreak*, s. 114, p. 70.
15 Ibid., p. 71.
16 Neitzsche, *The Gay Science*, s. 338, p. 269.
17 Neitzsche, *Beyond Good and Evil*, s. 146, p. 89.

13
Heidegger, Language, and Ecology

Charles Taylor

Heidegger's philosophy is anti-subjectivist, even as he puts it, polemically, "anti-humanist." There are certainly dark and worrying aspects to Heidegger's attack on humanism, but one consequence which seems clear and perhaps benign is that it aligns him with the ecological protest against the unreflecting growth of technological society. This is a drift one can discern in Heidegger's late work, well before one has come to grips with the philosophical insights it contains.

But there are many kinds of protest against technological society, which differ both in what they condemn in it, and in the grounds of their condemnation. On the first issue, some people condemn technology as such; others complain of its misuse. On the second, some point to the disastrous long-term consequences for human beings of runaway technology; others argue that we have reason to set limits to our domination of Nature, which go beyond our own long-term flourishing, that Nature or the world can be seen as making demands on us. This last is the path of the so-called "deep " ecology.

Here are two issues, with two major positions on each. One of the interesting things about Heidegger is that, on closer examination, he seems to fit into neither of the established positions on either issue. Heidegger's philosophy of ecology is something *sui generis*.

I cannot explore all of this here. I want rather to concentrate on working out to some degree Heidegger's position on the second issue. In this, he does come close to a "deep" ecological position. Indeed, one might want simply to attribute the second answer to him, that something beyond the human makes demands on us, or calls us. Only this source could not be identified with "Nature," or with the universe. Defining what the source is would bring us to the heart of one of the most puzzling features of his late philosophy. I want to start approaching it in this paper.

I believe this question can be most fruitfully approached through Heidegger's philosophy of language, and it is to this that I will devote the greater part of this essay. I shall return only at the end to indicate in what way our status as language beings can be thought to lay us open to ecologically relevant demands. I shall only be able to sketch this, but I hope that by that time this line of thought will have begun to appear convincing and potentially fruitful.

(1)   The late Heidegger's doctrine of language is itself strongly anti-subjectivist. He even inverts the usual relation in which language is seen as our tool, and speaks of language speaking, rather than human beings.[1] This formulation is hardly transparent on first reading. But I think we can understand it if we first set Heidegger against the background of an important tradition of thought about language which has flourished in the last two centries; and secondly, define his originality in relation to this tradition.

I shall call this line of thinking "expressive constitutive." It arose in the late eighteenth century in reaction to the prevailing doctrine about language which developed within the confines of modern epistemology, the philosophy articulated in different ways by Hobbes, Locke, and Condillac. On this view, language *is* conceived as an instrument. The constitutive theory, on the other hand, reacts against this, and Heidegger's conception of language speaking can be seen as a development of this early counter-response.

The contention between the two views can perhaps be understood in this way. The instrumental view is an "enframing"[2] theory. I shall use this term to describe attempts to understand language within the framework of a picture of human life, behavior, purposes, or mental functioning, which is itself described and defined without reference to language. Language can be seen as arising within this framework, and fulfilling a certain function within it, but the framework itself precedes, or at least can be characterized independently of language. By contrast, a "constitutive" theory gives us a picture of language as making possible new purposes, new levels of behavior, new meanings, and hence as not explicable within a framework picture of human life conceived without language.

The classical case, and most influential first form of an enframing theory was the set of ideas developed from Locke through Hobbes to Condillac. I have discussed this in "Language and Human Nature."[3] Briefly, the Hobbes–Locke–Condillac (HLC) form of theory seeks to understand language within the confines of the modern representational epistemology made dominant by Descartes. In the mind there are "ideas." These are bits of putative representation of reality, much of it "external." Knowledge consists in having representation actually square with the reality. But we can only hope to achieve this if we assemble our ideas according to a responsible procedure. Our beliefs about things are constructed, they result from a synthesis. The issue is whether the construction will be reliable and responsible, or indulgent, slapdash, and delusory.

Language plays an important role in this construction. Words are given meaning by being attached to the things represented via the "ideas" that represent them. The introduction of words greatly facilitates the combination of ideas into a coherent picture. This facilitation is understood in different ways. For Hobbes and Locke, they allow us to grasp things in classes, and hence make possible synthesis wholesale, whereas non-linguistic intuition would be confined to the painstaking association of particulars. Condillac thinks that the introduction of language gives us for the first time control over the whole process of association; it affords us "empire sur notre imagination."[4]

The constitutive theory finds its most robust early expression in Herder, in a critical response to Condillac. In a famous passage from the *Ursprung der Sprache*,

Herder repeats Condillac's fable – one might say "just so" story – of how language might have arisen between two children in a desert.[5] But he professes to find something lacking in this account. It seems to him to presuppose what it is meant to explain. What it is meant to explain is language, the passage from a condition in which the children emit nothing but animal cries to the stage where they use words meaningfully. The association between sign and some mental content is already there with the animal cry (what Condillac calls the "natural sign"). What is new with the "instituted sign" is that the children can now use it to focus on and manipulate the associated idea, and hence direct the whole play of their imagination. The transition amounts to their stumbling to the notion that the association can be used in this way.

This is the classic case of an enframing theory. Language is understood in terms of certain elements: ideas, signs, and their association, which precede its arising. Before and after, the imagination is at work and association takes place. What is new is that now the mind is in control. This itself is, of course, something that did not previously exist. But the theory establishes the maximal possible continuity between before and after. The elements are the same, combination continues, only the direction changes. We can surmise that it is precisely this continuity which gives the theory its seeming clarity and explanatory power: language is robbed of its mysterious character, is related to elements that seem unproblematic.

Herder starts from the intuition that language makes possible a different kind of consciousness, which he calls "reflective" (*besonnen*). That is why he finds a continuity explanation like Condillac's so frustrating and unsatisfactory. The issue of what this new consciousness consists in and how it arises is not addressed, as far as Herder is concerned, by an account in terms of pre-existing elements. That is why he accuses Condillac of begging the question. "The Abbot Condillac . . . had already revealed the entire essence of language before the first page of his book."

What did Herder mean by "reflection" (*Besonnenheit*)? This is harder to explain. We might try to formulate it this way: pre-linguistic beings can react to the things that surround them. But language enables us to grasp something *as* what it is. This explanation is hardly transparent, but it puts us on the right track. Herder's basic idea seems to be that while a pre-linguistic animal can learn to respond to some object appropriately in the light of its purposes, only the being with language can identify the object as of a certain kind, can, as we might put it, attribute such and such a property to it. An animal, in other terms, can learn to give the right response to an object – fleeing a predator, say, or going after food – where "right" means "appropriate to its (nonlinguistic) purposes." But language use involves another kind of rightness. Using the right word involves identifying an object as having the properties that justify using that word. We cannot give an account of this rightness in terms of extra-linguistic purposes. Rightness here is irreducible to success in some extra-linguistic task.[7]

Now to be sensitive to the issue of non-reductive rightness is to be operating, as it were, in another dimension. Let me call this the "semantic dimension." Then we can say that properly linguistic beings are functioning in the semantic dimension. And that can be our way of formulating Herder's point about "reflection." To be reflective is to operate in this dimension, which means acting out of sensitivity to issues of irreducible rightness.

But we need to extend somewhat our notion of the semantic dimension. My remarks above seemed to concern purely descriptive rightness. But we do more things with language than describe. There are other ways in which a word can be "le mot juste." For instance, I come up with a word to articulate my feelings, and thus at the same time shape them in a certain manner. This is a function of language which cannot be reduced to simple description, at least not description of an independent object. Or else I say something which re-establishes the contact between us, puts us once again on a close and intimate footing. We need a broader concept of irreducible rightness than just that involved in aligning words with objects.

Thus when I hit on the right word to articulate my feelings, and acknowledge that I am motivated by envy, say, the term does its work because it is the right term. In other words, we cannot explain the rightness of the word "envy" here simply in terms of the condition that using it produces; rather, we have to account for its producing this condition – here, a successful articulation – in terms of its being the right word. A contrasting case should make this clearer. Imagine that every time I feel stressed, tense, or cross-pressured, I take a deep breath, then exhale explosively out of my mouth, "How!" I immediately feel calmer and more composed. This is plainly the "right sound" to make, as defined by this desirable goal of restored equilibrium. The rightness of "How!" admits of a simple task account. That is because we can explain the rightness simply in terms of its bringing about calm, and do not need to explain its bringing about calm in terms of rightness.

This last clause points up the contrast with "envy" as the term that both articulates and clarifies my feelings. It brings about this clarification, to be sure, and that is essential to its being the right word here. But central to its clarifying is its being the right word. So we cannot simply explain its rightness by its *de facto* clarifying. You cannot define its rightness by the *de facto* causal consequence of clarifying; in other words, you cannot make this outcome criterial for its rightness, because you do not know whether it is clarifying unless you know that it is the right term. Whereas in the case of "How!" all there was to its rightness was its having the desired outcome; the bare *de facto* consequence is criterial. That is why normally we would not be tempted to treat this expletive as though it had a meaning.

Something similar can be said about my restoring the intimacy between us by saying, "I'm sorry." This was "the right thing to say," because it restored contact. But at the same time, we can say that these words are efficacious in restoring contact because of what they mean. Irreducible rightness enters into the account here, because what the words mean cannot be defined by what they bring about. Again, we might imagine that I could also set off a loud explosion in the neighborbood, which would so alarm you that you would forget about our tiff and welcome my presence. This would then be, from a rather cold-blooded, strategic point of view, the "right move." But the explosion itself "means" nothing.

What this discussion is moving us towards is a definition of the semantic dimension in terms of the possibility of a reductive account of rightness. A simple task account of rightness for some sign reduces it to a matter of efficacy for some non-semantic purpose. We are in the semantic dimension when this kind of reduction cannot work, when a kind of rightness is at issue which can't be cashed out in this way. That is why the image of a new "dimension" seems to me apposite. To move from non-linguistic to linguistic agency is to move to a world in which a new kind of issue is at play, a right use of signs which is not reducible to task-rightness. The world of the agent has a new axis on which to respond; its behaviour can no longer be understood just as the purposive seeking of ends on the old plane. It is now responding to a new set of demands. Hence the image of a new dimension.

If we interpret him in this way, we can understand Herder's impatience with Condillac. The latter's "natural signs" were things like cries of pain or distress. Their right use in communication could only be construed on the simple task model. Language arose supposedly when people learned to use the connection already established by the natural sign, between say, the cry and what caused the distress, in a controlled way. The "instituted sign" is born, an element of language properly speaking. Herder cannot accept that the transition from pre-language to language consists simply in taking control of a pre-existing process. What this leaves out is precisely that a new dimension of issues becomes relevant, that the agent is operating on a new plane. Hence in the same passage in which he declares Condillac's account circular, Herder reaches for a definition of this new dimension, with his term "reflection."

On my reconstruction, Herder's "reflection" is to be glossed as the semantic dimension, and his importance is that he made this central to any account of language. Moreover, Herder's conception of the semantic dimension was multifaceted, along the lines of the broad conception of rightness above. It did not just involve description. Herder saw that opening this dimension has to transform all aspects of the agent's life. It will also be the seat of new emotions. Linguistic beings are capable of new feelings which affectively reflect their richer sense of their world: not just anger, but indignation; not just desire, but love and admiration.

The semantic dimension also made the agent capable of new kinds of relations, new sorts of footing that agents can stand on with each other, of intimacy and distance, hierarchy and equality. Gregarious apes may have (what we call) a "dominant male," but only language beings can distinguish between leader, king, president, and the like. Animals mate and have offspring, but only language beings define kinship.

Underlying both emotions and relations is another crucial feature of the linguistic dimension, that it makes possible value in the strong sense. Pre-linguistic animals treat something as desirable or repugnant, by going after it or avoiding it. But only language beings can identify things as *worthy* of desire or aversion. For such identifications raise issues of intrinsic rightness. They involve a characterization of things which is not reducible simply to the ways we treat them as objects of desire or aversion. They involve a recognition beyond that, that they *ought* to be treated in one or another way.

(2)   Now this theory of language which gives a privileged place to the semantic dimension deserves the appelation "constitutive" in an obvious sense, in that language enters into or makes possible a whole range of crucially human feelings, activities, relations. It bursts the framework of pre-linguistic life-forms, and therefore renders any enframing account inadequate. But the constitutive theory which Herder's critique inaugurates has another central feature, that it gives a creative role to expression.

Views of the HLC type related linguistic expression to some pre-existing content. A word is introduced by being linked with an idea, and henceforth becomes capable of expressing it, for Locke.[8] The content precedes its external means of expression. Condillac develops a more sophisticated conception. He argues that introducing words ("instituted signs"), because it gives us greater control over the train of thoughts, allows us to discriminate more finely the nuances of our ideas. This means that we identify finer distinctions, which we in turn can name, which will again allow us to make still more subtle discriminations, and so on. In this way, language makes possible science and enlightenment. But at each stage of this process the idea precedes its naming, albeit its discriminability results from a previous act of naming.

Condillac also gave emotional expression an important role in the genesis of language. His view was that the first instituted signs were framed from natural ones. But natural signs were just the inbuilt expressions of our emotional states – animal cries of joy or fear. That language originated from the expressive cry became the consensus in the learned world of the eighteenth century. But the conception of expression here was quite inert. What the expression conveyed was thought to exist independently of its utterance. Cries made fear or joy evident to others, but they did not help constitute these feelings themselves.

Herder develops a quite different notion of expression. This is in the logic of a constitutive theory, as I have just described it. This tells us that language constitutes the semantic dimension, that is, that possessing language enables us to relate to things in new ways, e.g., as loci of features, and to have new emotions, goals, relationships, as well as being responsive to issues of strong value. We might say: language transforms our world, using this last word in a clearly Heidegger-derived sense. That is, we are talking not of the cosmos out there, which preceded us and is indifferent to us, but of the world of our involvements, including all the things they incorporate in their meaning for us.

Then we can rephrase the constitutive view by saying that language introduces new meanings in our world: the things that surround us become potential bearers of properties; they can have new emotional significance for us, e.g., as objects of admiration or indignation; our links with others can count for us in new ways, as "lovers," "spouses," or "fellow citizens"; and they can have strong value.

But then this involves attributing a creative role to expression. Bringing things to speech cannot mean just making externally available what is already there. There are many banal speech-acts where this seems to be all that is involved. But language as a whole must involve more than this, because it is also opening possibilities for us which would not be there in its absence.

The constitutive theory turns our attention toward the creative dimension of expression, in which, to speak paradoxically, it makes possible its own content. We can actually see this in familiar, everyday realities, but it tends to be screened out from the enframing perspective, and it took the development of constitutive theories to bring it to light.

A good example is the "body language" of personal style. We see the leather-jacketed motorbike rider step away from his machine and swagger toward us with an exaggeratedly leisurely pace. This person is "saying something" in his way of moving, acting, speaking. He may have no words for it, though we might want to apply the hispanic word "macho" as at least a partial description. Here is an elaborate way of being in the world, of feeling and desiring and reacting, which involves great sensititivty to certain things (like slights to one's honor: we are now the object of his attention because we unwittingly cut him off at the last intersection), and cultivated-but-supposedly-spontaneous insensitivity to others (like the feelings of dudes and females), which involves certain prized pleasures (riding around at high speed with the gang) and others which are despised (listening to sentimental songs); and this way of being is coded as strongly valuable; that is, being this way is admired, and failing to be earns contempt.

But how coded? Not, presumably, in descriptive terms, or at least not adequately. The person may not have a term like "macho" which articulates the value involved. What terms he does have may be woefully inadequate to capture what is specific to this way of being; the epithets of praise or opprobrium may only be revelatory in the whole context of this style of action; by themselves they may be too general. Knowing that X is "one of the boys" and Y is a "dude" may tell us little. The crucial coding is in the body expressive language.

The bike rider's world incorporates the strong value of this way of being. Let's call it (somewhat inadequately, but we need a word) "machismo." But how does this meaning exist for him? Only through the expressive gesture and stance. It is not just that an outside observer would have no call to attribute machismo to him without this behavior. It is more radically that a strong value like this can only exist for him when it is articulated in some form. It is this expressive style that enables machismo to exist for him, and more widely this domain of expressive body language is the locus of a whole host of different value-coded ways of being for humans in general. The expression makes possible its content; the language opens us out to the domain of meaning it encodes. Expression is no longer simply inert.

But when we turn back from this rather obvious case to the original description case, which was central to HLC theories, we see it in a new light. Here too expression must be seen as creative, language opens us to the domain it encodes. What descriptive speech encodes is our attribution of properties to things. But possessing this descriptive language is the condition of our being sensitive to the issues of irreducible rightness which must be guiding us if we are really to be attributing properties, as we saw above. So seeing expression as creative generates Herder's constitutive theory as applied to descriptive language.

This illustrates the inner connections, both historical and logical, between the constitutive theory and a strong view of expression. Either the espousal of the first can lead one to look for places where expression obviously opens us to its own content, which we will find in this domain of body language, and with emotional expression generally. Or else, the sense that expression is creative, which will likely strike us if we are attending closely to the life of the emotions, will lead us to revise our understanding of the much discussed case of description. In the case of Herder, the connections probably go in both directions, but if anything the second is more important than the first. The major proponents of the HLC were all rationalists in some sense; one of their central goals was to establish reason on a sound basis, and their scrutiny of language had largely this end in view. The proto-Romantic move to dethrone reason, and to locate the specifically human capacities in feeling, naturally led to a richer concept of expression than was allowed for in Condillac's natural cries, which were quite inert modes of utterance. From the standpoint of this richer notion, even the landscape of descriptive speech begins to look very different. But whatever the route, a road links the constitutive insight with the strong view of expression, so that the alternative to the enframing theory might with equal justice be called the constitutive-expressive.[9]

There are three further features of this view as it developed to its mature form which it would be useful to draw out here. The first is that attributing the central role to expression leads to a redefinition of what it is to acquire language. The crucial step is no longer seen as taking on board a *mental capacity* to link sign and idea, but as coming to engage in the *activity* of (overt) *speech*. In Humboldt's famous formulation, we have to think of language primarily as *energeia*, not just as *ergon*.[10]

This speech activity has an inescapable expressive-projective dimension; even when we are engaged in disinterested description, we are as speakers projecting a certain stance to our interlocutors and to the matter at hand. But it has another feature as well, and this is the second that I want to touch on here. It is conversation. The first and inescapable locus of language is in exchange between interlocutors. Language involves certain kinds of links with others. In particular, it involves the link of being a conversational partner with somebody; let's call this an "interlocutor." Standing to someone as an interlocutor is fundamentally different from standing to him/her as an object of observation or manipulative interaction. Language marks this most fundamental distinction in the difference of persons. I address someone as "you," speak of them as "him" or "her."

What this corresponds to is the way in which we create a common space by opening a conversation. A conversation has the status of a common action. When I open up about the weather to you over the back fence, what this does is make the weather an object for *us*. It is no longer just for you, and for me, with perhaps the addition that I know it is for you and you know it is for me. Conversation transposes it into an object which we are considering together. The considering is common, in that the background understanding established is that the agency which is doing the considering is us together, rather than each of us on our own managing to dovetail his/her action with the other.[11]

Thirdly, implicit in this Herder–Humboldt understanding of language is the recognition that the constitutive forms of expression, those that open us to a new range of meanings, go beyond descriptive language, and even beyond speech of any form, to such things as gesture and stance.

This suggests that the phenomenon which needs to be carved out for explanation is the whole range of expressive-constitutive forms, that we are unlikely to understand descriptive language unless we can place it in a broader theory of such forms, which must hence be our prior target. This view is strengthened when we reflect how closely connected the different forms are. Our projections are carried at once in linguistic (speech style and rhetoric) and in extra-linguistic (gesture, stance) form. Description is always embedded in acts which also projectively express. The idea that these could be treated as a single range was already pre-delineated in the definition I gave earlier of the semantic dimension. For even the projections of body language fit within its scope, as having their own kind of intrinsic rightness. The swagger of our bike rider is right in relation to the way of being he values, in a way which cannot be accounted for in terms of a simple task.

So constitutive theories go for the full range of expressive forms (what Cassirer called the "symbolic forms").[12] Now within these falls another sub-range not mentioned so far, the work of art, something which is neither expressive projection nor description. In a sense, the work of art played an even more important role in the development of expressivism than what I have been calling projection. We can see this in the conception of the symbol, as opposed to the allegory, which played an important role in the aesthetic of the Romantic period, and indeed, since. As described, for instance, by Goethe, the symbol was a paradigm of what I have been calling constitutive expression.

A work of art which was "allegorical" presented us with some insight or truth which we could also have access to more directly. An allegory of virtue and vice as two animals, say, will tell us something which could also be formulated in propositions about virtue and vice. By contrast, a work of art had the value of a symbol [13] when it manifested something which could not be thus "translated." It opens access to meanings which cannot be made available any other way. Each truly great work is in this way *sui generis*. It is untranslatable.

This notion, which has its roots in Kant's *Third Critique*, was immensely influential. It was taken up by Schopenhauer and all those he influenced, in their understanding of the work of art as manifesting what cannot be said in assertions in ordinary speech. And its importance for Heidegger in his own variant needs no stressing. I shall return to this shortly.

The work of art as symbol was perhaps the paradigm on which the early constitutive theories of language were built. In its very definition, there is an assertion of the plurality of expressive forms, in the notion that it is untranslatable into prose. From this standpoint, the human expressive-constitutive power – or alternatively, the semantic dimension – has to be seen as a complex and many-layered thing, in which the higher modes are embedded in the lower ones.

Outside of the attribution of properties, I mentioned above three other ranges of meanings which are opened to us by language: the properly human emotions, certain relations, and strong value. But each of these is carried on the three levels of expressive form that crystallized out of the above discussion: the projective, the symbolic (in works of art), and the descriptive. We express our emotions, and establish our relations, and articulate our values, in our body language, style, and rhetoric; but we can also articulate all of these in poetry, novels, dance, music; and we can also bring all of them to descriptive articulation, where we name the feelings, relations, values, and describe and argue about them.

(3) I have developed this portrait of the constitutive-expressive theory at length, because I think Heidegger's own views on language stand squarely within this

tradition. Heidegger is a constitutive theorist. By this I mean, not just that he happens to have such a theory of language, but also that it plays an essential role in his thinking.

There may be some question about this in relation to Heidegger's early writings, but his thinking after the "Kehre" seems to be articulating the central notions of the constitutive view. To describe language as the "house of being," for instance, is to give it a more than instrumental status. Indeed, Heidegger repeatedly inveighs against those views of language which reduce it to a mere instrument of thought or communication. Language is essential to the "clearing."

Heidegger stands in the Herder tradition. But he transposes this mode of thinking in his own characteristic fashion. While Herder in inaugurating the constitutive view still speaks in terms of "reflection," which sounds like a form of consciousness, Heidegger clearly turns the issue around, and sees language as what opens access to meanings. Language discloses. The deeper and darker and more difficult and problematic thesis, that language speaks, is something I want to go into shortly. But at least it is clear that language is seen as the condition of the human world being disclosed. The disclosure is not intra-psychic, but occurs in the space between humans; indeed, it helps to define the space that humans share.

This is already clear in "The Origin of the Work of Art,"[14] as is, incidentally, Heidegger's debt to the whole expressivist *topos* of the symbol. The work of art brings about the crucial constituting disclosure of a way of life, in a way that no set of mere descriptive propositions could. These could as descriptions be "correct"; that is, they could correctly represent reality. But the work of art is not a representation, at least not primarily. *"Ein Bauwerk, ein griechischer Tempel, bildet nichts ab"* ("A building, a Greek temple, does not represent") (30). It defines the objects of strong value: *"Das Tempelwerk fügt erst und sammelt zugleich um sich die Einheit jener Bahnen und Bezüge, in denen Geburt und Tod, Unheil und Segen, Seig und Schmach, Ausharren und Verfall die Gestalt und den Lauf des Menschenwesens in seinem Geschick gewinnen"* "It is the templework that first fits together and at the same time gathers around itself the unity of those paths and relations in which birth and death, disaster and blessing, victory and disgrace, endurance and decline acquire the shape of destiny for human being.") (31). It does this not for individuals, but for a people: *"Die waltende Weite dieser offenen Bezüge ist die Welt dieses geschichtlichen Volkes"* "The all-governing expanse of this open relational context is the world of this historical people." (31).

These crucial theses of the expressive-constitutive view are clearly recaptured by Heidegger in his own fashion, no longer as truths about "consciousness," but as crucial conditions of Being, or the clearing.[15]

(4)   But Heidegger is more than just a constitutive theorist. He also has his very original position within this camp, in particular in his late philosophy. Here we find dark sayings of the kind that I have adverted to above, that it is not humans that speak, but language. I do not claim to understand these fully, but I think they can be made partly intelligible if we develop further certain potentialities which are implicit in any constitutive theory, but which were not fully explored by his predecessors.

This theory rests on the central intuition that it is through language that disclosure to humans takes place. Animals may have their own kind of clearing, [16] but ours is constituted by language. In particular, ours is a world in which things have worth, in which there are goods in the strong sense: things which are *worth* pursuing.

Goods show up through finding expression, paradigmatically "symbolic," in terms of Goethe's distinction; as the goods of the Greeks showed up in the temple. Human beings build the temple. So constitutive theory puts a new question on the agenda, viz., what is the nature of this (in one obvious sense) human power of expression, which has such fateful consequences?

This is the basis for a massive parting of the ways. Different answers to this question are central to most traditions of "continental" philosophy, from the followers of Schopenhauer, through Heidegger and those he has influenced, to the deconstructionists and post-modernists. The issue has also been central to modernist poetics. Enframing theories, either in mainline semantics, or in post-Fregean theories of language like Davidson's, are on a completely different wavelength, because for them the question doesn't even exist. How could it? Only a constitutive theory can put it on the agenda. This, I think, is one of the most important sources of that talking past each other which we see when these two modes of philosophizing meet.

This issue connects up in a certain way with the very beginning of our philosophical tradition. Aristotle defined the human being as "zwon echon logon." This was usually tanslated as "rational animal." But Heidegger suggested that one go beyond the traditional interpretation that this rendering enshrines, and simply say: "animal possessing logos," with all the polysemy of that latter term, which nevertheless centers on language. Humans are language animals. They are beings that somehow possess, or are the locus of this constitutive power of expression. In order to know the essence of human beings, you have to understand this power, i.e., language in the broad sense in which constitutivists use the term. This will give you the *areté* of human beings, what life is proper for them. Aristotle can be read as proceeding in this way,[17] and so can Heidegger, even with all the massive differences between them.

So the task is: explain the constitutive dimension of language; explain the power of expression. One immediate temptation is to see it as *our* power, something we exercise; disclosure is what we bring about. For Heidegger this is a deeply erroneous view, i.e., not just a trivial mistake, but one that is generated out of the thrust of our culture and tradition. This reading can be called subjectivist. But in fact it can take a number of forms, and in order to understand them, we should examine what is at stake.

Language is essential to what we could argue is the central focus throughout Heidegger's philosophy, the fact/event that things show up at all. We can call this by one of Heidegger's terms, the "clearing" (*Lichtung*). Heidegger taught us to reorder the history of philosophy and culture in the light of how the clearing was understood.

One crucial point for Heidegger is that the clearing cannot be identified with any of the entities that show up in it. It is not to be explained by them as something they cause, or one of their properties, or as grounded in them. Later

Heidegger throught that some pre-Socratics had a vision which avoided this identification. But with Plato, Western culture starts on a fatal course. Plato's notion of the Idea places the clearing among beings. An Idea is not just another entity waiting to be discovered. It is not like the things that participate in it. It can be understood as self-manifesting. It gives itself to be understood. That is what underlies the image of light in which Plato frequently expounds the Ideas, and particularly that of the Good. This latter is likened to the sun; turning from the changing things of this world to the Ideas is likened to leaving the dark cave. Plato speaks of the soul turning to the illuminated side. And so on.

Plato, it can be said, had an ontic account of the clearing. It is still in an obvious sense a non-subjectivist one. But Heidegger thinks that it somehow put us on a slide towards subjectivism. Perhaps because the very act of ontically placing the clearing reflects a drive toward grasping it, exercising intellectual control over it; and this fully worked out will emerge in the will to power. But in any case, the Platonic understanding is transformed after Aristotle through a series of intermediate steps, each one more subjectivist, into a modern mode of thinking which explains the clearing through a power of the subject, that of representation. The understanding of reality as disposed through the power of a subject is greatly furthered by the medieval view of the world as the creation of an an omnipotent God. This at first coexists with Platonic and Aristotelian theories of the Ideas; it is the high noon of what Heidegger calls "onto-theology." But its inherent thrust pushes towards a definition of being as what it is through the disposition of subjective power.

In the modern age, this takes form at first in the idealism which emerges out of the central tradition of modern epistemology, and which Heidegger thinks is already implicit in its founding figures, in, e.g., Descartes and Locke. The real is what can be represented by a subject. This view culminates in various forms of non-realism. But for Heidegger the same thrust leads to our conceiving reality itself as emanating from will. It is not to be understood just in relation to the knowing subject, but to a subjectivity of striving and purpose. Leibniz is obviously one of the key figures in this development. But it reaches its culmination in the Nietzschean claim that everything is will to power.

Modern subjectivism onticises the clearing in the opposite way from Platonism. Now things appear because there are subjects which represent them, and take a stand on them. The clearing is the fact of representation; and this only takes place in minds, or in the striving of subjects, or in their use of various forms of depiction, including language.

But the real nature of the clearing is neither of the above. They can be seen as making equal and opposite mistakes. Each misses something important about it. The Platonic mode cannot acknowledge our role. The clearing in fact comes to be only around Dasein. It is our being there which allows it to happen. At least the representational theory grasps that. But it for its part cannot appreciate that the clearing doesn't just happen within us, and/or is not simply our doing. Any doing of ours, any play with representations, supposes as already there the disclosure of things in language. We cannot see this as something that we control or that simply happens within our ambit. The notion that it is simply in our heads already supposes in order to make sense that we understand our heads and ourselves as placed in a world, and this understanding doesn't happen only in our heads. This would be Heidegger's recreation of Hegel's disproof of the Kantian thing in itself. The idea that this clearing is our doing collapses into incoherence as well; it is only through the clearing that we have any idea of doing at all, that action is in our repertory.

So the clearing is both Dasein-related, and yet not Dasein-controlled. It is not Dasein's doing. Here we can see how for Heidegger enframing theories of language are redolent of modern subjectivism. They purport to understand language, i.e., that whereby the clearing comes to be, as a mode of representation which functions within a human life whose purposes are not themselves set by language. Language is enframed, and can be seen as performing a set of functions which can, except for respresentation itself, be defined non-linguistically. Language is something we can use; it is an instrument. This instrumentalization of the clearing is one of the furthest expressions of the will to power.

Heidegger's position can be seen from one point of view as utterly different from both Platonism and subjectivism, because it avoids onticizing altogether; from another point of view, it can be seen as passing between them to a third position which neither can imagine, one which is Dasein-related, but not Dasein-centered.[18]

Now it seems obvious that Heidegger found some of the background he needed to develop this position out of the constitutive-expressive tradition. Its understanding of expression, in particular of the symbol, begins to explore this middle ground. The symbol is both manifestation and creation, partakes of both finding and making. The philosophies that arose out of the Romantic phase (which can't necessarily themselves be called "Romantic"), e.g., those of Schelling and Hegel, begin to stake out a middle position. In a sense, they have something in common with Plato, and with the whole ancient and medieval conception of a cosmic order which embodies Ideas. For Hegel reality conforms to the Idea. But at the same time, they see the cosmos as crucially incomplete until brought to its adequate expression in human-sustained media – e.g., Hegel's Art, Religion and Philosophy. The Idea isn't a reality quite independent of the Being which can bring it to manifestation, i.e., human being. But this way of differing from the ancients does not take the standard modern form of locating the clearing in representation. The expression-articulation of the Idea is not a mere representation, but a kind of completing; at the same time, the completing is not itself just a human achievement. The human agent here is an emanation of cosmic spirit.

What we can see from this is that the idea of expression itself can nudge us towards a third way of locating the clearing. It gives us a notion of the clearing which is essentially Dasein-related; in this it is at one with the standard modern view. But it does not place the clearing simply inside us as a representation; it puts it rather in a new space constituted by expression. And in some versions it can acknowledge that the constituting of this space is not simply our doing.

Can acknowledge, but doesn't necessarily do so. There are two issues here which we can distinguish. The first concerns the ontic status of the clearing. The second is rather a clutch of issues, and touches the nature of the expressive power itself.

1   As to the first: the space of expression is not the same as, that is, it cannot be reduced to either ordinary physical space, or inner "psychic" space, the domain of the "mind" on the classic epistemological construal. It is not the same as the first, because it only gets set up between speakers. (It is Dasein-related.) It is not the same as the second, because it cannot be placed "within" minds, but rather is out between the interlocutors, as we saw in the previous section. In conversation, a public or common space gets set up, in which the interlocutors are together.

If we see the clearing as the space opened by expression, then the basis is there for a de-onticizing move, relative to the categories of our modern ontology, matter and mind. For this space is neither. The move is made possible, but it isn't taken right away. Hegel still draws heavily on the old onto-theology, and the Chain of Being, to ground the manifestations of spirit. Later, with Schopenhauer, a strange new twist is introduced. The ontic basis of expression is Will. But this is no longer seen as the benign source of being and goodness, but rather as the source of endless, disordered striving and suffering. This reversal undoubtedly helped to prepare the way for the move which Heidegger is the first to make explicitly, though one can perhaps see forerunners among those who prepared the way to modernist poetics, for example, Mallarmé. In declaring the ontological difference, Heidegger is realizing a potentiality opened by expressivism.

2   When we turn to the second gamut of issues, we can see that the expressivist turn did not put an end to subjectivism. On the contrary, it opens up a whole new range of forms, some of them among the most virulent. Here again, there is a potentiality, which may remain unrealized. What expressivism does is open the issue of the nature of the expressive power. The options are many. We can perhaps single out three sub-issues, which open up as it were a three-dimensional problem space, in which different thinkers and writers have located themselves.

A   If like the earlier theorists, e.g., Hegel, you see expression as bringing something to manifestation, then you can think of this reality as the self; and the essential activity is self-expression. Or one can identify it as something beyond the self; in Hegel's case, with a cosmic spirit or process. This is one dimension in which one can move towards subjective or objective poles.

B   But then, more radically, one can challenge the whole idea that expression manifests something; one can see it not as a bringing to light, but as a bringing about. The space is something we make. The potentiality for this more radical subjectivism is already there in the canonical notion of the symbol current in the Romantic era. The symbol manifests something; but this does not mean that it simply copies some model already in view. It rather creates the medium in which some hitherto hidden reality can be manifest. Prior to expression, this reality is not something which *can* be in view, and hence there can be no question of copying. Manifesting through the symbol therefore involves an element of creation, the making one might say of a medium in which the reality can for the first time *appear*. If we add, as did Hegel and others, that appearance was part of the potentiality of what comes to light, then this creation also counts as bringing this reality to completion.

Expression partakes of both finding and making. In the original variant, there is a balance between the two, but the second basically is in the service of the first. The radical step is to overturn this balance, and to see the clearing as something projected. Through the power of expression we make this space, and what appears in it should not be seen as a manifestation of anything. What appears is a function of the space itself. Once again, Mallarmé might be seen as one of the pioneers of this view, with his image of *le néant*. Nietzsche could be read as poised on a knife-edge between the two views, and a term like "transfiguration" remains ambivalent between them. But the major proponents of the radical, "creationist" view today are deconstructionists, particularly Derrida, with slogans like: *"il n'y a pas de hors-texte."*

C   There is a third issue on which one can be more or less subjectivist, and that is on the question of the "who?" of expression. Is it the work of the individual agent? Or is it rather something which arises out of the conversation, so that its locus is the speech community? Or should we think of the locutors themselves purely as artefacts of the space of expression, so that there is no "who" of expression at all? The first answer has been more or less discredited in the constitutivist tradition, for reasons which were touched on in the earlier sections. The second, Humboldtian one has been the most widespread. Each locutor, as s/he enters the conversation from infancy, finds their identity shaped by their relations within a pre-existing space of expression. In this sense, they are the creatures of this space. But as they become full members of the conversation, they can in turn contribute to shape it, and so no simple, one-sided relation of dependence can capture the reality of speakers and language, as the third theory supposes.

The third theory is exemplified by Derrida. *"Différance"* is the non-agent setting up the space of expression. This might be thought to be on the far anti-subjectivist end of the spectrum of this third question. But I believe that one should rather see the second, Humboldtian solution as the truly non-subjectivist one. The Derridean one is in fact the mirror image of the subjectivist outlook. It gets its plausibility from the implausibility of this outlook, which Derrida parades before us in its more extreme forms as the only alternative. But I haven't got space to argue this here.

These two main questions, the latter divided into three sub-issues, set up a problem space with many possible positions, combining different options on the various dimensions. The Derridean philosophy combines a radical "creationist" position on sub-issue B (hence question A, which asks what is manifested? does not arise), with a relegation of the locutor to purely derivative status when it comes to C. This is what gives his philosophy its strongly anti-subjectivist appearance, which I suggested is mere appearance. The rhetoric of the end of the subject masks the option in favour of a highly subjectivist stance on B. In fact, one might argue that the relegation of the locutor on C is just another consequence of the radical creationism on B. It is a corollary of the idealist thesis that there is no *"hors-texte."*

Heidegger stands quite differently in this space, I want to argue, so that Derridean readings gravely misperceive him. He is a "manifestationist" on sub-issue B; his strong anti-subjectivist stance is taken on sub-issue A. Expression is not self-expression; creative language is a response to a call. On sub-issue C, he comes quite close to the Humboldtian view. Statements like the famous one in Poetically Man Dwells: "For, strictly, it is language that speaks."[19] I understand as conveying his anti-subjectivist stand on A, rather than a proto-Derridean invocation of a super(non)agent.

This makes Heidegger come pretty close to a commonly held position in the constitutivist tradition on the second complex of issues (2), about the nature of the expressive power. Where he departs radically is rather on the first main issue (1), in his thoroughgoing insistence that the clearing is not to be ontically grounded. This might be confused with the creationist view of the expressive power on sub-issue B. But these are quite different questions. To see the clearing as not ontically grounded, or locatable, is not to see it as self-enclosed, as related to nothing outside it. A self-enclosed picture of the clearing would run clean against Heidegger's brand of anti-subjectivism.

What emerges with Heidegger is thus a novel position, one that was hard to imagine before he began to pose the questions of philosophy in his own peculiar way. The confusion between a de-onticized view of the clearing and a creationist one is easy to make if we operate in familiar categories. For most manifestationist readings of the space of expression were based on some firm ontic posits, which were thought to be the essential underpinnings of this reading, like Hegel's *Geist*, or Schopenhauer's Will, or Nietzsche's will to power, for that matter. Denying these seemed to mean opting for a view of the space of expression as purely made.

But Heidegger alters the whole philosophical landscape by introducing (1) the issue of the clearing and its ontic placing. Once we separate out this question from that of (2), the nature of the expressive power, we can combine a manifestationist view on this latter with a rejection of all ontic grounding. But on what, then, do we base this manifestationist view, if we can no longer recur to some ontic underpinnings of the familiar kind? On a reading of the space of expression itself. Otherwise put, the clearing itself, or language itself, properly brought to light, will show us how to take it. Heidegger as always moves to retrieve what is hidden, not in some distant point, but in the event of disclosure itself.

That is why I believe that articulating the themes of the constitutivist view of language can help in explaining Heidegger. He in fact draws on these, because he formulates the clearing through describing the action/event which makes it possible, and these are crucially linguistic.

(5)   Let me try to reconstruct Heidegger's *démarche* drawing on what has been said in earlier sections about language in the broad sense of the constitutivist tradition, that is, about the expressive power. We can follow the Aristotle-derived thread I mentioned at the beginning of this section: read the expressive power to glean the excellence, the *areté*, implicit in it.

Through language, a world is disclosed; a world in which features are located, which is also a locus of strong goods, of objects of the specifically human emotions, of human relations. So plainly one *telos*, or range of *telé*, which we can find in language prescribes that this disclosure be properly done: that the features be correctly located, that the goods be fully acknowledged, that our emotions and relations be undistortedly discerned. Some of this range of goals is carried out in what we define as science; other parts require other types of discourse, including in their own way literature and philosophy, and the other arts also have their articulative role.

This range of goals gives a manifestationist cast to the clearing. In the case of natural science, one might define the end as more like depiction, the representation of an independent object, but in, e.g., clarifying emotions, language also helps to constitute or complete; the model of the symbol is the appropriate one. Attributing this approach to language to Heidegger makes of him an uncompromising realist, and that is what I think he was.

But beyond these goals of first-order disclosure, there is a *telos* in the clearing to disclose itself, to bring itself undistortedly to light. If its goal is undistorted uncovering, then how can this uncovering itself be an exception? Showing up should itself show up. But this raises a problem, because Heidegger has argued that there is a tendency precisely to distort our understanding of the clearing. At least in the tradition determined by our Western "destining," we come to see language as our instrument, and the clearing as something that happens in us, and reflects our goals and purposes. At the end of this road is the reduction of everything to standing reserve in the service of a triumphant will to will. In the attempt to impose our light, we cover the sources of the clearing in darkness. We close ourselves off to them.

That this second-order disclosure is part of the *telos* of language comes clear in Heidegger's notion that the total mobilization of everything as standing reserve threatens the human essence.[20] For this is just the next stage in a basically Aristotelian line of argument. "The human is indeed in its nature given to speech."[21] So what goes against the *telos* of language goes against human essence.

But I can already sense that some readers may be uneasy at this Aristotelizing of Heidegger. So let me hasten to point out the difference. The human essence is not here derived from the ontic examination of a particular species of hairless ape, which happens to use language. We aren't deriving this from the nature of the "rational animal." It is, on the contrary, purely derived from the way of being of the clearing, by being attentive to the way that language opens a clearing. When we can bring this undistortedly to light, we see that it is not something we accomplish. It is not an artefact of ours, our "*Gemächte*." It must be there as the necessary context for all our acting and making. We can only act in so far as we are already in the midst of it. It could not happen without us, but it is not our doing. It is the basis for all the sense that our lives make; or that anything makes. Hence the sense of our lives must at least include as a central element the part we play in the clearing coming to be. This is not the major role that a creator would have, but a secondary one, helping it to happen, protecting and maintaining it. We have to "take care" of (*pflegen*) being, "spare" (*schonen*) it.[22] The human agent is "the shepherd of Being."[23]

Denying this role, trying to transform it into something else, acting as though we were in control, is going against our essence, and cannot but be destructive. The parallel with Aristotle's line of reasoning is unmistakable. It has been transposed, however, into a new key. Our essence is not derived from any ontic description, but from our role in relation to the clearing. That is why Heidegger sees his philosophy as non- even anti-humanist, aligning "humanism" as he does with an anthropocentric doctrine of human control.

But how do you acknowledge the way of being of the clearing? How do you make showing up undistortively show up? Disclosure is not some extra entity over and above the ones which show up. So meta-disclosure occurs in the way that first-order entities show up. And for Heidegger this means that they, or an important subset of them, have to show up as "things," and not simply as objects, or even worse, as standing reserve.

The thing about a "thing" is that in being disclosed it co-discloses its place in the clearing. Later Heidegger introduces the notion of the "four-fold" to explain this: mortal and divine beings, earth and sky. Take a humble entity like a jug. As it shows up in the world of a peasant, as yet unmobilized by modern technology, it is redolent of the human activities in which it plays a part, of the pouring of wine at the common table, for instance. The jug is a point at which this rich web of practices can be sensed, made visible in the very shape of the jug and its handle which offers itself for this use. So much for the human life which co-shows up in this thing.

At the same time this form of life is based on, and interwoven with, strong goods, matters of intrinsic worth. These are matters which make a claim on us. They can be called "divine." So these too are co-disclosed. Heidegger imagines this connection as arising from an actual ritual of pouring a libation from the jug. But I doubt if the Christian, Black Forest peasantry of Swabia (as against ancient Greeks) actually did this kind of thing; and it is sufficient to point out that the human modes of conviviality that the jug co-discloses are shot through with religious and moral meaning. Perhaps the pastor said grace, but even if he didn't, this life together has central meaning in the participants' lives.

The jug is something shaped and fashioned for human use. It is one of those objects which is already clearly identified as a locus of features. As such it stands on and emerges out of a vast domain of as yet unformed and unidentified reality. This is a field of potential future forming, but it is limitless, inexhaustible. All forming is surrounded by and draws on this unformed. If we are not closed to it, the jug will also speak of its history as a formed entity, of its emergence from unformed matter, of its continuing dependency on the unformed, since it can only exist as an entity as long as it is supported by the whole surrounding reality. It rests ultimately on the earth, and that is the word Heidegger uses for this dimension of co-disclosure.

Finally, the jug and the whole round of activities it speaks of, and the earth, are open to greater cosmic forces which are beyond the domain of the formable, and which can either permit them to flourish or sweep them away. The alternation of day and night, storms, floods, earthquakes, or their benign absence – these are the things that Heidegger gathers under the title "sky." They provide the frame within which the earth can be partly shaped as our world.

All these are co-disclosed in the thing. Heidegger says that it "assembles" (*versammelt*) them, and they "sojourn" (*verweilen*) in it.[24] When this happens, then the clearing itself can be said to be undistortively disclosed. The undistorted meta-disclosure occurs through this manner of first-order showing up. Being among things in such a way that they show up thus is what Heidegger calls "dwelling." It involves our "taking care" of them.

> Staying with things is the only way in which the fourfold stay within the fourfold is accomplished at any time in simple unity. Dwelling preserves the fourfold by bringing the presencing of the fourfold into things. But things themselves secure the fourfold *only when* they themselves *as* things are let be in their presencing. How is this done? In this way, that mortals nurse and nurture the things that grow, and specially construct things that do not grow.[25]

As is evident from this quote, "things" include more than made objects. They include living things. And they go beyond that: "But tree and pond, too, brook and hill, are things, each in in its own way."[26] So that part of what is involved in preserving the four-fold is the "saving the earth."[27]

Living among things in this way allows the four-fold to be manifest in their everyday presence. This is already an effect of language, because the four-fold can be co-disclosed only to us, who have already identified the thing itself, and marked out the four dimensions in language. But there is a more concentrated mode of language, where we try to bring to its own proper expression what is co-disclosed in the thing. We try to capture this in a deliberate formulation through an expressive form. Heidegger's own form of philosophizing (properly, "thinking") is an attempt to do this. But it can also be done in works of art. So the peasant woman, as she puts on her shoes, experiences her life in the fields and the seasons and the ripening corn. She "knows all this without observation or consideration." But in van Gogh's painting of the peasant's shoes, their thingly nature is shown as something we can contemplate, in an express formulation which we can consider and observe.[28]

But we close ourselves to all this when we turn away from living among things, and formulating what they co-disclose in art, and identify them as context free objects, susceptible of scientific study; and even more so when we are swept up in the technological way of life and treat them as just standing reserve. If we make these our dominant stance to the world, then we abolish things, in a more fundamental sense than just smashing them to pieces, though that may follow. "Science's knowledge, which is compelling within its own sphere, the sphere of objects, already had annihilated things as things long before the atom bomb exploded."[29]

So what does this tell us about language? It has a *telos*, and that requires that entities show up in a certain way. This is already made possible through language. But more, when it is lost, an essential role in its retrieval devolves on certain uses of language in philosophy and art, or in Heideggerese "*Denken*" and "*Dichten*". And when we understand the potential role that these can have, we understand that the original way of dwelling which we have lost flowed itself from some founding acts of one of the other.

So language, through its *telos*, dictates a certain mode of expression, a way of formulating matters which can help restore thingness. It tells us what to say, dictates the poetic, or thinkerly word, as we might put it. We can go on talking, mindful only of our purposes, unaware that there is anything else to take notice of. But if we stop to attend to language, it will dictate a certain way of talking. Or, otherwise put, the entities will demand that we use the language which can disclose them as things. In other words, our use of language is no longer arbitrary, up for grabs, a matter of our own feelings and purposes. Even, indeed especially in what subjectivism thinks is the domain of the most unbounded personal freedom and self-expression, that of art, it is not we but language which ought to be calling the shots.

This is how I think we have to understand Heidegger's slogan "*Die Sprache spricht*," rather than as a proto-Derridean invocation of a super(non)subject. That is why Heidegger speaks of our relation to this language in terms of a call (*Ruf*) which we are attentive to. "*Die Sterblichen sprechen insofern sie horen.*" And he can speak of the call as emanating from a "silence" (*Stille*).[30] The silence is where there are not yet (the right) words, but where we are interpellated by entities to disclose them as things. Of course, this does not happen before language; it can only happen in its midst. But within language and because of its *telos*, we are pushed to find unprecedented words, which we draw in this sense out of silence. This stillness contrasts with the noisy *Gerede* in which we fill the world with expressions of our selves and our purposes.

These unprecedented words (in fact, better "sayings," but "word" is pithier) are words of power; we might say: words of retrieval. They constitute authentic thinking and poetry.[31] They are on a different level from everyday speech; not because they are "heightened" speech; but rather because everyday speech is a kind of dulling, a falling off from, a forgetfulness of the more full-blooded disclosure they bring.[32] That is why I want to speak of retrieval.

(6) Heidegger is on to something very important, a power of words that enframing theories can make no sense of. It has tremendously positive uses, but also terrifyingly dangerous ones. Heidegger is characteristically only aware of the former. The danger comes from the fact that much can be retrieved from the grey zone of repression and forgetfulness. There are also resentments and hatreds and dreams of omnipotence and revenge, and they can be released by their own appropriate words of power. Hitler was a world-historical genius in only one respect, but that was in finding such dark words of power, sayings that could capture and elevate the fears, longings, and hatreds of a people into something demonic. Heidegger has no place for the retrieval of evil in his system, and that is part of the reason why Hitler could blindside him, and why he never thereafter could get a moral grasp on the significance of what happened between 1933 and 1945.[33]

But there is also a tremendous positive relevance of Heidegger's philosophy to modern politics, which is especially important today. I return here to the issue I raised at the outset. Heidegger's understanding of language, its *telos*, and the human essence can be the basis of an ecological politics, founded on something deeper than an instrumental calculation of the conditions of our survival (though that itself ought to be enough to alarm us). It can be the basis of in one sense a "deep" ecology.

For as I put it above, we can think of the demands of language also as a demand that entities put on us to disclose them in a certain way. This amounts in fact to saying that they demand that we acknowledge them as having certain meanings. But this manner of disclosure can in crucial cases be quite incompatible with a stance of pure instrumentality towards them. Take wilderness, for instance. This demands to be disclosed as "earth," as the other to "world." This is compatible with a stance of exploration, whereby we identify the species and geological forms it contains, for instance, as long as we retain the sense of the inexhaustibility of their wilderness surroundings. But a purely technological stance, whereby we see the rain forests as simply standing reserve for timber production, leaves no room for this meaning. Taking this stance is "annihilating" wilderness in its proper meaning, even before we step in and fell all the trees, to parallel Heidegger's remark about things and the atom bomb above.

This stance does violence to our essence as language beings. It is a destruction of us as well, even if we could substitute for the oxygen, and compensate for the greenhouse effect. This way of putting it might make it sound as though Heidegger's ecological philosophy were after all a "shallow" one, grounded ultimately on human purposes. But we have already seen how this misdescribes his view. For the purposes in question are not simply human. Our goals here are fixed by something which we should properly see ourselves as serving. So a proper understanding of our purposes has to take us beyond ourselves. Heidegger has perhaps in that sense bridged the difference between "shallow" and "deep" ecology, and come up with a genuine third position. As I indicated at the outset, his position is in a sense unclassifiable in the terms the issue is generally debated in. It breaks genuinely new ground.

Properly understood, the "shepherd of Being" can't be an adept of triumphalist instrumental reason. That is why learning to dwell among things may also amount to "rescuing the earth."[34] At this moment when we need all the insight we can muster into our relation to the cosmos in order to deflect our disastrous course, Heidegger may have opened a vitally important new line of thinking.

NOTES

1 "Denn eigentlich spricht die Sprache. . .," in "Dichterisch wohnet der Mensch," *Vorträge und Aufsätze*, vol.

2 "Enframing" is not used here in the sense of efficient ordering, which is the meaning of Heidegger's term, *Gestell*, standardly translated "enframing," although there is obviously an affinity between the two.

3 In *Human Agency and Language*, Cambridge, 1985.

4 See *Leviathan* (Oakeshott edition), Oxford: Blackwell n.d., chapter 4, p. 20; *Essay concerning Human Understanding*, 3.3.2; *Essai sur l'Origine des Connoissances humaines*, 1.2.4.45–6.

5 *Über den Ursprung der Sprache*, in *Johann Gottfried Herder's Sprachphilosophie*, Hamburg: Felix Meiner 1960, pp. 12–14.

6 *Ursprung*, p. 12.

7 I have argued for this reconstruction of Herder in terms of irreducible rightness at greater length in "The Importance of Herder" and "Heidegger versus Davidson."

268 Charles Taylor

8 *Essay*, 3.2.2.
9 Charles Guignon has used the term "expressive" for this view on language, in specific application to Heidegger. See his "Truth as Disclosure: Art, Language, History" in *Heidegger and Praxis*, ed. Thomas Nenon, supplement to *The Southern Journal of Philosophy* 28 (1989) pp. 105–20. It follows from the above that this is just as legitimate a term as "constitutive," or the double-barreled combination.
10 Wilhelm von Humboldt, *On Language*, translated by Peter Heath, Cambridge University Press, 1988, p. 49.
11 I have discussed this phenomenon of common space in "Theories of meaning," in *Human Agency and Language*, Cambridge, 1985.
12 Ernst Cassirer, *The Philosophy of Symbolic Forms*, Yale University Press, 1953.
13 "Symbol" is being used here in the way it was used in the tradition started by Goethe. When, in "The Origin of the Work of Art" (p. 20), Heidegger says the artwork is *not* a symbol, he is accepting a use of the term that treats it as synonymous with "allegory," which means pointing beyond itself. Goethe, on the contrary, was contrasting allegory and symbol.
14 Page numbers cited from *Holzwege*, Frankfurt: Klostermann 1972.
15 This claim seems to me indisputable as far as the late Heidegger is concerned. The question might arise about the author of *Sein und Zeit*, on the extent to which he was a constitutive theorist. I would argue that the Herder tradition was very much present in the earlier phase as well, although Heidegger had not yet drawn all the conclusions from it that shape his later philosophy. In particular, the discussions in *Sein und Zeit* about the "apophantic as" have, I think, to be understood in the light of some doctrine of the semantic dimension (ss. 32–3).
16 This seems at least to be Heidegger's view. "Self-revealing and self-concealing in the animal are one in such a way that human speculation practically runs out of alternatives. . . . Because the animal does not speak, self-revealing and self-concealing, together with their unity, possess a wholly different life-essence with animals." (*Vorträge und Aufsätze*, vol. III, Tübingen: Neske, 1954, p. 70).
17 *Ethics*, 1.7.
18 In "Heraklit" Heidegger explains that mortal *legein* does not define the *logos*, but nor does it simply copy (*nachbilden*) it. We have to find a third way between these two extremes. "Is there a path for mortal thinking to that place?" (*V&A* III, p. 21).
19 *Vorträge und Aufsätze*, vol. 2, Tübingen: Neske 1954, p. 64.
20 "Die Frage nach der Technik," in *Vorträge und Aufsätze*, vol. II.
21 *Unterwegs zur Sprache*, Gesamtausgabe, Vol. 12, p. 27.
22 "Bauen Wohnen Denken," in *V&A*, vol. II.
23 "Brief über den Humanismus," in *Wegmarken*, Frankfurt: Klostermann 1967, pp. 328, 338. "Der Mensch ist nicht Herr des Seienden. Der Mensch ist Hirt des Seins."
24 *V&A*, II, 27, 50.
25 "Bauen Wohnen Denken," pp. 25–6.
26 "The Thing," in ibid., p. 55.
27 "Building, Dwelling, Thinking," p. 25.
28 "The origin of the work of art," in *Holzwege*, Frankfurt: Klostermann 1972, p. 23.
29 *V&A*, II, p. 42.
30 *Unterwegs zur Sprache*, 27–9.
31 Heidegger's placing of "Dichten" alongside "Denken" reflects the fact that his view is substantially anticipated not only in the practice, but also in the self-understanding of some twentieth-century poets, notably Rilke. In the ninth *Duino Elegy*, Rilke offers his own understanding of the word of power. It is a word of praise: "Preise dem Engel die Welt. . .Sag ihm die Dinge. . .Zeig ihm, wie glücklich ein Ding sein Kann, wie

schuldlos und unser. "Praise the world to the angel. . . Tell him about the things . . . Show him how happy a thing can be, how blameless and ours. . . " The word "thing" here is taking on a special force, closely related to Heidegger's. Our task is to *say* them. And the list of examples is very reminiscent of Heidegger's. "Sind wir vielleicht *hier,* um zu sagen: Haus Brücke, Brunnen, Tor, Krug, Oostbaun, Fenster – höchstens, Säule, Turm. ("Are we *here* perhaps just to say: house, bridge, well, gate, jug, fruit tree, window – at most, column, tower. . ?") And this saying is a kind of rescue. "Und diese, von Hingang Tebenden Dinge verstehn, dass du sie rµhmst: vergänglich, traun sie ein Rettendes uns, den Vergänglichsten, zu." ("And these things that live, slipping away, understand that you praise them; transitory themselves, they trust us for rescue, us, the most transient of all.") This rescue is all the more necessary because of the rush of technological society to turn everything into a storehouse of power deprived of all form, as the seventh *Elegy* says. "Weite Speicher der Kraft schafft sich der Zeitgeist, gestaltlos wie der Spannende Drang, den er aus allem gewinnt. Tempel Kennt er nicht mehr." ("The spirit of the times makes vast storehouses of power, formless as the stretched tension it gathers from everything. Temples it knows no longer.") The concept of "standing reserve" was originally a poetic image of Rilke.

32   "*Eigentliche Dichtung ist niemals nur eine höhere else . . .uer Alltagssprache. Vielmehr ist umgekehrt das alltägliche Reden ein vergessenes und darum vermutztes Gedicht, aus dem kaum noch ein Ruren erklingt.*" ("Poetry proper is never merely a higher mode of everday language. It is rather the reverse: everyday language is a forgotten and therefore used-up poem, from which there hardly resounds a call any longer." *Unterwegs zur Sprache*, p. 28.

33   The different uses of words of power is discussed with characteristic insight by Vaclav Havel in his "Words on Words," the speech (he would have) delivered on receiving the German Book Prize. It is printed in the *New York Review of Books*, 18 January 1990, pp. 5–8. The Heideggerian provenance of some of his thinking on this score (partly via Patocka) is evident in the text.

34   "Building, Dwelling, Thinking." *V&A* II, 25.

14
Derrida and Heidegger: Iterability and *Ereignis*

Charles Spinosa

Followers of Heidegger are likely, when feeling tendentious, to find that Derrida's reading of Heidegger is self-aggrandizingly reductionist and that Derrida's work is simply a sophisticated version of what Heidegger diagnosed as nihilistic, Nietzschean, technological thinking.[1] Derrideans, with the encouragement of Derrida himself, read Heidegger as the forerunner Derrida has outstripped.[2] Derrida, it is said, learned from the failure of Heidegger's heroic attempt to overcome metaphysics and, in his bettering of Heidegger's deconstruction, has gone well beyond his teacher. Like compulsive shoppers, Richard Rorty and neo-pragmatists in his mold read both Heidegger and Derrida to see how much of each they can buy. It turns out that all of Heidegger, except early Heidegger's transcendental language and later Heidegger's nostalgia, can be bought by the pragmatists; and all of Derrida, except his transcendental language and his anti-metaphysical activism, can be bought as well. This state of affairs with its partisans and compulsive shoppers has stood in the way of getting a clear picture of how Derrida and Heidegger are really very close to each other and yet divided by fundamentally different intuitions about how human practices, and consequently human beings, work. The different intuitions show up in how each thinker understands language, in particular its moving force, and are focused in the difference between Heidegger's *Ereignis*[3] and Derrida's Iterability. Getting clear about what lies behind these terms, then, should give us a relatively clear and unmysterious picture of Heidegger's and Derrida's thought, show us that we should see them both as post-metaphysical and non-technological, and reveal that their unpragmatic content is large enough to make the price of assimilating them too exhorbitant for pragmatists.[4]

First, in order to develop a clear sense of what Heidegger and Derrida are claiming, we will need to lay out the meaning of a handful of roughly corresponding terms or notions. Ranging from the easy to the more difficult and giving Derrida's first, they are: system of differences and equipmental totality; trace and phenomenon; *différance* and the truth of being;[5] Derrida's version of Heidegger's ontological difference and the metaphysical version of the ontological difference; temporalization into present moments and pragmatic temporality; and, finally, temporalization and authentic temporalization. Then, in this context, the significance of Iterability and *Ereignis* can be worked out with particular reference to how both notions fit in with recognizable human behavior. Finally, showing how Heidegger and Derrida are neither metaphysical nor pragmatic will be a matter of drawing the consequences from the examples of Iterability and *Ereignis*.

1 Terms and positions

The main point of this section will be to get beyond the polemics and misunderstandings to show just how close Heidegger's and Derrida's positions are. To do this, the first thing to adapt to are the two different starting points for their thinking. Derrida typically focuses on language as the practice that reveals the most about how we are. Heidegger, instead, starts with simple (usually rural) activity such as a craftsman working on something in his shop. But this difference ought not come to much since Derrida says that the deep aspect of language–writing–structures any meaningful activity[6] and Heidegger thinks of language as a particularly revealing practice. They are both, then, starting with meaningful human activity. With no more preamble we may examine the first two sets of related distinctions.

Derrida takes over from Saussure the notion that language is a system of differences. By this, Derrida and Saussure mean that we do not respond to particular phonemes as such or to particular meanings as such but that we encounter word sounds or things (positivities) only in terms of the differences among the phonemes or meanings. Each phoneme or meaning is understood only in terms of its difference from the others. This notion is now fairly widely understood. Moreover, we encounter things in terms of a whole series of differences that are particularly charged for us; so we might say that if for us some of the particularly charged differences are true/false, real/imaginary, sensible/intelligible, discovered/invented, perceived/remembered, natural/ cultural, masculine/feminine, then anything we encounter will show up in terms of these differences. But we might easily imagine that if at another time or in a different culture holy/profane, saint/sinner replaced the first two charged diffe- rences, then things would show up differently for us. In living within this alternative set of charged differences, we would pass over some things that seem important to us now (such as the discipline of science) and other (now trivial) things would show up for us as of fundamental importance (such as the purity of one's soul). Again, if we replaced holy/profane with warlike/pastoral and saint/sinner with hero/shepherd, then things would show up in yet another wholly different way. The point to get from this is that "in language there are only differences *without positive terms.*"[7] This is to say, positive things like a saint or a sinner only show up, if they show up at all, as effects of the way a language's differences sort things out.

Heidegger's thinking is very close to this Saussurean/Derridean account. Indeed, when Heidegger says that there really is no such thing as "an equipment,"[8] he is making the same sort of point Derrida makes when he says that language has no positive terms. But Heidegger starts, as was said, with the situation of a craftsman at work in his shop. The craftsman shows up as involved in comporting himself in certain ways to make something. He shows up, that is, in terms of the skills and practices he embodies. And for the most part, these are skills and practices for dealing with equipment. But notice in terms of his involved activity, which Heidegger takes as basic, it does not make sense to say that the craftsman encounters a hammer or a nail alone. Rather, he encounters them as things *in order to* secure some planks of wood *towards* building a chest *for the sake of* enacting himself as, say, a cabinetmaker. The point is that he understands nothing, not even himself, independently of everything else in the shop that has some role in pursuing his occupation, his involved activity. A particular piece of string good, even exceptionally good, for tying together bamboo for making huts in the South Sea Islands would just not show up for him as such, even if it were hanging on his wall above his hammer. It would not show up as having such a use because he has no skills or practices for making such huts. He would pass over it or see it as waste material or as something to use in one of his normal activities. Thus, everything, even the craftsman himself, shows up in terms of a context of equipment, a world of involvement.

The differences between a system of differences and an equipmental context further narrow as we see how Derrida and Heidegger work with these notions. Because nothing can show up as wholly independent of either a system of differences or an equipmental context, Derrida becomes interested in traces and Heidegger in phenomena. These two, traces and phenomena, turn out to be roughly equivalent, though Derrida thinks that the trace goes beyond the phenomenon.[9] The trace is something that shows up in such a way that it is a ghost or sham of presence; its presence is shown as not really there; it is, as Derrida says, a "simulacrum" of its presence, it "dislocates itself, displaces itself, [and] refers itself."[10] The meaning of these claims comes out on two different levels. On the lower level, a word shows up as a trace when we respond to it with sensitivity to how its meaning is dependent on its context, how, that is, its meaning shifts as its context changes. We are alert to words in this way in reading works of literature where we expect that the meaning of its words will change as, say, more of a work is read and reread over the course of a life or lives. On the higher level, the trace refers to the way that no fixed or natural set of charged differences ever comes to hold sway over any system of differences. The "weave of differences" is always changing with history; so the trace also refers to this play (the changing of the charged differences) in the systems of difference. (This play, we shall come to see, is *différance*.)

Heidegger's phenomenon has precisely the same structure as the trace. It, like the trace, is not an appearance or just any old thing showing up, as common sense might suggest.[11] Rather, in Heidegger's terms, a phenomenon is "[t]hat which already shows itself in the appearance as prior to the 'phenomenon' as ordinarily understood and as accompanying it in every case."[12] Heidegger's point here is that the phenomenon he is interested in is, in effect, the way skillful coping in an equipmental totality allows any particular thing to show up. Like Derrida, Heidegger wants to see things in a way that is alert to the background understandings, activities, and structures that generate them. Both trace and phenomenon, then, are the aspect of anything that reveals how its particular context, linguistic and social, allows it to show up.

For Heidegger, the context that makes it possible for things to show up is usually understood not linguistically but rather as a particular way of being or revealing (a style of skillful coping) that is associated with a particular thing. This notion of particular ways of being (or revealing) is cashed out differently over the course of Heidegger's career. But even around the period of *Being and Time*, Heidegger already saw the history of the West – at least from Plato onwards – as the history of understanding being in terms of productivity.[13] This meant that the basic practice guiding our understanding of most other practices was the practice of a craftsman's productivity, his *techné*. So, for example, the power of Plato's ideas came from the sense that an idea preceded the way a craftsman formed his matter. Again, the notion of a Prime Mover or First Cause arose from fitting all beings into the mode of those made by a craftsman. This history of productivity took many different turns starting out with form/matter as the essential distinction, moving through essence/existence to subject/object.

Thus, phenomena show up not only in terms of a particular use (a hammer is in order to hammer, a car to transport oneself), but also in terms of a place in this history of being. They manifest a particular historical style of being. So, for example, one might find oneself engaged in a practice that reveals something of the pre-Platonic Greek way of being. We might suppose that a kind of training for, and taking part in, marathons might do this, especially if a particular harmony of thinking and acting is required.[14] If we think of early Greek culture as focused by competence, we might find its way of revealing things in certain academic practices where competence alone seems to count. Clearly, the sort of revealing in these practices is quite a bit different from the kind of revealing that goes on in, say, psychological testing or other subject/object, disciplinary practices. So phenomena that reveal that their showing up itself depends upon one particular historical way of making things show up are like the trace in that they reveal that revealing (another word for being)[15] in all its multiplicity could not ever be fully revealed unless history could be stopped. Here again, Derrida and Heidegger are on all fours.[16] Derrida even authorizes us to see an identity here, for he claims that the way Heidegger sees a usage (or a practice) is precisely as a trace in Derrida's sense. He only doubts that the being of usage or trace may be brought out in terms of a thinking dedicated to the essence of being.[17] Derrida has this doubt, as we shall see, because he does not read Heidegger intently enough.

In the course of giving an account of the terms, system of differences, equipmental context, trace, and phenomenon, Heidegger's "being" has come up and "*différance*" has been implicit. Can a clear sense now be given to these terms? Being amounts to revealing practices, which amount to "that on the basis of which beings are already understood."[18] But revealing always comes with one particular understanding or truth or essence.[19] The simplest way to make sense of this is to hear understanding, truth, or essence as style. Heidegger claims that, in the history of the West, we have had one style of revealing where things showed up as drawing humans to them, another where things showed up as signs telling human beings about creation, another where things showed up as objects organized for human intelligibility and control by necessary operations of the mind, and still others. These are all large-scale differences in the style of the revealing practices. To understand more fully what is meant here by "style," it will be easier to look more locally to those slightly different inflections of our general modern style in which things are revealed in different ways. We frequently see in our classes people whose style is rather careless and sloppy. They encounter chairs as things for resting the bodies they are forced to lug around. Work assignments are jobs to get done to please someone else. Reading, since it is boring, is best done when something else is going on for distraction's sake. This style pervades the lives of these people. The chairs are hard because they are not suited to relaxing. Sitting attentively erect is just not a way to encounter a chair in this style. Feeling a craftsman-like pride or concern about each sentence one is writing just does not fit with this relaxed way of approaching the world. And finally poring over a text for hours, writing summaries of arguments and objections in the margins, is a skill that has no place within this general way of approaching things. For people with different styles, one will pass over some things that will show up as crucial for another. In the cross-cultural limit, one person will live in a very different world from another. Since a style of revealing is the source and ground of how things show up, Heidegger thinks of it as an understanding of the truth or the essence of being.

Différance comes very close to Heidegger's notion of revealing (being) once we make adjustments for seeing things in terms of systems of differences instead of practices or components. Derrida writes:

> [W]e will designate as *différance* the movement according to which language, or any code, any system of referral in general, is constituted "historically" as a weave of differences.[20]

> Essentially and lawfully, every concept is inscribed in a chain or in a system within which it refers to the other, to other concepts, by means of the systematic play of differences. Such a play, *différance*, is thus no longer simply a concept, but rather the possibility of conceptuality, of a conceptual process and system in general.[21]

> *Différance* is the non-full, non-simple, structured and differentiating origin of differences.[22]

The point here is that *différance* is the movement that shifts the charges of particular differences (or re-constellates them) in any particular system of differences. As such, it is responsible for the particular set of important differences in any particular system at any time. This movement or play in any system of differences can be clarified in various ways. But for now, the way this *différance* works may be shown by looking at what is supposed to happen when Derrida shifts the charge in the speech/writing difference. Instead of seeing writing as different from and a deferred form of speech, Derrida wants, *in the first instance*,[23] writing to become the dominant term so that we see speech as an imitation of and as derived from writing.

Derrida is not trying to tell us that in the course of history, writing came first and then speech came as a representation of writing. Rather, he argues that the important feature of language is the way it bridges particular contexts, not the way it can be used as a tool to get someone nearby to do something. To put this as concretely as possible, Derrida claims that the request by the surgeon for a scalpel when he says, "Scalpel," and the response of the nurse of handing the surgeon a scalpel is *entirely* a derivative aspect of language. (And Derrida would argue this is no matter whether this use of language were glossed in terms of words indicating or pointing out things or as calling upon or activating particular skills for handling things.)[24] In fact, he would say any language use from the interior monologue to that of a close group of friends who are all sharing in a common project covers up the aspect of language that drives it. For in these situations, all the participants are already involved in the same practice. What is important about language, Derrida claims, is that it bridges different practices. The point of saying that an expression has meaning is to say that the expression retains that meaning from one context to the next. So, to go back to the surgeon example, saying "scalpel" does not get at what is linguistic in language, according to Derrida. For with a little more training and practice with the same nurse, this surgeon and nurse might, in the general course of things, work so well together that the surgeon need never say anything at all. The nurse might follow the procedure so well that when the surgeon holds out his hand, she finds herself already handing him the right scalpel. Handing the surgeon the scalpel could become as unarticulated as all the various ways of cutting the surgeon does in response to different textures of flesh and so on. What language does, the word "scalpel" in particular, is open the practice of surgical cutting to all sorts of other practices, like purchasing more scalpels from scalpel salesmen after the operation and allowing the surgeon to tell the hospital newspaper reporter that he saved the president's life by using a scalpel, and so on. This, Derrida thinks, is the defining aspect of language, and it is the aspect emphasized in writing, which is regularly used when two people are not working together in the same practice. Speech misses this point. Moreover, in having a culture where speech is understood as primary – a phonocentric culture – we are predisposed to think of ourselves as always involved in the same practice and to ignore all the different practices being bridged. By shifting the charge of the speech/writing distinction, speakers ought, in the first instance, to begin to see all the different practices being bridged. And, indeed, this seems to be happening. We speak now about mosaics and not melting pots. But, we want to object, Derrida did not get us to talk in terms of mosaics by reversing the charge of the speech/writing distinction. But this would be precisely Derrida's point. Of course, *he* did not do it. He, as Heidegger would also say, simply marked (or remarked upon) a shift that was taking place anyway. No person controls *différance*. That would be like thinking that someone controls language. We might as well say that a new way of revealing is happening this amounts to putting Derrida's insight about *différance* into Heidegger's language. And so far, that is so far as Derrida's and Heidegger's intuitions have been worked out, nothing is left out by this translation.

Why then is Derrida not content to speak as Heidegger? There are two reasons that keep getting confused with one another. The first is that Derrida simply has a mistaken view of part of what Heidegger argues and the second is because of a profound difference. Before getting to the profound difference, the confusion must be cleared up. This can be done by getting straight about the ontological difference, or ontological differences, since, for Heidegger, there are really two. The metaphysical version of the ontological difference is the difference between being, as the most general quality of beings (which Heidegger sometimes calls beingness), and particular beings. Heidegger thinks that from Anaximander on, the West has understood this metaphysical difference as that between Presence (the most general quality of beings) and present things. Heidegger gives at least two different accounts of why this happened and of its necessity. The simplest account to understand, though it seems to have the least necessity about it, is the one, already mentioned, that Heidegger developed early in his career. Thinkers, he says, tended to understand things showing up in terms of the then-current practices of production. The paradigmatic being was the one produced by the craftsman, something that, once finished, could stand alone without needing any more work; consequently, all beings were understood in terms of coming to presence (being crafted) and presence (the quality of existing fully and independently of a creator-craftsman). After all, in a tool-making, competence-centered culture, Heidegger would argue, presence, or the quality of being finished and ready for use, should seem the most general quality of anything at all. And just as Heidegger sees productive practices, in their various inflections, dominating the West, so presence shows up under various inflections as the most general quality of beings.

So far the account given of Heidegger's ontological difference concerns what Heidegger understands as the metaphysical version of the ontological difference. Focusing on this account, Derrida is led to think that Heidegger's contribution is almost entirely limited to thematizing explicitly for the first time that Western thought is constituted by thinking the presence of the present and then forgetting the distinction between presence and the present.[25] Derrida sets himself off from Heidegger by claiming that he is the one who first tries to understand the space within which the difference between presence and the present may be thought: "[I]t is the determination of being as presence or as beingness that is interrogated by the thought of *différance*," he writes.[26] But Heidegger himself understood that he was attempting to think the disclosive space or clearing in which this metaphysical understanding of the difference between being and beings could show up. For Heidegger this space is the one opened up by the real ontological difference, the one between being as revealing and the revealed. Indeed, in his later works, Heidegger's thinking of this deeper ontological difference takes two tracks. He thinks through the history of the West as the history of being in order to see the different modes of revealing and to get a sense of how they happen, how, that is, they are "sent" by revealing or being itself. And, secondly, he looks at marginal practices in the West where things are revealed in ways that do not fit with the dominant understandings of being guided by productive practices.[27] Indeed, as a matter of terminology, when thinking about the way things show up in marginal practices, he does not speak in terms of presencing or productivity but rather in terms of bestowal and gathering. (The meanings of these two terms will be worked out in the discussion of temporality.)

Since Derrida mistakenly thinks that Heidegger merely thinks of being as presencing and the ontological difference as the difference between presence and the present, his distinction between his project and Heidegger's turns out to be no distinction at all. His project, in fact, agrees entirely with Heidegger's. This can be seen fairly clearly by looking at the contrast Derrida draws between himself and Heidegger: "[T]he history of being, whose thought engages the Greco-Western *logos* such as it is produced via the ontological difference, is but an epoch of the *diapherein*."[28] If for *diapherein*, we read Heidegger's *ontological* difference and not the *metaphysical* one, we have Derrida reproducing Heidegger. To get at their profound difference, we must develop an understanding of how Heidegger sees non-metaphysical revealing, that is how he understands revealing from early to late in terms other than presencing. We must see, in other words, how Heidegger's understanding of human practices as temporal leads to things showing up in terms of bestowing and gathering. For this we must turn to Derrida's and Heidegger's sense of temporality.

Both Derrida and Heidegger think our everyday way of encountering time is misleading and consequently draws us to inadequate temporal understandings.[29] For Heidegger, our inadequate formulations of time come from our absorption in handling things. In our involved comportment, we organize things according to what is appropriate when. "It is appropriate to put the handles on *after* we make the drawers," our cabinetmakers say. "The varnish takes as long to dry as it takes for me to build this rack for the top shelf," another cabinetmaker might add. Both these statements reveal an understanding of time in terms of a particular sense of what ultimately should get done (the cabinet should be made), what has already been done (supplies have been collected and the wood has been varnished), and what the ultimate goal and what has been done leave open for one's current occupation (building drawers or making the rack). As these statements show, in doing what is appropriate, we articulate our activity according to a temporality where the present is of first importance and where the future and past show up as a matter of taking stock of where we are in the process. Heidegger argues that the time of the philosophers, with its divisible nows and the rest, derives from this pragmatic time.[30]

Derrida describes a similar sense of normal time, only, as expected, his model is not based on artisans working but on a philosopher reading a text very closely. He writes:

[T]he movement of signification is possible only if each so-called "present" element, each element appearing on the scene of presence, is related to something other than itself, thereby keeping within itself the mark of the past element, and already letting itself be vitiated by the mark of its relation to the future element, this trace being related no less to what is called the future than to what is called the past, and constituting what is called the present by means of this very relation to what it is not: what it absolutely is not, not even a past or a future as a modified present.[31]

Heidegger would find this account too abstract; Derrida's present is exceedingly close to a now point. But Derrida saves his account, from a Heideggerian attack, first by thinking in terms of an actual activity – close reading – and, second, by realizing that the past and the future are not modified present moments but part of the structure of the activity of having any meaningful experience at all. For a meaningful experience cannot be a wholly unique (wow) moment but, for the sake of intelligibility, must always sort with other similar or identical experiences and become the ground for other meaningful experiences.[32]

That both Derrida and Heidegger think that these relatively pragmatic accounts of time are inadequate points to an important claim for both of them. As is well known, Heidegger holds that there is authentic and inauthentic temporalizing (and activity). For Derrida, likewise, human activity (writing) has in it something like a hierarchy. But Derrida has regularly been seen as someone who demolishes all hierarchical distinctions. Could he have one of his own? We need to see first what is at stake in higher-order kinds of temporalizing.

For Heidegger what makes human acitivity distinctive is not that it is so good at producing things or even that in any culture (or equipmental context) all the activity is co-ordinated. Rather, he is interested in two things. First, he notes that the co-ordinated activity of any culture (or equipmental context) has a particular style, which we describe in meaningful ways, and, second, that style can change. So, for example, productivity comes in various sorts of styles. Producing can occur in the style of subjects and objects where things are accomplished by large organizations in which each member works on some little task. We have, then, individual subjects that need to be controlled and uninteresting interchangeable objects (neither things nor finished works). This description obviously amounts to production as Foucault describes it in a disciplinary society where each worker engages in part of the project and is watched by a mighty panoptic subject. Or producing could occur in the way of the small craftsman who gets drawn by a particular piece of material to work it in a certain way. He might very well see the chair as coming out of the wood. His skilled labor reveals what the wood can do. These different styles of production would show up, especially according to later Heidegger, as radically different ways of being or of revealing. The fact that there are such different styules in our history shows as well that these styles change. That there are styles of revealing and that they change is what Heidegger thinks is most important about revealing. Moreover, it is the activity of holding on to a style, including holding on to it in such a way that it changes, that provides the ground for authentic temporalizing.

The paradigmatic experience of this kind of temporalizing is, for Heidegger, receiving a new vision of how things are, finding a story that makes sense of your life, finding that your puttering around at something has finally clicked and now you can do it as you never could before. From early to late, Heidegger describes this kind of temporalizing as a receiving, a bestowal, or allotment, and with any bestowal or allotment goes a gathering together or a consolidating of the new sense of things.[33] Here we may see bestowal or allotment as a way of describing what we mean when we say, about some interpretation or some way of doing things that really works, "It just came to me" or "It just dawned on me that . . ."

Gathering is Heidegger's name for the way the new insight or the new way of doing something brings all the disparate aspects of the matter or activity together. When, for instance, we suddenly get a new reading of a text, part of getting the sense that our new reading is illuminating is the activity of collecting together in terms of the new reading all sorts of aspects of the text we had ignored or forced into shape before. This sort of activity is, at least, a good first approximation of this gathering.[34] This general activity of bestowal and gathering, though, has a particular temporal structure. A bestowal is a case where the future has opened up and bestowed or allotted some new way of dealing with all the things that we were *already* coping with. This opening up upon what is already, Heidegger thinks, is the structure of the authentic future and past. The present then shows up as the activity of coming alive to one's coping because of the new clarity that has been bestowed upon it. This present is not a matter of seeing what to do *now* but of sensing, perhaps even celebrating, how everything fits together. We get a rough sense of this difference between the pragmatic present and the authentic present by comparing the way things show up as present to be worked on when we are carrying out chores as opposed to the way things show up as present during a toast at a wedding feast when the entire life of the couple and ourselves are there in the articulation of the occasion. A more fully developed concrete example that shows how this bestowing/gathering temporalizing works and is related to the temporality of producing things should put these matters in order.

Many people, but men in particular, in my generation worked throughout college and professional school in order to establish lives with large amounts of personal ease and nonchalance. Our activity in the classroom, our jobs, our love lives were all held together by a general style of producing a freedom from the ties that would force us into compromises we did not want to make. This meant that we worked very hard to develop niches for ourselves in our public lives. In our private lives, we worked on the little things that we could control. We developed sophisticated cooking skills, gardening skills, home-repair skills, personal-finance skills, athletic skills, skills for easy-going romances, and all the tastes that go along with all of these. But slowly life started to dull. And suddenly starting a family has come to many men my age to seem just the thing to do. But it is not the idea or concept of starting a family that comes to this group of men. Rather, suddenly, life is felt as something directed towards having a family. In the light of this future, everything takes on a new look. All the sophisticated skills now show up in an intensified, collected way as means of forming a family where the husband need not dominate his wife and where the father can nurture the baby. So having a family has come out of the future to make sense of the past and to redirect the current ways of coping with things, yielding an intense feeling of the connectedness or integrity of all the small skills. So, yes, it is still appropriate to boil the water before putting in the pasta, but before it was appropriate in order to produce (in terms of lived sentiments) pasta with precisely the right *al dente* texture. Now it is appropriate in order to produce (in terms of lived sentiments) the right family moment. So it is in this sense that authentic temporalizing – the temporality of receiving a particular general meaning or style – is the source of pragmatic temporalizing – the temporality of the way things show up in terms of coping with them.[35] Authentic temporalizing is the source of what makes pragmatic time count for something. Put another way, bestowing and gathering are the source of presencing.

Derrida's full account of temporalizing differs quite a bit, and even explicitly, from Heidegger's, and it is in terms of this difference that we may begin to see his profound disagreement with Heidegger. As we have seen, Derrida focuses on shifts in the charged differences in a system of differences. These shifts are the activity – though, Derrida insists, not activity in the regular ontic sense of the word – of *différance*. Moreover, he argues that these shifts cannot be directly experienced. This is what he means when he says that *différance* cannot be thought on the basis of the present. And so far he makes good sense. No one experiences the actual shift in vision and feeling entailed by falling in love. Though once we are in love, we realize that our way of dealing with things and people has changed (our world changed). In a like manner, once any one of Derrida's shifts has occurred, we find ourselves belatedly making sense of things according to the new ordering occasioned by the shift. This is what Derrida means when he talks about an essential belatedness in our lives. But, although we may reorder various projects of our lives around the shift in the play in the system of differences, we do not and cannot bring the shift itself into present direct experience in that reordering. For this reason, Derrida claims that Heidegger's gathering, collecting in a newly intensified way the meaning of the bestowal or shift, ought not to count as a genuine part of authentic temporalizing. For that gathering could only disguise the radical unexperienceable quality of the shift. Thus, thinking in terms of bestowal or allotment is a mistake because the inflection of both of those terms makes sense only if gathering or regathering is a genuine activity, rather than a cover-up of a radical shift. Take away the genuineness of gathering, and the change that the terms "bestowal" and "allotment" get at becomes better depicted as a relieving (as in one guard relieving another)[36] or as a displacing of one world with another. For Derrida, then, an adequate account of temporalizing sees it as a matter of constantly trying to make sense of, or take account of, some completely incomprehensible advent in our lives. Our present, then, is always belated, always following a past advent that we cannot comprehend. The future, on a first impression, bifurcates, either looking like more belated activity trying to clarify the past shift or looking totally incomprehensible and showing up as the possibility of an incomprehensible shift. But, on second thought, any account of a totally incomprehensible futural shift will be understood in the terms of the current belated activity, so the future will show up as an impure advent, indescribable and already falsely described.

Derrida says that a life temporalized this way would look like accounts of life given by Nietzsche and Freud. For simplicity's sake, the picture of one of Freud's compulsives will do here. The Ratman, for instance, finds himself moving about stones in the path of his girlfriend's carriage and each time justifying what he is doing in clever ways. But the point of Freud's account is that the Ratman is responding to something unconscious, as Derrida says, a shift in a system of differences that could never be conscious. It is wholly other.[37] So the poor Ratman's attempts at consolidation or gathering are wholly out of touch with what motivates them.

This sort of talk, and example, may seem unpersuasive to Heideggerians. And shifting from the Freudian model to the Nietzschean one is not likely to help very much. But Derrida's point becomes more trenchant if put in Heidegger's terms. An aspect of Heidegger's being (characterized here as human practices for revealing things and people) is that new understandings of being (new ways of revealing) are sent, but this sending cannot be responded to in the way we generally respond to a thing. In responding to a style of revealing in the practices, human beings can at best deal more consistently with things and people in a way more appropriate to the general style. Presumably this means dropping the old, worn-out ways of treating things and people and developing new ones. So men in my generation stop dealing with things in terms of personal growth and freedom and start dealing with them in terms of family and fatherhood. (The arugula, which made every salad a hit, now shows up as something the children have to be taught to like). But all of this activity, Derrida objects, has to do with things. It is not aimed at the revealing practices or, even more important, at the way a particular way of revealing comes about. It wholly misses the shift. True temporalizing ought to get at the temporal structure of our activity when we are attending to revealing itself, and that occurs, he argues, strictly in terms of our experience of belatedness. Any other relation to revealing such as the gathering involved in reordering one's dealing with the old everyday matter of one's life is "forbidden":

> The structure of delay in effect forbids that one make of temporalization (*temporization*) a simple dialectical complication of the living present as an originary and unceasing synthesis – a synthesis constantly directed back on itself, gathered in on itself and gathering.[38]

Which view is right? Does it make sense to claim, as Heidegger does, that gathering is a genuine aspect of the human activity of responding to one's revealing practices? Or must we agree with Derrida that no way of dealing with things can put us into a special, authentic relation with the current way of revealing? The point here will not be to answer these questions, but rather to make them show up in very concrete ways as two very different pictures of how the revealing practices work. To see this difference concretely, we must turn to Iterability and *Ereignis*.

2 Iterability and *Ereignis*

The main points of this section will be to show (1) why Derrida sees revealing practices (the system of differences or writing) as only authentically revealing when the practices or system is changing its way of revealing (as it always is at one speed or another), and (2) why Heidegger thinks that authentic revealing occurs when one is simply in touch with the current *appropriate* way of revealing (and therefore implies that there is a certain deep stability in the revealing practices).

Iterability reveals best Derrida's sense of the constant change of charged differences. Put another way, Iterability shows that language or any meaningful practice can only manifest itself if structured by *différance*. How does this work? Derrida's argument begins rather simply. Repeating or recalling or reporting, he argues, is implicit in any human speech practice. In fact, some variant of repeating is implicit in any meaningful human practice whatsoever. For a meaningful event, either a speech act or a vision or a mood or whatever, could only be meaningful if we had some way of getting at it, of bringing it to our attention, independent of the original context in which it occurred. (This point was made before with the surgeon example.) If some event were so unique that it could not be prescinded from its context and did not show up for us with this potential already apparent, then we could not have any means of recalling it outside of that original context. And even if we were to return to its original context and the event were to recur, we could have no way of identifying it as the same event we experienced before. Without marking the experience in some way that is at least partly independent of the context of the experience, we would simply be awash in the experience each time it was repeated. Derrida wants us to think of language and meaningful experience as innately intertextual; this is just to say that we could have no way of identifying any experience at all even in the first instance, if it did not show up, somehow, already prescinded from its context. Without such abstracting, an experience would remain wholly embedded and unnoticed to begin with. In arguing this way Derrida is on all fours with at least one interpretation of Wittgenstein's private language argument. He simply tells us that signs, meanings, or experiences must be recognizable outside of their original context in order to be meaningful.

Derrida adds, though, that this feature of meaning practices, this Iterability, shows that the meaning of words or experiences cannot be controlled by the speaker. In the first instance all this means is that as soon as a speaker's words leave his mouth, others will determine them according to their own lights. But this claim does not seem to reveal very much. For most of human experience shows that this difference in understanding is relatively minimal, except when very complicated ideas are being expressed. So when someone says to another, removed from the original situation, that, for instance, he heard A make an ungenerous comment regarding B the day before, the identities of A and B and of ungenerous comments are altered only to the slightest degree as the context changes from A and his intimates on the first day to one of A's intimates and an outsider on the second day. The degree of A's ill-temper towards B may be understood to be slightly greater or less than in fact it was. But, for the most part, the identities remain fairly stable, or else change occurs in predictable ways as words are reported from context to context. Now if the report were of a very difficult text's meaning or the contexts crossed large historical or cultural distances, then the disparity of understanding from context to context might be greater but, generally speaking, different contexts are not all that different or are well co-ordinated with each other.

Derrida claims however, that the changes in meaning attendant upon Iterability are more radical than our simple commonsensical account would suggest. He wants to exhibit from the phenomenon of Iterability not only that the receiver may misunderstand the speaker's meaning but also that the speaker never really controls his meaning even for himself at the very beginning. The meanings of his own words might change for him at the very instant he speaks them. This is quite a telling claim, if it can be justified, so, first, let us see that Derrida in fact makes it. Here Derrida starts with the normal view that a mark, a saying, will be less stable the greater the distance from its original utterance, but then he adds that he has merely put things this way for pedagogical reasons:

> What holds for the receiver holds also, *for the same reasons*, for the sender or the producer. To write is to produce a mark that will constitute a sort of machine which is productive in turn, and which my future disappearance will not, in principle, hinder in its functioning, offering things and itself to be read and to be rewritten. When I say "my future disappearance" . . . it is in order to render this proposition more immediately acceptable. I ought to be able to say [instead of] my disappearance, pure and simple, *my nonpresence in general*, for instance *the nonpresence of my intention of saying something meaningful*, my wish to communicate, from the emission or production of the mark.[39]

To drive this slightly muddled point home, that in the general case, the speaker is not present to his own meaning and hence the subject is not the ground of his meanings, Derrida adds: "the situation of the writer . . is, concerning the written text, basically the same as that of the reader."[40]

To develop an intuition of what Derrida thinks of as the general case of language use or of having meaningful experiences, a concrete example is needed. We need to see an example of a speaker's words *actually* changing the context that gives meanings to his words, pulling that context out from under him. To see this, suppose we have a newly arrived Easterner in California who finds that people seem to misunderstand his jokes, are rather numb to his ideas, seem to respond to the things he says with the wrong affects, and so on. His mood would be one of confusion, irritation, annoyance. He would feel, in general, out of sorts, and things would show up to him in this way, as either perpetuating his view that things are all slightly off in California or that Californians show signs here and there of getting with it. Everything he says or feels about himself he would understand in the context of this mood. But as he speaks more and more, he might very well find himself uttering words that before he had only used in a joking way back in the East, in imitation of, say, Woody Allen, and now too so far as he clearly intends them it is to repeat them in this same old way. "I guess I'm just not laid back," he says. But, suddenly, precisely as he utters these words, everything changes. He sees that, in actual living fact and not just as a matter of course, he *is* not laid back and that *is* why people have been misunderstanding him, his gestures, and his expressions generally. In uttering these words, he sees himself as transformed. He understands his being anew and with clarity. Moreover, the people who were numb, cold, and impossible to get through to now show up as laid back, as having a different but definable way of being. His mood suddenly shifts from being out of sorts to being focused and curious about the new world he is adventuring into. Indeed, in the course of uttering *ces mots justes*, the meaning of the very words has changed and so has the speaker's identity and his context.[41]

This, I think, is what we ought to take as the paradigmatic Derridean experience of language and other meaningful experiences. It is one where the meaning of our sentences, such as it is, transforms us. It does not get at something that we already are but transforms us in a way that just happens to fit with our circumstances. It is for this reason that Derrida can say that *différance* is not a word or a concept.[42] It is supposed to transform us and consequently itself when it is used. It is also for this reason that Derrida can claim that the human subject is a function of language.[43] A speaker is created and recreated in his or her speaking. But the speaker is never ultimately the center or meaning giver of his or her speech.

One small and one larger point now need to be made. First, if language transforms us in this way, then it may seem to do so because it is a resource rich with meanings. But to think this is precisely to miss Derrida's point. Meanings are not stable, but generate new meanings only loosely related to the old. This transformational working of language impoverishes any rich sense of meaning. Another way to put this is to say that meaning for Derrida ought to be experienced as wonder and not as something that co-ordinates our practices, that makes them resonate together. Meaning is wonder not resonance.

Second, we should like to see an argument for why an experience that most people would take to be marginal at best should be understood by Derrida to be the most deeply revealing and indeed, in some sense, the most typical case of language use.[44] Before presenting an argument we should see, again, that it is in fact the case that Derrida sees language or revealing practices as transformational. Here, in one of Derrida's most recent writings, he tells us that although the norms of minimal intelligibility change slowly, they are always in the process of changing and have only been slowed by unnatural cultural power formations such as, one may assume, logocentrism and phallocentrism:

> [T]he norms of minimal intelligibility are not absolute and ahistorical, but merely more stable than others. They depend upon socio-institutional conditions, hence upon nonnatural relations of power that by essence are mobile and founded upon complex conventional structures that in principle may be analyzed, deconstructed, and transformed; and, in fact, these structures are in the process of transforming themselves profoundly and, above all, very rapidly . . . *"deconstruction" is firstly this destabiliszation on the move*.[45]

The picture that we see here is that the shared practices[46] that allow for things and people to show up (to become intelligible), if left to their own nature, would change in a more rapid and noticeable way than they do today. This is to say that Iterability as exemplified above would show itself in normal language use. But the workings of intelligibility are jelled or gummed up, and the culprit for gumming up the works is metaphysical practices, the hold of which deconstruction will weaken. (Here we glimpse the political side of deconstruction that neo-pragmatist commentators of Derrida such as Fish and Rorty slight.)[47] But this brings us back to our original question, why believe at all that our revealing practices are naturally in a state of flux?

The best place to turn for Derrida's reasons for this claim is his recent writing on the law.[48] His point in this legal writing is to clarify the indeterminancy in the meaning of judicial decisions. According to Derrida, as we might expect, this indeterminancy of meaning is due to the poverty of meaning that exists in any meaningful experience. (For meaningful experience is, as described, transformational, full of wonder, and not resonant.) So interpreting the law, on the level Derrida describes it, is much like any other form of interpretation. Following this line of thought, Derrida, first, makes the Wittgensteinian point[49] that laws (rules in general) cannot determine their own interpretation. They can only show up as determinate against a background of practices or form of life (system of differences) that determines them in one way or another. But the fact that we have a judicial system with lawyers and judge's rulings and the rest shows that our practices for revealing people and things do not fully determine any particular rule. And, indeed, no particular single set of practices could fully determine the meanings of any set of laws or rules, because meaningful words, signs, rules, etc., depend, as has been argued, on having implicitly a sort of impoverished generality that bridges (and generates new) contexts or sets of practices.[50] So far so good. But how is it that these revealing practices work at all since they do not work according to any rational rules that could be set out?

Derrida sees the determination of a law in everyday life as occurring by means of a running together or competition of examples,[51] exemplary rulings situated in the past, each claiming priority and singularity, with one winning the day at a particular instant because of some contingent likeness to the present situation. "We are," Derrida says, noting our general condition, "in a realm where, in the end, there are only singular examples. Nothing is absolutely exemplary."[52] Roughly, the picture that Derrida sets up is one where in interpreting, that is, in the activity of giving meaning to particular things and people, human beings understand new things in terms of how close they come to one or another formerly experienced thing. Something shows up as a bird because it comes closer (for some wholly contingent, momentary reason) to examples of birds than examples of insects or man-made flying objects. One chess master might think that the feel and lay of pieces on the chess board require move A and another chess master might think the same situation requires move B, because one master has habituated himself to a slightly different set of examples from those that the other master has habituated himself to.[53]

This picture, sketchy as it is, should now give us clear grounds for seeing how Derrida's thought holds together. First, if the background practices for revealing work by using a loosely co-ordinated cache of examples (here Derrida has replaced sets of charged differences with caches of examples), then shifts in the relative exemplariness of various examples ought to happen frequently. Indeed, any particular interpreting, speaking, writing, whatever, would involve a complicated assignment of more weight to certain examples and less weight to others. Doing this would understandably produce a sense of wonder at the change in the way things and people show up. So the experience of transformation implied in seeing Iterability as the central feature of language ought to happen more regularly. We can also see now why it does not.

Under the delusive metaphysical regimen that tells us that we ought to have a secure, fundamental way of interpreting things, we have grown to ignore and repress experiences that would make us aware of this jostling around of examples. So, for instance, if experience in our culture is set up so that men normally take a firm judicial decision with clear winners and losers as the most exemplary kind of decision and women normally take as paradigmatic a tentative compromise that tries to accommodate the needs of all those involved, then we will determine that the way women understand decisions bespeaks infirmity and a weak will. A man who suddenly has a womanish response to a decision is clearly, at best, having a bad day. Social structures supporting this invidious distinction are the sort of nonnatural, metaphysically inspired structures that Derrida claims we have set in place. It is clear as well that deconstruction, which makes us sensitive to small changes in what is exemplary and to how certain examples are unnaturally maintained, is a movement that will loosen the hold of the unnatural metaphysical, logocentric, phallocentric structures. Presumably, its goal is not to demolish these structures so much so as to weaken their hold and to put them in their place, to let them be employed only when properly solicited.

Finally, we may now see, too, how this view of the Iterability in the revealing practices fits with Derrida's view of temporality. Derrida, we remember, saw true temporalizing as an effect of belatedness. The notion was that understanding (in the normal sense) occurred as an after-effect of the wonder of a meaning-giving event. And consolidating the effects of a particular meaning-giving event was a privative kind of activity. Now we see that Derrida makes these claims because he understands these background revealing practices as working by means of loosely co-ordinated examples whose authority shifts to accord with the different sorts of situations in which people find themselves. These shifts in relative authority are experienced as the primary meaningful or wonderful event, and they are primary because they manifest most fully the unstable nature of the practices. The consolidating that does, in fact, take place covers up the looseness of the co-ordination of the practices and consequently does not constitute a deep response to the practices that reveal things and people.

In contrast, Heidegger considers the clearing or background practices that reveal people and things to be tightly co-ordinated, and finds that this co-ordination does not, in the richest instances, arise from the imposition of stabilizing metaphysical practices. Consequently, acting in accord with a mode of co-ordination of the revealing practices is a genuine response to the revealing itself. Working out the sense of *Ereignis*, Heidegger's rather mysterious word which means happening, appropriation, owning, will show how this according oneself with a style of revealing can be genuine. We shall also see (1) that Heidegger's "metaphorics of proximity," of "neighboring, shelter, house, service, guard, voice, and listening," is *not* associated with a "simple and immediate presence,"[54] and (2) that Heidegger's understanding of *Ereignis* does not show that he thinks the metaphysics of presence a necessary aspect of Western revealing as Derrida seems to think.

Ereignis is Heidegger's counterpart to Derrida's Iterability. Like Iterability for Derrida, *Ereignis* is the essential aspect of language. To see that Heidegger believes this, we have to keep in mind, as a rough first approximation, that language for Heidegger allows for the revealing of things in such a way that it is understood that they show up differently, under different aspects, in various modes of revealing. We need also to keep in mind that the essence of *Ereignis* is *Eignen* or owning. With just this much, we can at least see what Heidegger means when he claims *Ereignis* is the essential moving force of language and also says: "The ruling power [*Regende*] in [the] showing of saying is owning [*Eignen*]."[55] Explaining more precisely what this sentence means and how, in particular, *Ereignis* moves Heidegger's thinking in the opposite direction from Derrida's will be the point of the rest of this section.

When thinking of language, Heidegger, as Derrida accuses,[56] focuses on speech. Indeed, in his first stab at language in *Being and Time* and even later, Heidegger focuses on people speaking to others who dwell with them and are concerned with the same things.[57] Nothing could start out farther from Derrida's account. But what Heidegger wants us to notice is not the closed situation in which *speaking* occurs – which Derrida thinks language itself opposes – but rather that the situation and the people are given to each other by the speaking itself.[58] This sets up a sort of dilemma. For language, according to Heidegger, turns out to be something of a grab bag. It is "pervaded by all the modes of saying and of what is said, in which everything present or absent announces, grants or refuses itself, shows itself or withdraws."[59] So we move rather quickly from a closed, local setting to a language, which like Derrida's, constitutes many different contexts. To put this in the terms used earlier, language is constituted by a collection of ways of cutting up the world that go with various expressive styles of revealing.[60] It might very well seem that in looking at language so generally, Heidegger has discovered babble and not language at all. The question, for Heidegger, is how something so multifarious as language produces local situations at all.

In order to understand Heidegger's solution, two aspects of the way he sees linguistic practices must become clear. First, Heidegger thinks that speaking is a matter of listening to what language is saying or showing. What he has in mind here is relatively plain. We can see it when we begin to take up any particular practice, like playing chess or discussing how Heidegger's thinking works. The practice, chess or Heidegger's thinking, already has ready-made articulations suitable to the sorts of things the practice does. We hear instructors talk in terms of pawns and knights and queen's gambits or we hear them speak of Dasein and the truth of being, presencing, and so on. And when we speak, we use these terms as we have heard others use them in various contexts with the hope, each time, of coming to a better understanding of the phenomenon the words pick out and why it is an important one. What we want to have happen is what the Easterner had happen when he learned that he was not laid back. We want to understand more completely how the meaning of the words gets filled in. But this experience, as Heidegger would have us see it, is not a transformation so much as a deepening. We develop a richer understanding of a practice we are already involved in. We are listening, we may say now, to hear the inner sense of our words in the way they articulate the practice in which we are engaged.

But a deep problem remains. For if language is as multifarious as Derrida argues and Heidegger begins by conceding, then how can anyone's listening strike just the right vein of articulations suited to a particular revealing practice? For in repeating the words of an instructor, these words might get filled in in a way that runs against the particular practice the student started out in. So, for instance, a student might very easily hear a philosopher's example about *les mots justes* as revealing a peculiar historical fact about the current philosophical moment, that philosophers at this particular time for particular historical reasons find *les mots justes* attractive for their examples. Confusion would *seem* to fall away as he progressed to think more and more about the history of philosophical examples. But the student would be led wholly out of the philosophic practice in which he began. And this could happen over and over again. What is to keep the student from doing this? On a Derridian account, nothing would prevent this, nothing, that is, but for the nonnatural, metaphysical authority in our practices insisting on keeping disciplines completely distinct and ordered according to their supposed natural kinds. But Heidegger claims that there is another aspect of language, *Ereignis*, which is the tendency of the revealing of language to reveal particular things in the mode that is best suited to the kind of thing they are. Since this may be both hard to believe and to understand, let us show first that this is in fact what Heidegger thinks. Here Heidegger first says that it is *Ereignis* that allows people to speak and then claims that speaking by way of *Ereignis* means revealing beings in the way most suited to them:

> *Ereignis* grants to mortals their abode within their nature, so that they may be capable of being those who speak. If we understand "law" as the gathering that lays down that which causes all beings to be present *in their own*, in what is appropriate for them, then *Ereignis* is the plainest and most gentle of all laws.[61]

What does Heidegger mean by claiming that *Ereignis* tends to make sure that a thing is revealed in the mode of revealing best suited to it? Heidegger gets at this when he speaks of revealing a thing in its primordial being. In doing this, he frequently writes as though by primordial being, he means revealing the thing in terms of the style of revealing predominant at its origin. One can see relatively easily what he means by this. It would not be unusual to think that, for instance, the richest way to understand technological equipment like data processors of various kinds would be in terms of the technological mode of revealing, where everything shows up as available for flexible use. To try to appreciate a computer printout the way one might appreciate a hand-written letter, noticing the care with which the letters were shaped and the boldness or elaborateness of the shaping of the letters, would surely be mistaken. A fountain pen, however, would best be understood according to the subject/object kind of revealing (prominent when it was invented) where people show up as complicated subjects trying to understand themselves and objects. In this mode of revealing, the fountain pen could be appreciated for the kinds of stoke one could make with it, the intricate ways that it would allow one to express his or her subjectivity. Likewise, a hand-written letter would obviously be best suited to being appreciated through this mode of revealing. The point is that one kind of revealing will be best suited to bringing out the usable aspect of any piece of equipment most fully. So far as equipment is concerned, this account runs with common intuitions.

But what about natural objects? Should we regard them as flexible material to be used up or as producing the sublime effects to be cherished as the Romantic poets did? Should we regard them as having the kind of energy they had for the ancient Greeks or as signs from God that tell us of the order in His creation as the Medievals thought? Here the answer is not so obvious, for obviously here we cannot be expected to respond to natural things according to the revealing that was current when they were invented. But primordiality need not cause us to recur to actual originary moments. A primordial relation to natural objects would be the one that, like the relation to the computer printout or the fountain pen, gives us a way of dealing with the thing that resonates with the thing in such a way that we become more sensitive to our relation with the thing as one that focuses our shared revealing practices. Put a little more concretely, a primordial relation with a thing is one where the thing makes us sensitive (generally in the spirit of thanks or celebration) to the way of life we lead that makes us take cognizance of the thing in the first place. A couple of instances should show how this works. For many of us now who find that the conservation of natural things makes sense, the most primordial way of responding to them is in terms of practices attached to old pantheistic ways of seeing things. For under this view, all natural things seem worthy of celebration, and this yearning for celebration awakens us to our ecological way of life. Others, of course, may well find that, because such sanctifying practices too easily grant the worthiness of *every* natural thing, they empty out nature's vital energies. These country people who hunt, let's say, to supplement their diet would live in such a way that natural things show up most richly, that is resonate with their way of life, when understood as prizes to be taken in a genuine struggle.

If we allow, then, that this tendency named *Ereignis* could lead us to respond to things in the way that makes them resonate most intensely with our way of life, then speaking, which is where *Ereignis* occurs, would be a way of letting any particular thing show itself in its ownmost (most resonant) being. Moreover, *Ereignis* would be the tendency in language that counters the Derridian Iterability. But, we want to know, What is the evidence that such a thing as *Ereignis* goes on at all?

There are two ways to show *Ereignis* in our practices, *Ereignis*, that is, as distinguished from frantic, neurotic attempts at metaphysical closure. For the first, we can return to the story of the *mot just*, of the Easterner who discovers that he *is not laid back*. For Derrida this event would look like an event of transformation. For Heidegger, this event would be a matter of the Easterner owning up or coming into his own. (Here is the sense of owning in *Ereignis* that Heidegger is at some pains to bring out.)[62] We need not go so far as to say that the Easterner has found his single true identity but we may say that he has come upon a way of revealing (as positively not laid back) that reveals and unites many aspects of his style of daily life.

Perhaps, though, a better way to see this is to think in terms of sagas which, according to Heidegger, capture saying's natural essential sense.[63] We imagine that sagas held their high places in various cultures because they collected together various practices and showed, in a glamorizing way, how the practices were connected together. So we might easily imagine that a fishing culture might very well have in it a great flood saga where ship-building became an essential activity. Such a saga would reveal the essential place in the culture of people other than the fishermen by collecting the shipbuilders and paddle-makers and making them important too. Of course, this culture could as well have another saga about the lost founding figure who was nurtured by sea hawks, and this saga would collect, among other things, nurturing practices and, in collecting them, glamorize them and make them important. We see similar effects in our own culture now. Towards the end of the 1960s and beginning of the 1970s, films about con artists and small-time criminals seemed to give us a fix on the way we, Americans, felt that we were involved in revealing practices that were hypocritical. At the beginning of the 1980s popular films captured a sense of naive confidence, and this spoke to and of the way we were having things show up. In these cases, the films brought us in touch with our own ways of revealing things and people.

But how are these ways of collecting, the sagas or the films, different from the neurotic activity that Freud describes and that Derrida uses to characterize this collecting and gathering, this resonating kind of meaning? Is it not the case that becoming attached to these films, like the neurotic's attachment to his explanations, hides the changes in the revealing practices. It certainly seems to resemble what is going on in the neurotic's case. But neurotics' explanations seem neurotic precisely because they do not resonate with many of our shared social practices. These explanations always come short of what they need to explain, and, somehow sensing this, their authors add to these accounts solutions that try to bridge this gap in a too completely meticulous way. The neurotic account seeks a closure that makes us hear in it a flatness that fails to achieve the sort of reasonable but open and forthright explanation the neurotic himself seeks. This, however, is simply not the case with the way sagas or films work. They do allow us to get a fix on the way that we are revealing things. They do make us feel more at home with what we are doing. Furthermore, they open us up to further distinctions, so we do not find ourselves displacing one explanation with another or seeking closure. Rather the films, and our thinking about them, give us a *general* sense of what we are about and allow us to be at home with, and therefore open to, more and more of our own practices.

But does not all this seeking for a particular work of art, saga or film, to reveal our way of revealing to us constitute the motivation of metaphysics? Are we not seeking a foundation? And if we are not seeking a final foundation, are we not seeking some sort of second best thing to it? Are we not, then, as Derrida accuses, living beyond metaphysics but longing for proximity with some quieting location, some consolation, some truth of being?[64] The answer to these questions goes directly to how we understand revealing practices to be constituted. For

Heidegger, they are made up, like language, of many styles of revealing, but the various styles are collected together as substyles of larger styles. This collecting does not produce a single style that co-ordinates all the other styles. But it does mean that various new ways of revealing, various changes, let us say, in the importance of various examples (various exemplary moves in chess, for example), generally remain within one particular general style of revealing. In fact, we could have no experience of deepening resonance unless *Ereignis*, as the tendency to give us things in their richest, most resonant manner, could bring these changes of paradigms into proximity with one of the appropriate styles of revealing. Without these general styles, one thing revealed in a particular way would not resonate with other things picked out in other particular ways.[65] Having noted this, we may see, finally, that the activity of *Ereignis*, as this collecting, is the source of all of Heidegger's metaphorics of proximity.

But, finally, we want to ask on Derrida's behalf, are not all of Heidegger's styles various aspects of the metaphysics of presence? For does not this metaphysics finally collect every way of revealing? On the one hand, we know that Heidegger cannot mean this because he does uncover non-metaphysical ways of revealing. He calls them by odd names such as things thinging, artworks working, language speaking. But, on the other hand, matters are not so certain, for what are we to make of the following quotation Derrida relies upon in his polemic?[66] Does not Heidegger here confess that all ways of revealing in the West understand being as presence?

> In the sending of the destiny of being, in the extending of time, there becomes manifest a dedication, a delivering over into what is their own, namely of being as presence and of time as the realm of the open. What determines both, time and being, in their own, that is, in their belonging together, we shall call *Ereignis*.[67]

Once we understand that, by "*Ereignis*," Heidegger means the tendency to make things show up in the most resonant way, we can see that Heidegger is simply saying here that some time around the fifth century *BC*, the style of revealing apropriate to craftsmen producing things urged itself upon the early philosophers as a sort of *mot juste* that they were lucky enough to receive as the most resonating (gathering) account of how things showed up in general. Focusing on terms that articulated this practice seemed to bring poeple and things into their own, and the West has thought out of this Greek understanding ever since. But all of this resonant collecting, this metaphysical talking, occurs strictly within a more general tendency of the revealing practices to deal with things in a way most suited to those things and to collect different styles of revealing together as substyles. Nothing in this quotation says that productivity exclusively determines thinking in the West. Nothing says that revealing or being must be exclusively thought in terms of presence. Heidegger simply says that the story of productivity, of presence, has the strongest hold upon us. Who would deny it? Thinking about *Ereignis*, though, ought to loosen that hold, and yet not wed us to Derrida's notion of loosely stuctured practices.

3 Rorty's neo-pramatist reading

If the main point here has been to show that neither Derrida nor Heidegger is trapped within a thematics of presence and that, therefore, neither is metaphysical, then it may seem that this paper comes to a conclusion similar to Rorty's general conclusions about Derrida and Heidegger. Rorty, after all, evaluates both thinkers according to their different, not necessarily metaphysical, magical words.[68] And it turns out that Heidegger's magical words work for deconstructing the closure of the tradition; Derrida's work for deconstructing Heidegger.[69] But what Rorty wants most is the Nietzschean gaiety of new beginnnings that Derrida gives us with his Iterability and *différance*. Rorty sees this in new vocabularies replacing old. Yet he also wants to retain the Heideggerian gratitude that makes sense only when a new understanding is focused by a gathering activity.[70] One ought not to feel gratitude for stark Derridean transformations, because those transformations are not supposed to enrich meaning but to impoverish it. Rorty, in short, wants both wonder and resonance. But what Derrida and Heidegger have shown is that these two ways of understanding linguistic practices depend upon radically different views about how revealing practices work. To have both wonder and resonance, Rorty should give a third, independent account of how the practices work. It seems that Rorty's adoption of the Kuhnian picture of revolutions in vocabulary followed by periods of normal science which builds connections among the new words is a start in this direction. But, to make sense of this, we need an account of what could impose this Kuhnian order on Iterability and *Ereignis*. And this sort of account is precisely what Rorty resists for being too philosophical. The account would necessarily focus on something cross-cultural and transhistorical, a condition for the possibility of things showing up, and the transcendental is a price Rorty will not pay.

NOTES

1 Richard Rorty speaks in this Heideggerian voice – though not directly imagining a confrontation with Derrida – in his "Heidegger, Contingency, and Pragmatism," in this volume [(pp. 223–4).]. In Charles Taylor's "Heidegger, Language, and Ecology," also in this volume (p. 261), we see him – speaking about Derrida in a Heideggerian voice – locate Derrida's position as a particularly extreme form of the subjectivist outlook. This is to say that Taylor locates Derrida's position where Heidegger rightly or wrongly located Nietzsche's.

2 Jacques Derrida, *Positions*, trans. Alan Bass, Chicago: University of Chicago Press, 1981, pp. 52, 54. See also Gayatri Chakravorty Spivak's Preface to Jacques Derrida's *Of Grammatology*, Baltimore: The Johns Hopkins University Press, 1976, pp. xiv–xix, xxxviii, xlviii–1. Herman Rapaport's book *Heidegger and Derrida*, Lincoln: University of Nebraska Press, 1989, chronicles how close Rapaport things Heidegger came to doing Derridian deconstruction at various points in his career.

3 *Ereignis*, most literally tanslated as "enowning" is standardly glossed as an event of appropriation or more simply as appropriation. I am leaving the term in the German, not because I find the translations misleading in any particular way, but because "appropriation" or "event of appropriation," while good translations, already implicitly contain the sort of interpretation I plan to work out in detail. I would prefer not to help out my interpreation by a trick of translation.

4 It is especially important to make this point, at least for Derrida, since he has claimed that on occasion what he is doing could be construed as pragrammatology. (See Jacques Derrida, "Afterword: toward an ethic of discussion," *Limited Inc*, trans. Samuel Weber, Evanston, Ill.: Northwestern University Press, 1988, p. 151.) Unfortunately, on the occasion where he made this claim, Derrida did not take the time to separate his effort from that of the pragmatists and neo-pragmatists.

5 To be consistent and avoid confusion, I will always write the tanslation of *"Sein"* as "being" with a lower case "b" even in quotations, unless the grammar of the sentence requires otherwise.

6 Jacques Derrida, "Signature Event Context," *Limited Inc*, trans. Samuel Weber and Jeffrey Mehlman, 1971; Evanston, Ill.: Northwestern University Press, 1988, p. 9.

7 Jacques Derrida, *"Différance,"* *Margins of Philosophy*, trans. Alan Bass, Chicago: University of Chicago Press, 1982, p. 11.

8 Martin Heidegger, *Being and Time*, trans. John Macquarrie and Edward Robinson, New York: Harper & Row, 1962, p. 97.

9 Derrida, *"Différance,"* p. 23.

10 Ibid., p. 24.

11 Heidegger, *Being and Time*, p. 54.

12 Ibid., pp. 54–5.

13 Martin Heidegger, *Basic Problems*, trans. Albert Hofstadter, Bloomington, Indiana: Indiana University Press, 1982, pp. 106–12. For a later and similar account, see Martin Heidegger, "The question concerning technology," *The Question Concerning Technology*, trans. William Lovitt, Harper Colophon–Harper & Row, 1977, pp. 6–12.

14 I think that Albert Borgmann's claims about running are best understood in this way. See Albert Bormann, *Technology and the Character of Contemporary Life*, Chicago: University of Chicago Press, 1984, p. 207.

15 Martin Heidegger, *Nietzsche*, trans. Frank A. Capuzzi, 4 vols, New York: Harper & Row, 1982, 4, p. 212.

16 A significant difference between the two, however, could be shown to come out of their views of the history of the West. Derrida has a Nietzschean view, that history is the repetition of various systems of differences, which like so many perspectives or world pictures are ontologically fundamentally the same so far as none of them reveals the play in systems of difference any more than any other. At best, the play, the changing of the charged differences, can only be revealed, Derrida says, in a dissimulation. It is always a sort of mysterious other, like the unconscious (Derrida, *"Différance,"* p. 6). So Derrida sees historical change as a sort of zero-sum game, a general economy, as he calls it, a moving set of world pictures that always leave *différance* out or disguised. Heidegger, on the other hand, thinks that while revealing (or being) cannot be fully revealed within the world, it can be revealed mediately by works of art, thinker's words, the founding of states, and the founding of religions (Martin Heidegger, "The origin of the work of art," *Poetry, Language, Thought*, trans. Albert Hofstadter, New York: Perennial Library–Harper & Row, 1971, p. 62). So cultures can have better and worse relations to "the source or their intelligibility." I use the phrase "source of their intelligibility" as a neutral term to get at the determining aspects of both *différance* and being; therefore "source" is not to be understood as a self-sufficient ground. The relation of *différance* to being will be developed later.

17 Here are Derrida's words: "[I]t is at this moment when Heidegger recognizes *usage* as *trace* that the question must be asked: can we, and to what extent, think this trace and the *dis* of *différance* as *Wesen des Seins*? Does not the *dis* of *différance* refer us beyond the history of Being, and also beyond our language, and everything that can be named in it?" (Derrida, *"Différance,"* p. 25).

18 Heidegger, *Being and Time*, pp. 25–6.

19 Here I use the terms "truth and essence" in a Heideggerian way. So these terms do not get at any sort of conceptual definition but rather the "truth" or "essence" of something or of the revealing practices in the way that it or they work.

20 Derrida, *"Différance,"* p. 12.

21 Ibid., p. 11.

22 Ibid., p. 11.

23 I say "in the first instance" because Derrida has a grander design than just reversing the speech/writing difference. That grander design will come out in the discussion of Iterability.

24 These are two ways of taking Heidegger's early account of everyday language in *Being and Time*, pp. 195–210, 260–5. I add the adjective "everyday" here because it is evident that at the same time as the writing of *Being and Time* or very shortly after it, Heidegger had a different way of describing artistic language. See Martin Heidegger, *Basic Problems*, pp. 171–3.

25 Derrida, *"Différance"* pp. 21, 22, 23. See also Jacques Derrida, "The ends of man," *Margins of Philosophy*, p. 128; and *"Ousia* and *Gramme,"* *Margins of Philosophy*, pp. 63–7.

26 Derrida, *"Différance,"* p. 21

27 A good example of this marginal revealing is presented in Heidegger's essay on the thing. See Martin Heidegger, "The Thing," *Poetry, Language, Thought*, pp. 165–86.

28 Derrida, *"Différance,"* p. 22.

29 Derrida, however, is quite suspicious of any account that attempts to come up, as Heidegger does, with some sort of pure, originary time. He argues that all accounts of time must be infected with their inadequate, vulgar counterparts. See Jacques Derrida, *Ousia* and *Gramme,"* pp. 45–6, 60, 63. Indeed, as we shall see, his more adequate conception of time is really based on the denial of any adequate conception of time at all.

30 Heidegger, *Being and Time*, pp. 458–72.

31 Derrida, *"Différance,"* p. 13.

32 This point will be developed more fully in discussing Iterability.

33 Heidegger, *Being and Time*, p. 463.

34 Heidegger in his later writings thinks that this gathering has a particular structure; it brings together mortals, earth, sky, and divinities. He also thinks the early Greeks understood language as utltimately a kind of gathering. This he thinks is the sense of the verbal form of *logos, legein*. These sophisticated workings out of gathering need not be developed here.

35 Heidegger, *Basic Problems*, pp. 228, 268–9; and Heidegger *Being and Time*, pp. 377, 457, 472–80.

36 See Jacques Derrida, "From Restricted to General Economy: A Hegelianism Without Reserve," *Writing and Difference*, trans. Alan Bass, Chicago: University of Chicago Press, 1978, pp. 262–5, 271–2. I thank Steven Knapp for pointing out this aspect of Derrida's work to me See also on this matter Alan Bass's footnote 23 in Derrida, *"Différance,"* pp. 19–20.

37 Derrida, *"Différance,"* pp. 19–21.

38 Ibid., p. 21.

39 Derrida, "Signature Event Context," p. 8.

40 Ibid., p. 8.
41 Both Charles Taylor and Richard Rorty have similar cases of *mots justes*, and I have benefited from their analyses, but the case here of *ces mots justes* differs in important ways from theirs. In Charles Taylor's case, it is important to see that the speaker's words get it right about some particular thing already implicit in his situation. This is not the point here. Presumably there are lots of different ways of getting at the differences of Californians and Easterners. An Easterner might as well say that Californians have lost all their European ethnicity or he might sense that Californians are deeply flaky or purists of a peculiar sort of any of dozens of other things. On the other hand, this example is meant to differ from Rorty's examples of new words in that in its use as *un mot juste* it is immediately fully meaningful. Rorty argues, for instance, that the first time Derrida used *différance*, "that collocation of letters, it was, indeed, not a word, but only a misspelling. But around the third or fourth time he used it, it had *become* a word" ("Deconstruction and Circumvention," p. 102). This is to say that, for Rorty, a new use of an expression remains at first something mostly meaningless and only gets its meaning as new practices gather around it. But this misses Derrida's point about *différance* and his other words. They are not words in any normal sense; they transform us in our use of them. They then have whatever meaning it is that gets the transformation going. But obviously this cannot be a deep resonating meaning. It is more the wonder of seeing a new vista.
    The relevant texts are: Charles Taylor, "Heidegger, Language, and Ecology," in this volume (p. 250); and Richard Rorty, "Deconstruction and circumvention," *Essays on Heidegger and Others*, Cambridge: Cambridge University Press, 1991, p. 102; and Richard Rorty, *Contingency, Irony, and Solidarity*, Cambridge: Cambridge University Press, 1989, p. 18.
42 Derrida, *"Différance"* p. 11.
43 Ibid., p. 15.
44 In claiming that such transformational language use is typical, Derrida, at least, has not distanced himself very far from Heidegger who himself, in his later writings, claims that a particular kind of poetic language use, which will be described later, is the typical and most revealing language use. See Heidegger, "Language," *Poetry, Language, Thought*, p. 208.
45 Derrida, "Afterword," p. 147; emphasis mine.
46 Notice that with his use of the term "norms," Derrida reveals that he could acquiesce to the more Heideggerian "practices" or comportments.
47 See Stanley Fish, "With the compliments of the author," *Doing What Comes Naturally*, Durham, North Carolina: Duke University Press, 1989, pp. 37–67, esp. 57; and Rorty, "Deconstruction and circumvention," pp. 98–101. Rorty develops the case he presented in "Deconstruction and Circumvention" in his "Two meanings of 'logocentrism'"; and "Is Derrida a transcendental philosopher?" *Essays on Heidegger and Others*, pp. 107–18, 119–28.
48 Jacques Derrida, "Force of law: the mystical foundation of authority," *Cardozo Law Review* 11 (1990), pp. 919–1037.
49 I follow roughly John Searle's reading of Wittgenstein here. See John R. Searle, "Skepticism about rules and intentionality," forthcoming.
50 Derrida, "Force of Law," pp. 961–7.
51 Ibid., p. 967
52 Ibid., p. 977.
53 Hubert and Stuart Dreyfus have elaborated a worked-out account of this in their book *Mind over Machine*, New York: The Free Press–Macmillan, 1986.
54 Derrida, "The ends of man," p. 130.
55 Martin Heidegger, "The way to language," *On the Way to Language*, trans. Peter D.

Hertz, New York: Harper & Row, 1971, p. 127; and Martin Heidegger, "Der Weg zur Sprache," *Unterwegs zur Sprache*, 1959; Frankfurt-am-Main: Vittorio Klostermann, 1985, p. 246, vol. 12 of *Gesamtausgabe* (the Hertz translation has been altered slightly). Heidegger makes the connection between *Ereignis* and *Eignen* explicit; see Heidegger, "The way to language," p. 128; and Heidegger, "Der Weg zur Sprache," p. 247.

56 Derrida, "The ends of man," p. 132, n. 36.
57 Heidegger, "The way to language," p. 120.
58 Ibid., p. 121.
59 Ibid., p. 122.
60 Since this is a surprising claim for Heidegger to make, I shall include this quotation here: "Speaking, *qua* saying something, belongs to the design of the being of language, the design which *is pervaded by all the modes of saying and of what is said*, in which everything present or absent announces, grants or refuses itself, shows itself or withdraws. *This multiform saying from many different sources* is the pervasive element in the design of the being of language. With regard to the manifold ties of saying, we shall call the being of language in its totality 'Saying' – and confess that even so we still have not caught sight of what unifies those ties" (Heidegger, "The way to language," pp. 122–3; emphases mine). Although language looks like a hodgepodge here, Heidegger's last sentence should be noted. That unity is what he and this essay go on to explore.
61 Ibid., p. 128; emphasis mine.
62 Ibid., p. 128.
63 Ibid., p. 123. Heidegger adds, though, that the sense of Saying he is after is not precisely that of the saga.
64 Derrida, "The ends of man," pp. 135–6.
65 If we line up Heidegger's view of the revealing practices, or clearing as he calls it, with Derrida's view, we see something very interesting. Heidegger's view is that the clearing consists of various loosely connected sets of revealing practices each set tightly co-ordinated by its particular paradigms. For a time, Heidegger would say, a particular set can dominate a particular culture. And, over time too, new paradigms and new sets may establish themselves. Against this, Derrida's view is that the"clearing" (Heidegger's term) consists, in its natural state, of loosely co-ordinated practices. Paradigms come forth in a moment and then die off just as quickly. To common sense the Derridion view, with its constant change, will look like a prescription for constant breakdowns and confusion. So why does Derrida see the clearing this way? What motivates his view?
    It is well known that Derrida develops his position from the margins of texts and behavior. The reason for this should not seem obscure. For it is on the margins of texts and behavior that one can actually see the traces of revealing practices. Even when John Searle, Derrida's most notorious antagonist, teaches his students about the Background – Searle's term, roughly speaking, for the revealing practices – he himself retreats to the margins of our activity. He tells his students, for instance, a funny story of how it became clear to him that a mug of beer could only show up for him on the basis of many unthematized, non-intentional skills and capacities. For years he had known, Searle says, how to handle mugs of beer. But then at some point in the 1970s, he grabbed his mug and, because it was made of plastic amd much lighter than he had expected, he ended up tossing his beer up in the air. The point of the story is that he had a skill for handling the weight of beer in mugs that he never really thought about, until the practices for making beer mugs changed. Then, the breakdown occurred and one aspect of the background skill became apparent. Stories

such as these could be multiplied and must be in order to make people sensitive to the background revealing practices. Derrida, like John Searle, is quite good at making us see them, only Derrida calls them by various names indicating the situation in which the practices revealed themselves.

The difference, however, between Derrida and Heidegger or Derrida and Searle is that Derrida seems to have read the state of the revealing practices when they became apparent back into their normal state. That is, Derrida seems to claim that it is a natural, normal feature for revealing practices to be constantly shifting. He then has to give an account of how this constant shifting is disguised and covered up by repressive social practices. Heidegger saw this kind of move as the traditional philosophers' mistake of reading breakdown phenomena back into the normal situation and then constructing an account of how the true state of the normal is hidden. So, for instance, in *Being and Time*, Heidegger suggests that philosophers developed the notion that people always act on the basis of beliefs and goals (either conscious or unconscious ones) because people normally only notice how they act in breakdown situations, and in breakdown situations, where they can no longer simply cope, the do indeed act deliberately on the basis of explicit beliefs and goals (Heidegger, *Being and Time*, pp. 102–7). Philosophers took aspects of the breakdown situation – explicit beliefs and goals – and assumed that these mental states underlay any directed action, just as Derrida takes another aspect of a different kind of breakdown situation – that the background becomes apparent when it is shifting – and generalizes that the background is continuously changing. Against the first, traditional generalization, Heidegger argued that most everyday behavior is transparent in the sense that, for instance, the activity of opening a door and taking a seat in a classroom is not accompanied by an experience of any beliefs and goals (Heidegger, *Basic Problems*, p. 163). Moreover, Heidegger claims, no one need have a theory of how door knobs work and the beliefs that there is a relatively flat surface and no chasm on the other side of the door in order to stride into a classroom. Against Derrida's generalization, Heidegger would argue likewise that for the most part the background revealing practices are relatively stable and that that is why our experience is characterized for the most part by resonance and not wonder. (For more on Heidegger's account of this traditional mistake, see Hubert L. Dreyfus, *Being-in-the-World*, Cambridge, Mass.: The MIT Press, 1991, pp. 60–87. For more on John Searle's account of the Background, see his *Intentionality*, Cambridge: Cambridge University Press, 1983, pp. 141–59. The suspicions developed in this note were worked out in conversations with Hubert Dreyfus and John Searle.

66 Derrida, "The ends of man," p. 132, n. 35. Derrida also suggests, without this quotation from "Time and Being," that thinking the difference between being and beings even if this difference does not cash out presence and the present draws one to another kind of presence and a repetition of metaphysics. Metaphysics itself, he argues, is constituted on trying to think another kind of presence. See Derrida, *"Ousia and Gramme,"* generally, but pp. 63–7 in particular.

67 Heidegger, "Time and Being," p. 19.

68 Rorty, "Deconstruction and circumvention," p. 104.

69 Ibid., pp. 105–6.

70 Richard Rorty, "Heidegger, Contingency, and Pragmatism" (this volume pp. 224–5). Rorty ingeniously redescribes Heideggerian gratitude as Deweyan.

Index